T0212217

Lecture Notes in Computer Science 12782

More information about this subseries at http://www.springer.com/series/7409

Norbert Streitz · Shin'ichi Konomi (Eds.)

Distributed, Ambient and Pervasive Interactions

9th International Conference, DAPI 2021
Held as Part of the 23rd HCI International Conference, HCII 2021
Virtual Event, July 24–29, 2021
Proceedings

 Springer

Editors
Norbert Streitz (iD)
Smart Future Initiative
Frankfurt, Germany

Shin'ichi Konomi
Faculty of Arts and Science
Kyushu University
Fukuoka, Japan

ISSN 0302-9743   ISSN 1611-3349 (electronic)
Lecture Notes in Computer Science
ISBN 978-3-030-77014-3   ISBN 978-3-030-77015-0 (eBook)
https://doi.org/10.1007/978-3-030-77015-0

LNCS Sublibrary: SL3 – Information Systems and Applications, incl. Internet/Web, and HCI

This Springer imprint is published by the registered company Springer Nature Switzerland AG
The registered company address is: Gewerbestrasse 11, 6330 Cham, Switzerland

Foreword

Human-Computer Interaction (HCI) is acquiring an ever-increasing scientific and industrial importance, and having more impact on people's everyday life, as an ever-growing number of human activities are progressively moving from the physical to the digital world. This process, which has been ongoing for some time now, has been dramatically accelerated by the COVID-19 pandemic. The HCI International (HCII) conference series, held yearly, aims to respond to the compelling need to advance the exchange of knowledge and research and development efforts on the human aspects of design and use of computing systems.

The 23rd International Conference on Human-Computer Interaction, HCI International 2021 (HCII 2021), was planned to be held at the Washington Hilton Hotel, Washington DC, USA, during July 24–29, 2021. Due to the COVID-19 pandemic and with everyone's health and safety in mind, HCII 2021 was organized and run as a virtual conference. It incorporated the 21 thematic areas and affiliated conferences listed on the following page.

A total of 5222 individuals from academia, research institutes, industry, and governmental agencies from 81 countries submitted contributions, and 1276 papers and 241 posters were included in the proceedings to appear just before the start of the conference. The contributions thoroughly cover the entire field of HCI, addressing major advances in knowledge and effective use of computers in a variety of application areas. These papers provide academics, researchers, engineers, scientists, practitioners, and students with state-of-the-art information on the most recent advances in HCI. The volumes constituting the set of proceedings to appear before the start of the conference are listed in the following pages.

The HCI International (HCII) conference also offers the option of 'Late Breaking Work' which applies both for papers and posters, and the corresponding volume(s) of the proceedings will appear after the conference. Full papers will be included in the 'HCII 2021 - Late Breaking Papers' volumes of the proceedings to be published in the Springer LNCS series, while 'Poster Extended Abstracts' will be included as short research papers in the 'HCII 2021 - Late Breaking Posters' volumes to be published in the Springer CCIS series.

The present volume contains papers submitted and presented in the context of the 9th International Conference on Distributed, Ambient and Pervasive Interactions (DAPI 2021), an affiliated conference to HCII 2021. I would like to thank the Co-chairs, Norbert Streitz and Shin'ichi Konomi, for their invaluable contribution in its organization and the preparation of the proceedings, as well as the members of the Program Board for their contributions and support. This year, the DAPI affiliated conference has focused on topics related to the design of intelligent environments, interaction in smart cities, and the Internet of Things, as well as intelligent environments for learning and cultural heritage.

I would also like to thank the Program Board Chairs and the members of the Program Boards of all thematic areas and affiliated conferences for their contribution towards the highest scientific quality and overall success of the HCI International 2021 conference.

This conference would not have been possible without the continuous and unwavering support and advice of Gavriel Salvendy, founder, General Chair Emeritus, and Scientific Advisor. For his outstanding efforts, I would like to express my appreciation to Abbas Moallem, Communications Chair and Editor of HCI International News.

July 2021   Constantine Stephanidis

HCI International 2021 Thematic Areas and Affiliated Conferences

Thematic Areas

- HCI: Human-Computer Interaction
- HIMI: Human Interface and the Management of Information

Affiliated Conferences

- EPCE: 18th International Conference on Engineering Psychology and Cognitive Ergonomics
- UAHCI: 15th International Conference on Universal Access in Human-Computer Interaction
- VAMR: 13th International Conference on Virtual, Augmented and Mixed Reality
- CCD: 13th International Conference on Cross-Cultural Design
- SCSM: 13th International Conference on Social Computing and Social Media
- AC: 15th International Conference on Augmented Cognition
- DHM: 12th International Conference on Digital Human Modeling and Applications in Health, Safety, Ergonomics and Risk Management
- DUXU: 10th International Conference on Design, User Experience, and Usability
- DAPI: 9th International Conference on Distributed, Ambient and Pervasive Interactions
- HCIBGO: 8th International Conference on HCI in Business, Government and Organizations
- LCT: 8th International Conference on Learning and Collaboration Technologies
- ITAP: 7th International Conference on Human Aspects of IT for the Aged Population
- HCI-CPT: 3rd International Conference on HCI for Cybersecurity, Privacy and Trust
- HCI-Games: 3rd International Conference on HCI in Games
- MobiTAS: 3rd International Conference on HCI in Mobility, Transport and Automotive Systems
- AIS: 3rd International Conference on Adaptive Instructional Systems
- C&C: 9th International Conference on Culture and Computing
- MOBILE: 2nd International Conference on Design, Operation and Evaluation of Mobile Communications
- AI-HCI: 2nd International Conference on Artificial Intelligence in HCI

List of Conference Proceedings Volumes Appearing Before the Conference

1. LNCS 12762, Human-Computer Interaction: Theory, Methods and Tools (Part I), edited by Masaaki Kurosu
2. LNCS 12763, Human-Computer Interaction: Interaction Techniques and Novel Applications (Part II), edited by Masaaki Kurosu
3. LNCS 12764, Human-Computer Interaction: Design and User Experience Case Studies (Part III), edited by Masaaki Kurosu
4. LNCS 12765, Human Interface and the Management of Information: Information Presentation and Visualization (Part I), edited by Sakae Yamamoto and Hirohiko Mori
5. LNCS 12766, Human Interface and the Management of Information: Information-rich and Intelligent Environments (Part II), edited by Sakae Yamamoto and Hirohiko Mori
6. LNAI 12767, Engineering Psychology and Cognitive Ergonomics, edited by Don Harris and Wen-Chin Li
7. LNCS 12768, Universal Access in Human-Computer Interaction: Design Methods and User Experience (Part I), edited by Margherita Antona and Constantine Stephanidis
8. LNCS 12769, Universal Access in Human-Computer Interaction: Access to Media, Learning and Assistive Environments (Part II), edited by Margherita Antona and Constantine Stephanidis
9. LNCS 12770, Virtual, Augmented and Mixed Reality, edited by Jessie Y. C. Chen and Gino Fragomeni
10. LNCS 12771, Cross-Cultural Design: Experience and Product Design Across Cultures (Part I), edited by P. L. Patrick Rau
11. LNCS 12772, Cross-Cultural Design: Applications in Arts, Learning, Well-being, and Social Development (Part II), edited by P. L. Patrick Rau
12. LNCS 12773, Cross-Cultural Design: Applications in Cultural Heritage, Tourism, Autonomous Vehicles, and Intelligent Agents (Part III), edited by P. L. Patrick Rau
13. LNCS 12774, Social Computing and Social Media: Experience Design and Social Network Analysis (Part I), edited by Gabriele Meiselwitz
14. LNCS 12775, Social Computing and Social Media: Applications in Marketing, Learning, and Health (Part II), edited by Gabriele Meiselwitz
15. LNAI 12776, Augmented Cognition, edited by Dylan D. Schmorrow and Cali M. Fidopiastis
16. LNCS 12777, Digital Human Modeling and Applications in Health, Safety, Ergonomics and Risk Management: Human Body, Motion and Behavior (Part I), edited by Vincent G. Duffy
17. LNCS 12778, Digital Human Modeling and Applications in Health, Safety, Ergonomics and Risk Management: AI, Product and Service (Part II), edited by Vincent G. Duffy

38. CCIS 1420, HCI International 2021 Posters - Part II, edited by Constantine Stephanidis, Margherita Antona, and Stavroula Ntoa
39. CCIS 1421, HCI International 2021 Posters - Part III, edited by Constantine Stephanidis, Margherita Antona, and Stavroula Ntoa

http://2021.hci.international/proceedings

9th International Conference on Distributed, Ambient and Pervasive Interactions (DAPI 2021)

Program Board Chairs: **Norbert Streitz,** *Smart Future Initiative, Germany* and **Shin'ichi Konomi,** *Kyushu University, Japan*

- Andreas Braun, Luxembourg
- Paul Davidsson, Sweden
- Jun Hu, Netherlands
- Michael Koch, Germany
- Nicos Komninos, Greece
- Artur Lugmayr, Australia
- Irene Mavrommati, Greece
- H. Patricia McKenna, Canada
- Tatsuo Nakajima, Japan
- Guochao Peng, China

- Carsten Röcker, Germany
- Denisa Reshef Kera, Spain
- Boris De Ruyter, Netherlands
- Christoph Stahl, Luxembourg
- Reiner Wichert, Germany
- Chui Yin Wong, Malaysia
- Woontack Woo, Korea
- Takuro Yonezawa, Japan
- Chuang-Wen You, Taiwan

The full list with the Program Board Chairs and the members of the Program Boards of all thematic areas and affiliated conferences is available online at:

http://www.hci.international/board-members-2021.php

HCI International 2022

The 24th International Conference on Human-Computer Interaction, HCI International 2022, will be held jointly with the affiliated conferences at the Gothia Towers Hotel and Swedish Exhibition & Congress Centre, Gothenburg, Sweden, June 26 – July 1, 2022. It will cover a broad spectrum of themes related to Human-Computer Interaction, including theoretical issues, methods, tools, processes, and case studies in HCI design, as well as novel interaction techniques, interfaces, and applications. The proceedings will be published by Springer. More information will be available on the conference website: http://2022.hci.international/:

General Chair
Prof. Constantine Stephanidis
University of Crete and ICS-FORTH
Heraklion, Crete, Greece
Email: general_chair@hcii2022.org

http://2022.hci.international/

Contents

Learning and Culture in Intelligent Environments

Smart Cities

Integrating Inter-field Data into Space-Time to Grasp and Analyze Activities in Town

Kenro Aihara[1,2,3]($\boxtimes$) (iD) and Atsuhiro Takasu[1,2] (iD)

1 National Institute of Informatics, Tokyo, Japan
{kenro.aihara,takasu}@nii.ac.jp
2 The Graduate University for Advanced Studies, Tokyo, Japan
3 Joint Support-Center for Data Science Research, Research Organization of Information and Systems, Tokyo, Japan

Abstract. The development of open data by local governments and data platforms for each field is progressing. These are broad ranged data on each area, such as traffic, disaster prevention, retail and services, and are expected to be useful information sources both for citizens and visitors. On the other hand, although these data are usually deployed in a network reachable place, when they have to be handled individually according to its own format, and in some cases, conversion both in format and in semantics are required, which is a barrier to use.

In this paper, on the premise of the existence of a data platform that is developed for each field, the functions necessary for a data linkage infrastructure that enables them to be integrated and used are shown. In particular, a methodology which integrates each piece of information into space-time space is proposed. And also the paper shows an interactive visual dashboard to grasp and analyze activities in town. This application aims to provide information to help managing town.

Keywords: Integration of heterogeneous contents · Data linkage · Smart city · GIS

1 Introduction

The development of open data by local governments and data platforms for each field is progressing. These are broad ranged data on each area, such as traffic, disaster prevention, restaurants and services, and are expected to be useful information sources for citizens and visitors. On the other hand, these data are usually deployed in a network reachable place, but when they have to be handled individually according to its own format, and in some cases, conversion both in format and in semantics are required, which is a barrier to use.

By the way, in existing information services for tourists, especially smartphones application services for tourists, the content provided are selective and limited in some specific fields and target areas covered. That is, there is a problem

© Springer Nature Switzerland AG 2021
N. Streitz and S. Konomi (Eds.): HCII 2021, LNCS 12782, pp. 3–14, 2021.
https://doi.org/10.1007/978-3-030-77015-0_1

on coverage in content. In addition, there are many cases where has a problem with the cost of maintaining and updating content, and the content may often be obsolete.

Given the existence of data platforms developed for each field, the paper presents the data linkage challenges that enable them to be integrated and used.

In assumption that the main purpose of analysis in common interactive analytics is from the viewpoint of proximity in space-time, the integration of data results in the problem of mapping overspace-time. One of the main application areas of utilization is smart city applications. Specifically, they are applications from a macro perspective such as grasping the flow in the region and analyzing economic activities reflected in logistics and distribution, and from a micro perspective such as smartphone services to support the behavior of migrants in the city. For both perspectives, the key is spatiotemporal integration. An example of an application that uses various integrated data for the latter smartphone service is described in the separate manuscript [1], so in this paper, the former is taken as an example, and the utilization of integrated data mainly in marketing analysis is described. Here, the paper deals with the superposition of data in the retail, mobile, and public sectors.

In this paper, research background is described at first. Next, the basic approach about integrating heterogeneous data is shown. The paper describes the underlying data for mapping in space-time. Then, data are grounded on the map by using such fundamental data. Some issues in the converting process are shown. Finally, the paper also shows an interactive analytics as an example of exploiting integrated data.

2   Background

2.1   Cyber-Physical Systems (CPS)

Cyber-physical systems (CPS) are a promising new class of systems that deeply embed cyber capabilities in the physical world, either on humans, infrastructure or platforms, to transform interactions with the physical world [3,6]. CPS facilitates to use the information available from the physical environment. Advances in the cyber world such as communications, networking, sensing, computing, storage, and control, as well as in the physical world such as materials and hardware, are rapidly converging to realize this class of highly collaborative computational systems that are reliant on sensors and actuators to monitor and effect change. In this technology-rich scenario, real-world components interact with cyberspace via sensing, computing and communication elements.

More than big data systems, social CPS is the operating system of urban society. It provides a user environment that supports the agency of people in decision-making. Social CPS focuses human aspects in the parallel world because human is not only subject to exploit such systems but also object to be observed and be affected by the systems. Information flows from the physical to the cyber world, and vice-versa, adapting the converged world to human behavior and social dynamics. Indeed humans are at the center of this converged world since information about the context in which they operate is the key element to adapt the CPS applications and services.

The need for social CPS in building sustainable, safe, and secure urban societies is growing. The prerequisite basic technologies are maturing rapidly. Remaining efforts include opening data silos maintained by the private sector and the government, and analyzing massive, complex data that cannot be completely described by a single monolithic model. Social CPS is filled with tantalizing challenges for research and development.

2.2 Open Data

Open Definition describes open data as "Open means anyone can freely access, use, modify, and share for any purpose (subject, at most, to requirements that preserve provenance and openness)." [5] Although the idea of open data has been around for a long time, the term "open data" has been used to refer specifically to the activities of open-data government initiatives, such as data.gov, data.go.uk, and data.go.jp, in recent years. To promote government transparency, accountability, and public participation, governments make information publicly available as machine-readable open data.

Linked Open Data (LOD) is Linked Data which is released under an open license, which does not impede its reuse for free [2]. Linked Data is structured data which is interlinked with other data to share information to enable to be processed semantically by computers. Tim Barners-Lee advocated the five star rating scheme of LOD as follows:

1. Available on the web (whatever format) but with an open licence, to be Open Data
2. Available as machine-readable structured data (e.g. excel instead of image scan of a table)
3. as (2) plus non-proprietary format (e.g. CSV instead of excel)
4. All the above plus, Use open standards from W3C (RDF and SPARQL) to identify things, so that people can point at your stuff
5. All the above, plus: Link your data to other people's data to provide context

Usually, when considering the use of open data by machine processing, it is considered that three or more stars are required.

2.3 Marketing Analysis

The market for marketing analysis, especially digital marketing, is expected to double in the last five years. Traditional marketing analysis has mainly focused on analysis of changes along the time axis and periodicity by using conventional methods, such as association rules, cluster analysis, regression, and time series analysis. At present, customer behavior and needs are diversifying and fluctuating rapidly, so it is becoming necessary to analyze the spatiotemporal axis with a relatively small spatiotemporal cube, and it is urgent to introduce these in each company. In marketing analysis, poin-of-sales (POS) transaction data with customer information added have been acquired, and are the main target data for analysis. The focus is shifting from analyzing past data to predicting the future. In this research, the authors superimpose the floating population data in the mobile field, the food business license list in the public sector, and the postal code data and administrative boundary data as fundamental data.

3 Integration of Inter-field Data

3.1 Issues on Integration

Generally, various types of data are managed and provided in an autonomous distributed manner. From the viewpoint of data linkage, the same data has different formats, structures, and expressions, and is an obstacle to cross-use. At present, data that should be connected is not connected. There are the following issues regarding data linkage:

- a large variety of data, a large amounts of data
- distributed management of data
- data written in different ways
  - the same data in different formats
  - the same data in different structures
  - the same data in different expressions

The difference between formats may correspond to 2-star class of five star rating scheme of LOD shown in Sect. 2.2, while the difference between structures is regarded as 3-star class. In order to actually use different data by computational integration, a match at the expression level, that is, a 4-star class is required. In particular, when trying to use data in different fields, the use of words is generally quite different, and there are many technical issues in realizing these integration.

In many cases, integration between different formats can be handled by converting the file format of structured electronic files. For example, tabular data is interoperable in csv format. In the case of semi-structured data, such as XML and JSON, is often used, and in the case of GIS data, Shapefile is also common.

Even if the format is interoperable, differences in data structures are often a significant issue. Deterministic solution may be difficult when the union compatibility in the relational model is not established, such as when the correspondence between data items is not obvious even between tabular formats or when the domain is different. In addition, the integration of tabular and semi-structured data and the integration of different semi-structured data further increase the difficulty of deterministic and mechanical matching.

When unstructured data is targeted, deterministic matching is quite difficult, so calculate a plausible matching with a probabilistic approach and accept it as it is, or use it as a suggestion and judge suitability manually.

Even if the format is interoperable and the difference in data structure can be absorbed, the difference in data representation, that is, semantics may become a problem. In recent years, research and development aimed at integrated use of data by absorbing differences between structures and expressions by using ontology technologies such as knowledge graphs and the Semantic Web have been promoted. For example, Semantic Web Challenge on Tabular Data to Knowledge Graph Matching[1] is performed for matching tabular data, and assigning a Knowledge Graph property to the relationship between two columns (CPA task – Columns-Property Annotation), the top-level suggestions show an average F1 score of 99% [4].

3.2   Integration of Heterogeneous Data

As mentioned above, here the authors aim to integrate data through mapping into space-time space, which is one of specific forms of integration, before integration at the general semantic level. This is because the integrated data is used in a realistic application that supports analysis along the spatiotemporal axis, and analyists usually may be supported by visualization on the spatiotemporal axis. Therefore, the data attributes corresponding to the location and time are targets to be integrated by converting their expressions. In particular, marketing data and people's activies in town are superimposed on space-time.

3.3   Mapping and Converting with Fundamental Data

To map values of attributes on location, some fundamental data may be able to be usuful. To begin with, you need to know the variations of notation on location.

Geographic Coordinate System. Now that smartphones have become widespread and the location of mobile objects can be easily obtained by GPS, the latitude and longitude of geographic coordinate system is the most commonly used expression of location. Latitude and longitude change the coordinates of the same point depending on the geodetic system, so it may be necessary to convert them, but GIS utility softwares, such as GDAL[2], are developed and spread, and there is no technical difficulty as long as the scale in meters is used. A lot of interactive analytics tools use a map interface which handles geographic objects with latitude and longitude, so all location data must be grounded in latitude and longitude space finally.

There are some common file formats for geographical representation. One is GML, which is an XML-based notation defined by Open Geospatial Confortium (OGC). Another standard format is GeoJSON, which can describe geographical features, such as points, line strings, and polygons, in JSON format. In contrast to other standard formats, GeoJSON is written and is maintained by open group of developers. Therefore, it is particularly suitable for handling on the web and

---

[1] https://www.cs.ox.ac.uk/isg/challenges/sem-tab/2020/.
[2] https://gdal.org/.

mobile applications, and seems to be widely used as a de facto standard in recent years. Yet another common format is the format created for ArcGIS, a commercial GIS tool known as Shapefile. A lot of GIS softwares can import and export data in Shapefile format, so this file format is often used, especially in the distribution of static maps. This paper uses GeoJSON format by default because JSON is directly editable in a human readable format and can be processed natively by many open softwares supporting GIS including not only specific tools but also general softwared like database systems, such as PostgreSQL and Elasticsearch[3]. Therefore, preferable geografic reprensentation for integratation must be expressed with latitude and longitude in GeoJSON format.

Postal Address. Postal addresses are a well-known form of location addressing in communication between people. Although there are differences in notation and numbering depending on the country or region, people can identify a specific place on the map according to the rules. On the other hand, there is a weakness that it is not possible to describe in areas such as pinpoint designation of places and areas without buildings, and it is less descriptive to indicate the position. To use a postal address as a location description, converting it into a geographical coordinate system is necessary. Such conversion is called geocoding. In fact, address notation is ambiguous, including omissions and errors, often resulting in incomplete conversions. In addition, since the address description has a low resolution, it is often difficult to pinpoint the position identification only by the address.

Usually pinpoint geocoding service may be commercial, but administrative boundary data, e.g. polygons of each town, are provided as open data. In Japan, boundary data at the town level is distributed from the Government of Japan in Shapfile, GML, and KML formats.

Postal Code. Postal codes, or zip codes, are often used in association with the postal address. The postal code is originally given for the purpose of delivering mail, so it is considered that a code is assigned to the delivery block. That is, each code may correspond to a town and its resolution is even lower than the postal address. Its low resolution has both positives as well as negatives. From the perspective of privacy protection, which has become increasingly important in recent years, postal codes are often used to identify residences rather than postal addresses or geographical coordinates.

Therefore, in order to ground the data with the postal codes to the geographical coordinate system, it is necessary to identify the town blocks corresponding to each code and derive the polygons for such blocks.

Grid. Another addressing system to identify space is grid, or mesh, which is a tessellation of a flat tiles. One of common grid systems is Geohash, which encodes

---

[3] https://www.elastic.co/.

a geographic location into a single letter string. It is a hierarchical spatial data structure which devides space into 32 backets of grid shape in lower level.

In Japan, "Grid Square Code" is widly used[4]. Fundamental data, such as maps and route network data, are often supplied in Grid Squre Code.

Distance Marker. Distance markers, or kilometer posts or mileposts, are often used in traffic management such as roads and railroads. Once road origins and paths are defined, the position on the path can be described as the distance from the orign along the path. For example, in the maintainance task for the road, distance markers are used as a recording location for incidents. Care must be taken when converting distance markers to a coordinates system. When you look up the coordinate of the distance marker, you must calculate the distance from the origin when along the linestring of the path, but its distance can be obtained precisely only when the coordinate is given. That is, converting latitude and longitude coordinates on a path to distance markers is straight forward, but not the other way around.

3.4 Simulation

In this section, simulation with real data is described. Figure 1 shows overview of flow of integration.

Data. We prepared the following data:

- Fundamental data
  - Boundary Data at the Town Level from e-Stat[5]
  - Postal Code Data[6]
  - List of Food Business Licenses of Sapporo City as Point-Of-Interests data[7]
  - List of Environmental Hygiene Services of Sappory City as Point-Of-Interests[8]
- Transaction data
  - POS transaction data with customer attributes of convenience stores
- Trajectory data
  - Point-type Floating Population data of Agoop[9]

The goal of integration is that analyists can handle both POS transaction data in retail industry and trajectory data in mobility sector in the same geographical and time space. Therefore, Both data must be mapped into GeoJSON format by using fundamental data. Point-Of-Interests are organized from the open data platform of Sappro city.

---

[4] JIS X 0410:2002, http://www.stat.go.jp/data/mesh/.

[5] https://www.e-stat.go.jp/help/view-on/map/boundary_data.

[6] http://www.post.japanpost.jp/zipcode/download.html.

[7] https://ckan.pf-sapporo.jp/dataset/sapporo_food_business_licences.

[8] https://ckan.pf-sapporo.jp/dataset/sapporo_environmental_hygiene_services.

[9] https://www.agoop.co.jp/service/point-data/.

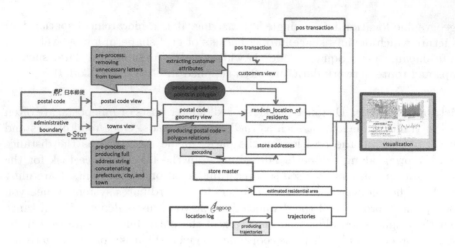

Fig. 1. Overview of integration flow

Converting Postal Code to Corresponding Polygons. Fields related to postal code itself and prefecture, city, and town in postal code data is defined as follows:

administrator's code (JIS X0401, X0402) 5-digit
postal code 7-digit
prefecture name string
city name string
town name string

Unfortunately, description in town name is some problematic, in actual. For example, there are some supplemental and summative descriptions, such as "only if not listed below" (as defalut) and "x-th street (y-th to z-th avenue)". Of course people can understand what such description means but they need to be processed semantically and logically for machines. Fields are well-formed and seem to easy to be mapped.

On the other hand, the administrative boundary data is provided in Shapefile format, so first it must be converted in GeoJSON format. After the conversion, you can find definitions of data fields as follows:

PREF (prefecture code) 2-digit
CITY (city code corresponding to the prefecture) 3-digit
S_AREA (town code) 6-digit
PREF_NAME string as prefecture name
SITYO_NAME string as county level name
CITY_NAME string as city name
S_NAME string as town and street level description
geometry polygons in GeoJSON format

To integrate postal codes and administrative boundary data, you must join the field of town name in postal code and the field of S_NAME in boundary data in addition to prefecture-city level matching. As mentioned above, the field of town name contains some supplemental (but noisy) strings, so in addition to simple string matching, some heuristics to solve the gap in semantics are needed.

You may realize that there is diffference between administrative levels in this example; postal code data has only two levels above city, namely, prefecture and city, while administrative boundary data has three: prefecture, county as "sityo", and city. That is, there is a difference in structure level. It is considered that the difference is caused by the difference in each purpose. To match the occurrence in dynamic data and fundamental data above, you need to take an approach such as approximate matching, or similarity search, instead of exact matching of character string. Such strategies are also heuristic and can be a barrier to automatic integration. For matching of address string, variations of full address string may be needed; one is produced by concatenating prefecture, county, city, and another is from prefecture and city, and so on. And also some normalization replacement may be needed in numbers and reserved letters.

Converting Postal Address to Corresponding Location. Lists of local businesses in open data of Sapporo city contains only postal address to identify its location. To map its location into the geographical coordinates, geocoding is needed. Fortunately, the notation of postal address is well controlled, normalized, and correct in the lists, so the conditions for geocoding are better. If you need to position the locaion in town level, approximate matching for postal address in previous section can be used instead of geocoding.

4   An Example of Using Integrated Data: Interactive Analytics

This section describes an example of an interactive analytics for marketing research. The system is implemented as Kibana's dashboard. Kibana is visualization tools for no sql database of Elasticsearch. Prior to loading data into elasticsearch, integration of POS transaction data, trajectory data have been made by using normalization, join, and some heuristics on relational database of PostgreSQL with PostGIS extension. Figure 2 illustrates an overview of system architecture.

4.1   Preparation of POS Transaction Data

For marketing analysis, the customer attributes of his/her residence in postal code format is attached to some transaction data. To put it simply, the sales data is added to the entire polygon corresponding to the postal code. But here, in order to grasp the degree of scattering according to different zoom levels of viewed area, the location of each customer's residence is randomly assigned inside the corresponding polygon of the designated postal code.

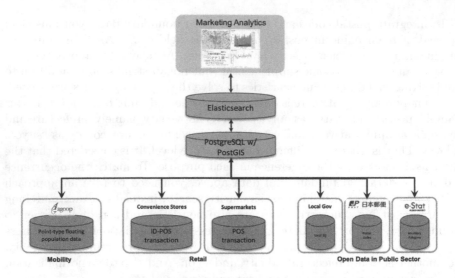

Fig. 2. Overview of system architecture

4.2   Preparation of Trajectories Data

Point-type floating population data of Agoop is a collection of records of position of user of specific smartphone applications with pseudonymized user identifier and timestamp originally. For each individual, sequences of points as trajectories are produced according to some rules, such as cutting policy when the distance between consective two points are apart. Each trajectory has the locations and the timestamps of start and end, length of its path, duration of travel, and stuck motions.

4.3   Overview of Visualization

Figure 3 illustrates the system of intaractive analytics. As a function of the dashboard of Kibana, it is possible to interactively set a filter based on the target time range and the range of attribute values on the top of the window. Examples of trajectories are shown in Fig. 4. Blue lines denotes trajectories and stuck points are illustated as pins. Green grids include destinations of movable objects. This example shows the situation refecting trajectories and destinations which passed through designated area.

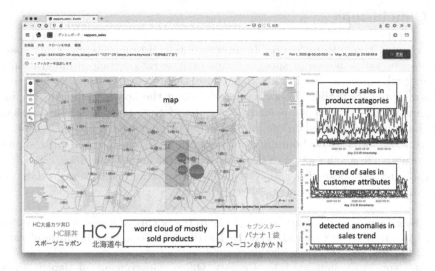

Fig. 3. Snapshot images of the intaractive analytics tool

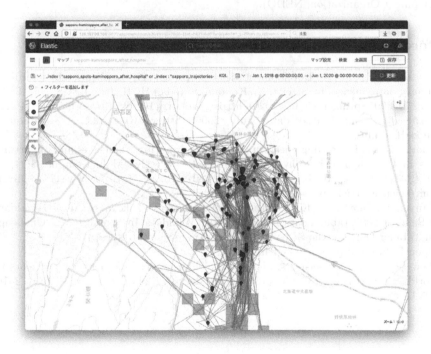

Fig. 4. Snapshot images of trajectories (Color figure online)

5   Conclusions

In this paper, the authors focused to integrate data through mapping into space-time space, which is one of specific forms of integration, before integration at the general semantic level. This is because the integrated data is used in a realistic application that supports analysis along the spatiotemporal axis, and analyists usually may be supported by visualization on the spatiotemporal axis. Data have to be grounded on the map by using fundamental data, such as postal codes and administrative boundary polygons. In addition, the paper also showed an interactive analytics as an example of exploiting integrated data.

Applying methodologies and systems for integrating heterogeneous data and verification through experiments are future issus.

Acknowledgments. The authors would like to thank City of Sapporo, Secoma Campany, Ltd., HOKUNO Co., Ltd., and the Distribution Economics Institute of Japan (DEIJ) for their cooperation with this research.

This work was supported by Cabinet Office, Government of Japan, Cross-ministerial Strategic Innovation Promotion Program (SIP), "Big-data and AI-enabled Cyberspace Technologies" (funding agency: the New Energy and Industrial Technology Development Organization, NEDO).

References

1. Aihara, K., Takasu, A.: Development of one-stop smart city application by interdisciplinary data linkage. In: Streitz, N., Konomi, S. (eds.) HCII 2020. LNCS, vol. 12203, pp. 379–390. Springer, Cham (2020). https://doi.org/10.1007/978-3-030-50344-4_27
2. Berners-Lee, T.: Linked data, July 2006. https://www.w3.org/DesignIssues/LinkedData.html
3. Conti, M., et al.: Looking ahead in pervasive computing: challenges and opportunities in the era of cyber-physical convergence. Pervasive Mob. Comput. **8**(1), 2–21 (2012). https://doi.org/10.1016/j.pmcj.2011.10.001, http://www.sciencedirect.com/science/article/pii/S1574119211001271
4. Nguyen, P., Yamada, I., Kertkeidkachorn, N., Ichise, R., Takeda, H.: MTab4Wikidata at SemTab 2020: tabular data annotation with Wikidata. In: Semantic Web Challenge on Tabular Data to Knowledge Graph Matching (SemTab) (2020)
5. Open Definition: http://opendefinition.org/
6. Poovendran, R.: Cyber-physical systems: close encounters between two parallel worlds. Proc. IEEE **98**(8), 1363–1366 (2010). https://doi.org/10.1109/JPROC.2010.2050377

Crowdsourced Urban Annotations and Augmented Reality as Design Thinking Tools to Navigate and Interact with Urban Data

Omar Al Faleh[(✉)]

New York University, New York, NY 10012, USA
Omar.faleh@nyu.edu

Abstract. Urban data and urban analytics have become global phenomena as modern cities move towards institutionalizing the collection and the availability of statistical and urban-sensing data. Projects like the Citizen Sense, Smart Citizen, SONYC, and the New York City Open Data projec are but a few of many global initiatives that study and highlight the importance of working with urban data as means to annotate, measure, and build a smart city (Picon 2015) or a sentient city (Shepard 2011) whose present and futures rely heavily on the policies and strategies of collecting and analyzing urban data. Are urban data objective and un-opinionated snapshots of reality? Will presentation strategies and mediums influence how data is interpreted and used in designing the futures of the city? Are statistical and sensor data true representations of urban reality or are there other data that also needs to be considered, like oral histories and inter-city migration trails, to present a more accurate picture? This paper presents an HCI centric design research that addresses some of the questions and concerns regarding urban statistics and urban data as meta descriptors of the city, and as blueprints of the metropolis of the future.

Keywords: Conceptual design and planning · Design methods and techniques · Design thinking · Mixed reality and environments · Social design · UX (User Experience)

1 Background

The development of data-centric urban management methods, which became prevalent in the last few decades, have roots in the practices and policies of the plague-stricken Europe of the 17th century, where city states kept records of the number of residents in each house and a daily record of those residents' well-being and health. These records included daily observations and counts of sickness, death, irregularities and complaints, and were then transmitted to the authorities that managed and distributed medical treatment to prevent anyone from concealing their sickness (Foucault 1975). The same frame of thought that keeps records of urban data to regulate access to public services has led to the creation on the US Census bureau whose mission is to collect data in urban areas to decide on percentages of representation in congressional bodies in the united states and decide on

© Springer Nature Switzerland AG 2021
N. Streitz and S. Konomi (Eds.): HCII 2021, LNCS 12782, pp. 15–28, 2021.
https://doi.org/10.1007/978-3-030-77015-0_2

the distribution of public funding for elements of public life like hospitals, education, and transportation[1].

While one's experience in the city is continuous for most cases, post-industrial cities are marked by invisible divisions that separates the city into neighborhoods, blocks, boroughs, and other divisions that sometimes denote different distribution of services, wealth, race, and ethnicities. These urban clusters are called census tracts, which are small, relatively permanent statistical subdivisions of a county that average about 4,000 inhabitants[2], making the size and delineation of such tracts change from city to another, and from one neighborhood to another. Creating divisions enables us to study the city on different scales, which places the decision-making process in the hands of different authorities based on the scale in which the data was sampled. For example: the mathematical average of income and employment levels will change based on the scale of the studied sample, making the policies that are directly related to a family's median income differ in scope between regulating the entire borough of Manhattan, the upper west side of Manhattan, and the tracts north and south of the intersection of Amsterdam Ave & 78th street (Fig. 1).

Fig. 1. Census tracts divisions in New York (Screenshot from the Opportunity Atlas project: https://www.opportunityatlas.org/ - last accessed on March 20th 2020)

---

[1] https://www.census.gov/history/.

[2] https://www2.census.gov/geo/pdfs/education/CensusTracts.pdf.

Similarly, census tracts split Alphabet City in the east village of Manhattan into three different tracts, with the southern block showing almost half the income of the northern block, making the southern block a "poor" neighborhood compared to the "closer to the average Manhattanite income" northern block, both of are located 6 streets apart (Figs. 2 and 3).

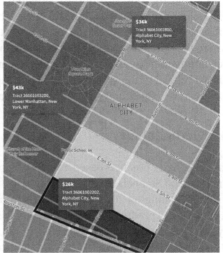

Fig. 2. Income variation in the upper west side (Opportunity Atlas) (screenshot from the Opportunity Atlast project: https://www.opp ortunityatlas.org/ - last accessed on March 20th 2020)

Fig. 3. Income variation in Alphabet city (Opportunity Atlas) (screenshot from the Opportunity Atlast project: https://www.opp ortunityatlas.org/ - last accessed on March 20th 2020)

While topographical representations show those areas as different discrete blocks with different colors and shading, the city remains a place for continuous flow and mobility. Social scientists like Saskia Sassen observe the social and economic interdependency between the rich and poor areas within the city, and also between the urban and suburban settlements: "a topographic representation of rich and poor areas of a city would simply capture the physical conditions of each – advantages and disadvantages. It would fail to capture the electronic connectivity that can make even poor areas into locations on global circuits" (Sassen 184).

2   Problem Statement

Sassen's work demonstrates that attempting to understand city dynamics by mapping or transcribing city blocks into a schematic relationship of discrete adjacent divisions (neighborhoods, census tracts, etc.) is not representative of the urban continuity and the complex intermobility within the city, which is characterized by the constant flow between neighborhoods that are not necessarily within similar socioeconomic indicators.

This is more true as we observe that census data are collected and validated at large once every 10 years, which means that what is considered a data-centric representation of the city can be a decade old descriptor of an urban reality that might have completely changed, depending on what year we're looking at this data.

Therefore, this research starts from the proposal to move beyond the traditional two-dimensional representation of overlaying socioeconomical divisions in a city map, and into a more complex representation of vertically-layered accumulation of statistical data, subjective observations, experiential reflections, narrative representations, socioeconomical divisions, mobility and intermobility, all supported by one continuous urban infrastructure. This is mainly inspired by the work of Antoine Picon and Carlo Ratti, where they propose that, while maps are linked to the desire to manage cities better, the development of new tools for visualization (or simulation) of the urban realm constitutes a refusal of the top-down dashboard approach in favor of new mediums that resist technocratic power and promote more collaborative urban life (Picon and Ratti 2019).

3 Methodology

Inspired by a practice-based research approach in design (Zimmerman et al. 2017; Sanders and Stappers 2013), and following the Research Through Design method (Martin and Hannington 2012), which starts from the theory and the conceptual as a basis for technological production and interaction design, this research follows an iterative design cycle. The original concept is broken into sequential design phases and production milestones where each phase start with a conceptual process of ideation and prototyping, followed by a technical production phase that includes product testing and validation by potential end users, whose feedback is then synthesized to inform and, potentially change, the requirements and considerations for any subsequent design iterations.

This iterative process is also dependent on the availability and reliability of data sources and urban statistics, as they are principle design element in the lifecycle of the app. This is to an extent where the availability and format of the data can potentially influence and reshape the final product and the emerging interaction patterns.

4 Concept

The general idea of this project is to design an experiential urban walk that allows users to access the hidden annotations of the city through mobile technology. The walk will be a non-traditional narrative experience which tells the story of the different neighborhoods in the city through presenting the users with data and annotations in situ instead of the traditional top-down view like google maps or similar forms. This way, understanding urban realities though data access becomes an embodied experience that is equally multi-sensory and location specific. However, the data we are discussing here should not be limited to statistics and numbers, but should also include user-generated, crowd-sourced data that transcends the geographical dispositions of urban divisions and census tracts, and move into the form of a location-specific annotation with various media types like text, images and sounds.

The idea is to enable every day urban dwellers to tag and annotate different areas of their cities with their own subjective reflections, allowing them to post messages and texts, take photos or upload existing images, and record and upload sounds. In essence, this enables the creation of mediated meta tag annotation system for the city, which also serves as a location-specific narrative archive. When accessed together during the urban walk, users will be presented with a fuller picture about the urban reality: from census-level statistics to comments and images that were added by users that once stood in their place.

In this context, this project is a knowledge-first platform to empower data-driven decision making about urban issues: from design and policy decisions to choosing one's next home, to the simple task of familiarizing oneself with the nature and the vibes of the city and its different neighborhoods through the eyes of fellow urbanites. This tool could indirectly answer questions like: is this a safe neighborhood to live in? is this a diverse neighborhood? What are the locals' working status in this neighborhood? And how did this street corner look like in 2011?

Such significant undertaking led to designing this project to be built in different phases:

1. Data collection and normalization.
2. Designing a web server to serve this normalized data.
3. Designing a prototype of a mobile client that consumes this data as one walks in the city by accessing the device's location.
4. Designing a tool for crowd-sourcing data annotation, which allows people to add their own location-specific media to the already existing database.
5. Designing the mobile augmented reality experience that reads from the data collected above.

In this paper, we will go over the first four, already completed, phases and discuss the implications of the current design on the future consumer application: a mobile application that allows for the retrieval and the representation of such data in-situ. This application will use mobile augmented reality as a tool and as a lens that allows the process of revealing the invisible and bringing forth a hidden dimension of the city.

5 Data

To better the illustrate the concepts of spatial divisions vs. urban continuity, this project uses two different datasets in tandem: the census bureau's data as an unopinionated dataset, and a collection of already existing opinionated, user-generated set of annotations that are not necessarily descriptive of any statistical content, rather presenting a subjective reflection on the nature or the spirit of the neighborhood. The contrasting nature of the different types of data pose interesting frictions in terms of the way they operate in space:

– Census data works on a well-defined spatial disposition that has clear two-dimensional borders while user generated data is anchored to a specific location point.
– Census data is reflective of a top-down depiction of realities in the city, including bias and discrimination, while crowdsourced annotations present a bottom-up interpretation, resistance, and subjective representation of these realities.

5.1 Census Data

Census data was acquired from the Opportunity Atlas project website, which is the result of a collaboration between the Census Bureau and researchers at Harvard University and Brown University. The Opportunity Atlas makes their data set available, including census data for each of the areas we are exploring, labelled and identified by tract numbers. These data include the household income, incarceration level, teenage birth, employment, high school graduation, college graduation, number of working hours per week, hourly wage, people who still live within the same commuting zones and within the same tract as adults, along with income data for US born and foreign born individuals, among other data indicators.

Census data is classified by tracts, which, as discussed earlier in this paper, describes a subdivisions of a county that houses around 4,000 people, which means that census tract covers larger blocks in the city, and they get larger as we move away from downtown Manhattan where the population density is significantly higher than that of Queens or Brooklyn for example. The implication is significant on the experience design for the consumer application, as it implies walking for longer periods of times before the user can see any real change in data representation, especially when adjacent tracts display similar figures. Therefore, more granular data annotations with more frequent changes are definitely needed.

5.2 Hoodmaps

According to the City Lab online publication "Hoodmaps[3] are crowdsourced, color-coded maps that feature more than 2,000 cities around the world, letting users draw and highlight parts of each city depending on what kind of urbanite they think is most likely to be found there. Each city is divided into six color-coded categories: hipsters, "normies," suits, tourists, "uni" (students), and rich. Users can also add tags wherever they want to say something that goes beyond one of the six categories." (Echenique).

Developed by Pieter Levels, who's originally from Amsterdam, his intention was to allow visitors who have never been in the city before to find about the "real" places that embody the spirit of the city, not the tourist areas that do not really represent the local scenes. Therefore he created this system that allows people to write their own narrative take on the city by using very few words, and tagging specific areas of the city with them. Hoodmaps geo-tags all their user annotations, and places them on an open source map, annotating neighborhoods, streets, corners, or entire blocks with different tags.

Having contacted the developer to ask for their permission to use the data, I had access to a database of tags and entries, which was already indexed and identified by geolocation coordinates.

6 The Product

6.1 The Database and Server

Working with the data sources mentioned above, I downloaded the census data for the five boroughs of New York, which included data for more than 3000 census tracts,

---

[3] https://hoodmaps.com/.

and normalized them into one table by cross-referencing the census tract numbers and neighborhood names using an R script to handle the large amount of data. The resulting data was inserted into a MySQL database. Hoodmap data, which was already normalized and available as a json file, was also transformed by another R script into a CSV file that can be cross-referenced with the census data, and was inserted into the same database in a different table.

The next challenge was to work on a system to retrieve the census data based on specific geo coordinates. Since all census data are indexed by tract number, not by geolocation coordinates (Longitude and Latitude), I had to find a conversion method that is fast, almost real-time, and flexible enough to still work with future census updates.

Looking into the Census office website I found a public HTTP API that accepts Longitude and Latitude coordinates and returns the corresponding tract number, so I built an HTTP server that uses NodeJS and ExpressJS to handle that conversion for me. That server would take any query with a specific geo location point (Longitude and Latitude), make a server-side request to the Census open API with those parameters, which will in turn retrieve the corresponding census tract number and return it to my NodeJS server. The server then would query the MySQL database with this newly retrieved track number to retrieve the needed census data and return them to the consumer that made the initial request (Fig. 4).

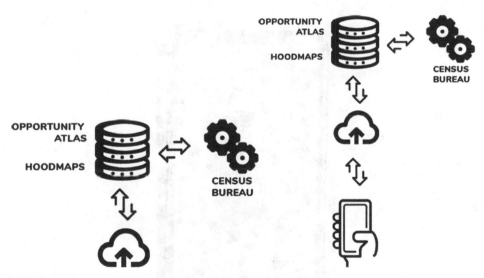

Fig. 4. Database and census API communication   **Fig. 5.** Application lifecycle

The Node/ExpressJS server was extended to provide a set of authenticated RESTful API endpoints which allow reading and writing to the database by multiple 3rd party consumers. Using an OAuth2.0 mechanism to secure any incoming API requests, the server can return census data and Hoodmaps tags to any incoming authenticated request with a valid geolocation coordinates, making any needed server-to-server request to the Census Bureau's API endpoint to get the exact tract number by location coordinates as described before. The server is deployed using the Heroku cloud service, and connects to an Amazon S3 bucket to upload and retrieve media annotations.

6.2 The Mobile App Prototype

The mobile experience prototype is intended to validate the functionality and validity of the initial assumptions, and the inner workings of the server and database. The mobile application loads the data from the server using on the user's location as they navigate in the city streets.

The Application, which was developed in React Native for iOS, periodically queries the user's position using the phone's GPS and send a request to the server every 0.2 miles to retrieve the data based on the user's current location. The NodeJS server will then query the Census API to translate the location into the corresponding Census tract number and use that number to query the right data from the MySQL database and return them to the mobile app for display (Fig. 5).

With a simple display, the app shows a red dot in the center of the screen to represent the user's location, and places the hoodmap tags in approximate geographic positioning, displaying how far they are from the user's location. The bottom of the screen shows the census metrics that are relevant to the user's location, and they update as users move from one census tract to another (Fig. 6).

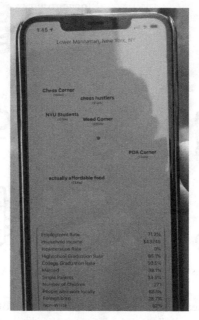

Fig. 6. First app prototype (Color figure online)

This app shows the need for an augmented, more granular data annotations to enrich the experience and make the process more engaging, since data remained scarce, and the display stayed static across multiple blocks, only updating tag distance and orientation in reference to the user's red dot.

6.3 City Data Story

The next phase of development was to design and build a tool that enables people to complement, contrast, protest, or expand on the already existing database by adding other location-specific datasets that consist of images and sounds. The new tool allows for crowdsourcing user-generated visual and audible tags about the city. Like Hoodmaps, the annotation media is tagged to a specific location and is left on the map, but unlike Hoodmaps which explicitly asks users to stereotype their city, the tool encourages people to contemplate on how to represent the spirit of the neighborhood with one image or a sound recording. These new annotations, combined with the already existing database, can add up to a richer user experience.

The Website, City Data Stories[4] is an online tool that allows people to upload their images and sounds to a specific location on the map and contribute to writing an audio-visual narrative of their city. This responsive website leverages google maps for geolocation and annotation placement and uses Google's Geolocation API and Places API to facilitate location searching in the map in the search field.

The website invites people to visit an *About* page, which has a two minutes introduction video about the project, explaining the concept and showing users how to upload their annotations through screen recordings instructions. The Go to map button takes users to the main view of the website, the map view (Fig. 7).

Fig. 7. City data stories - main map view

---

[4] https://datastories.city/.

The map view centers itself by default on Washington Square Park in Manhattan, right across the street from the library building of the New York University. The map shows an overlay of the Hoodmaps tags, scaled by the number of votes, which makes tags with higher votes more legible than those with lower votes.

Over those tags are the image and sound layers, which show all the annotations that users have uploaded to the site within the viewing square pf the map and the zoom level. The interface has an address search text field that allows people to search for a specific address, an intersection or a business or landmark. Below the search field are three filter that allow people to toggle visibility of the different attributes by type to allow for a clearer perspective of the map (Fig. 8).

Fig. 8. Annotation details

Image and Sound annotation icons are clickable, which allows visitors to see a bigger image or a sound player in a popup that overlays the website. Annotation details include a bigger size image, a title, and a description. The name of the person who uploaded the annotations. The uploaded annotations are not meant to be images or sounds without context, uploaded media only become annotations when their geographical positioning is contextualized through title and description.

Users can add their own annotations by clicking on the Add Yours button on the top-right side of the browsers, which takes them into another map view without the annotation clutter (Fig. 9).

Fig. 9. City data stories website - add yours instructions

First time users are greeted with a popup message the first time they access the website which explains to them the process of uploading annotations and provides hints on how to choose images or sound to upload, and why (Fig. 10).

Fig. 10. City data stories website - add yours instructions

When users click on a point in the map, an upload dialogue is generated with a short instructions blurb and a button to select the file we want to upload. There are two tabs on top of the upload dialogue, which allow the users to choose whether they are uploading an image or a sound (Fig. 11).

After the file is selected, users are greeted with another dialogue where they get to enter the details of the file they are uploading. While captions (description) and username are optional, media title is mandatory as people need to express why they think that their media is relevant to that location.

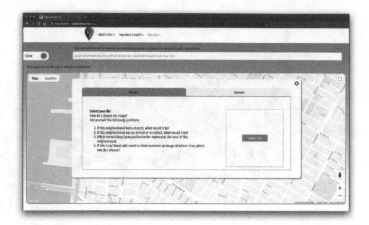

Fig. 11. City data stories website - add yours instructions - upload dialogue

The website incorporates a reporting system where users can report any content they deem inappropriate, which will alert the site admin to either investigate or simply delete the delinquent content.

The City Data Stories website is built with HTML5, SASS/CSS3, and ReactJS as the main framework. Communication with the NodeJS backend happen through authenticated Restful API calls. The website is also designed to be responsive to mobile devices and has passed the W3 accessibility test online.

7 Testing

After the website was built and deployed on a live server, it was time to test and evaluate the final product with two different user bases: one that was familiar with my project and original idea, which mostly consisted of class cohorts at the NYU Integrated Digital Media thesis class, and another group than was never informed about the project's concept, but were directly or indirectly working in domains that are related to architecture, urban design, or design in general.

The questions were sent to participants as a google questionnaire, with a set of questions around the concept, design, user experience, and accessibility.

7.1 Concept

The concept was received well in general with largely positive feedback. One commentator called the app "a visual Wikipedia", and another called it "yelp for the city". However, the recurring theme in the comments were concerns about privacy and security, and whether the app retains any of the user's personal information or share their information and media with any 3rd party.

There was also a sense of hesitation about willingness to participate and annotate vs. the willingness to navigate and view the annotations. One interesting suggestion was to enable the annotations in street view in addition to map view. This way, media will not be solely anchored to a two-dimensional location, rather oriented and placed in space in a position that contextualizes it within the context of the current environment.

7.2 Design

Design feedback was lukewarm, with comments about the need to reconsider and improve the color scheme. Some comments described the map view as cluttered since the Hoodmaps tags were creating graphical noise that makes the map look unreadable. A possible roadmap includes mimicking the Hoodmaps' system which only shows higher-rating tags on more global zooms, increasing tags visibility as users zoom-in.

There were comments asking for camera access to directly take photos and upload images to the map. The majority of comments preferred using pan & zoom as ways to navigate towards a clearer view on the map rather than using filters. Some asked for the ability to navigating annotations from the detailed view through arrows.

8 Conclusion and Future Work

This research aims to build a set of tools that bring urban data into the hands of city dwellers and everyday people. This idea starts from the proposal that data can be curated to tell a story about the city where data is not only a collection of hard numbers and statistics, rather augmented with images, sounds, stories, and interpretations. The tool that I describe in this paper enables for the creation of location-specific urban media annotations that contrast and augment the spatially spread statistical census data. This tool will feed into the larger concept behind this research, which is the creation of an experiential urban walk that allows for the navigation of an annotated dimension of the city by using augmented reality as a tool and a lens that allow us to reveal this hidden dimension without completely disconnecting from the physical reality.

This project can be viewed as a platform that can be shaped into many things: a platform for activism and resilience of society, a narrative for creating and designing experiences, a democratic platform that allows for individual contribution to the definition and the story of the city, and a platform that enables decision making, not necessarily from a professional perspective, but also from the point of view of everyday users and city dwellers.

The next immediate steps in the development of this project will be split into two phases: refining the existing annotation tool to address the feedback from the user testing, and build the augmented reality urban walk, which will be largely informed by the development process of the mobile app prototype as described earlier in this paper, and expanded to display the data in Augmented reality rather than flat representations on the screen.

Thinking of this project as a platform rather than a product means that the door is open for future possibilities and variations over the same idea without having to redesign or reconceptualize the project from scratch. Some immediate future implementations include allowing users to create and share urban excavation pathways with their friends, creating curated urban walks, creating historical walks, and curating urban soundscapes.

References

Echenique, M.: Hoodmaps Wants You to Stereotype Your Neighborhood - CityLab. City Lab (2017). https://www.citylab.com/life/2017/08/hoodmap-stereotype-your-city-hipsters/538218/

Foucault, M.: Discipline and Punish: The Birth of the Prison. Vintage (2012)

Hanington, B., Martin, B.: Universal Methods of Design Expanded and Revised: 125 Ways to Research Complex Problems, Develop Innovative Ideas, and Design Effective Solutions. Rockport Publishers, Gloucester (2019)

Picon, A.: Smart Cities: A Spatialised Intelligence. Wiley, New York (2015)

Picon, A., Ratti, C.: Mapping the future of cities: cartography, urban experience, and subjectivity. New Geograph. **9**, 62–65 (2019)

Sassen, S.: Unsettling Topographic Representation. Sentient City: Ubiquitous Computing, Architecture, and the Future of Urban Space, Mark Shepard (ed.). MIT Press Cambridge (2011)

Shepard, M.: Towards The Sentient City. Sentient City: Ubiquitous Computing, Architecture, and the Future of Urban Space, edited by Masrk Shepard, Architectural League of New York, New York, Cambridge (2011)

Zimmerman, J., Forlizzi, J., Evenson, S.: Research through design as a method for interaction design research in HCI. In: Proceedings of the SIGCHI Conference on Human Factors in Computing Systems (2007)

The Inclusion of Citizens in Smart Cities Policymaking: The Potential Role of Development Studies' Participatory Methodologies

Diogo Correia[1]($\boxtimes$) , José Feio[2] , Leonor Teixeira[3] ,
and João Lourenço Marques[4]

[1] Management, Industrial Engineering and Tourism, Governance, Competitiveness and Public Policies, Department of Economics, University of Aveiro, 3010-193 Aveiro, Portugal
diogo.correia@ua.pt

[2] University of Oxford, Oxford, UK

[3] Department of Economics, Management, Industrial Engineering and Tourism, Institute of Electronics and Informatics Engineering of Aveiro, University of Aveiro, 3010-193 Aveiro, Portugal
lteixeira@ua.pt

[4] Department of Social, Political and Territorial Sciences, Governance, Competitiveness and Public Policies, University of Aveiro, 3010-193 Aveiro, Portugal
jjmarques@ua.pt

Abstract. Smart Cities emerged in the 90s. Since then the concept has passed from several phases from a purely techno-centric vision to see technology as a means and not an end in itself. Alongside this evolution, the role of citizens has been changing. Nowadays, citizens are seen as taking part in the co-design and co-creation of Smart Cities. However, standard participatory development methodologies are still lacking to guide policymakers.

This paper will critically evaluate the role of citizens in smart cities' governance. Smart City governance can be seen as a specific type of policymaking. Accordingly, knowledge from other disciplines that explore policymaking can be useful in highlighting flaws and future opportunities for smart cities governance. The present work explores this when it comes to the role of citizens in policymaking. It makes use of the knowledge from development geography, and reviews how citizens participation has been understood in smart cities governance. It does so by combining a review of the literature as well as interviews with Portuguese smart cities policymakers. This paper brings these insights together. The results show that while smart city policymakers recognize the importance of including citizens in policymaking, the practical application of this is still very limited. This can be enhanced by using knowledge from development geographies approach to similar problems as well as via the development of tools and guidelines. Future research should explore both of these aspects.

Keywords: Citizen · Smart cities · Development studies · Participation · Inclusion and Co-creation

© Springer Nature Switzerland AG 2021
N. Streitz and S. Konomi (Eds.): HCII 2021, LNCS 12782, pp. 29–40, 2021.
https://doi.org/10.1007/978-3-030-77015-0_3

1   Introduction

Smart city governance is a type of policymaking. It is distinct from other policymaking types as it focuses on local level changes that have a specific purpose, i.e. make cities smarter. Despite the definition of what can be considered a smart city and therefore the object of smart city policymaking is beyond this article's scope, this article addresses two key differences drawing on the above. First, smart city policymaking, as compared to, for example, national-level policymaking in areas such as health and employment, involved markedly different actors such as local level policymakers and enterprises, which might create different policymaking dynamics. Second, this has led to smart city policymaking being studied by a different academic community. While national-level policymaking is often studied in university departments of public and social policy, smart city's governance is often studied in engineering departments. This leads to a creation of a diverse academic community which approaches policymaking in multiple ways.

There have been recently some works which have attempted to bridge knowledge from other academic communities into smart cities. In a previous paper, the authors attempted to show the importance of knowledge from social policy to smart cities' future [1]. This paper follows this by bringing together the two issues outlined above. It explores the dynamics between actors relevant for smart city policymaking. In specific, it explores the role of citizens in smart cities policymaking. Moreover, it does so by exploring debates on the inclusion of citizens in local policymaking, which have taken place in the discipline of development geography.

There is a great agreement in the literature about the importance of the citizen being included in the co-creation, however, there is little presence of information on what methods, tools, and timings there should be promoted their participation, and empirical examples of best practices that have revealed positive results.

When thinking about the citizens' role, it is useful to have a theoretical understanding of policymaking. There are various ways of understanding the several steps in policymaking and several theories about relevant factors for its development. One broad way of understanding policymaking is to see it as a cycle which starts with agenda setting (i.e. the recognition of a problem which needs to be tackled), followed by policy formulation (i.e. the development of a policy solution to the identified problem), legitimation (i.e. the recognition by relevant actors of the need to put forward the policy solution), implementation (i.e. the act of putting in place the policy solution), evaluation (i.e. the assessment of whether the policy solution has effectively addressed the identified problem), and finally the policy maintenance, succession or termination (i.e. a decision about how to change or not the policy in place which can then lead to a new agenda setting moment) [2, 3].

Different stakeholders such as Non-governmental Organizations (NGOs), the general public and policymakers can play a role in different policy cycle parts. Moreover, their influence on policymaking will significantly depend on which elements of the cycle they are involved.

This understanding of the policy cycle should motivate scholars to understand not just whether certain actors are involved in policymaking but in which parts of it and in which ways [4]. This article aims to do so for one specific stakeholder, citizens, as well as for one specific type of policymaking, smart cities policymaking.

2 Theoretical Background

2.1 Learnings from Zero Carbon Cities and the Importance of Participation

When considering smart cities' future, it is useful to look back at previous disruptive conceptualizations and their consequences. One of the most predominant was the concept of Zero Carbon Cities.

Drastic cuts in emissions on 95% from all sources will be necessary in the developed world. Therefore, new urban developments are being announced, taking into account ambitious targets for carbon emissions and reducing energy consumption [5], preserving sustainable urban development with the minimal ecological footprint.

Zero carbon cities (or carbon neutral) aim to become a city that does not emit carbon to the atmosphere. To achieve that goal, this term has been used to name the cities built from the scratch, with vast amounts of investment to fulfill that, and attract and nurture technology companies.

A diverse set of projects were being put in place to fulfill that ambition. Among them are Songdo in Korea, Masdar City in Abu Dhabi, UAE, and Dongtan in Shangai, China. In Songdo, South Korea, a city was built from scratch. This was a highly technologically advanced urban space, and its objective was to have 50% of green spaces with smart waste management between other smart city technologies [6]. A similar project was started in Masdar, Abu Dhabi, to make a zero waste and zero-emission city. The city is still under construction and aims to be a car-free city by favoring public transport and autonomous electric vehicles [7]. In Dongtan, Shanghai a similar project in an agricultural land located in the third biggest island of China, has a half a million target population. It has the goal of achieving 100% consumption of renewable energy by 2030 [8].

These cities' projects, sometimes referred as "Smart Cities in box" [9], have been noticing several constraints and turned cities into ghost cities because people did not relate themselves with the built artificial environment and did not want to live there. In a nutshell, Ghost Cities were born from the concept of Zero Carbon Cities, megalomaniac projects in which cities were created entirely from scratch but whose occupation and habitability fell far short. These cities were thought with the first stage of Smart Cities in mind, having its development been largely pushed from corporations to residents.

This draws the attention to the growing importance of the theme of inclusion and participation. People have to be capable of using technology to benefit from it [10].

The inclusion of Citizens in the creation and design of Smart Cities comes to oppose the underlying assumptions of Zero Carbon Cities.

The adaptation of smart cities policies and ideologies towards the future rather than creating cities from zero seems to be the only way [11]. Thus, may not be the most technological or the most efficient but are intended to promote policies and solutions designed jointly with citizens to improve existing living conditions, understanding together which problems exist in cities and which solution best serves the purposes of citizens and with which they are identified more for their resolution. Moreover, if citizens are not consulted in any stage of the process, there is a risk that they will not adopt the proposed solution.

2.2 The Role of Citizens in Smart Cities

Smart Cities appeared in the 90s to face the challenges raised from urbanization and globalization witnessed by cities [12–15]. The concept was primarily associated with technologies and had a techno-centric vision where Information and Communication Technologies (ICTs) would solve all the emerging problems [16, 17]. For some time, technological companies sold this vision and led cities' innovation. After Hollands [18] criticized the direction things were going, the focus passed to promote sustainability and citizens' quality of life. ICTs were a means and not an end [19]. That was also fueled by the 2008 world's financial crisis and population acknowledgment of the global warming effects [20].

Nowadays, cities have gone from being developed for citizens to being developed with citizens. The focus has changed from the technology diffusion to meet corporate and economic interests and citizens having a passive role to focus on people, governance, and policy where citizens act as co-creators and contributors for the city [21]. Cities are increasingly promoting a co-creative dynamic environment where the opportunity is given to citizens for co-creation in a technology-cities-people involvement.

Smart Cities public participation literature is centered in finding the best ways to engage citizens in urban designing using computing technologies, empowering them not just as data collectors but also as designers [22].

Mueller, Lu, Chirkin, Klein and Schmitt [23] created the concept of Citizen Design Science, as the new way to integrate citizens' ideas and wishes in the urban planning process combining crowdsourcing opinions through ICTs with design tools. Salim and Haque [24] proposed a taxonomy of urban computing, addressing user interaction modes, provocations, and scale of participation, in mobile crowdsensing, urban probes, participatory urbanism, interactive public display, and also interactive urban intervention. Memarovic et al. [25] defined three levels of engagement in public spaces: passive (people just observe), active (interact with the display) and discovery (learn and appreciate the contents stimulated). Through a workshop with various stakeholders, Forlano and Mathew [26] set up a collaborative designing process from brainstorming to prototype a 25–30 years future city scenario. Marsal-Llacuna and López-Ibáñez [27] developed a Smart Urban Planning Method based on reverse engineering principles. Through web-based surveys and data mining tools, citizens were asked about their urban activities in the previous 24 h and their desired scenarios for urban activities to ultimately find the optimal land use.

City's sustainability and mostly social sustainability can only be achieved by the community's engagement, which can be enhanced through digital modes of participation rather than just the conventional [28].

Simonofski, Asensio, De Smedt and Snoeck [29] proposed the CitiVoice Framework where citizens participate in the three different phases: as democratic participants in decision making, co-creators of ideas and solutions, and users. It also defines the criteria as hierarchically organized into dimensions and sub-dimensions. Boukhris, Ayachi, Elouedi, Mellouli and Amor [30] proposed a tool based on multicriteria decision making based on citizens' opinions. This hybrid model of weighting and options ranking is applied in deciding the allocation of the budget among several projects.

Because of the diminished noted existing research of citizen involvement in Smart Cities, Granier and Kudo [31] studied several Japanese cities and communities through interviews and analysis of official documents and concluded that public participation is not at the city governance level, but instead as participants in the co-production of public services (e.g. energy production and distribution).

Webster and Leleux [32] defined as mechanisms of Smart city participation and co-production: hackathons, living labs, fab labs and maker spaces, smart urban labs, citizens' dashboard, gamification, open datasets, and crowdsourcing. The survey of Szarek-Iwaniuk and Senetra [33] 's case study made to Olsztyn's residents revealed that ICTs and mostly online surveys contribute and encourage the public to participate in decision-making. However, other options must not be forgotten to combat exclusion.

Although social media should not be considered as the primary tool for citizen participation, the Díaz-Díaz and Pérez-González [34] 's case study of the Santander City Brain shows a collaborative tool designed to promote open innovation by the share of ideas, comment and vote, which proves that a social media adapted method can represent an effective way to set the political agenda and influence political discourse. Moreover, in the organization chart, it can be noted democratic and non-democratic parts in the process.

Citizens can increasingly play an active role not just in data collection but also in decision making. Furthermore, for this are necessary methodologies capable of extracting the maximum value of the citizen.

Although Smart Cities concept are new, we must not forget that politicians still run cities. Therefore, the Political Party in charge, the agenda, and the wills of city's policymakers shall be considered. The Smart City initiatives have to be aligned with the policy agenda, which has its cycle [35]. The governance of a city is made up of electoral cycles. What does not change is the people who inhabit it. In planning the strategy to be adopted by these ecosystems' decision-makers it is necessary to listen and brainstorm with the different "Stakeholders", never underrating in the final decision the importance of the "citizens voice".

2.3 The Role of Citizens in Development Initiatives

Scholars of smart cities are not the first to consider the role of citizens in policymaking. The discipline of development geography has been one of the first to address these and consider the citizens' role in development initiatives in the Global South. Therefore, in any debate about the involvement of citizens in policymaking, the literature from development geography to provide relevant insights to it.

The debates in this discipline can be subdivided into three main phases. Top-down interventions marked the first phase, which happened in the post-World War II (WWII) decades [36]. These were often defined and constructed by international organizations such as the International Monetary Fund and the World Bank with very little involvement of the people affected by reforms. These reforms often took the form of deregulation of the economy. They assumed that this was a solution that could be applied regardless of the local context. This phase is often referred to as the Washington Consensus [37]. John Williamson [38] defined in 1989 ten sets of specific recommendations related to this, which included free trade, floating exchange rates, free markets, and macroeconomic stability.

The second phase came to life as a critique to the Washington Consensus [39]. It was recognized that there was a need to involve the people affected by policies in their development [40]. This appealed to both the new right and the left of the political spectrum to do development in the new millennium. Participatory development then emerged as the dominant paradigm. It was seen as a way of gathering the local knowledge of individuals to promote more efficient programs.

Moreover, it was also seen as a way to empower the poor and marginalized by giving them a voice and recognition in the development process [41]. This led to the emergence of partnerships between international organisations and local NGOs. For example, NGOs like the Slum Dwellers International and organisations such as the UN have since then worked to promote informal settlers' involvement in the development of their own urban space.

A third phase came as a critique to this move towards participation. Authors such as Cooke and Kothari [42] argued that it was not enough to involve citizens in the policymaking process. It is essential to ask who is being involved and what way. They argued that most participatory development interventions did not empower individuals but rather use local people as tokens rather than provide any real change. This is not a critique to participation itself but rather to specific ways of involving citizens [43]. What is needed is a complex understanding of the local context, which sees the power relations inherent to human relations and the struggles and conflicting interests between individual communities and intra-community groups

This development of understanding first policymaking as a top-down process and then moving towards engaging with citizens to understand then and address the complexities of this engagement can be seen as three critical phases in the move towards more significant and more empowering citizens' involvement policymaking. Therefore, this paper will explore how policymakers in cities understand citizens' involvement in smart cities policymaking and attempt to place this understanding in one of these three phases to better grasp what still needs to be done in this field.

3   Methodology

3.1   Data Collection, Data Analysis and Sample

In terms of methodology, this research uses qualitative methods to explore citizens' role in smart cities. Specifically, how it is perceived, who are the actors that define the structure of these policy processes, and who is involved.

In terms of data collection, in-depth interviews were conducted with eight policymakers from different Portuguese cities. This covered a range of cities from different regions of the Portuguese territory, with different characteristics, the smallest one with around 20 000 people and the largest one with around 240 000. The interviews were conducted via Zoom between January and February 2021. These were then transcribed. These interviews focused on understanding how policymakers think about and consider the role that citizens play in smart cities policymaking efforts.

In terms of data analysis, a thematic analysis was conducted. This followed an inductive approach. Accordingly, the transcriptions of the interviews were scanned, and emerging codes from the data were identified. The data was then coded according to these. The following sector presents them.

In terms of ethical considerations, this research's main ethical issue has to do with the anonymity of participants. This is especially the case due to the small number of interviews conducted. Interviews were therefore anonymized. For these purposes, no names of cities or policymakers will be referred. Interviewees (policymakers) will be numbered and only this information will be provided below in Table 1.

Table 1. Policymakers and cities sample data

	City (Population)	City (Location)
Policymaker 1	45 000	South
Policymaker 2	20 000	Center
Policymaker 3	240 000	North
Policymaker 4	35 000	North
Policymaker 5	140 000	Center
Policymaker 6	40 000	North
Policymaker 7	210 000	South
Policymaker 8	190 000	North

4 Results

This section presents the results from the thematic analysis of the interviews. Data was aggregated to highlight the similarities between the interviewees' answers to the need, type and challenges of citizens involvement.

4.1 The Need to Involve Citizens

All policymakers considered it is essential to involve citizens in the policymaking process. For example, Policymaker 1 considered it was essential to involve citizens through "initial opinion studies, which would increase commitment and gather contributions". Policymaker 5 considered that, despite their city does not actively involve citizens, "it is important to do so at an early stage to evaluated pros and cons and post-implementation to understand the satisfaction with a certain solution".

4.2 Types of Citizens Involvement

Another aspect that emerged from the interviews is the different ways of engaging with citizens. Following from the literature reviewed in previous chapters Table 2 outlines the different types of engagement across Policymakers. Two aspects become apparent. First, there is a wide range of citizens involvement across the various cities, from citizens not being involved at all to them taking part in the design and trial of solutions. This suggests that even within the same country, the local context is still determinant when it comes to citizens involvement. Second, besides variety, some cities already have a high level of involvement of citizens with focus groups, forum discussions and involvement in designing solutions.

Table 2. Types of involvement per Policymaker (PM) interviewed

	Citizens are not involved	Passive Participation	Active Participation	Co-design of Solutions	Co-creation of Strategies
PM 1		Questionnaires about policy options			
PM2	People are not motivated to get involved				
PM 3				Design and trial of solutions	
PM 4			Discussion Forums and Mobile Apps		
PM 5	Participation is not promoted				
PM 6	People are not motivated to get involved				
PM 7			Focus Groups and Mobile APPs		
PM 8		Requests for suggestions and feedback via email			

4.3 Problems Associated with Involvement of Citizens

Citizens are Not Used to Being Involved. It was acknowledged that this is not a common practice and that "citizens are not used to be consulted" (Policymaker 2). One aspect which was mentioned across all interviews was that there was a cultural barrier to participation. It was argued that Portuguese citizens are not used to neither motivated for civic participation and strategic thinking necessary for smart cities policymaking. Citizens are involved in electoral campaigns but not in the policymaking processes that follow. Policymaker 6, for example, argues that after these campaigns, "there is no specific moment of discussion" for the involvement of citizens. Policymakers argued that citizens "do not give the information they are looking for" as often they focus a lot on their interests rather than on the city as a whole.

Citizens Do Not Have the Necessary Information to Be Involved. It was also argued that citizens engagement is hampered by a lack of knowledge on their part. Citizens are argued not to have critical thinking regarding smart cities. Policymaker 6, for example, argued that in participatory budget exercise "none of the proposals related to smart cities" but rather to individuals' interests. It was argued for the need to separate between what is qualified participation and what is not.

Often Only the More Radical Voices Are Spoken. Various policymakers also mentioned that in different forms of engagement such as participatory budgets or via social media, it is often the most extreme vocal voices. This shapes the debate in a way that ignores the concerns of the majority of citizens.

Lack of Human Resources. Engaging with citizens is argued to require much commitment from policymakers. Most of them argue that this requires dedicated teams to inform citizens and sort out the information they provide. In often strained human resources, this is a problem outlined by many of the policymakers interviewed.

Lack of Methodological Standard Approaches. Throughout the years the Government has promoted the enhancement of cities' participatory budgets, however, these are unanimously seen by policymakers has a non-effective method. They refer that the logic of territorially distributing money across multiple projects is manipulated by the interests of some groups for local interventions rather than that the promotion of global well-being or a vision for the future. However, they also say that they lack other tools to involve citizens in a standard way.

5 Discussion

When analyzing the above responses, one is able to place how these Policymakers understand the involvement of citizens in relation to the literature of development geography reviewed in Sect. 2.3. It is clear that all Policymakers recognize the importance of involving citizens in policymaking. This suggests that phase one is not a good description of the current state of play in smart cities policymaking. One can also note that while they recognize this importance, many Policymakers outline problems in involving citizens and various constraints associated with it. However, some Policymakers also recognize a highly developed understanding of power dynamics and how it is important to consider whose voice is being heard. This suggests that smart cities policymaking is currently in between the phase 2 and phase 3 of development geography understanding of the involvement of citizens in policymaking.

One should also pay attention not just to what is mentioned but also to what is not. When talking about the problems associated with citizens participation, most Policymakers put the onus on the citizens. It is the citizens who are not motivated and the citizens who are not well informed and that do not participate in the right way. However, one could easily turn the table around and say that it is the Policymakers who are not motivating the citizens enough, providing with the necessary information and explaining to them what type of insight they are looking for. Again, looking at the literature in development geography it becomes clear that it is possible to do high level engagement with citizens even if they lack knowledge and are not experienced in policymaking – a lot of development initiatives take place in countries of the Global South which have very low levels of education and in which citizens are often even further away from policy and politics than in countries of the Global North like Portugal. It is then clear that the problems outlined by Policymakers can be addressed by them and the responsibility for them should not necessarily be put on the citizens.

This research has two main limitations. First, only a small number of policymakers were interviewed which limits the generality of the findings. Second, the study only considers the perspective of policymakers. While this provides a good overview of the situation in this country it also limits the findings to the smart cities state of art in it.

In terms of future work, it becomes clear that at least in a Portuguese context there is a lack of knowledge about methodologies to involve citizens in smart cities policymaking. Most cities rely on participatory budgets while most Policymakers recognize that these are not adequate. Future research should explore the practical side of involving citizens, developing methodologies and guidelines for it. The goal to fully involve citizens will likely require involving them as early as possible. However, this is missing and requires guidance and research.

6 Conclusions

In conclusion, the need to include citizens in smart cities policymaking is unanimous. However, what is also unanimous is the many problems associated with this such as the inability of citizens to be able to have a holistic view and strategical thinking required to bring added value. This paper has argued that policymakers need to start viewing problems from their own perspective. It has placed the current thinking about citizens involvement within debates which took place in the discipline of development geography. This can allow for future research to explore insights from this discipline and use them in the development of citizens involvement in smart cities. Overall, by interviewing policymakers involved in smart cities it becomes clear that there is a need to develop practical tools to help them involve citizens in policymaking complemented with guidelines on how to deal with aspects such as inherent power relations within groups.

Acknowledgements. This work was financially supported by the research project DRIVIT-UP – DRIVIng forces of urban Transformation: assessing pUblic Policies (POCI-01-0145-FEDER-031905), funded by FEDER funds through COMPETE 2020 - Programa Operacional Competitividade e Internacionalização (POCI). It is developed within the research unit on Governance, Competitiveness and Public Policy (UIDB/04058/2020)+(UIDP/04058/2020), and the Institute of Electronics and Informatics Engineering of Aveiro (UIDB/00127/2020), both funded by national funds through FCT - Fundação para a Ciência e a Tecnologia.

References

1. Correia, D., Feio, J.: The Smart City as a social policy actor. In: International Conferences ICT, Society, and Human Beings (2020)
2. Head, B.W.: Three lenses of evidence-based policy. Aust. J. Public Adm. **67**(1), 1–11 (2008)
3. Jasanoff, S., et al.: Science and decisionmaking. Hum. Choice Clim. Chang. Soc. Framew. **1**, 1–87 (1998)

4. Leach, M., Scoones, I., Wynne, B.: Science and citizens: globalization and the challenge of engagement, vol. 2. Zed Books (2005)
5. Kennedy, S., Sgouridis, S.: Rigorous classification and carbon accounting principles for low and Zero Carbon Cities. Energy Policy **39**(9), 5259–5268 (2011)
6. Carvalho, L.: Smart cities from scratch? A socio-technical perspective. Cambridge J. Reg. Econ. Soc. **8**(1), 43–60 (2015)
7. Reiche, D.: Renewable Energy Policies in the Gulf countries: a case study of the carbon-neutral 'Masdar City' in Abu Dhabi. Energy Policy **38**(1), 378–382 (2010)
8. Cheng, H., Hu, Y.: Planning for sustainability in China's urban development: status and challenges for Dongtan eco-city project. J. Environ. Monit. **12**(1), 119–126 (2010)
9. Calzada, I., Cobo, C.: Unplugging: deconstructing the smart city. J. Urban Technol. **22**(1), 23–43 (2015)
10. Coe, A., Paquet, G., Roy, J.: E-governance and smart communities: a social learning challenge. Soc. Sci. Comput. Rev. **19**(1), 80–93 (2001)
11. Shelton, T., Zook, M., Wiig, A.: The 'actually existing smart city'. Cambridge J. Reg. Econ. Soc. **8**(1), 13–25 (2015)
12. Tan, M.: Creating the digital economy: strategies and perspectives from Singapore. Int. J. Electron. Commer. **3**(3), 105–122 (1999)
13. Gibson, R.W., Kozmetsky, D.V., Smilor, G.: The Technopolis Phenomenon: Smart Cities, Fast Systems, Global Networks, vol. 38, pp. 141–143 (1992)
14. van Bastelaer, B.: Digital cities and transferability of results. In: Proceeding 4th EDC Conference Digital cities, no. October, pp. 61–70 (1998)
15. Mahizhnan, A.: Smart cities: the Singapore case. Cities **16**(1), 13–18 (1999)
16. Ahvenniemi, H., Huovila, A., Pinto-Seppä, I., Airaksinen, M.: What are the differences between sustainable and smart cities? Cities **60**, 234–245 (2017)
17. Mora, L., Bolici, R., Deakin, M.: The first two decades of smart-city research: a bibliometric analysis. J. Urban Technol. **24**(1), 3–27 (2017)
18. Hollands, R.G.: Will the real smart city please stand up? Intelligent, progressive or entrepreneurial? City **12**(3), 303–320 (2008)
19. Nam, T., Pardo, T.A.: Conceptualizing smart city with dimensions of technology, people, and institutions. In: ACM International Conference Proceeding Series, pp. 282–291 (2011)
20. Lom, M., Pribyl, O., Svitek, M.: Industry 4.0 as a Part of Smart Cities, no. June, pp. 0–11 (2016)
21. Cohen, B.: The 3 Generations of Smart Cities (2015). https://www.fastcompany.com/304 7795/the-3-generations-of-smart-cities
22. Gooch, D., et al.: Amplifying Quiet voices: challenges and opportunities for participatory design at an urban scale. ACM Trans. Comput. Interact. **25**(1), 1–34 (2018)
23. Mueller, J., Lu, H., Chirkin, A., Klein, B., Schmitt, G.: Citizen design science: a strategy for crowd-creative urban design. Cities, **72**(August 2017), 181–188 (2018)
24. Salim, F., Haque, U.: Urban computing in the wild: a survey on large scale participation and citizen engagement with ubiquitous computing, cyber physical systems, and Internet of Things. Int. J. Hum. Comput. Stud. **81**, 31–48 (2015)
25. Memarovic, N., Langheinrich, M., Alt, F., Elhart, I., Hosio, S., Rubegni, E.: Using public displays to stimulate passive engagement, active engagement, and discovery in Public spaces. In: ACM International Conference Proceeding Ser. no. June 2016, pp. 55–64 (2012)
26. Forlano, L., Mathew, A.: From design fiction to design friction: speculative and participatory design of values-embedded urban technology. J. Urban Technol. **21**(4), 7–24 (2014)
27. Marsal-Llacuna, M.L., López-Ibáñez, M.B.: Smart urban planning: designing urban land use from urban time use. J. Urban Technol. **21**(1), 39–56 (2014)

28. Bouzguenda, I., Alalouch, C., Fava, N.: Towards smart sustainable cities: a review of the role digital citizen participation could play in advancing social sustainability. Sustain. Cities Soc. **50**(November 2018), 101627 (2019)

29. Simonofski, A., Asensio, E.S., De Smedt, J., Snoeck, M.: Hearing the voice of citizens in smart city design: the citivoice framework. Bus. Inf. Syst. Eng. **61**(6), 665–678 (2019)

30. Boukhris, I., Ayachi, R., Elouedi, Z., Mellouli, S., Ben Amor, N.: Decision model for policy makers in the context of citizens engagement: application on participatory budgeting. Soc. Sci. Comput. Rev. **34**(6), 740–756 (2016)

31. Granier, B., Kudo, H.: How are citizens involved in smart cities? Analysing citizen participation in Japanese 'smart Communities'. Inf. Polity **21**(1), 61–76 (2016)

32. Webster, C.W.R., Leleux, C.: Smart governance: opportunities for technologically-mediated citizen co-production. Inf. Polity **23**(1), 95–110 (2018)

33. Szarek-Iwaniuk, P., Senetra, A.: Access to ICT in Poland and the co-creation of Urban space in the process of modern social participation in a smart city-a case study. Sustain, **12**(5) (2020)

34. Díaz-Díaz, R., Pérez-González, D.: Implementation of social media concepts for e-Government: case study of a social media tool for value co-creation and citizen participation. J. Organ. End User Comput. **28**(3), 104–121 (2016)

35. Chen, S., Karwan, K.: Innovative cities in China: lessons from Pudong New District, Zhangjiang High-Tech Park and SMIC village. Innov. Manag. Policy Pract. **10**(2–3), 247–256 (2008)

36. Mathur, H.M.: Participatory development: some areas of current concern. Sociol. Bull. **46**(1), 53–95 (1997)

37. Gore, C.: The rise and fall of the Washington consensus as a paradigm for developing countries, **28**(5) (2000)

38. Williamson, J.: The Washington consensus revisited. Econ. Soc. Dev. into XXI Century, 48–61 (1997)

39. Cornwall, A.: Whose Voices ? Whose Choices ? reflections on gender and participatory development **31**(8), 1325–1342 (2003)

40. Mosse, D.: Authority, gender and knowledge: theoretical reflections on the practice of participatory rural appraisal. Dev. Change **25**(3), 497–526 (1994)

41. Mohan, G., Stokke, K.: Participatory development and empowerment: the dangers of localism. Third World Q. **21**(2), 247–268 (2000)

42. Cooke, B., Kothari, U.: Participation: the new tyranny? Zed books (2001)

43. Hickey, S., Mohan, G.: Participation: from tyranny to transformation: exploring new approaches to participation in development. Zed Books (2004)

The Importance of Theory for Understanding Smart Cities: Making a Case for Ambient Theory

H. Patricia McKenna[⊠]

AmbientEase, Victoria, Canada

Abstract. This paper seeks to develop a theoretical foundation for ambient theory as a theory in support of advancing definitions and understandings of smart cities and regions. Through a review of the evolving research literature for the ambient and for smart cities, a conceptual framework is formulated consisting of components and characteristics constituting ambient theory for smart cities and regions. The framework is then operationalized for use in this paper, exploring the practical application of ambient theory in smart cities and regions. Using a case study approach together with an explanatory correlational design, elements such as technology-driven services, creative opportunities, and access to public data are explored. Drawing additionally on other works where this approach is employed, elements such as awareness, information and communication technologies (ICTs), interactivity, and sensing are provided as further examples showing the potential for promising relationships in support of ambient theory for smart cities. Ambient theory as advanced in this paper is discussed in terms of theory usefulness, parsimony, and type. Future directions are identified for explorations of ambient theory going forward for both research and practice in contributing to definitions and understandings of smart cities and regions.

Keywords: Adaptability · Ambient human-computer interaction · Ambient theory · Awareness · Correlation · Creativity · Information and Communication Technologies (ICTs) · Interactivities · Sensing · Smart cities · Smart environments · Theory building

1 Introduction

In the context of grand challenges for human-computer interactions (HCI), Stephanidis et al. (2019) [1] highlight the need for "the conceptualization of theories, methodologies" arguing that "tools of a proactive and more generic nature" are needed to "more accurately adapt to the increased interactivity of new technologies." Streitz, Charitos, Kaptein, and Böhlen (2019) [2] address such grand challenges focusing on ambient intelligence (AmI) in relation to contexts for design in smart environments and societies. And yet, to understand AmI it is worth noting that in exploring the notion of "digital future", Dourish and Bell (2011) [3] describe and contextualize ubiquitous computing as it emerged from the research lab of Xerox PARC, speaking in terms of the "competing narratives" also

© Springer Nature Switzerland AG 2021
N. Streitz and S. Konomi (Eds.): HCII 2021, LNCS 12782, pp. 41–54, 2021.
https://doi.org/10.1007/978-3-030-77015-0_4

emerging from other research labs such as ambient intelligence from Phillips, pervasive computing from IBM, proactive computing from Intel, to name a few, providing different "research agendas." Other initiatives said to be associated with ubiquitous computing include that of the Internet of Things (IoT) at MIT [3]. Nakashima, Aghajan, and Augusto (2010) [4] clarified earlier on that although "networks, sensors, human-computer interfaces, pervasive computing and Artificial Intelligence" including "robotics and multiagent systems" are understood to be "all relevant" to AmI, it is however "AmI which brings together all these resources" along with "many other areas to provide flexible and intelligent services to users acting in their environments." And while acknowledging much larger phenomena such as ambient intelligence, Thibaud (2015) [5] chooses to highlight "microscopic transformations, mundane moments and background processes that support ordinary ambiances." In doing so, Thibaud (2015) [5] explores "the development of a sensory ecology of everyday life" noting that "it is as if we are witnessing a fundamental shift that is redefining how we think about the current ambient world."

In response, this paper provides a formulation of ambient theory for smart cities and regions; explores the potential for ambient theory to contribute to evolving understandings of smart cities; and advances ambient theory as "a tool of a proactive nature" in support of designs, developments, and implementations involving people more meaningfully and taking their needs into consideration when interacting with technologies and with each other in smart environments. Where ambient intelligence (AmI) focuses on systems to support people and their needs [2, 6], this paper addresses the ambient in terms of people and their multisensory capabilities as articulated by Thibaud (2015) [5] and Lévy (2008) [7], introducing ambient theory to complement and extend existing theory for smart cities [8], environments, regions, and beyond [9].

1.1 Background

Harrison et al. (2010) [10] identify and define information technology (IT) foundations and principles for smart cities focusing on instrumented, interconnected, and intelligent. Harrison and Abbott Donnelly (2011) [11] describe smart cities as "a field in want of a good theoretical base" proposing a theory of smart cities enabled through "instrumentation" as in, that which "makes the invisible visible." The importance of messiness in ubiquitous computing is highlighted by Dourish and Bell (2011) [3], recognizing "that the practice of any technology in the world is never quite as simple, straight forward, or idealized as it is imagined to be" such that, "mess is never far away" and that "technological realities are always contested." Streitz (2019) [12] describes the aspect of AmI environments where "computation is perceived as dissolving in behavior as well as into the physical environmental context" such that "the computer 'disappears' as a 'visible' distinctive device" which may occur "physically due to being integrated into the environment" on the one hand, "or mentally from our perception" on the other hand. Mosannenzadeh and Vettorato (2014) [13] provide a review of the research literature in search of a definition for the smart city concept and provide a conceptual framework based on keyword analysis, whereas a global definition is said to be lacking (Neirotti et al., 2014) [14] and fuzziness in understanding the smart city concept persists according to Lara et al. (2016) [15]. Ramaprasad, Sánchez-Ortiz, and Syu (2017) [16] provide a unified definition of smart city in the form of an ontology intended for use by smart city researchers and city officials. Batty (2020) [17] introduces the notion of high and low frequency cities associated with rapid change and slow change, respectively, calling for "more extensive science" and evolving urban theory to accommodate complexity, data mining, artificial intelligence (AI) and machine learning.

1.2 Definitions

Definitions are provided for key terms used in this paper based on the research literature.

Ambient. McCullough (2013) [18] defines ambient in a variety of ways such as, "that which surrounds but does not distract" and "a continuum of awareness and awareness of continuum."

Awareness. Drawing on the work of Gaver et al. (1992) [19], Streitz et al. (2007) [20] provide a definition of awareness in a workplace context "as the pervasive experience of knowing who is around, what sort of things they are doing, whether they are relatively busy or can be engaged, and so on" where the elements of "presence" and "availability" are important.

Smart Cities. Townsend (2013) [21] defines smart cities as "places where information technology is combined with infrastructure, architecture, everyday objects, and even our bodies to address social, economic and environmental problems."

2 Theoretical Perspective

In developing a theoretical perspective for this paper, a review of the research literature is provided for the ambient in Sect. 2.1; ambience and ambiance in Sect. 2.2; smart cities and the ambient in Sect. 2.3; enabling formulation in Sect. 2.4 of a conceptual framework for ambient theory for smart cities.

2.1 The Ambient

McCullough (2013) [18] identifies the importance of awareness in describing the ambient as "a continuum of awareness" and "an awareness of continuum" pointing possibly to the characteristics of persistence and pervasiveness. Crawford and Ballif (2014) [22] suggest that Rickert (2013) [23] advanced "an ambient theory" in relation to "materiality" in arguing that "the virtual" is a space that can be experienced, such that the notion of "virtuality" is described as "the mode of being-in-networks" adding that, "it is not less authentic than face-to-face existence, just different in the affordances, hinderances, and intensities." For Rickert (2013) [23], the terms "artificiality" and "virtuality" are considered to be "similarly poor descriptions for something better understood as ambient invention and creation." According to Rickert (2013) [23], among the benefits of the ambient is the understanding "of action as *material, affective, ecological*, and *emergent*." Papastergiadis, Barakin, and McQuire (2016) [24] explore "ambient screens" in order to consider "the extent to which urban interactions with large screens are indicative of new modes of perception, awareness, and subjectivity" that is referred to as "ambient awareness" and described as "a mode of inhabiting mediated cities." Citing the work of Benjamin (1986) [25], Papastergiadis et al. (2016) [24] note that "the ambient refers to a mode of attention that enables a discernment of what is a relevant point from a field of multiple references" where "the process of discernment requires an ability to stretch consciousness, derive information from multiple reference points, including new visual technologies" so as to "develop a sensibility." In this context, Papastergiadis et al. (2016) [24] describe ambient awareness as "a sensibility that attends to the field by relating elements that are peripheral to each other and organizing them into a new form" and that such forms "are themselves fleeting and contingent." Papastergiadis et al. (2016) [24] also refer to the notion of an "ambient perspective" in describing "the sensory processes that are in play in the casual observer's reaction to urban screens" noting that the "tendency toward the interlinking of human and nonhuman 'agency' that we have described as ambient awareness has also variously been described as 'ambient intelligence'," citing the work of Aarts, Harwig, and Schuurmans (2001) [26]. Sengupta (2020) [27] describes the notion of ambient computing as "the use of computers and the internet without consciously using them" involving "intelligent agents" that use "a combination of hardware, software, human-device interaction, user experience and machine learning."

2.2　Ambience and Ambiance

Over time, as described in this section, researchers have used the variant spellings of ambience and ambiance.

Ambience. In moving toward the development of ambient theory, Rickert (2013) [23] describes ambience as "material and spatial" and "embedded in place" to form "a plastic, open-ended, and evolving event." Papastergiadis et al. (2016) [24] employ the term "ambience" in describing "the density and spread of information" and "new technologies for handling contingency." Streitz et al. (2019) [2] note that "the term 'ambience' is an important aspect of the concept of ambient intelligence" in that AmI "stresses the environmental character of these systems and the experiences they evoke." Further, Streitz et al. (2019) [2], drawing on the work of Aarts and De Ruyter (2009) [28], state that "the concept of ambience in AmI implies that computation becomes non-obtrusively integrated into everyday objects and spaces."

Ambiance. Thibaud (2015) [5] refers to "the 'setting of ambiance' in urban spaces" where discussions of ambiance and atmosphere emerge. According to Thibaud (2015) [5], "from a theoretical point of view the notion of ambiance is not fundamentally different from the notion of atmosphere" yet in terms of relationships, "ambiance tends to emphasize more the situated, the built and the social dimensions of sensory experience" with a focus on "design activity" whereas "atmosphere is more affective, aerial and political oriented" focusing on "philosophical, ontological and geographical issues." Thibaud (2015) [5] employs "experience design" in relation to perspectives on urban design in terms of "ambiance, *operating modes*" including "establishing the sensory as a field of action, composing with affective tonalities, giving consistency to urban situations, maintaining spaces over time and playing with imperceptible transformations." Thibaud (2015) [5] claims that "ambiance cannot be precisely located because it has more to do with a pervasive field" emerging from the "coalescence of the various factors making up a situation." Contributing to theory building efforts, Piga et al. (2016) [29] engage in "mapping ambiances." It is worth noting that the recent International Congress on Ambiances (2020) [30] places a focus on "the renewal of the forms of feeling in a world that is undergoing major changes" highlighting the "emergence of potential new kinds of senses and sensibilities" at the axes of "new sensitizations", "human and non-human sensitivities", and "artificial and extended sensibility."

2.3   Smart Cities and the Ambient

The notion of awareness emerges as a key element in the construction of smart artefacts in ambient environments as described by Prante, Stenzel, Röcker, Streitz, and Magerkurth (2004) [31]. Awareness also emerges in relation to ambient displays and privacy issues, as an example of smart artefacts, as described by Streitz, et al. (2007) [20] in terms of "affordances for awareness" in the context of "augmented and shared environments" for "interaction and experience design" around distributed teams enabled by information and communication technologies (ICTs). Drawing on the work of awareness researchers [19], Streitz, et al. (2007) [20] point to the importance of "information about presence and availability" as key to awareness. By introducing ICTs, together with "sensing technology into everyday objects of our environments", Streitz, et al. (2007) [20] describe the notion of "smart environments" preferring 'smart' to 'intelligent' "to avoid a too anthropomorphic association" giving way to a "new quality of interaction and 'behaviour' (of artefacts)." A distinction is made between "system-oriented, importunate smartness" and "people-oriented, empowering smartness" where the former features action and decision-making "without a human in the loop" while the latter includes "the human in the loop and in control as much as possible and feasible" promoting the perspective that "smart spaces make people smarter" while "designing 'experiences' with the help of smart or augmented spaces" [20]. As such, "awareness about our physical and social environment" is extended "by providing observation data and parameters that – in many cases – are 'invisible' to our human senses" citing the examples of "pollution data or computer network traffic" thus giving way to "new experiences" [20]. With this information, Streitz, et al. (2007) [20] argue that "the world around us becomes the interface" and yet, people have always been able to sense the presence of smoke through scent and sight; the presence, force and direction of the wind; not to mention the information revealed through well-worn paths. In the context of explorations of collaborative and "awareness technologies", Brewer, Williams, and Dourish (2007) [32] highlight the importance of design for meaningful use(s) in support of appropriation and daily practices "through real use." According to Streitz, et al. (2007) [20], "a core function of smart environments" is the "collecting and processing of personal information" where "privacy and ubiquity" would "seem to be in a constant conflict" giving rise to the need for "zones of interaction" (e.g., ambient, notification, and interaction zones) enabling "differentiated services" by distance or proximity as well as "awareness moments" and "experiences of awareness".

Gams et al. (2019) [6] describe ambient intelligence (AmI) as "an experience of the user with respect to the services provided by" intelligent systems, identifying the tendency "to consider AmI to be something artificial" as in, "something made by human beings." McKenna (2017) [33] speaks in terms of "urbanizing the ambient" as a pathway toward "engaging people in meaningful discussion about the smart city phenomena" offering a framework for enriching spaces, things, and designs in smart cities using "noticing, idea generation, and the sharing of content about the city" as mechanisms for focusing on awareness, attention, and attunement. Streitz (2019) [12] argues for the need to keep people in-the-loop and more meaningfully involved. Mora, Deakin, Zhang, Batty, de Jong, Santi, and Appio (2020) [34], working on theory building in the smart cities space using "middle-range theory", call for an interdisciplinary theoretical perspective advancing the notion of "sustainable smart city transitions." Gregor (2006) [35] described "mid-range theory" as "moderately abstract" with "limited scope" that "can easily lead to testable hypotheses." In an exploration of smart learning environments and journeys, Lister points to the importance of "the ambient and pervasive interactions landscape of future connected learning cities" supporting "learning as and when need or curiosity necessitates" (2021) [36].

Indeed, ambient theory may serve to complement and extend existing smart city and urban theory, going beyond "instrumentation" as proposed by Harrison and Abbott Donnelly (2011) [11]. As such, this work posits that, in view of the need for theory to support understandings of smart cities and the ambient dimension of urban life in the 21st century (Nakashima, Aghajan, and Augusto, 2010) [4] – including the digital, the sensory, and other less visible elements (McKenna, 2019) [37] – ambient theory may assist in providing more definition to the smart city concept along with a stronger theoretical foundation since theory is said to be underdeveloped in the smart cities domain [8, 38]. From a human geography perspective in cities, people and their multi-sensorial capabilities [7] are emphasized in urban spaces incorporating thinking by Beaude (2015) [39] who articulated the notion of the Internet as an extension or innovation of space with implications for urban digital layers and environments.

2.4   Ambient Theory

The ambient theory conceptualization in this work, as depicted in Fig. 1, posits that smart cities and regions are characterized by, and concerned with, awareness involving people and technologies, contributing to smart environments, and new action potentials.

More specifically, the ambient theory proposition requires:

a) awareness in the form of two key components – awareness in relation to technologies and to people
b) awareness-based spaces, that foster an evolving interplay of one or more elements, such as – adaptive, dynamic, emergent, interactive, pervasive
c) *meaningfully* involving people in action, whether in planning, design, development, implementation, evaluation, or creative use(s) of the ambient dimension of technologies.

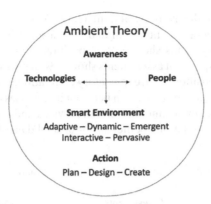

Fig. 1. Ambient theory components and characteristics in smart cities and regions.

To the extent that ambient theory is based on the presence or absence of the three factors described above (a-c), it can be said to exhibit some degree of parsimony and simplicity while also being interdisciplinary. By contrast, the middle-range theory of sustainable smart city transitions proposed by Mora et al. (2020) [34], given the complexity involved with cross-case analysis, is said to be lacking in parsimony. Ambient theory is intended for use in smart environments, particularly in smart cities and regions where awareness and sensing are present, as in, technologies supporting enhanced awareness and spaces accommodating more aware people and their multisensorial capabilities. While the domain for ambient theory is smart cities, it is worth noting that this domain encompasses many other domains or sub-domains, including energy, transportation/mobility, and so forth. As such, awareness, sensing, and meaningful involvement denote conditions indicative of when and where ambient theory will hold in the context of smart cities, environments and regions.

3 Application of Ambient Theory to Smart Cities

This paper employs an exploratory case study approach in combination with an explanatory correlational design. Using an online space, people were invited to sign up for the study, providing demographic details (e.g., age range, city, gender) and the option to self-identify in one or more categories (e.g., community member, educator, student, city official, business, etc.). Respondents included people in small to medium to large-sized cities in Canada, the United States, Ireland, Greece, Israel, and beyond. Data collection included use of a pre-tested survey instrument and a pre-tested interview protocol where respondents were asked to assess various aspects of smart cities based on their everyday experiences. In parallel with this study, data were also collected systematically through group and individual discussions with a wide array of people in several Canadian cities. Overall, an analysis was conducted for n = 78 involving 41% females, 59% males for people ranging in age from their 20s to their 70s.

Survey respondents were asked to assess the extent to which they associate smart cities with technology-driven services and the extent to which factors such as creative opportunities contribute to the livability of a smart city. As shown in Table 1, on a seven-point Likert-type scale, with 1 = not at all and 7 = absolutely, for technology-driven services, respondent assessments show 50% at position 5 and 50% at position 7. For creative opportunities, respondent assessments show 25% at position 3; 50% are assessed at position 6; and 25% at position 7. An explanatory correlational design (Creswell, 2018) [40] is then used to calculate the correlation between items assessed. When correlated, a relationship emerges between technology-driven services and creative opportunities in the form of a Spearman correlation coefficient for ordinal data of .70.

Table 1. Correlation between Technology-driven services and Creative opportunities.

Element	Assessments	Correlation
Technology-driven services	50% (5); 50% (7)	.70
Creative opportunities	25% (3); 50% (6); 25% (7)	

Correlations in this range (.66 to .85), according to Creswell (2018) [40], are said to be "very good" with "good prediction" potential. As suggested perhaps by Table 1, involving people through creative opportunities in the widespread and often disappearing [20] or invisible embedding of infrastructures in support of the [12] presence and pervasiveness of technologies in urban spaces may contribute to greater potential for success in smart cities. While such technologies may enable the designing of experiences [20], the involving of people more meaningfully and creatively would seem to be needed to support awareness, and in more fully appreciating smart environments where "the world around us becomes the interface" combining the "digital or virtual" with the "real" to form integrated "hybrid worlds."

Streitz, et al. (2007) [20] point to the data dimension of smart environments, identifying the "collecting and processing of personal information" as "a core function" and data are explored in this work in the form of access to public data. As shown in Table 2, respondent assessments for access to public data show 50% at position 6 and 50% at position 7. As such, assessments for the extent to which factors such as creative opportunities contribute to the livability of a smart city when correlated with assessments for the extent to which access to public data contributes to the success of a smart city project, a Spearman correlation coefficient of .70 emerges. Findings associated with creative opportunities

Table 2. Correlation between Creative Opportunities and Access to public data.

Element	Assessments	Correlation
Creative Opportunities	25% (3); 50% (6); 25% (7)	.70
Access to public data	50% (6); 50% (7)	

make it perhaps worth recalling and considering the claim by Rickert (2013) [23] that, "virtuality" and "artificiality" are "better understood as ambient invention and creation."

As with the study underlying this work, in Table 3, relationship development in support of awareness in smart cities and regions improves upon other recent work [41] here *awareness,* using *heightening urban sensibilities* as a proxy, is correlated with *interactions,* using *interactive public spaces* as a proxy. As shown in Table 3, when awareness is correlated with interactivity, a Spearman correlation coefficient for ordinal data of .81 emerges.

Table 3. Correlation between Awareness and Interactivity (using proxies) in smart cities.

Element	Proxy	Correlation
Awareness	Heightening urban sensibilities	.81
Interactivity	Interactive public spaces	

If, as advanced in this work, awareness is an indicator of the ambient in smart cities along with associated indicators such as interactivity, predictive capabilities for ambient theory so far would seem to be promising.

It is worth noting that when information and communication technologies (ICTs) were explored in relation to privacy in other recent work [42], as shown in Table 4, a correlation of .57 emerges and Creswell cautions that correlations in the .35 to .65 range "are useful for limited prediction."

Table 4. Correlation between ICTs and Privacy.

Element	Correlation
ICTs	.57
Privacy	

Noting the challenges and tensions between "privacy and ubiquity", Streitz, et al. (2007) [20] proposed "zones of interaction" to accommodate "awareness moments" and "experiences of awareness." Also, of note in Tables 1, 2, 3 and 4 are variables for ambient theory identified in this work that pertain to both people and technology and include interactivity, sensing, and pervasiveness, to name a few, in relation to awareness. As such, the examples presented in the Tables highlight that, along with technologies in support of awareness (e.g., ICTs), ambient theory posits the need for people, their experiences, and their awareness potentials to also be supported. It is worth noting that in explorations of smart environments involving the Internet of Things (IoT), Curry et al., (2018) [43] place an emphasis on factors pertaining to awareness and user experience. And finally, in the context of big data and learning analytics, Wise and Shaffer (2015) [44] point to the importance of theory in assisting to identify "what variables a researcher should attend to" as well as "how to interpret a multitude of micro-results" in order to "make them actionable."

4   Implications, Limitations, and Mitigations of Ambient Theory

This paper advances ambient theory as a theory for smart environments, cities, and regions while pointing to implications going forward as well as limitations and mitigations of this work.

Implications.   The awareness component of ambient theory will be important in anticipating the methods and tools which will be necessary in applying the ambient theoretical framework in smart environments. The examples provided in Sect. 3 of this paper, associated with Tables 1, 2, 3 and 4 for exploring awareness in smart cities, use a hybrid methodology, combining a case study approach with an explanatory correlational design. The potential practical impact of the proposed theoretical framework on the design and evaluation of smart cities applications and services could contribute to emergent people-related factors for meaningful involvement, in addition to those described in this paper.

Taking into consideration work by Higgins (2004) [45] on "making a theory useful", the Table examples in Sect. 3 of this paper also serve to demonstrate the usefulness of ambient theory by beginning to show the use of ambient theory for practical assessments in everyday spaces. In this way, some idea may begin to emerge concerning what ambient theory is, and what it is not. It is worth noting that Gregor (2006) [35], in discussing theory in the context of information systems, provides guidance on types of theory (e.g., analyzing, explaining, predicting, design and action, etc.) and their interrelationships, providing opportunities going forward for the discussion of ambient theory in terms of predictive capabilities, analyzing, design, action, and so on.

Attentive to the value of taxonomies [46] and typologies [47] for theory development, this paper points to opportunities going forward for consideration of typologies [42] and taxonomies in support of ambient theory for smart cities.

Limitations and Mitigations.   Among the possible limitations of this paper is that of generalizability which may be mitigated by drawing on the generalizability framework developed by Lee and Baskerville (2003) [48]. For example, it could be said that the empirical findings from case study and correlational research described in Sect. 3 of this paper, in the context of ambient theory, pertain to "analytical generalizability" described by Yin (2017) [49] in case study research which is advanced by Lee and Baskerville as "empirical to theoretical (ET) generalizability." As such, this type of generalizability is possibly important for future studies of ambient theory and smart cities going forward. It is also possible that this paper provides an early-stage example of the notion by Lee and Baskerville (2003) [48] of "(TT) generalizability" involving "generalizing from concepts to theory" where this work "generalizes from theoretical propositions in the form of concepts" as derived from the literature review "to the theoretical propositions that make up a theory" as described in Sect. 2.4 around the conceptual framework for ambient theory.

5 Conclusion

This paper seeks to further develop a theoretical foundation for the ambient in smart environments by proposing ambient theory for smart cities and regions. To this end, a conceptual framework describing the components and characteristics of ambient theory for smart cities and regions is formulated together with a three-part proposition guiding the use and operationalization of ambient theory. Use of ambient theory is then demonstrated in relation to research where a case study and explanatory correlational design is used to explore the nature of relationships among elements in smart environments pertaining to people and their interactions with technologies. As such, ambient theory is intended to describe and to model environments and spaces characterized by awareness in relation to people and technologies. Other associated features of smart environments include, but are not limited to, attuning, sensing, and interactivity. Guided by the "theory contribution canvas" developed by Gregor (2017) [50], this work makes a contribution to urban theorizing by formulating ambient theory for smart cities and regions while opening spaces for dialogue and practice.

Going forward it will be important to further interrogate and validate ambient theory to determine whether and to what extent it is a good theory, along with its application to smart cities and beyond. While limitations of this paper may pertain to generalizability, this is mitigated by proposing empirical to theoretical (ET) generalizability [48] as a type of analytical generalizability [49] as in, "generalizing to theory" and possibly even "TT generalizability" [48], generalizing from concepts to theory. The audience for this paper will be researchers concerned with urban theory and smart cities theory; urban practitioners including city officials, community members, and planners and developers concerned with people and technology interactions and experiences; and those concerned with improving livability aided by meaningfully involving people in aware and ambient human-computer interaction in urban spaces, environments and regions.

References

1. Stephanidis, C., et al.: Seven HCI grand challenges. Int. J. Hum. Comput. Interaction **35**(14), 1229–1269 (2019). https://doi.org/10.1080/10447318.2019.1619259
2. Streitz, N., Charitos, D., Kaptein, M., Böhlen, M.: Grand challenges for ambient intelligence and implications for design contexts and smart societies. J. Ambient Intell. Smart Environ. **11**, 87–107 (2019)
3. Dourish, P., Bell, G.: Divining a Digital Future: Mess and Mythology in Ubiquitous Computing. MIT Press, Cambridge (2011)
4. Nakashima, H., Aghajan, H., Augusto, J.C. (eds.): Handbook of Ambient Intelligence and Smart Environments. Springer, New York (2010). https://doi.org/10.1007/978-0-387-93808-0
5. Thibaud, J.-P.: The backstage of urban ambiances: When atmospheres pervade everyday experience. Emotion Space Soc. **15**, 39–46 (2015)
6. Gams, M., Gu, I.Y.H., Härmä, A., Muñoz, A., Tam, V.: Artificial intelligence and ambient intelligence. J. Ambient Intell. Smart Environ. **11**, 71–86 (2019). https://doi.org/10.3233/AIS-180508
7. Lévy, J. (ed.): The City: Critical Essays in Human Geography. Routledge Contemporary Foundations of Space and Place. Routledge, New York (2008)

8. Batty, M.: Big data, smart cities and city planning. Dialogues Hum. Geogr. **3**(3), 274–279 (2013). https://doi.org/10.1177/2043820613513390. PMID:29472982
9. Brenner, N.: New Urban Spaces: Urban Theory and the Scale Question. Oxford University Press, New York (2019)
10. Harrison, C., et al.: Foundations for smarter cities. IBM J. Res. Dev. **54**(4), 1–16 (2010)
11. Harrison, C., Abbott Donnelly, I.: A theory of smart cities. In: Proceedings of the 55th Annual Meeting of the ISSS. International Society for Systems Sciences (2011)
12. Streitz, N.: Beyond 'smart-only' cities: redefining the 'smart-everything' paradigm. J. Ambient Intell. Hum. Comput. **10**(2), 791–812 (2018). https://doi.org/10.1007/s12652-018-0824-1
13. Mosannenzadeh, F., Vettorato, D.: Defining smart city: a conceptual framework based on keyword analysis. TeMA – J. Land Use Mobility and Environ. (2014). https://doi.org/10.6092/1970-9870/2523.
14. Neirotti, P., De Marco, A., Cagliano, A.C., Mangano, G., Scorrano, F.: Current trends in smart city initiatives: Some stylized facts. Cities **38**, 25–36 (2014). https://doi.org/10.1016/j.cities.2013.12.010
15. Lara, A.P., Da Costa, E.M., Furlani, T.Z., Yigitcanlar, T.: Smartness that matters: towards a comprehensive and human-centered characterization of smart cities. J. Open Innov. Technol. Market Complexity **2**(1), 9 (2016). https://doi.org/10.1186/s40852-016-0034-z
16. Ramaprasad, A., Sánchez-Ortiz, A., Syn, T.: A Unified Definition of a Smart City. In: Janssen, Marijn, et al. (eds.) EGOV 2017. LNCS, vol. 10428, pp. 13–24. Springer, Cham (2017). https://doi.org/10.1007/978-3-319-64677-0_2
17. Batty, M.: Defining smart cities: high and low frequency cities, big data and urban theory. In: Willis, K.S., Aurigi, A. (eds.) The Routledge Companion to Smart Cities, pp. 51–60. Routledge, London (2020)
18. McCullough, M.: Ambient Commons: Attention in the Age of Embodied Information. The MIT Press, Cambridge (2013). https://doi.org/10.7551/mitpress/8947.001.0001
19. Gaver, W.W., et al.: Realizing a video environment: EuroPARC's RAVE system. In: Proceedings of the ACM Conference on Human Factors in Computing Systems (CHI 1992), New York, pp. 27–35. ACM Press (1992)
20. Streitz, N., et al.: Smart artefacts as affordances for awareness in distributed teams. In: Streitz, N., Kameas, A., Mavrommati, I. (eds.) The Disappearing Computer. LNCS, vol. 4500, pp. 3–29. Springer, Heidelberg (2007). https://doi.org/10.1007/978-3-540-72727-9_1
21. Townsend, A.M.M.: Smart Cities: Big Data, Civic Hackers and the Quest for a New Utopia. W. W. Norton & Company, New York (2013)
22. Crawford, N., Ballif, M.: Book review: Rickert's Ambient Rhetoric. Present Tense: A Journal of Rhetoric in Society, vol. 4, no. 1 (2014). Accessed 13 Oct 2020
23. Rickert, T.: Ambient Rhetoric: The Attunements of Rhetorical being. University of Pittsburgh Press, Pittsburgh (2013)
24. Papastergiadis, N., Barakin, A., McQuire, S.: Conclusion: Ambient screens. In: Papastergiadis, N. (ed.) Ambient Screens and Transnational Public Spaces. 1 edn. Hong Kong University Press, HKU, Hong Kong (2016)
25. Benjamin, W.: Illuminations. Translated by Harry Zohn. Schocken Books, New York (1986)
26. Aarts, E., Harwig, R., Schuurmans, M.: Ambient intelligence. In: Denning, P.J. (ed.) The Invisible Future, pp. 235–50. McGraw-Hill, New York (2001)
27. Sengupta, D.: Taxonomy on ambient computing: a research methodology perspective. Int. J. Ambient Comput. Intell. (IJACI) **11**(1), 1–33 (2020). https://doi.org/10.4018/IJACI.2020010101
28. Aarts, E., de Ruyter, B.: New research perspectives on ambient intelligence. J. Ambient Intell. Smart Environ. **1**(1), 5–14 (2009)

29. Piga, B.E.A., et al.: Mapping ambiances: a synopsis of theory and practices in an interdisciplinary perspective. Ambiances, tomorrow. In: Proceedings of 3rd International Congress on Ambiances, Volos, pp. 367–372. hal-01414063

30. Ambiances international network. Ambiances, Alloaesthesia: Senses, Inventions, Worlds, 4th International Congress on Ambiances (2020). https://ambiances2020.ambiances.net

31. Prante, T., Stenzel, R., Röcker, C., Streitz, N., Magerkurth, C.: Ambient Agoras - InfoRiver, SIAM, Hello.Wall. In: Extended Abstracts and Video Proceedings of the ACM Conference on Human Factors in Computing Systems (CHI 2004), Vienna, pp. 763–776 (2004)

32. Brewer, J., Williams, A., Dourish, P.: A handle on what's going on: combining tangible interfaces and ambient displays for collaborative groups. In: Proceedings of the Tangible and Embodied Interaction Conference (2007)

33. McKenna, H.P.: Urbanizing the ambient: why people matter so much in smart cities. In: Konomi, S., Roussos, G. (Eds.) Enriching Urban Spaces with Ambient Computing, the Internet of Things, and Smart City Design, pp. 209–223. IGI Global (2017). https://doi.org/10.4018/978-1-5225-0827-4.ch011

34. Mora, L., et al.: Assembling sustainable smart city transitions: an interdisciplinary theoretical perspective. J. Urban Technol. (2020). https://doi.org/10.1080/10630732.2020.1834831

35. Gregor, S.: The nature of theory in information systems. MIS Q. **30**(3), 611–642 (2006)

36. Lister, P.: What are we supposed to be learning? Motivation and autonomy in smart learning environments. In: Streitz, N., Konomi, S. (eds.) HCII 2021. LNCS, vol. 12782, pp. 533–547. Springer, Cham (2021)

37. McKenna, H.P.: Ambient Urbanities as the Intersection between the IoT and the IoP in Smart Cities. IGI Global, Hershey (2019)

38. Roy, A.: The 21st century metropolis: new geographies of theory. Reg. Stud. **43**(6), 819–830 (2009). https://doi.org/10.1080/00343400701809665

39. Beaude, B.: Internet: a unique space of coexistence. In: EPFLx: SpaceX Exploring Humans' Space: An Introduction to Geographicity. Massive Open Online Course (MOOC), edX, Fall (2015)

40. Creswell, J.W.: Educational Research: Planning, Conducting, and Evaluating Quantitative and Qualitative Research, 6th edn. Pearson, Boston (2018)

41. McKenna, H.: Beyond confluence, integration and symbiosis: creating more aware relationships in smart cities. In: Ahram, T., Karwowski, W., Vergnano, A., Leali, F., Taiar, R. (eds.) IHSI 2020. AISC, vol. 1131, pp. 1063–1068. Springer, Cham (2020). https://doi.org/10.1007/978-3-030-39512-4_161

42. McKenna, H.P.: Seeing Smart Cities through a Multi-Dimensional Lens: Perspectives, Relationships, and Patterns for Success. Springer, New York (2021). https://doi.org/10.1007/978-3-030-70821-4

43. Curry, E., Hasan, S., Kouroupetroglou, C., Fabritius, W., Ul Hassan, U., Derguech, W.: Internet of Things enhanced user experience for smart water and energy management. IEEE Internet Comput. **22**(1), 18–28 (2018). https://doi.org/10.1109/MIC.2018.011581514.

44. Wise, A.F., Shaffer, D.W.: Why theory matters more than ever in the age of big data. J. Learn. Anal. **2**(2), 5–13 (2015). https://doi.org/10.18608/jla.2015.22.2

45. Higgins, E.T.: Making a theory useful: lessons handed down. Pers. Soc. Psychol. Rev. **8**(2), 138–145 (2004)

46. Gill, S.K., Cormican, K.: Support ambient intelligence solutions for small to medium size enterprises: Typologies and taxonomies for developers. In: IEEE International Technology Management Conference (ICE) Milan, pp. 1–8 (2006). https://doi.org/10.1109/ICE.2006.7477074.

47. Doty, D.H., Glick, W.H.: Typologies as a unique form of theory building: toward improved understanding and modeling. Acad. Manag. Rev. **19**(2), 230–251 (1994)

48. Lee, A.S., Baskerville, R.L.: Generalizing generalizability in information systems research. Inf. Syst. Res. **14**(3), 221–243 (2003). https://doi.org/10.1287/isre.14.3.221.16560

49. Yin, R.K.: Case Study Research: Design and Methods (Sixth Edition). Sage, Thousand Oaks (2017)

50. Gregor, S.: On theory. In: The Routledge Companion to Management Information Systems. Routledge, London, 1 edn. pp. 57–72. (2017)

Research on Cross-channel Switch Behavior of Users from Smart Government APP to Government Service Platform Under PPM Framework

Siyuan Wu, Yuwen Wang, and Guochao Peng[✉]

Sun Yat-sen University, Panyu District, Guangzhou 510000, China
penggch@mail.sysu.edu.cn

Abstract. Based on the Resource Dependence Theory and Network External-ity Theory, this paper discusses the influencing factors and mechanism of users' switch from smart government apps on mobile to government service platform on computer. A conceptual model of switch behaviors was constructed by the PPM framework (Push-Pull-Mooring, push-pull-anchor). So as to provide inspiration for exploring the trend of smart government and assisting the integration and utilization of government digital resources.

Keywords: Smart government · Government apps · Government service platform in computer · Switch behaviors · Push-pull-mooring framework

1 Introduction

With the development of smart cities and digital government, the government has gradually formed government service centers and self-service kiosk on offline, government portal and government service platform on PC, government service apps and WeChat government applets on mobile, which in order to continuously promote the realization of service goals such as "Online Approval" and "One Visit at Most". These are gradually form a multi-level and unified "one network". The rapid development of "smart government" has laid the foundation for the modernization of the government's governance system and governance capability. Smart government services represented by government service platform on PC and government service apps are becoming important channels for government information disclosure and government service provision.

With the launch of the first mobile APP "Mobile Nanjing", various smart government apps such as "Beijing Tong", "Smart Wuxi" and "Ningbo Citizen Tong" have been released. Citizens can download the government APP provided by the government anytime and anywhere smart services, such as traffic business, real-time road conditions, appointment registration, and government affairs.

As of July 1, 2019, China has built 31 provincial government service apps [1]. However, many government affairs apps in China have lagged, disconnected, stuck and other phenomena, with low overall scores, low user satisfaction, and low utilization

© Springer Nature Switzerland AG 2021
N. Streitz and S. Konomi (Eds.): HCII 2021, LNCS 12782, pp. 55–67, 2021.
https://doi.org/10.1007/978-3-030-77015-0_5

rates [2], causing a great waste of government resources. At the same time, in order to further speed up the realization of the goal of "One Pass for All" and other goals, integrated government service platforms have gradually emerged throughout the country. According to the evaluation data of the 46th "Statistical Report on Internet Development in China", as of June 2020, China's national government service platform has connected 32 regions and 46 State Council departments, and the platform has registered 126 million real-name users; in addition, 31 provincial governments have established government service platforms covering the three levels of provinces, cities, and counties [3].

Faced with the diversity and optionality of government services, citizens have shown a trend of switch from government apps on mobile to government service platform on computer on the contrary. However, the previous studies on smart government mostly focused on concept discussion, new technology adoption and continuance. It is difficult to explain the cross-channel migration phenomenon of users from government apps to government service platform using the current adoption and continuance theory.

Therefore, based on the theory of resource dependence and the theory of network externality, a switch behavior model was constructed from three levels of push factors, pull factors and mooring factors on the basis of PPM framework (Push-Pull-Mooring) to explore into the key factors and mechanism of users' switch from government apps on mobile to government service platform on computer. It is conducive to exploring the trend of smart government, so as to provide improvement measures for the design and management of smart government, help the integration and utilization of government digital resources, and provide certain theoretical support for the research on the deep usage behaviors of government service users.

2 Literature Review

2.1 Smart Government

Smart government is a concept derived from "smart government". This article defines it as the government relies on network systems (such as the Internet of Things and the Internet) to realize seamless connection between management and service through advanced information technology, thus providing people with more user-friendly service choices, more thorough demand analysis and more convenient smart response, such as intelligent response systems such as government apps, government applets, government service platform and other smart response systems.

The previous research on smart government mainly focused on two aspects: (1) The discussion of concepts. For example, some scholars believe that smart government is a stage of e-government [4]; However, other scholars believe that smart government is a new mode of government services to improve the performance of government departments and the efficiency of government services [5]. At present, there is no unified concept to define smart government the academic circle. (2) Research on how to build smart government. For example, Kalsi [6] uses ICT and other technologies to optimize government processes and improve service quality; Lv [7] uses three-dimensional geographic information system and cloud computing technology for three-dimensional processing and visualization of city operation information; Manda uses integrated information systems to support smart government decision-making [8], and so all.

The above literature review shows that the previous studies on smart government mainly focused on theoretical research and technology mining, and seldom involved the research on user behaviors after technology implementation and application. How to make full use of the existing information technology and platform to establish convenient and beneficial smart government is an important issue to be considered in the process of smart government construction, and it is also the key to maximize the value of smart government.

2.2 User Switch Behavior

In the mid-1990s, researchers began to apply the migration theory in the field of population geography to the user switch behaviors in the field of marketing. User switch is defined as the behavior process that users begin to use new products/services to replace existing products/services, that is, when users are faced with a variety of products and services from different operators, they switch to other products/services when they have stopped or have not completely stopped using the current products/services [9].

There are three main types of user switch behaviors: (1) User switch between products/services under different channel, such as the switch from PC search to mobile phone search [10], the switch from traditional paper reading to digital reading [11], and the switch from offline education to online education [12]; (2) User switch between homogeneous products/services under the same channel, such as the switch between mobile personal cloud storage services [13], the switch between mobile payment apps [14], and the switch from free to paid knowledge Q&A platforms [15]; (3) User switch between heterogeneous products/services under the same channel, such as the switch between mobile instant messages [30]. This study belongs to the first category, that is, the switch behaviors of users from government apps to government service platform under the different channel.

At present, there have been diversified studies on user switch behaviors in various fields, and the influencing factors and theoretical models are different due to different application situations in different fields. In the field of mobile payment, Wang [14] explored the relationship between switch rewards, privacy concerns, habits and users' switch behaviors based on the characteristics of mobile payment. In the field of social media, Chang[9] found that dissatisfaction with the original apps, the attraction of the new apps and the switch costs will promote the switch behaviors of users; Lin[16]discussed the relationship between trust, perceived value, perceived risks, habits and actual switch behaviors based on trust theory and technology acceptance theory. In the field of medical and health care, 나비랑 [17] conducted a research survey on the switch intention of fitness center participants and found that the relationship benefit perception and relationship immersion have an impact on the switch intention; 자밀라 explored the relationship between the medical purpose of medical tourism, the quality of medical services, the willingness to revisit and the intention to switch [18].

2.3 Cross channel User Switch Behavior

Scholars' research on the switch behavior of users in different channels are shown in Table 1. Due to different scenarios, the factors that affect the switch are different, but most of them consider factors such as perceived convenience, perceived usefulness, trust, and habits. The switch channels are diversified, such as from computer to mobile, offline to online, paper media to e-reading, and so on. These studies have provided enlightenment and thinking for the research on the switch behavior of users' government services, but the switch behavior of users in government services is still a new area of concern. The switch path and switch mechanism of users in the government service field have yet to be resolved, and whether the relevant influencing factors Applicability to government services needs to be further verified.

Table 1. Research on the switch behavior between PC and mobile

Research object	Switch orientation	Influencing factors	Author	Year
Mobile payment	PC payment → Mobile payment	Cognitive trust, Emotional trust, Perception ability	Gong, Xiang [19]	2020
Mobile search	PC search → Mobile search	Perceived association, Perceived context, Perceived convenience, Habits, Relative disadvantages	Chen Minghong [10]	2019
Traffic	Car → Public transit	Convenience, Flexible service, Commuting obstacles	Alexandra S. [20]	2019
Education	Offline education → online education	Learning convenience, Service quality, Perceived price, E-learning motivation, Perceived usefulness, Learning participation, Conversion cost, Social presence, Learning, Habit	Yu-Hsin Chen [12]	2019
Mobile payment	PC payment → Mobile payment	Satisfaction, Trust, Perceived similarity, Perceived attractiveness	Cao,Xiongfei [21]	2018
E-commerce	PC → Mobile	Perceived value difference, Perceived technological difference	Cao,Yuzhi [22]	2015

(*continued*)

Table 1. (*continued*)

Research object	Switch orientation	Influencing factors	Author	Year
Health service	PC → Mobile	Relationship benefit perception, Emotional immersion, Relationship immersion	나비랑 [17]	2015
E-reading	Paper reading → E-reading	Social influence, Compatibility, Complexity, Convenience, E-book content, price, conversion cost	Chiang, H. S [11]	2014

The previous studies on user switch behaviors involved a wide range of research, including social media, e-commerce, mobile payment, health care and other fields, but few researchers paid attention to the research on user switch in smart government. Therefore, this paper will explore the key factors and mechanism of user switch from government apps to government service platform, so as to provide improvement measures for the design and management of smart government, and at the same time help enrich the theoretical basis of government service users' usage behaviors.

3   Research Theories and Hypothetical Models

PPM (Push-Pull-Mooring) framework is the main example of migration research, which was first applied to population migration. In 1966, Lee systematically summarized the "thrust-pull force" theory in his article "Migration Theory" [23]. In 1995, Moon introduced the concept of "mooring factors" into the push-pull theory [24]. In 2005, Bansal et al. formally established a unified PPM framework using migration theory to explain the switch of consumers between different services [25]. Therefore, based on PPM framework, this paper constructs a switch behavior model from three levels of push factors, pull factors and mooring factors to explore the influence path and mechanism of user switch from government apps on mobile to government service platform on computer.

3.1   Push Factors

Push factors refer to the factors that urge users to migrate from a place. In this research, it refers to the unfavorable factors of the original product/service, that is, the user's perception of the difference between the mobile government apps and the PC government service platform, and the satisfaction with the government APP.

Perceived Differences

Perceived differences in this paper refer to various differences that users feel when using different devices or smart government platforms in different situations. In the context of smart government, perceptual differences include four dimensions: system difference, initialization difference, compatibility difference and convenience difference (as shown in Table 2). Due to differences in equipment, scenarios, and systems, there is a difference between the use of government service functions on mobile phones and the use of users on computers. Compared with the old-fashioned user interface, crashes, freezes, and government APPs that need to be updated from time to time, the PC-side government service platform is smoother and more convenient in terms of usage and usage scenarios. For example, when a government app version is updated according to the needs of the operator, users need to update it, while the government service platform does not need to install and update steps; When users need to upload/download government materials and files, the mobile app has a weaker operating experience than the PC terminal. When users obviously perceive the difference between the two, or even when they obviously perceive that a certain mode is more user-friendly, they will have psychological deviation, thus causing the switch intention.

Table 2. Four dimensions of perceived differences

Concept	Definition
System difference	Users perceive the differences in system and performance between government apps and government service platform (such as system operation speed, buffering and loading, and choppiness)
Initialization difference	Users perceive the differences between the initialization of g government apps and government service platform (such as authorization, login, update, settings, etc.)
Compatibility difference	Users perceive the difference in the compatibility of government apps and government service platform with their life and equipment
Convenience difference	Users perceive the difference in convenience between government apps and government service platform

H1: Users' perceived differences between government apps and government service platform significantly affects their switch intention.

Satisfaction

Satisfaction is one of the core constructs in Expectation-Conformation Theory (ECT). In 1980, Oliver [26] studied the relationship between consumer satisfaction and continuance and found that satisfaction is a reference for consumers to repurchase a product or reuse a service next time. In other words, if consumers are lowly satisfied with the original product/service, the phenomenon of consumers migrating to other products/services may occur. When they are dissatisfied with the original product/service, they are likely to turn to alternative products to obtain a better user experience [27], which will result in the intention to abandon or stop using the original product/service, and there will be a willingness to switch, so the user will be interested in the original government APP Satisfaction is negatively correlated with switch behavior.

H2: Users' satisfaction with government app significantly affects their switch intention.

3.2 Pull Factors

Pull factors refer to the factors that attracts users to switch to a place. In this study, it refers to the favorable factors of new products/services, namely, user satisfaction with the PC-side government service platform, reference network scale, total network scale, perceived usefulness and perceived government investment.

Network Externality Theory (NET)
Network effect means that the benefits users get from products/services will increase with the increase of the number of users in the same network, which is called network externality [28]. Network Externality Theory points out that the utility of a certain product includes not only the "basic utility" brought by the product itself, but also the "network benefits" caused by the user scale [13]. Obviously, network externality is very important in the process of technology diffusion. Lin pointed out the role of direct and indirect network externalities in IT [29], in which scholars used reference network scale and total network scale to measure direct network externalities.

Reference Network Size and Total Network Size are one of the key constructs in the network externality theory. By reference to Cheng et al.'s definition of two concepts, this paper defines reference network size as the number of users' friends, colleagues, relatives or others that use mobile government service applets in their social circle; and defines total network size as the total number of users who perceive the use of the PC-side government service platform. If users and people around them use the same equipment or system, it will be more convenient for them to connect and share, transmit files, exchange information, etc. Therefore, the reference network size will affect users' switch intention. At the same time, as the total network scale of users increases, product/service developers will gradually introduce new services and functions to ensure that their own interests increase. This is specifically reflected in the government services that the government will gradually add new government service items to ensure convenience for citizens and Respond to citizens, so that users can obtain more network resources and service quality. Therefore, the total network size of users will also affect their willingness to switch.

H3: Users' reference network size for government service platform significantly affects their switch intention.
H4: Users' total network size for government service platform significantly affects their switch intention.

Perceived Usefulness

Perceived usefulness is one of the important constructs of TAM proposed by Davis. Perceived usefulness is the degree to which users subjectively belive that a certain system can improve work efficiency. Previous studies have proved that there is a positive correlation between perceived usefulness and switch intention [13]. This study defines perceived usefulness as the degree to which users believe that using the PC-side government service platform is more effective and efficient than the government APP. The core essence of the PC-side government service platform is to provide government services to users and citizens better and faster, and to deliver government policies and information to the public in a timely manner. It is also the key to the full popularization of government services from offline to online. The way. With the help of computer equipment and webpage systems, computer storage has larger storage capacity and longer storage time than mobile phones, making it easier to edit, upload, download and print required documents and materials, and can improve the efficiency and experience of users in handling government affairs. Therefore, the higher the user's perceived usefulness of the PC-side government service platform, the stronger the willingness to switch.

H5: Users' perceived usefulness of government service platform significantly affects their switch intention.

Perceived Government Investment

Resource Dependence Theory (RDT) is an important theory school for research on organizations. It emphasizes that the demand for resources constitutes the dependence of organizations on the outside, and the importance of resources determines the degree of dependence [32]. The government's use of various resources and technologies to build various government service platforms and channels to serve the people is a process of resource dependence, thus users' switch intention will be related to their perception of government investment. The construction and service quality of government service platforms depend on government resources. When users feel the increase of government investment in government service platform on computer, they can probably feel the improvement of the quality and efficiency of government service platform, thus showing the intention to switch.

H6: Users' perceived government investment in government service platform significantly affects their switch intention.

3.3 Mooring Factors

Mooring factors, i.e. hindering factors, refer to factors that hinder the switch of users from one place to another. In this research, it refers to the obstacles to the switch from the original product/service to the new product/service, that is, the user's habits and switch cost in the process of switchring from the government APP to the PC-side government service platform.

Habits

Bhattacherjee believe that when users are accustomed to using a certain product/service, their use tends to be a natural unconscious behavior, and they are unlikely to carefully compare the relative advantages between different products/services, which will hinder the switch of users [33]. When users are accustomed to the use of government apps, they may not devote too much energy to other new ways of handling government affairs, thus hindering their switch intention.

H7: Users' habits significantly affect their switch intention.

Switch Costs

Switch costs refer to the costs that users bear when switchring to another product/service, including but not limited to time and money. Switch costs in the field of information technology have been widely considered. Jones et al. divided switch costs into three types: continuity costs, learning costs and sunk costs [34]. However, government service apps are different from social media apps. The products/services of government are public goods/services, namely there is no charge, so users basically have no sunk costs and continuity costs when they switch between government service products. Therefore, this paper integrates the switch costs into three dimensions: evaluation cost, learning cost and setting cost (as shown in Table 3). Switch costs play an important role in the switch between government apps and government service platform. When users feel that the evaluation cost, learning cost and setting cost are too high, they will be unwilling to switch from the perspective of self-interest and convenience, that is hindering their intention to switch.

Table 3. Three dimensions of switch costs

Concept	Definition
Evaluation cost	The time and effort related cost to study and analyze products/services and make switch decisions
Learning cost	The time cost of learning new products/services
Setting cost	The cost of time and effort spent on signing up and completing personal information on a new product/service

H8: Switch costs of users significantly affect their switch willingness.

3.4 Switch Intention and Switch Behaviors

The relationship between behavioral intention and actual behavior has been widely explored by researchers, and many researchers have also proved that intention and behaviors are significantly related, such as Venkatesh [35], Ajzen [36] and Lin [16]. Ajzen [36] put forward the theory of planned behavior to explain the relationship between intention and behavior, believing that all factors that may affect behaviors indirectly affect the performance of behaviors through behavioral intention. Therefore, this study also agrees that push factors, pull factors and mooring factors affect switch behaviors by affecting switch intention, that is, switch intention will positively affect switch behaviors.

H9: Users' switch intention significantly affects their switch behaviors.

Based on the above research hypothesis, the research model is proposed in this paper, as shown in Fig. 1.

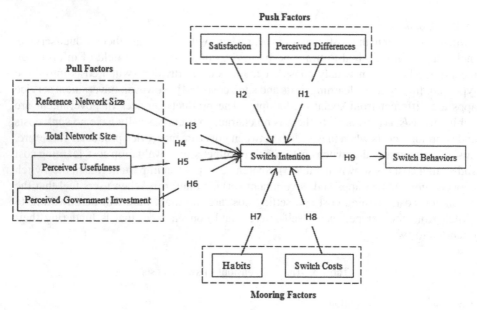

Fig. 1. Research model

4   Conclusion and Future Outlook

The government APP and government service platform, as a way and platform for smart government affairs in the new environment, play a very important role in providing government services to citizens and delivering government information in a timely manner. In the face of limited financial and social resources, how to make full use of existing information technology is the key to maximizing the value of smart government affairs. Based on the Resource Dependence Theory and Network Externality Theory, this paper discusses the influencing factors and mechanism of users' switch from smart government apps on mobile to government service platform on computer. A conceptual model of switch behaviors was constructed by the PPM framework (Push-Pull-Mooring, push-pull-anchor).The nine hypotheses of this model can be verified by empirical research, such as questionnaire survey, experimental research, grounded theory, etc. So as to provide inspiration for exploring the trend of smart government and assisting the integration and utilization of government digital resources.

At the theoretical level, this research draws on the resource dependence theory and externality theory in organization and economics, combined with the current development of online government htm services, and based on the PPM framework, constructs the switch behavior model of users' smart government APP to government service platform. And this model also makes up for the shortcomings in previous studies that have paid little attention to the transfer behavior of government service users, enriches the relevant research and theoretical basis of government service users' use behavior, and provides new ideas and directions for future research in the field of government services.

At the practical level, this research found that users will transfer behavior between the government APP and the government service platform when using online government services, and this transfer behavior is affected by multiple factors, including perception differences, satisfaction, and perception Usefulness, perceived government input and transfer cost all have a positive impact on the user's willingness to transfer. How to use these factors to improve the current use of government APP is the responsibility and obligation of relevant government departments, it is also an important way to realize smart government affairs. For example, the government can increase the promotion of government affairs APP, design more humane government affairs APP interactive interfaces, and improve the smoothness of government affairs APP system operation.

There are some areas in this research that can be improved and further studied. In the future, we can consider using questionnaire survey to expand the sample extraction for further research, or using experimental research to explore causal relationship, etc. At the same time, variables that affect users' switch behavior in the field of smart government affairs may include user emotional commitments, privacy concerns, perceived usefulness, peer influence, context, and trust. Future research can fully consider these variables that affect transfer willingness. In addition, the current academic research on transfer behavior is not deep enough, mainly focusing on quantitative research. In the future, qualitative research can be considered to explore the deeper transfer motivation and behavior mechanism behind the transfer behavior.

Acknowledgement. This research was supported by two grants respectively funded by the Natural Science Foundation of Guangdong (No.: 2018A030313706) and the National Natural Science Foundation of China (No.: 71974215).

References

1. Party School of the Central Committee of C. P. C (China National School of Administration). Mobile Government Service Development Report. https://www.gov.cn/guowuyuan/2019-07/22/content_5412804.htm. Accessed 30 Dec 2020
2. Tian, L., Guochao, P., Fei, X.: Research on the status and problems of mobile application of smart city in China. Libr. Inf. Serv. **63**(08), 65–73 (2019)
3. China Internet Network Information Center. The 46th Statistical Report on Internet Development in China [EB/OL]. https://www.cac.gov.cn/2020-09/29/c_1602939918747816.htm

4. Lemke, F., Taveter, K., Erlenheim, R., Pappel, I., Draheim, D., Janssen, M.: Stage models for moving from e-government to smart government. In: Chugunov, A., Khodachek, I., Misnikov, Y., Trutnev, D. (eds.) EGOSE 2019. CCIS, vol. 1135, pp. 152–164. Springer, Cham (2020). https://doi.org/10.1007/978-3-030-39296-3_12
5. Shola, S., Naaz, R., Chishti, M.A.: Ethics aware object oriented smart city architecture. China Commun. 14(5), 160–173 (2017)
6. Kalsi, N.S., Kiran, R.: A strategic framework for good governance through e-governance optimization. Program Electron. Libr. Inf. Syst. 49(2), 170–204 (2015)
7. Lv, Z.H., Li, X.M., Wang, W.X., et al.: Government affairs service platform for smart city. Future Gener. Comput. Syst. Int. J. EScience 81, 443–451 (2018)
8. Manda, M.: Towards "smart governance" through a multidisciplinary approach to e-government integration, interoperability and information sharing: a case of the LMIP project in South Africa. In: Janssen, Marijn, et al. (eds.) EGOV 2017. LNCS, vol. 10428, pp. 36–44. Springer, Cham (2017). https://doi.org/10.1007/978-3-319-64677-0_4
9. Chang, I., Liu, C.C., Chen, K.: The push, pull and mooring effects in virtual migration for social networking sites. Inf. Syst. J. 24(4), 323–346 (2014)
10. Chen, M., Qi, X., Lu, X., et al.: Understanding users' searching behavior switching from PC to mobile. From a dual perspective of enablers and inhibitors. Procedia Comput. Sci. 162, 355–360 (2019)
11. Chiang, H.S., Chen, C.C.: Exploring switch intention of users' reading behaviour an e-book reader case study. Electron. Libr. 32(4), 457–434 (2014)
12. Chen, Y.-H., Keng, C.-J.: Utilizing the Push-Pull-Mooring-Habit framework to explore users' intention to switch from offline to online real-person English learning platform. Internet Res. 29(1), 167–193 (2019)
13. Cheng, S., Lee, S.-J., Choi, B.: An empirical investigation of users' voluntary switching intention for mobile personal cloud storage services based on the push-pull-mooring framework. Comput. Hum. Behav. 92, 198–215 (2019)
14. Wang, L., (Robert) Luo, X., Yang, X., Qiao, Z.: Easy come or easy go? Empirical evidence on switching behaviors in mobile payment applications. Inf. Manage. 56(7), 103–150 (2019)
15. (Chris) Zhao, Y., Liu, Z., Chen, S., et al.: From free to fee: exploring the factors that influence the askers' switching behavior on online Q&A platforms. Proc. Assoc. Inf. Sci. Technol. 56(1), 517–520 (2019)
16. Lin, C.N., Wang, H.Y.: Understanding users' switching intentions and switching behavior on social networking sites. Aslib J. Inf. Manage. 69(02), 201–214 (2017)
17. 나비랑., 남상백., 이성진.: The influence of relationship benefit perception on relation immersion and switch intention. Korean J. Sports Sci. 24(6), 701–716 (2015)
18. 자밀라., 변정우.: The effect of medical tourism destination image on revisit and switch intention. Focused on medical service quality mediation effect. J. Tour. Leisure Res. 31(9), 173–195 (2019)
19. Gong, X., Zhang, K.Z., Chen, C., Cheung, C.M., Lee, M.K.: What drives trust switch from web to mobile payment services? The dual effects of perceived entitativity. Inf. Manage. 57(7), 103–250 (2020)
20. Kang, A.S., Jayaraman, K., Soh, K.L., et al.: Convenience, flexible service, and commute impedance as the predictors of drivers' intention to switch and behavioral readiness to use public transport. Transp. Res. Part F Psychol. Behav. 62, 505–519 (2019)
21. Cao, X.F., Yu, L.L., Liu, Z.Y., Gong, M.C., Adeel, L.: Understanding mobile payment users' continuance intention: a trust switch perspective. Internet Res. 28(2), 456–476 (2018)
22. Cao, Y., Lu, Y., Gupta, S., et al.: The effects of differences between e-commerce and m-commerce on the consumers' usage switch from online to mobile channel. Int. J. Mob. Commun. 13(1), 51–70 (2015)

23. Lee, E.S.: A theory of migration. Demography **3**(1), 47–57 (1966)
24. Moon, B.: Paradigms in migration research: exploring "Moorings" as a schema. Prog. Hum. Geogr. **19**(4), 504–524 (1995)
25. Bansal, H.S., Taylor, S.F., James, Y.S.: "Migrating" to new service providers: toward a unifying framework of consumers' switching behaviors. J. Acad. Market. Sci. **33**(1), 96–115 (2005)
26. Oliver, R.L.: A cognitive model of the antecedents and consequences of satisfaction decisions. J. Market. Res. **17**(4), 460–469 (1980)
27. Fan, L., Suh, Y.-H.: Why do users switch to a disruptive technology? An empirical study based on expectation-disconfirmation theory. Inf. Manage. **51**(2), 240–248 (2014)
28. Katz, M.L., Shapiro, C.: Network externalities, competition, and compatibility. Am. Econ. Rev. **75**(3), 424–440 (1985)
29. Lin, C.P., Bhattacherjee, A.: Elucidating individual intention to use interactive information technologies: the role of network externalities. Int. J. Electron. Commer. **13**(1), 85–108 (2008)
30. Zhou, T., Lu, Y.: Examining mobile instant messaging user loyalty from the perspectives of network externalities and flow experience. Comput. Hum. Behav. **27**(2), 883–889 (2010)
31. Lin, T.-C., Huang, S.-L.: Understanding the determinants of consumers' switching intentions in a standards war. Int. J. Electron. Commer. **19**(1), 163–189 (2014)
32. Ozturk, O.: Bibliometric review of resource dependence theory literature: an overview. Manage. Rev. Q. 1–28 (2020)
33. Bhattacherjee, A., Limayem, M., Cheung, C.M.K.: User switching of information technology: a theoretical synthesis and empirical test. Inf. Manage. **49**(7), 327–333 (2012)
34. Jones, M.A., Mothersbaugh, D.L., Beatty, S.E.: Why customers stay: measuring the underlying dimensions of services switching costs and managing their differential strategic outcomes. J. Bus. Res. **55**(6), 441–450 (2002)
35. Venkatsh, V., Speier, C., Morris, M.G.: User acceptance enablers in individual decision making about technology: toward an integrated model. Decis. Sci. **33**(2), 297–316 (2002)
36. Ajzen, I.: The theory of planned behavior. Organ. Behav. Hum. Decis. Process. **50**(2), 179–211 (1991)

Users Adaptation and Infusion of Smart City App

Bingqian Zhang, Caihua Liu, Yongxin Kong, Yuwen Wang, and Guochao Peng[✉]

School of Information Management, Sun Yat-sen University, Guangzhou 510006, Guangdong, China
penggch@mail.sysu.edu.cn

Abstract. Smart city app is an important link in the process of urban intelligence. However, many users fail to make full use of system functions after adoption. To solve this problem, this paper analyzes the adaptive information behavior of users. It adopts grounded theory-based qualitative research to conduct personal in-depth interviews and focus group interviews with 23 interviewees, and builds a model of influencing factors on the adaptive behavior of smart app users. The research shows that emotional perception, smart environment, users' personal characteristics and non-linear tasks are the main influencing factors on users' adaptive behavior, and technology exploration behavior has a positive effect on technology utilization behavior.

Keywords: Adaptive information behavior · Smart city app · Grounded theory · Process model

1 Introduction

In recent years, with the development of the new generation of information technologies (ITs) such as the IoT, cloud computing and mobile Internet, modern cities are moving forward from digitalization and networking to automation and intelligence. Smart city construction aims to improve the efficiency and transparency of public utilities and services, create a more sustainable urban environment, improve citizens' living standards and quality of life, and promote economic development [1].

The popularity of mobile Internet has impacted the reform of urban management. Smart city apps emerging with mobile Internet have become the main way for citizens to participate in smart city governance. Smart city apps make use of IoT technology devices (such as wireless sensors, GPS, GIS, detector, high-definition camera, etc.) installed on physical infrastructure to realize real-time perception and monitoring of various key data in the city. These IoT data will be transmitted to the cloud backend database in real time, aggregated, processed and analyzed with the data provided by public service departments, and finally delivered to the user. Therefore, compared with the traditional e-government and hospital appointment, the smart city apps take real-time data transmission as the core, and connect the urban IoT and physical infrastructure,

N. Streitz and S. Konomi (Eds.): HCII 2021, LNCS 12782, pp. 68–81, 2021.
https://doi.org/10.1007/978-3-030-77015-0_6

public service departments and institutions, as well as citizen users, featured with real-time, mobility, integration, etc.

A literature has investigated the smart city apps released by 201 cities with the highest level of smartness in China. The results show that among the 201 cities, local governments of 140 cities have released multiple smart city apps, a total of 333, covering 7 administrative regions in East and South China, with a wide range of distribution. In terms of functions, the apps provide 17 main functions and 52 column settings, covering various areas of civic life such as transportation, medical treatment, payment and appointment. However, the statistics of user ratings of smart city apps show that the average score of 333 apps is 2.99, which is below the median score of 3. In terms of specific scores, 50.5% of the apps are in the low range of 1.0–2.99. The low user ratings means that China's smart city apps currently have low user satisfaction and poor experience. At the same time, the low number of downloads, low loyalty, and the existence of "one-time use" among users are the key to restrict the further development of the apps. "Failed" smart city apps will not only lead to huge waste of hardware infrastructure investment, but also bring negative impact on the life of citizens and the image of local government [2].

As for the smart apps and services in the society, most of the literature focuses on the fields of computer science and artificial intelligence such as system design and algorithm optimization, but rarely discusses the use and participation behavior of users from the perspective of information system (IS). The user behavior of smart city apps has the following two obvious characteristics: First, because of the limitations of usage scenarios, users generally do not use the app again after completing the service or using certain functions, making it a "disposable" app. Therefore, it is necessary for users to expand their use and deeply use system functions, so as to improve the retention rate and utilization rate of smart city apps after adoption. Second, reports have pointed out that smart apps have poor compatibility, link failure, flashback, abnormal data and other prominent problems [3]. These system operation problems are the key factors that lead to negative emotions and negative behaviors of users such as boycott, neglect and quit.

Existing studies on the use behavior of smart technologies and smart apps are mostly focused on adoption and continuous use [3, 4]. However, most studies simply summarize the use behavior in a one-dimensional structure, such as active or inactive, use or not use, and have not subdivide the various use behavior of users in the later stage of adoption.

For this end, this paper tries to use the grounded theory-based qualitative research to analyze the concept of user's adaptive use behavior and explore the development law and formation mechanism of the behavior. This has great theoretical value and practical significance for improving users' usage and participation, realizing the effective connection of residents, government, service providers and resources in the city, and building a truly "intelligent and humanized" service platform for smart cities.

2 Literature Review

2.1 The Concept of User Adaptation and Infusion

Adaptive information behavior refers to that users actively study, explore, adjust, merge and retain the existing system functions according to different task requirements, so as to improve the utilization efficiency of the system [5]. The researchers of user information behavior point out that encouraging users to make full use of the technology already implemented is an important way to realize the value of information system [6]. However, a major problem in the implementation of information system is poor use effect after the implementation of the system. The organizations or users rarely make full use of the information system, so it is difficult to realize the return on investment or the expected impact [7]. The use and information behavior of users are the key factors that determine the successful implementation of IT/IS. Therefore, in order to solve the problem that users do not make full use of the apps, scholars propose to shift the research focus from "building system" to "using system".

The initial stage of IT adoption and use is an important part of the research on the use of information systems [8], which has been extensively discussed in the existing literature on IT/IS use behavior. However, IT/IS adoption is only the beginning of successful implementation of an information system. For the more complex post-adoption stage, user behavior mainly falls into the following two parts. The first part is user continuance behavior, which is also the focus of research on IT/IS user behavior. The Expect-Confirmation Model of IS Continuance (ECM) proposed by Bhattacherjee et al. has become the classical theoretical basis for studying the continuous use of information systems including the application of smart technology [9, 10]. The second part is the habit formation in the use of IT and IS, that is, the tendency of individuals to actively use the information system [11]. This part emphasizes the pre-influencing factors of habitual use and the subsequent influence on the system and environment, as well as the influence of habitual use on users' interaction with the information system (for example, intent of use, innovation, etc.) [12].

Although research on the continuance and habit of IT/IS use is critical, the relevant researches have not adequately addressed the nature of IT use after adoption. The post-adoption active use behavior of users is usually equated with continuous use or habitual use, and is loosely summarized as increased intensity or higher frequency of use [13]. Therefore, some scholars have discussed the specific ways of using IS or IT after adoption.

The researchers point out that users will experience a gradual familiarization process after accepting IT or IS. In the initial stage, users use few system functions to complete the assigned tasks; as users become more familiar with the system, they may not be satisfied with their current usage and explore a wider range of more useful features to achieve task goals, which is adaptive informational behavior [14].

Although the academic circle has put forward many related concepts (such as deep use, extended use, enhanced use, effective use, etc.) from different perspectives, the specific behaviors studied are roughly the same that is, users use more system or technical functions to improve their task performance, which includes existing tasks and broader potential tasks [15]. For example, Schwarz proposed the concept of deep use, which refers to the use of more functions to deepen the use of different technical functions [16]. Burton et al. proposed that deep use means that users' use of IS has reached the extent of making full use of the deep structural features of IS [19]. Wang et al. (2006) embodied deep use as users seeking multiple ways to make full use of IS [18]. Bagayogo et al. defined enhanced use as the use of previously unused functions, the use of IT functions to perform new tasks, and the extension of existing IT/IS functions, etc. [15]. At the individual user level, Burton et al. defined effective use as the use of a system in a way that contributes to the realization of the use goal of the system [19].

2.2 Factors Influencing Adaptive Information Behavior

Most researches around the topic of deep use are about the extended use of IT/IS functions, and the existing researches on the extended use of IS mostly focus on the factors that influence the extended use of users. Hsieh and Wang (2007) combined the technology acceptance model (TAM) with the information system continuance model (ISC) and pointed out that perceived usefulness and perceived ease of use have a positive effect on the deep use behavior. Unlike continuance behavior and adoption behavior, satisfaction does not have a direct impact on the deep use behavior [20]. Hsieh et al. studied the extended use behavior of customer relationship management system in enterprises based on sensemaking theory, and pointed out from the technical level and the working system level that users' perceived technology quality and perceived service quality have a positive effect on the deep use behavior of the system [6]. Tanja and Jurij took the intelligent business system as the research object, and explored the influence of objective system factors (such as system quality, organizational environment, etc.) and behavioral factors (such as perceived effort, social influence, promotion conditions, etc.) on users' deep use. They divided the extended use behavior into three dimensions: use range, use intensity, and use fusion [13]. Hsu et al. improved the IS success model and pointed out that service quality, system quality and information quality had a significant positive effect on user satisfaction, which further influenced the extended use of ERP system by employees, thus determining whether ERP could be successfully implemented [21].

In terms of smart technologies and apps in the context of smart cities, most studies focus on the extended use behavior of smart medical IT/IS. Raymond et al. took the electronic medical record system (EMR) as the research object and affirmed that the extended use of EMR system by doctors can significantly improve the service performance. They also pointed out that the more functions available in the EMR system, the higher the perceived ease of use, and the greater the possibility of extended use of EMR system [22]. From the perspective of social influence theory, Wang et al. took perceived ease of use and perceived usefulness as control variables, and discussed the social influence factors (rewards, punishments, social image and group norms) on doctors' intention of extended use of electronic health record systems (EHR) [23]. For the smart technology of wearable medical devices, some scholars pointed out that user concerns such as users' privacy and health information concerns would affect their coping behaviors, which would affect the extended use behavior of patients in learning and using wearable medical devices [24] (Table 1).

Table 1. Related research on adaptation behaviors

Author	Adaptive behavior	Research object	Main theoretical basis	Research method	Kernel variable
Tanja and Jurij [13]	Extended use	Business intelligence system (BIS)	Technology, Organization and Environment (TOE) framework	Qualitative research	Personal characteristics, quality characteristics, organizational factors, macro-environment characteristics, performance concepts, results demonstration, effective perceptions, social influence, favorable conditions
Bagayogo et al. [15]	Enhanced use	ERP system, Office system		Grounded theory	Innovation track, real-time use range and adaptation
Hsieh et al. [6]	Extended use	ERP system	TAM theory, ISC continuance theory	Questionnaire survey	Expectation confirmation, satisfaction, perceived usefulness, perceived ease of use
Hsieh et al. [20]	Extended use	CRM system	Sensemaking theory	Questionnaire survey	Technical quality, service quality, employee participation, system coordination
Hsu et al. [21]	Extended use	ERP system	IS success model	Questionnaire survey	Service quality, system quality, information quality, satisfaction
Li et al. [16]	Routine use Innovative use	Business intelligence system (BIS)	Intrinsic motivation theory	Questionnaire survey	Intrinsic achievement motivation, intrinsic cognitive motivation, intrinsic stimulus experience motivation, perceived usefulness

(continued)

Table 1. (*continued*)

Author	Adaptive behavior	Research object	Main theoretical basis	Research method	Kernel variable
Liang et al. [25]	System exploration and extended use	ERP system	Effective use theory, adaptive structure theory	Questionnaire survey	System complexity, work autonomy, innovation atmosphere, task diversity
Marakhimov and Joo [24]	Extended use	Wearable medical devices	Coping theory, user adaptation coping model	Questionnaire survey	Health concern, health information concern, privacy concern, challenge arousal, threat arousal, emotional coping, problem coping
Reymond et al. [22]	Extended use	Electronic medical record system (EMR)		Questionnaire survey	Perceived ease of use, functional coverage, and satisfaction
Wang et al. [23]	Extended use	Electronic health record system (EHR)	Social influence theory	Questionnaire survey	Reward, punishment, social image, group norms

Previous studies have mostly combined TAM and TPB theories to discuss the influencing factors on users' adaptive behavior. However, the following problems indicate that the existing theories at the adoption stage are not sufficient to explain the adaptive use behavior of smart city app users:

1. The function settings and interface layout of the mobile app tend to be unified and homogenized;
2. The improvement of users' information literacy and the increase of digital native users;
3. After the initial adoption stage, users already have a certain understanding of smart city apps.

Therefore, factors such as perceived usefulness and perceived ease of use do not play an obvious role in the adaptive use stage, and the motivation of the adaptive use stage needs to be further explored. In addition, the influencing factors of the adaptive use stage are mostly about the system characteristics, ignoring the influence of task characteristics and social environment factors on the adaptive use of the system. Specifically, in terms of psychological, emotional and cognitive factors, most studies take satisfaction as the core variable. However, the single variable of satisfaction cannot fully capture the sentimental and emotional experience of users in the post-adoption stage. It is necessary to further analyze the cognitive motivations of users' adaptive use by combining the characteristics of smart city apps.

3　Research Design and Data Analysis

Considering the exploratory nature of this research and the purpose of establishing an adaptive information behavior process model, it is appropriate to adopt the grounded theory-based research method. As a qualitative research method, grounded theory can construct theories from empirical data to explain overall research problems and phenomena [26].

The research firstly collects data through open and semi-structured interviews, and then draws on the open coding, axial coding and selective coding proposed by Strauss et al. to conduct a three-stage analysis. The coding process uses NVivo11 as an auxiliary tool to conduct comparative analysis and coding consistency test on the interview data, and build an adaptive behavior process model of smart city app users after reaching theoretical saturation.

3.1　Data Collection

This paper conducted sampling interviews with 25 users. The interviewees were between 23 and 57 years old, and their occupations involved middle school teachers, college teachers, housewives, civil servants, employees of enterprises, Taobao shopkeepers and on-the-job graduate students. These interviewees were representative.

The research adopted the semi-structured interview, and the main questions of the interview outline included "Will your behavior change in information inquiry and other aspects over time?", "For what reasons will you start using new functions?", "Do you have any emotional or psychological fluctuations or changes at this stage? Will it affect your behaviors such as information acquisition", "What will you do when encountering difficulties or unfamiliar functions?", etc. Further questioning and discussion may be conducted based on the answers of the interviewees. In this stage, one-on-one interviews and focus group interviews were used. The one-to-one interview can get to know the usage characteristics and psychological cognition of the interviewees as deeply as possible, while the focus group interview can make the interviewees' thinking more divergent and enlighten each other, thus making the interview content more comprehensive.

3.2　Coding Analysis

In the open coding stage, the researchers reviewed the interview data word by word, refined the original language of each interviewee and formed a concept. Through several comparisons, the data was preliminarily classified and initial category coding was given. A total of 84 categories have been formed during this coding stage.

In the axial coding stage, with the continuous collection of interview data and the emergence of new concepts, the concepts and categories formed in the open coding stage were further compared, analyzed, classified and adjusted to form the main category according to the internal correlation and logical relationship. At the same time, it summarized the behavior stage and behavior related conditions in terms of time dimension, and initially straightened out the influencing factor model of the adaptive use of smart city apps.

In the selective coding stage, the researchers repeatedly compared the axial coding results with the existing literatures and theories, further sorted out the relationship between the main categories and built a process model for the adaptive behavior of smart city app users (see Fig. 1).

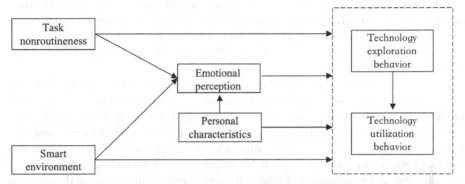

Fig. 1. Influencing factors and process modelfor the adaptive behavior of smart city app users

The research selects the interview data of 6 interviewees for theoretical saturation test, and carries out the same three-stage coding and categorization process for this part of the interview data. The results show that no new concepts, categories and correlation relations emerge. Therefore, it can be considered that the process of research on categorization has good reliability and validity, and the theory has reached saturation.

4 Research Findings

4.1 Model Description

Task nonroutineness smart environment, personal characteristics and emotional perception are the main influencing factors of adaptive use. Among them, emotional perception plays a role of mediating variable, which is jointly affected by task nonroutineness, smart environment and personal traits. If users perceive good operation quality and convenience in the early stage of use, it will prompt users to use more smart city app functions to deal with tasks or query information. In addition, the smart city app is a utilitarian information system, and the characteristics of tasks have an important impact on the activation of new functions. Complex and diverse task nonroutineness prompt users to explore the system more. At the same time, users with high information literacy and strong innovation will have clearer needs for intelligence, and tend to use smart apps in a deeper level. In addition, the intelligence degree of the user's surrounding environment also affects the user's adaptive use. The higher the intelligence degree, the more comprehensive the user's use of smart city apps.

In the adaptive use stage, users will carry out technology exploration behaviors such as learning and exploration, to improve their use experience and system knowledge [27]. As interviewee No. 5 said, "I dare not click at will for fear that I may click the wrong place and the system will fail. My daughter taught me how to operate and I do as she says." Digital native users will explore the system directly in a more efficient way. As the interviewee No. 3 pointed out, "I skipped the guidance steps at the beginning, which are too troublesome to remember after reading. I like to explore the new functions by myself." This is because digital native users have higher information literacy and use experience, and tend to interact with the system more efficiently and get real-time feedback when processing information [29]. The exploration behavior will have an impact on extended use. On the one hand, it will expand the scope of use of system functions and enable more new functions; on the other hand, it will increase the frequency of use of new functions and the app.

In addition, if the user perceives that the current use performance cannot match the task requirements, the user will replace the mastered functions with more efficient and simpler ones to improve the system service performance and promote the adaptive use of smart app content [28]. As the interviewee No. 18 pointed out, "I originally made an appointment in the system for local handling when the driver's license was renewed. But I thought it was too troublesome to go to the vehicle administration office. I then checked other functions in the system and found that I could apply remote renewal directly. So, I applied for remote renewal and received a new license sent from the original license issuing place, saving me a lot of time."

4.2 Theoretical Elements of Smart City Apps Adaptation and Infusion

Task nonroutineness refer to new, complex, and diverse task forms generated when users use smart city apps. Specifically, it includes the completion level tasks such as living payment (such as paying utility bills), business processing (such as real estate registration), business appointments (such as marriage registration appointments), etc.; information query tasks such as human and social information query, work progress query, cost information query, life information query, etc.; and information acquisition tasks such as local news information, real-time traffic information, public health information, etc. The impact of task nonroutineness on adaptive IT/IS use behavior has been verified in numerous empirical studies. Bagayogo et al. investigated users' enhanced use behavior of IT and found that the complexity of the user's task at hand positively affected their enhanced use [15]. Liang et al. investigated the extended use of complex systems by employees in conjunction with the ERP system, and found that the diversity of employees' tasks at hand ultimately positively affects their extended use [25] (Table 2).

Smart environment refers to the intelligence degree of the surrounding environment in which users use smart city apps, including public environment (such as government publicity, the intelligence degree of the whole society, etc.), family environment (such as the intelligent atmosphere of family, acquaintances' recommendation, etc.), and technical environment (the intelligence degree of the system environment) (Table 3).

Table 2. Coding paradigm of the core category "Task nonroutineness"

Core category	Sub-categories	Initial concept	Example of quotation
Task nonroutineness	Task completion	Living payment; business handling; business appointment	A02: "For example, when you register for marriage, you have to queue up for a long time if you go to the Civil Affairs Bureau directly, so you need to make an appointment in advance."
	Information query	Human and social information inquiry; work progress inquiry; cost information inquiry; life information query	
	Information acquisition	Local news information; real-time traffic information; public health information	

Table 3. Coding paradigm of the core category "Smart environment"

Core category	Sub-categories	Initial concept	Example of quotation
Smart environment	Public environment	Government publicity; public advertising	A05: "My daughter recommended this app to me and taught me some basic operations."
	Family environment	Acquaintances recommendation; children's influence; follow trends	
	Technical environment	Response speed; stable operation ability; equipment adaptability; information accuracy;	

As a new type of smart app, the user groups are highly differentiated in terms of information literacy and digital savvy, which can be divided into digital immigrants and digital natives. Most digital natives were born in the technological era after the 1980s. They have high digital savvy and information literacy, can actively explore in the information system according to personal information needs, and are keen on new technologies. However, digital immigrants were born earlier and have to go through a difficult learning process for new technologies and information systems. Therefore, the user's personal characteristics have an important influence on the adaptive behavior of smart city apps (Table 4).

Table 4. Coding paradigm of the core category "Smart environment"

Core category	Sub-categories	Initial concept	Example of quotation
Personal characteristic	Personal innovation	Innovation consciousness; innovation ability	A12: "I have used similar apps before, so I am familiar with them quickly."
	Information literacy	App use awareness; App use ability; literacy	
	Knowledge and experience	System cognition; functional knowledge; use experience	

The user's emotional perception mainly includes trust, emotional attachment and perceived convenience. In the process of use, users' emotional perception will be affected by smart environment, personal characteristics and other aspects, which in turn will affect the development of adaptive behavior. Therefore, users' emotional perception is an important mediator variable that affects adaptive behavior (Table 5).

Table 5. Coding paradigm of the core category "Emotional Perception"

Core category	Sub-categories	Initial concept	Example of quotation
Emotional perception	Trust	Authoritative trust; service ability trust; security trust	A16: "I think this app is run by the government, which is quite authoritative. I don't worry about my privacy information being leaked, so I often use the services."
	Emotional attachment	Habit; love; support; involuntarily	
	Perceived convenience	Use convenience; life convenience; service convenience	

When analyzing the adaptive behavior of enterprise information systems, scholars pointed out that technological exploration is manifested by employees' attempts to use new methods or innovative use of existing technologies to complete work, so as to achieve the purpose of improving work performance [5, 30]. In the context of smart apps, technological exploratory adaptive behavior means that users update their existing cognition and knowledge reserves of apps through learning or exploration, and try to use new functions or new technologies to solve task requirements (Table 6).

Table 6. Coding paradigm of the core category "Technology exploration behavior"

Core category	Sub-categories	Initial concept	Example of quotation
Technology exploration behavior	Exploration intention	Explore more new functions; explore function combination; explore efficient alternatives; explore personalized settings	A20: "When I come across a function that I haven't used before, I just click it and see how it works and what the process is."

After users have enough knowledge about the system and new functions, they will use the new system functions to complete personal tasks or meet information needs, that is, technology utilization adaptive behavior [5, 30]. Full utilization and adaptation of new functions can improve the utilization rate of system functions and task performance [19], which mainly includes extended use behavior and integrated use behavior in smart APP. Integrated use behavior is more manifested as the combination of user's personalized settings and functions, such as setting and adding common functions, or combining the "hot news" function and the "local news" function (Table 7).

Table 7. Coding paradigm of the core category "Technology utilization behavior"

Core category	Sub-categories	Initial concept	Example of quotation
Technology utilization behavior	Extended use behavior	Use more functions; enable new functions; increase the frequency of use; alternative use;	A11: "After I got how to use the function search bar of app, I don't have to search in the menu bar for a long time. I can directly use the search bar to find the function I want to use".
	Integrated use behavior	Combined use; reconstruction use; personalized settings	

5 Conclusion and Suggestion

This paper adopted the grounded theory of procedural school to systematically explore the adaptive behavior process of smart city app users. The research first collected data through questionnaire survey and in-depth interview, followed by three-stage coding, and built a model of influencing factors on adaptive behavior.

In theory, the research broke through the thinking restrictions of research adoption and continuance, and analyzed the information behavior of smart app users from the perspective of post-adoption adaptive behavior. On the one hand, the research explored the internal motivations of adaptive behaviors from four aspects: environment, tasks, emotions, and users; on the other hand, the research identified the main categories of different adaptive behaviors through coding analysis, and clarified the concepts of adaptive behaviors in terms of technological exploration and technological utilization, expounded the mutual influence of adaptive behaviors, and systematically interpreted adaptive behaviors. The research helps to fully understand the complex evolution process of the information behavior, enriches and deconstructs the connotation of adaptive behavior, and provides a theoretical basis for it.

This research is a grounded theory-based qualitative research. Due to the limitations of research methods, there will inevitably be some personal subjective factors of the researcher in the coding process. In addition, the influence intensity of emotional perception, social environment and other factors, as well as the influence of adaptive behaviors on user performance, needs to be analyzed through quantitative research, in order to reveal the process and results of adaptive behaviors of smart city mobile service users more completely and accurately.

Acknowledgement. This research was supported by two grants respectively funded by the Natural Science Foundation of Guangdong (No.: 2018A030313706) and the National Natural Science Foundation of China (No.: 71974215).

References

1. Nam, T., Pardo, T.A.: Conceptualizing smart city with dimensions of technology, people, and institutions. In: Proceedings of the 12th Annual International Conference on Digital Government Research, 12–15 June 2011
2. Peng, G.C.A., Nunes, M.B., Zheng, L.: Impacts of low citizen awareness and usage in smart city services: the case of London's smart parking system. IseB **15**(4), 845–876 (2017)
3. Hsiaoping, Y.: The effects of successful ICT-based smart city services: from citizens' perspectives. Govern. Inf. Q. **34**(5), 556–565 (2017)
4. Gracia, D.B., Casaló-Ariño, L.V., Pérez-Rueda, A.: Determinants of multi-service smart-card success for smart cities development: a study based on citizens' privacy and security perceptions. Govern. Inf. Q. **32**(2), 154–163 (2015)
5. Bala, H., Venkatesh, V.: Adaptation to information technology: a holistic nomological network from implementation to job outcomes. Manage. Sci. **62**(1), 156–179 (2016)
6. Hsieh, P.A., Rai, A., Xu, S.X.: Extracting business value from IT: a sensemaking perspective of post-adoptive use. Manage. Sci. **57**(11), 2018–2039 (2011)
7. Jasperson, J., Carter, P.E., Zmud, R.W.: A comprehensive conceptualization of post-adoptive behaviors associated with information technology enabled work systems. MIS Q. **29**(3), 525–557 (2005)
8. Venkatesh, V., Morris, M.G., Davis, G.B., Davis, F.D.: User acceptance of information technology: toward a unified view. MIS Q. **27**(3), 425–478 (2003)
9. Bhattacherjee, A.: Understanding information systems continuance: an expectation confirmation model. MIS Q. **3**(25), 351–370 (2001)
10. Bhattacherjee, A., Perols, J., Stanford, C.: Information technology continuance: a theoretical extension and empirical test. J. Comput. Inf. Syst. **3**(2), 17–26 (2008)
11. Limayem, M., Cheung, H.C.M.K.: How habit limits the predictive power of intention: the case of information systems continuance. MIS Q. **31**(4), 705–737 (2007)
12. Guinea, A.O.D., Markus, M.L.: Why Break The Habit Of A Lifetime? Rethinking the roles of intention, habit, and emotion in continuing information technology use. MIS Q. **33**(3), 433–444 (2009)

13. Grublješič, T., Jaklič, J.: Conceptualization of the business intelligence extended use model. Data Process. Better Bus. Educ. **55**(3), 72–82 (2015)
14. Saga, V.L., Zmud, R.W.: The nature and determinants of IT acceptance, routinization, and infusion. In: Proceedings of the IFIP TC8 Working Conference on Diffusion, Transfer and Implementation of Information Technology, pp. 67–86 (1993)
15. Bagayogo, F.F., Lapointe, L., Bassellier, G.: Enhanced use of it: a new perspective on post-adoption. J. Manage. Inf. Syst. **15**(7), 322–357 (2014)
16. Li, X., Hsieh, P.A., Rai, A.: Motivational differences across post-acceptance information system usage behaviors: an investigation in the business intelligence systems context. Inf. Syst. Res. **24**(3), 659–682 (2013)
17. Straub Jr., B.J.W.: Reconceptualizing system usage: an approach and empirical test. Inf. Syst. Res. **17**(3), 228–246 (2006)
18. Wang, W., Butler, J.E.: System deep usage in post-acceptance stage: a literature review and a new research framework. Int. J. Bus. Inf. Syst. **1**(4), 439–462 (2006)
19. Burton-Jones, A., Grange, C.: From use to effective use: a representation theory perspective. Inf. Syst. Res. **24**(3), 632–658 (2013)
20. Po-An Hsieh, J.J., Wang, W.: Explaining employees" extended use of complex information systems. Euro. J. Inf. Syst. **16**(3), 216–227 (2007)
21. Hsu, P.F., Yen, H.J.R., Chung, J.C.: Assessing ERP post-implementation success at the individual level: revisiting the role of service quality. Inf. Manag. **52**(8), 925–942 (2015)
22. Raymond, L., et al.: Improving performance in medical practices through the extended use of electronic medical record systems: a survey of Canadian family physicians. Med. Inf. Decis. Making **15**(27), 1–15 (2015)
23. Wang, W., Zhao, X., Sun, J., Zhou, G.: Exploring physicians' extended use of electronic health records (EHRs): a social influence perspective. Health Inf. Manage. J. **45**(3), 134–143 (2016)
24. Marakhimov, A., Joo, J.: Consumer adaptation and infusion of wearable devices for healthcare. Comput. Hum. Behav. **76**, 135–148 (2017)
25. Liang, H., Peng, Z., Xue, Y., Guo, X., Wang, N.: Employees' exploration of complex systems: an integrative view. J. Manage. Inf. Syst. **32**(1), 322–357 (2015)
26. Wang, F.: Explaining the low utilization of government websites: using a grounded theory approach. Govern. Inf. Q. **31**, 610–621 (2014)
27. Luo, Y., Ling, H.: Exploration and exploitation of information systems usage and individual performance. Procedia Comput. Sci. **22**(1), 863–872 (2013)
28. Thatcher, A.J.B.: Moving beyond intentions and toward the theory of trying: effects of work environment and gender on post-adoption information technology use. MIS Q. **29**(3), 427–459 (2005)
29. Vodanovich, S., Sundaram, D., Myers, M.: Digital natives and ubiquitous information systems. Inf. Syst. Res. **21**(4), 1–13 (2010)
30. Gupta, A.K., Smith, K.G., Shalley, C.E.: The interplay between exploration and exploitation. Acad. Manag. J. **49**(4), 693–706 (2006)

IoT, Sensors and Smart Environments

Re-imagining Indoor Space Utilization in the COVID-19 Pandemic with Smart Re-configurable Spaces (SReS)

Poorvesh Dongre[✉][iD], Mark Manuel[iD], and Denis Gračanin[iD]

Virginia Tech, Blacksburg, VA 24060, USA
{poorvesh,mmark95,gracanin}@vt.edu

Abstract. The outbreak of COVID-19 has put various restrictions on human lifestyle. At the beginning of the outbreak, almost all public spaces were closed to minimize the spread of this virus. Even as public spaces open up, they have several restrictions. Such restrictions include limited occupancy in common rooms to ensure social distancing and this can lead to increased occupancy costs inside buildings. The strategy of "Design as a cure" has been long used by architects and urban planners to minimize the spread of infectious diseases in urban environments. Re-configuring the space layout and optimizing the heating, ventilation, and air condition (HVAC) operations were some immediate solutions proposed by building designers to minimize the risk of COVID-19 infection in buildings. This paper explores the use of smart re-configurable spaces (SReS) to improve the efficiency of indoor space utilization while maintaining a safe indoor environment. We used an existing smart building design framework to design SReS for a common area/lounge in one of the cadet resident halls at Virginia Tech. User requirements were measured by conducting an interview with the residential coordinator and focus groups among the cadets. The concept of generative design was used in Revit 2021 to design various layouts of the lounge. Towards the end, we create a layout for maximum occupancy and suggest various re-configuration strategies. Future work includes modeling and evaluating the human-building interaction of SReS in virtual reality (VR).

Keywords: Smart re-configurable spaces · Generative design · Smart built environment · Adaptive architecture

1 Introduction

The outbreak of COVID-19 caused huge losses to life and property worldwide. A consequence of the pandemic was that it closed down all public spaces and forced humans to perform all activities virtually from home. The re-opening of public spaces was allowed with restrictions on space occupancy, the requirement of wearing masks, and the sanitation of frequently touched surfaces. The centers for disease control and prevention (CDC) guidelines mandates a distance of 6

© Springer Nature Switzerland AG 2021
N. Streitz and S. Konomi (Eds.): HCII 2021, LNCS 12782, pp. 85–99, 2021.
https://doi.org/10.1007/978-3-030-77015-0_7

feet among individuals in public spaces as they re-open. Such obligations have reduced the number of people that can occupy a space at a given time and have therefore increased space occupancy costs in public spaces. All this has caused a great deal of inconvenience to people worldwide. Public spaces become unavailable on full occupancy and in some cases users are required to pay a premium to safely access such facilities. Architects and urban planners have long used the strategy of "Design as a cure" to minimize the spread of infectious diseases in urban environments. In the 14th century, cities cleared overcrowded living spaces and expanded their borders to prevent the spread of the bubonic plague. In the 20th century, modern architects designed curative environments that included large windows and balconies to promote the circulation of air and sunlight [1]. These environments also had flat surfaces that would not collect dust, and white paint to emphasise cleanliness [2]. Similarly, in the age of COVID-19, architects, building designers and urban planner have suggested some strategies to minimize the spread of COVID-19. Architects recommend changing the spatial configuration to minimize social interaction in built environments [3]. Megahed and Ghoneim in their vision of antivirus-built environment suggested using Artificial Intelligence (AI) in the built environment as an immediate measure to prevent the contamination of COVID-19 infection [4]. Other solutions given by building designers include optimizing the heating, ventilation, and air condition (HVAC) operations in buildings [5].

This paper explores the use of smart re-configurable spaces (SReS) to automatically change the spatial configuration of a room in a building based on occupancy needs while maintaining a safe indoor environment. Our vision for SReS is that they automatically change the spatial layout of building components such as walls, furniture, etc. based on user needs to maximize space utilization. We use a common room (lounge) in one of the cadet residence halls at Virginia Tech, Blacksburg, VA as our case study for this research. A smart building design framework proposed by Dasgupta et al. is used to model the application of SReS in this particular residence hall [6]. User requirements were assessed by conducting an interview and focus groups. Designs were generated by using generative design in a 3D modeling software Revit. The results of our study include a layout that maximizes the occupancy of the lounge area and several possible re-configurations to fulfill user (cadet) needs.

2   Related Work

The concept of SReS is inspired from the fundamentals of adaptive architecture. Schnädelbach defines adaptive architecture as a multi-disciplinary field of study that is concerned with buildings that can adapt to their environments and users automatically or through manual intervention [7]. Examples of manually adapted architecture include Shōji, the Rietveld's Schröder house, Holl's Fukuoka housing, and Ban's Naked House. Examples of technologically enhanced adaptive architectural prototypes include TU Delft's Muscle Tower, Reciprocal Space, Re-configurable Wall System, Living Wall, and the Exo-Building.

The TU Delft's Muscle Tower is a flexible frame that automatically reacts to human movement [8]. Reciprocal Space and Re-configurable Wall System change the shape of the walls based on the surrounding environment [9]. Living Wall consists of an electronically augmented wallpaper that changes its patterns on human interaction [10]. Exo-Building is a tent like structure that imitates a person's physiological states [11]. The smart reconfiguration service presented by Gračanin et al. as shown in Fig. 1 recognizes the activities-of-daily-living (ADL) of users and changes the space configuration by moving the walls and furniture [12].

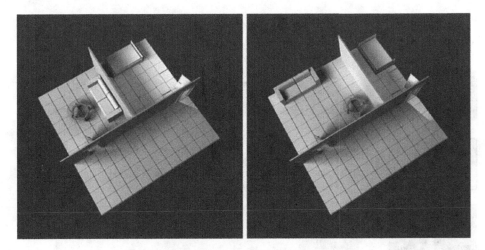

Fig. 1. An illustration of two interchangeable configurations for a living room. **Left:** Default configuration of a typical living room and bedroom. **Right:** Reconfiguration of the space for social activities [12].

The idea of an adaptive solar façade (ASF) that can change its geometry based on environmental and human inputs was used by Tabadkani et al. [13]. They used Grasshopper, a plugin tool for Rhino, to generate 1800 origami-based dynamic design models. The method of using computers to generate and evaluate various design alternatives is called generative design (GD). This study also uses the GD tool in Revit to create several layouts of the lounge area in the cadet residence hall at Virginia Tech. The use of GD for space planning is becoming popular among building design researchers. Nagy et al. proposed a novel workflow for GD and applied it for designing an office space [14]. Goldstein et al. introduced a tool called SpaceAnalysis to help designers create their own GD workflows [15]. Villaggi et al. included the result of surveys to capture their qualitative preferences in the GD workflow to design a 49,000 square foot office space [16]. GD was also used in the urban space planning of a neighborhood development project in Alkmaar, Netherlands [17].

We use Revit over other GD tools because Revit is a more compatible tool for building information modeling (BIM). BIM is an intelligent 3D modeling process to plan, design, construct, and manage buildings and infrastructure projects more efficiently. It also provides a standardized way to store, share and exchange building information. A smart built environments (SBE) is equipped with sensors, sensor networks, controllers, actuators and interfaces that perform the function of collecting, storing, analyzing, and presenting the building data. BIM with its information exchange capabilities can also provide data to the SBE [18].

3   Methodology

The implementation of our study is based on the SBE design framework proposed by Dasgupta et al. [6, 19]. An illustration the framework is shown in Figure 2.

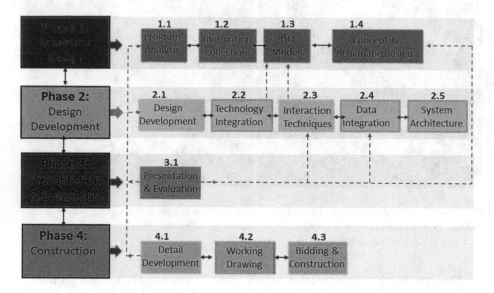

Fig. 2. Smart built environment (SBE) design framework [6, 19].

According to this framework, the first step in designing a SBE is "schematic design". It involves use of Models and Theories of Human Computer Interaction (HCI) to identify the user requirements and create a "schematic design" that can fulfill user requirements. For this research, we conducted an interview and focus groups with our target audience to identify the user requirements. Analysis of data collected from interview and focus groups was done using qualitative coding. 3D design and modeling software by Autodesk were used to create schematic designs. More on this is discussed in the Data Collection and Analysis section of this paper.

The second step in designing a SBE framework is "design development". In this step we design various room layouts to suit the identified user requirements. GD was used to improve the efficiency of layout design. This also confirms to the technology integration component of the SBE design framework. We followed the approach given by Villaggi et al. of using the qualitative data in GD workflow and generated multiple layouts to suit the user requirements [16]. The idea here is that lounge area after getting equipped with smart re-configurable capabilities will change itself based on these layouts. This step also includes Technology Integration, Interaction Techniques, Data Integration, and System Architecture. Details of designs developed using the GD process and discussions on other phases of this step are given in the Results section of this paper.

The third step in SBE design framework is "presentation and evaluation". This includes showing the generated layouts to the cadets and to the residential administration. It also includes assessing the human-building interaction (HBI) between the cadets and lounge SReS system. Getting feedback on the generated layouts and HBI is not a part of this paper and will be address in future work.

The last step in SBE design framework is "construction". It includes Detail development, Working Drawing, and Bidding and Construction. As of now, there are no plans for "construction" because this research project is just meant to check the feasibility of SReS.

4 Data Collection and Analysis

Schematic Design
Focus Groups. We conducted focus groups among student cadets who reside in an ROTC residence hall at Virginia Tech, Blacksburg to understand their space usage requirements in the lounge area. All cadet participants have an engineering background but to ensure diversity we grouped together sophomores and seniors in the session. The discussion in our focus groups included topics regarding ADL, lounge area usage (time spent and activities performed), changes in lounge area usage post COVID-19, and potential application of SReS in lounge area. The focus group sessions were audio-recorded, with the consent of the students, and this was later transcribed into text. The transcribed document was manually checked to remove possible errors in transcription. Analysis of the focus group data was done using qualitative coding techniques in MAXQDA 2020. Qualitative coding is the process of labeling a passage in the text as codes to identify different themes in qualitative data. Some codes were hard coded based on questions asked and some were coded in-vivo depending on their relevance to our research.

Interview. We also conducted a two-part interview with the residential coordinator of the same residence hall to check if there are any complaints, rules, or regulations that we should be cognizant of while designing for the lounge area. During the first part of the interview, we asked them some simple background information (job responsibilities and years of experience), typical lounge area usage and occupancy, impact of COVID-19 on lounge area usage and occupancy, room reservation systems (if any), common complaints or issues about using the lounge area, and their opinion on the application of SReS in the lounge area. Data collection and analysis for the interview was same as that for the focus groups. In the second part of our interview, we took a tour of the lounge on 4th floor of the hall. The objective of this tour was to allow us to create a spatial map of the lounge area. We needed this spatial map, as building plans for this particular residence hall were not available to us due to the privacy concerns. We used a Microsoft Hololens 2 headset to scan the lounge and create a spatial map. Using this headset, we were able to generate a 3D mesh of the lounge area. This 3D mesh data was processed in Autodesk's 3ds Max software before finally transferring it to Revit for schematic design development. The 3D mesh and final 3D model (schematic design) of the lounge area are shown in Fig. 3

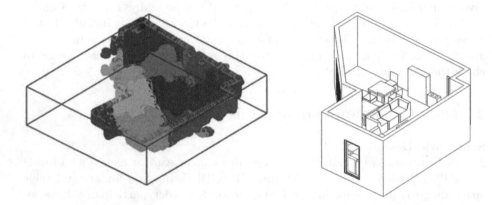

Fig. 3. Illustration of the 3D model building process. **Left:** 3D mesh from Microsoft Hololens 2. **Right:** 3D model in Revit.

5   Results

5.1   Design Development

General Findings from Focus Groups and Interviews. We learned that there were a total of 14 lounges in the building, approximately 3 per floor. Post COVID-19, each lounge has been given an occupancy limit. This is to enforce the mandated 6-feet social distancing policy that is widely-used as a preventative measure against the spread of COVID-19. The larger lounges now occupy a maximum six students, while the smaller can house between 2 and 4 students at a time. The larger lounges were given to different ROTC companies (groups of cadets) and companies tended to be quite possessive about them. This is because these lounges are typically filled with company memorabilia and other artifacts. Each of these spaces have a sign-in sheet that serves as a make-shift reservation system that lets other cadets know for how long the space will be in use. Senior cadets get reservation priority over junior cadets. Scheduling conflicts are handled internally among the student cadets. To build upon this, we propose the inclusion of an improved reservation-system through our SReS system design.

Qualitative Coding of Focus Groups and Interviews. As mentioned earlier, qualitative coding is the process of labeling a passage in the text as codes. For this research we hard coded some of the codes based on the questions asked during the focus groups and the interviews. These hard codes included: ADL, Lounge Uses, COVID Impact, Rules, and SReS application. ADL codes captured the typical activities in a student cadet's everyday routine. The daily activities mentioned in focus groups and interviews include "studying", "training", and "meeting". Among these "studying" and "meeting" are typically performed inside the residence halls and the lounges are a common place for cadets to usually study or meet. This is also reflected in code "lounge uses" that covers the typical activities cadets used the lounge for. Illustrative quotations from the focus groups and interviews are shown below.

Residential coordinator quotes:
"I have seen people from other companies in a same lounge space. But that was also during the day when studying was taking place."
Student cadet quotes:
"So I use the lounges like, even last year to study. I'm a night owl and I would go at like, from 10pm to 3am. So I spent a lot of time in them."
"We use the lounges, like whenever we had like, one on one meetings, and I feel that things like collections for company duties and stuff like that."

Other lounge uses include "memorabilia" and "leisure". Illustrative quotations from the focus groups and interviews on these are shown below.

Residential coordinator quotes:
"Halloween decorations, because you want them to still have fun, but still follow regulations. And so I have slowly but surely had to move a few things out of the hallways that might have been considered a tradition for them and I want to make sure they can maintain their traditions. But let's put it in a lounge."
Student cadet quotes:
"Another big one that I know a lot of people use it for is if they're trying to get away from the roommate for a little bit. Or, you know, if your roommates got something on and you can't bother them, so you'll go to one of the lounges instead, especially if you don't feel like leaving the dorms entirely."
"Well, our company has a PlayStation. So someone set that up, and they would play video games in there. Another a sophomore has a VR headset. So they set up the VR headset, and they would have like congregations in there and play."

COVID Impact reflects some of the issues that cadets are facing in their respective student resident halls. The major issues that were discovered because of

COVID include "reduced occupancy" in lounges and "loneliness". Illustrative quotations on COVID Impact are shown below.

Residential coordinator quotes:

"So they talk about loneliness. But they also talk about a lack of privacy. Because like, especially if you have a roommate, you're never alone. And so it's hard for students who are trying to have counselling sessions with someone always in the room, or someone trying to have a private, you know, emotional conversation, like with a parent or family member, like there's always someone there."

Student cadet quotes:

"I know, a couple of times, we had to have meetings outside. Because there was too many people to meet in even one of the big common rooms."

"I used the largest to hang out with my girlfriend away from my roommate and every single time there were pretty much taken."

The code Rules highlight some of the spoken and unspoken regulations that students have to follow in the ROTC residence halls. Some of these include keeping the hallways vacant, not bringing food into the lounges, keeping the room doors open, and having a door card at all times. The requirement of keeping the hallways vacant has resulted in some of cadets putting extra items in the lounge area. These extra items (typically, floor/company spirit items) take up space and this can further reduce the occupancy limits of lounges. The code SReS Application focuses on the potential applications that cadets believe SReS can be used for in the lounge area. We received positive feedback from our interview and focus groups to implement SReS in the lounge area. There were also some interesting ideas suggested during the focus groups such as bigger rooms being split into smaller rooms, stacking chairs, and collapsible furniture.

Generative Design. Based on the findings from the qualitative coding exercise, we came up with the following objectives for SReS design development in the lounge area:

1. To design a layout that maximizes occupancy in the lounge
2. To design re-configurations that can provide flexible study and meeting spaces in the lounge
3. To provide sufficient space for keeping memorabilia and other artifacts

To begin with we developed a GD script in Dynamo (a visual programming tool for Revit) to check the maximum occupancy and safe seat positions in the current layout of lounge area. The script asks the designer to select the Revit family instances (furniture items) from the 3D model and stores the location of these instances on that floor as a list. A function was used to create various paths through the work spaces. This function creates a circular boundary around the floor and creates inbound curves spaced at various resolutions. The points where this curve passes over the furniture items gives the locations that have are safe for social distancing, i.e. six feet apart. Data.Remember node and Data.Gate node from the GD Add-ons in Dynamo run various iterations on the curve to find the safe seats. Finally, the furniture items that are located at safe distances are highlighted with a Green color in Revit. Running this script on the 3D model of lounge gave us a maximum occupancy of four. The current lounge layout and the best seat arrangement for this layout as selected from GD study is shown in Fig. 4.

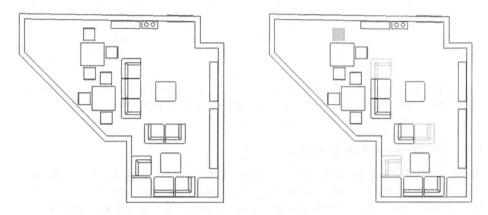

Fig. 4. Seat arrangements in lounge. **Left:** Current lounge layout. **Right:** Best seat arrangement. (Color figure online)

In the next step, we used the pre-installed GD studies in Revit to find the layout configuration that can allow maximum occupancy. The pre-installed GD studies in Revit that were used for this research include Grid Object Placement, Stepped Grid Object Placement, and Randomize Object Placement. Grid Object Placement study aligns elements on X and Y axes in a rectangular grid to generate alternatives for placing objects in a room whereas the Stepped Grid Object Placement study uses a diamond grid to do the same. Randomize Object Placement study randomly places the elements in clusters over a given space. Single seat sectional couches were used to create these arrangement because the lounge is already equipped with some of those. Moreover sectional couches are more comfortable to sit and have a side rest that can be used to keep notebooks and laptops. The Grid Object Placement study gave a rectangular arrangement of sectional couches in lounge area with a maximum occupancy of eight. The Stepped Grid Object Placement gave a maximum occupancy of three with sectional couches arranged in a diamond shape. The Randomize Object Placement study did not give any result. The best arrangements as a result of running Grid Object and Stepped Grid Object placement studies on the 3D lounge model is shown in Fig. 5.

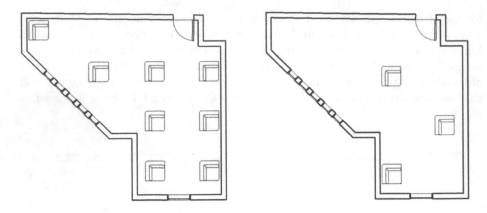

Fig. 5. Illustration of best layouts from the generative design (GD) study. **Left:** Lounge layout from grid object placement. **Right:** Stepped grid object placement.

5.2   Technology Integration

After finalizing our layouts, we moved on to brainstorming about the mechanisms that will help us implement the "re-configurable" aspects of SReS. Building on the current reservation-based system, our SReS will allow students to book time slots for when they plan to use the lounge area. To reserve a space in the lounge, students will have to select a time and specify the number of co-members and the purpose of their reservation. From our focus groups and interviews we determined that the primary reason for students to use the lounge was to either hold meetings or to study. For each time slot, furniture and partition walls will be moved automatically to create desired layouts based on the reservation requirements. For instance, consider a case in which eight students (the maximum safe occupancy determined from our generated layouts) would like to use the lounge to study individually. For this specific case, upon parsing the reservation request from these eight students, the SReS will determine that eight separate groups/entities require to use the space at the given reservation time. In response to this, the SReS will re-arrange its furniture and partition walls to match the layout shown in Fig. 5 (Left).

The SReS must be able to switch between different layouts, while ensuring that the safety of the current space occupants is not compromised. This can be done by considering the safe changing of layouts as an obstacle avoidance problem, where each moving component needs to ensure that it does not damage the occupants, itself, or any other component in during its movement. This aligns with the three laws of SBE safety proposed by Gracanin et al. [20].

Sensor-actuator pairs will control the movement of individual pieces of furniture and/or walls. To ensure that moving SReS components do not threaten the safety of their occupants, there needs to be an intelligent agent that oversees all state transformations within the space. This can include a smart BIM-model that keeps track of the current state of the SReS, along with a Rule Engine (a set of hierarchical state conditions) that validates the safety of each SReS component movement [20]. Only one SReS component will be allowed to move at a time and all motion will be halted if the sensors on a moving component detect a possible collision with any other entity. Only unoccupied and unobstructed SReS components are allowed to change their positions. Communication between the sensors, actuators, Rule Engine and the BIM-model will be constant and robust. To ensure the safety of its occupants, the SReS also needs to communicate every instance of a potential safety violation. Flashing LED light strips and audio warnings were suggested as potential modes of communicating hazards, during our focus group meetings. We will focus more on this aspect in the next iteration of this work.

5.3   System Architecture

SReS builds upon the idea of flexible and context-sensitive spaces presented by Gracanin et al. [12]. They use a service based framework as shown in Fig. 6 to explain the System Architecture of SReS. These spaces are typically imbued with embedded devices, sensors and actuators, making them capable of recognizing and acting upon the current state of the space. In the service-based framework, the activities of daily living (ADL) and space usage patterns is measured with the IoT Layer and Data Layer. The IoT Layer provides connectivity and communication to the embedded devices, sensors and actuators and the Data Layer provides data collection and fusion. However, the addition of these sensors also introduces an added level of complexity into the design of the space [21]. The configuration layer allows users to manage the space configuration. The UI layer supports multi-modal interactions between the SReS and users across a variety of interfaces.

6   Discussion

The cadets were unique as a target population for an SReS case study as they have various regulations to abide by. Even in their residences cadets have to always live by the rules. Analysis of the data collected from focus groups and interview revealed that cadets primarily use the lounge for studying and meeting. The outbreak of COVID-19 has put more restrictions on the already rule-bound lives of cadets. They do not have constant access to the lounges in resident halls anymore due to the reduced occupancy restrictions and so a lot of them are forced to stay inside their rooms to study and attend online classes. The culture in the corps encourages storing of memorabilia and other artifacts in lounge which further puts a restriction on the occupancy of the lounge. The lounges also serve as a get-away space for cadets to have some private and/or leisure time. This is another reason why the residence hall lounges need to be made more accessible for these cadets. This research uses the idea of SReS to increase the occupancy of a lounge in one of the cadet residents at Virginia Tech and make it more accessible while maintaining social-distancing guidelines. We use

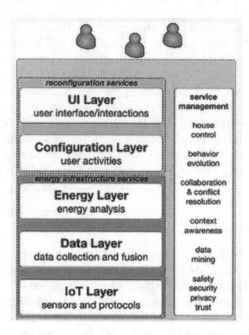

Fig. 6. Service centric framework for smart re-configurable spaces (SReS) framework [12].

a custom script in GD to first check the maximum occupancy and optimal seat arrangement in the lounge. Maximum occupancy as instructed by the residence hall administration is six, but the GD study reveals that occupancy should not be more than four. GD is further used to find a lounge layout that can occupy more cadets and our layout results reveal that occupancy can be increased to as much as eight (a hundred percent increase). The layout that supports eight people was generated using the Grid Object Placement study in Revit and is shown in Fig. 5 (Left). We use this layout as the default configuration in our lounge SReS system.

The lounge SReS in the cadet residence hall will have movable single-seat sectional couches and movable partition walls. Since cadets primarily use the lounge for studying and meeting, there can be many possible configurations depending on the meeting group size. As mentioned, the lounge can occupy a maximum of 8 people at a time, (while adhering to the six-feet apart social distancing rule). Therefore, at full occupancy the total number of re-configurations possible are 20. These include 4 groups of 2, 5 groups of 3, 4 groups of 4, 3 groups of 5, 2 groups of 6, 1 group of 7, and 1 group of 8 which is the default configuration. Figure 7 shows how the configuration can change if two cadets want to meet and the others want to study.

As shown, the middle couch will move towards the one at the corner while maintaining a distance of six feet and a movable partition wall will create a meeting space. A similar approach can be followed if cadets want to meet and

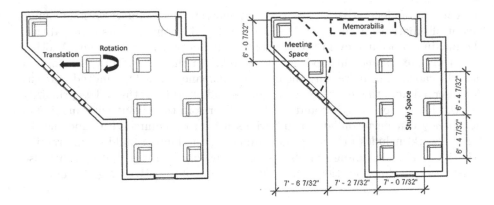

Fig. 7. Re-configuration for a meeting of 2 and studying of 6 scenario. **Left:** Single seat sectional couch rotating and translating to new position. **Right:** Partition wall comes up to create meeting space.

study in different combinations. If all cadets want to only study or if all of them want to only meet the then they can use the default configuration. In case of partial occupancy, only one portion of the lounge SReS system will re-configure whereas the remaining will continue to remain in default configuration. As shown in Fig. 7 (Right), the space along the door of lounge is reserved for memorabilia and artifacts. SReS furniture components (couch, walls) will not move into this space while re-configuring themselves. One potential limitation is the range of SReS component is that the translation of sectional couch on full occupancy is restricted to a few inches only. For instance, in the previously discussed example of two meeting and others studying, the translation of the sectional couch is only by a few inches from its original position. There is approximately a 6 in. translation perimeter for all couches which cannot be crossed to ensure social distancing.

7   Conclusion and Future Work

This research explores the applicability of smart re-configurable spaces (SReS) in the lounge area of cadet residence hall at Virginia Tech. Prior research used SReS in a typical home but little research has been conducting into the application of SReS in public spaces. For SReS to be successful in public spaces it needs the capability to manage the dynamic behavior of various people in that space. To this end, we used the smart built environment (SBE) framework proposed by Dasgupta et al. to approach the SReS design process [6,19]. The organization of this paper also follows the steps enlisted in SBE design framework starting from "schematic design development" to "design development". Focus groups and interviews were conducted to get the user requirements and subsequently the schematic design was developed. For detailed design development we used the concept of Generative Design (GD) to generate and evaluate various lounge layout alternatives. A custom GD study developed by the authors revealed that the maximum occupancy in the lounge with its current layout is four. Another GD study pre-installed in Revit generated a layout that can occupy a maximum of eight cadets thus increasing the current occupancy limit by hundred percent. As observed from the results of focus groups and interviews, the cadets primarily use the lounge for studying and meeting. Therefore the layout with maximum occupancy can be reconfigured in various ways to accommodate cadet needs. Future work includes modeling and evaluating the human-building interaction (HBI) in the cadet lounge SReS system using virtual reality (VR). This also constitutes the "presentation and evaluation" step of the SBE design framework.

References

1. Chang, V.: Cholera outbreaks and the 1918 flu transformed architecture. The coronavirus will do it again. Slate Mag. (2020)
2. Budds, D.: Design in the age of pandemics. Curbed, March 2020
3. Dietz, L., Horve, P.F., Coil, D.A., Fretz, M., Eisen, J.A., Van Den Wymelenberg, K.: 2019 novel coronavirus (COVID-19) pandemic: built environment considerations to reduce transmission. Msystems 5(2) (2020)
4. Megahed, N.A., Ghoneim, E.M.: Antivirus-built environment: lessons learned from Covid-19 pandemic. Sustain. Cities Soc. **61**, 102350 (2020)
5. Daniela, D., et al.: COVID-19 and living spaces challenge. Well-being and public health recommendations for a healthy, safe, and sustainable housing. Acta Biomed. **91**(9–S), 61–75 (2020)
6. Dasgupta, A., Handosa, M., Manuel, M., Gračanin, D.: A user-centric design framework for smart built environments. In: Streitz, N., Konomi, S. (eds.) HCII 2019. LNCS, vol. 11587, pp. 124–143. Springer, Cham (2019). https://doi.org/10.1007/978-3-030-21935-2_11
7. Schnädelbach, H.: Adaptive architecture-a conceptual framework. In: Geelhaar, J., Eckardt, F., Rudolf, B., Zierold, S., Markert, M. (eds.) Proceedings of MediaCity: Interaction of Architecture, Media and Social Phenomena, Weimar, Germany, pp. 523–555 (2010)
8. Oosterhuis, K., Biloria, N.: Interactions with proactive architectural spaces: the muscle projects. Commun. ACM **51**(6), 70–78 (2008)
9. Menges, A., Sheil, B., Glynn, R., Skavara, M.: Fabricate: Rethinking Design and Construction. UCL Press, London (2017)
10. Buechley, L., Mellis, D., Perner-Wilson, H., Lovell, E., Kaufmann, B.: Living wall: programmable wallpaper for interactive spaces. In: Proceedings of the 18th ACM International Conference on Multimedia, pp. 1401–1402 (2010)
11. Schnädelbach, H., Irune, A., Kirk, D., Glover, K., Brundell, P.: ExoBuilding: physiologically driven adaptive architecture. ACM Trans. Comput.-Hum. Interact. (TOCHI) **19**(4), 1–22 (2012)
12. Gračanin, D., Eltoweissy, M., Cheng, L., Tasooji, R.: Reconfigurable spaces and places in smart built environments: a service centric approach. In: Stephanidis, C. (ed.) HCI 2018. CCIS, vol. 852, pp. 463–468. Springer, Cham (2018). https://doi.org/10.1007/978-3-319-92285-0_63

13. Tabadkani, A., Shoubi, M.V., Soflaei, F., Banihashemi, S.: Integrated parametric design of adaptive facades for user's visual comfort. Autom. Constr. **106**, 102857 (2019)
14. Nagy, D., et al.: Project discover: an application of generative design for architectural space planning. In: Proceedings of the Symposium on Simulation for Architecture and Urban Design, pp. 1–8 (2017)
15. Goldstein, R., Breslav, S., Walmsley, K., Khan, A.: SpaceAnalysis: a tool for pathfinding, visibility, and acoustics analyses in generative design workflows
16. Villaggi, L., Stoddart, J., Nagy, D., Benjamin, D.: Survey-based simulation of user satisfaction for generative design in architecture. In: De Rycke, K., et al. (eds.) Humanizing Digital Reality, pp. 417–430. Springer, Singapore (2018). https://doi.org/10.1007/978-981-10-6611-5_36
17. Nagy, D., Villaggi, L., Benjamin, D.: Generative urban design: integrating financial and energy goals for automated neighborhood layout. In: Proceedings of the Symposium for Architecture and Urban Design Design, Delft, the Netherlands, pp. 265–274 (2018)
18. Zhang, J., Seet, B.C., Lie, T.T.: Building information modelling for smart built environments. Buildings **5**(1), 100–115 (2015)
19. Dasgupta, A.: Towards a unified framework for smart built environment design: an architectural perspective. Master's thesis, Virginia Polytechnic Institute and State University, Blacksburg, VA, 7 May 2018
20. Gračanin, D., D'Amico, A., Manuel, M., Carson, W., Eltoweisy, M., Cheng, L.: Biologically inspired safety and security for smart built environments: position paper. In: Proceedings of the 3rd Workshop on Bio-Inspired Security, Trust, Assurance and Resilience (BioSTAR 2018), 2018 IEEE Security and Privacy Workshop (SPW), pp. 293–298, 24 May 2018
21. Luria, M., Hoffman, G., Zuckerman, O.: Comparing social robot, screen and voice interfaces for smart-home control. In: Proceedings of the 2017 CHI Conference on Human Factors in Computing Systems, pp. 580–628. ACM (2017)

Pervasive Smart Objects: Framework for Extending Smart-Object Services

Kota Gushima(✉), Yukiko Kinoshita, and Tatsuo Nakajima

Waseda University, Okubo 3-4-1, Shinjuku, Tokyo, Japan
{gushi,yukiko-kinoshita,tatsuo}@dcl.cs.waseda.ac.jp

Abstract. Although various types of smart objects have already been developed, the use of these devices has not yet penetrated widely into people's everyday lives. Therefore, we constructed a design framework to increase the pervasiveness of smart-object services. This study consisted of two parts: defining a design space for smart objects, and developing a design framework using the defined design space. First, we analyzed 26 smart-object products to obtain the design space for smart-object services. These products were cited from various research projects regarding smart objects and were used to identify the features of smart objects. As a result, we obtained five dimensions: information acquisition method, perception, information provision by device, information conversion level, and target of service. Afterward, we performed a case study based on the design space, with the mindset of widening the applicability of the case study, and developed a design framework with the design space as the core to increase the pervasiveness of smart-object services. The resulting framework consists of four phases. Based on the application of this framework to other case studies, we then obtained valuable insights regarding the use of this design framework.

Keywords: Smart objects · Ambient media · Ubiquitous computing · Design framework

1 Introduction

It has been more than 25 years since Mark Weiser advocated for ubiquitous computing [24], wherein technologies disappear into the background of people's everyday lives. This concept is used in many areas of information technology. Public displays often seen at bus and train stations, for example, are a commonplace application that incorporates ubiquitous computing.

Smart objects have an important role in realizing the concept of ubiquitous computing. According to Kortuem et al. [18], smart objects are defined as "autonomous physical/digital objects augmented with sensing, processing, and network capabilities. Smart objects carry chunks of application logic that let them make sense of their local situation and interact with human users." Research on smart objects has advanced significantly since their inception, and a variety of smart-object applications, such as in smart homes, have been developed in the process. For example, a smart plant system

© Springer Nature Switzerland AG 2021
N. Streitz and S. Konomi (Eds.): HCII 2021, LNCS 12782, pp. 100–121, 2021.
https://doi.org/10.1007/978-3-030-77015-0_8

notifies its user of the amount of water in the plant through the use of ambient light [23]. Similarly, many smart objects used in everyday life utilize ambient media, which aim to speak to the background of human consciousness. Research on ambient media has been undertaken since the 1990s. Furthermore, in recent years, with the development of optical see-through head-mounted displays (HMD) such as Microsoft HoloLens, it has become possible to develop not only physical smart objects but also digital smart objects [12]. We believe that, through the use of information technologies, the real world can be extended physically and digitally, and potentially deliver necessary information to end users more efficiently.

However, although various types of smart objects have already been developed, the use of these devices has not yet penetrated widely into people's everyday lives. For example, although the concept of a smart home was developed 10 years ago, this has not yet been adopted widely among the general populace. Because services that use smart objects depend on certain situations and on certain supporting devices, these services are limited and are not adequately pervasive. As a result, general adoption of smart-object services is yet to be realized. At the same time, these kinds of services have always been threatened by security issues, which will have to be resolved for smart-object technology to be more widespread in the future.

With this research, we aim to develop a framework for designing smart-object services that can be utilized in a wider range of situations. Design frameworks support the feasibility of new services by providing processes of development or defining components of these services. To develop a design framework, we should first define a design space for smart-object services to determine the features necessary for these services. This design space can be helpful for visualizing the particularities of a service during its design.

We refer to the design space of Internet of Things (IoT) services, which includes a virtuality that we have developed in past research [10]. In that design space, we focused only on the IoT. By contrast, smart objects include a variety of objects, and not only IoT, but also ambient media. Therefore, to obtain knowledge for designing smart-object services, an analysis of such services is necessary. In particular, because the aspects of ambient media used in smart objects have not yet been incorporated into our previous design space, we define a new design space for smart objects based on this analysis. Finally, we summarize the design space in table format for ease of use.

Afterward, we develop a framework based on this design space. By focusing on the process of considering whether a service can be extended, we extract design steps for the framework. Concretely, we disassemble a case study based on the table-formatted design space and develop the framework based on a process wherein we determine how the case study can be applied to a wider range of situations. Finally, we verify the framework on two other case studies, specifically on whether the applicability of these cases can be extended.

Our contributions are as follows:

1. By analyzing smart objects, we clarify their features and develop a design framework for smart-object services, specifically on how these services can be utilized in a wider range of situations.

2. By analyzing existing services using our design framework, we prove that our framework helps to determine possibilities for utilizing these services in a wider range of situations.

2 Background: Design Space for Virtuality-Introduced Internet of Things

In this section, we describe the IoT-service design space that we have developed a priori [11]. To create this design space, we analyzed 138 IoT products proposed in Kickstarter, and three case studies involving virtuality. We then extracted the design space with the help of focus groups.

Services and products using IoT technology are currently being used in actual society. In our previous research, we aimed to investigate IoT products to extract their characteristics. We analyzed cutting-edge IoT products, i.e., those that have not yet been mass-produced, and extracted the characteristics of those products that are expected to trend in the future. To accomplish this objective, we investigated IoT products proposed in the famous crowdfunding platform Kickstarter, and by July 25, 2017, we found a total of 138 products related to IoT.

Based on our analysis, we classified the results into three categories and devised the following dimensions for this design space.

2.1 Dimension 1: Taxonomy of IoT

As a result of this survey, we divided the analyzed IoT products into two categories: (1) customizable IoT and (2) static IoT. Customizable IoT enables users to customize functions and modules. Many customizable IoT products are similar to the board-based products Arduino and Raspberry Pi. Static IoT, on the other hand, provides specific functions to users who utilize the static functions provided by their IoT devices.

2.2 Dimension 2: Visualizing Degree

In this subsection, we describe our three case studies, wherein virtuality was exhibited, and present an overview of the dimensions of the design space that resulted from our case-study analysis. These case studies were (1) Virtual Aquarium, (2) HoloMoL, and (3) Ambient Bot. These services influence people via virtual worlds and virtual objects, and have a wide variety of purposes and methods. We were then able to obtain the dimensions of the design space by extracting knowledge of design applications. The second dimension was named "visualizing degree," which identifies how to incorporate virtuality into how information is expressed into the real world. Details on this dimension are as follows:

Visualizing Degree 0. In this degree, such as in Virtual Aquarium, products present information through physical devices, such as physical displays and projectors to visualize information, and therefore additional space is required for their installation. This degree of service is useful in certain locations, such as toilets and bathrooms, where these devices can be installed. For example, Augmented Go is a service that allows users to learn strategies of Go using a projector [16]. Other research studies to extend the real world using physical displays and projectors have also been conducted [21].

Visualizing Degree 1. In this degree, the product uses see-through HMD to extend the physical object. An example of a service that exhibits this degree is HoloMoL, which overlays virtual objects on physical objects and places virtual objects in the real world. Compared to degree 0, this degree is superior in terms of mobility because it does not depend on additional physical devices.

Visualizing Degree 2. In this degree, products can present information without physical constraints. For example, Ambient Bot floats around the user without the limitation of the real world and can access information anywhere. Nonetheless, products that exhibit this visualizing degree have to be designed such that they can be well integrated into real space, even though they are not physically restricted. Expressions that do not fit in the real space can cause a loss of immersion of virtuality, and thus designers must focus on blending digital expressions into real space.

2.3 Dimension 3: Virtuality Level

Based on these two dimensions, we conducted a focus group discussion to collect ideas for IoT services involving virtuality. The participants were 10 Japanese students (male: 8, female: 2, average: 22.3 years old). In this focus group discussion, the participants discussed current IoT products that were proposed on Kickstarter. The number of people in each group was three or four persons. From the findings obtained, we determined a new dimension: the virtuality level.

Virtuality Level 0 application visualizes information. Virtuality Level 1 provides a virtual context that is valuable to the users, to provide them with information more efficiently. The difference between the two virtuality levels is that Virtuality Level 0 applications express information visually, such as in textual form, which is then layered onto the real world. On the other hand, Virtuality Level 1 applications express information that is ambiently integrated in the real world by integrating the virtual context. For example, in a Virtuality Level 0 application, the data obtained from sensors are identified by number and text, whereas in a Virtuality Level 1 application, the data are translated and identified as virtual objects located in the real world. To develop a Virtuality Level 1 application, creators have to incorporate AR and VR technologies to render virtual objects that make the experience believable.

3   Modification of Design Space

In this part of the study, we analyze existing smart objects, especially ambient-media research products, to develop a new design space for services that use smart objects. We examine a total of 26 research products. From our analysis, we determine the features of these products and sort similar features to find new dimensions for the new design space.

Table 1. Analysis template based on dimensions of design space.

Information acquisition method	Display of media			Target of service
	Perception	Information provision by device	Information conversion level	
			(Reasons for assigned levels are explained here.)	

Finally, we devise a new design space for smart objects, as outlined in Table 1. In the following section, we describe the process of defining the dimensions of the design space extracted via the analysis.

3.1 Information Acquisition Methods

First, we clarify how these smart objects are classified, which is referred to as Dimension 1 of the previous design space. For this aspect, we determine that all examined products are characterized by methods for acquiring information to be expressed by these products. In this section, we categorize these methods for acquiring information.

Category 1: Customizable Service. The first category of methods for obtaining information is through customizable services. Many smart-object products can be customized by their users. For example, Sideshow [2] summarizes notifications generated by a personal computer as a ticket and visualizes the information on the side of the display. With Sideshow, it is possible to customize the service such that it focuses on only the necessary notifications from among all possible notifications that may otherwise overflow in a personal computer. Another example of a customizable service is Calm Automation [4], which is a DIY Toolkit that allows the user to customize the information to be displayed, including the method for displaying the information. This service uses a device that combines a smartphone application and a specific device characterized by minimal interactions, such as up, down, and rotation. For example, to learn about the weather, the user can draw a sun and clouds on paper and paste the pictures onto the device. Afterward, the user would customize the device through its smartphone application to show the picture of the sun when it is sunny, and the picture of the clouds when it is cloudy. This product can report a variety of information based on customizations by the user on the device and its smartphone application.

A limitation of customizable services is that they often require sensor devices and input devices. However, as discussed later, there are several workarounds to these limitations. We assume that a service is automatically classified under this category if it is a customizable service.

Category 2: Non-customizable Service. The second category of methods for obtaining information is through non-customizable services. The services in this category can be classified in more detail. We describe its four subcategories as follows:

Subcategory 1: Non-usage of Devices for Obtaining Information. Products that cannot be customized can be divided based on two attributes: products using sensor devices, and products not using sensor devices. An example of a service that does not use sensor devices is the Ambient Birdhouse [22]. This service plays videos as though birds are visiting the birdhouse at regular intervals. This product includes cards that are illustrated with bird pictures and provide detailed information on the birds. By touching a card onto the birdhouse device, the user can watch videos of the bird featured on the card. Another example of service that does not use a sensor device is Scope [6], which provides a circular space on the monitor specifically for notifications because it focuses on providing notifications on the display unobstructed. The system also does not require any additional devices to acquire information. Scope is similar to Sideshow but does not allow its users to select which notifications to display.

Subcategory 2: Environmental Sensing. There are two types of service that require devices to acquire information. The first type requires sensor devices, whereas the second type requires input devices. The first type of devices can be further classified according to the object to be sensed, also referred to as environmental sensing. An example of a service that uses environmental sensing is Dangling String [25], which is connected via Ethernet and senses congestions in the network in a given location. Specifically, it senses the packets passing through a LAN cable. The system then shakes the strings to visualize the congestion. Another example of environmental-sensing devices are low-res lighting displays [14], which produce lighting displays based on energy data acquired from the environment, e.g., inside a house. As demonstrated with these examples, environmental sensing is a method that utilizes sensing devices on a prescribed location and acquires information regarding the environment directly from the environment itself.

Subcategory 3: Personal Information Sensing. The second type of service requiring sensor devices operates through what is termed as personal information sensing. An example is the Digital Family Portrait [20], which is designed specifically for family members that live far away. In this system, multiple icons are displayed around photographs of family members living in remote areas. The system displays information such as the person's health condition, and his or her involvement with other people. The system therefore requires sensors to collect the relevant personal information.

Subcategory 4: Usage of Input Devices. This subcategory of services requires the use of input devices, which implies that their respective systems include functionalities for interactions with users. An example of this system is Lumitouch [3], which is an interactive pair of photo frames. When a user picks up one of the photo frames, its paired photo frame then lights up. Depending on how the user touches the frame, he or she can send his or her emotions, which are represented by colors. Another example is the Notification Collage [9], which is similar to a digital notice board typically used in companies. Notes and video chats can be displayed and shared on the bulletin board, providing participants with an opportunity to engage in conversations among their colleagues. The shared display can be placed in a public space or as a display on an individual's desk. The service requires a smart board as its input device. Through the use of input devices such as this, active data gathering from the users is made possible. In Table 2, we summarize the categories and services that we have analyzed.

Table 2. Classification based on methods of acquiring information.

Customizable service	Non-customizable services			
	Non-usage of devices for obtaining information	Services requiring sensor devices		Usage of input devices
		Environmental sensing	Personal information sensing	
Calm Automation Ambient notification with shape-changing circuits in peripheral locations Information Percolator Kandinsky Sideshow Table fountain Lamp Ultrasonic humidifier Water lamp Pinwheels Ambient Orb My Yahoo! web portal Apple's dashboard	NotifiVR Ambient Birdhouse Scope What's Happening	CityCell NotifiVR ClassBeacons Low-res lighting displays Dangling String Informative art	Digital Family Portrait	CityCell Lumitouch Notification Collage

3.2 Methods for Displaying Media

In this section, we discuss how smart-object services display or provide their acquired information.

Perception. With regard to perception, the most common approach of providing information is to target the user's vision by showing information as media. The second most common approach is to target the user's auditory senses. For example, in NotifiVR [8], which is a system that seeks ways of providing important notifications via an HMD, the vision of the user is covered with the HMD, where notifications are shown on the display. A method of providing notifications via audio is also being proposed. Systems such as NotifiVR can also utilize tactile feedback, i.e., neither visual nor auditory, such as notifications through vibrations. Another example is the ultrasonic humidifier [7], which is a humidifier that controls three states, i.e., Off, Pulse, and Overflow, via notification of an event. This device then displays information regarding the humidity. However, in reality, it is considered almost impossible to sense the humidity, although information can still be received through observations of the condition of the humidifier. In Table 3, we outline the results of our investigations regarding perception.

Table 3. Classification based on perception.

Visual sense		Auditory sense	Other
Calm Automation	Kiumra	Ambient Birdhouse	NotifiVR
Ambient notification	Lumitouch	NotifiVR	Ultrasonic humidifier
with shape-changing	Notification Collage	Dangling String	
circuits in peripheral	Scope	Table fountain	
locations	Sideshow		
CityCell	Table fountain		
ClassBeacons	Lamp		
Low-res lighting	Ultrasonic humidifier		
displays	Water lamp		
Ambient Birdhouse	Pinwheels		
NotifiVR	What's Happening		
Dangling String	Ambient Orb		
Digital Family Portrait	My Yahoo! web portal		
Informative art	Apple's dashboard		
Information Percolator			
Kandinsky			

Information Provision by Device. For a smart object to be able to provide information to its user, its service should be able to produce media for displaying the information. These two functionalities are closely related, as discussed in the previous section. Many such systems require devices for expressing information visually, auditorily, or through other means. The type of device used depends on the service. Several of these services use generic-type monitors and mobile terminals, whereas some other services represent information using built-in media, such as ambient media. Numerous types of devices are independently being developed for these services, and as such, methods for information provision by device cannot be practically categorized.

Information Conversion Level. When acquired information is converted into representations for the end users to utilize, it is necessary to consider the degree of information conversion. The information conversion level refers to the degree of abstraction in the expression of acquired information. It is similar to the virtuality level explained in Sect. 2. The difference is that the information conversion level focuses not only on virtual objects but also on physical objects expressing information.

The information conversion level reveals whether the service produces an expression that everyone can understand, or whether it will be an expression that only a specific person could understand. For example, because Notification Collage shows the information that the user wants to share as it is, the information conversion level is low, and users know who shared what, regardless of whether these users are familiar with the system or otherwise. By contrast, Pinwheel [5] is a system with which wind turbines are made to rotate according to input information, such as heart rate and weather forecasting, which users can customize. This type of information regarding windmills may not be understandable to most people. The information conversion level of this application is therefore quite high, because only the people who are familiar with the system can understand it. By comparison, Digital Family Portrait displays icons around the pictures of people. Whereas outside observers can intuitively assume that the displayed information is related to the persons in the photos, they may not understand what the system actually intends to communicate without further explanation. Therefore, the information conversion level is said to be lower than that of Pinwheel, but higher than that of Notification Collage. Figure 1 visualizes the information conversion levels of a sampling of systems.

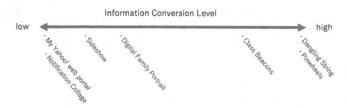

Fig. 1. Classification of services based on information conversion level.

3.3   Target of Service

In this section, we examine the entities to whom the service designer wants to convey information. Based on this criterion, services can be categorized as either targeting the public, targeting a community, or targeting an individual.

A service is said to target the public if it is meant to be used by an unspecified population, i.e., there is no specific designation on who can use the system. An example of such a system is CityCell [19], which is an artistic system that combines objects with hexagonal lights. Its main functionality is to recognize people's positions. When the system detects people from afar, the objects on the CityCell light up. If these people approach the system, they can then operate the objects using their smartphones. They can also rearrange the lighting objects by directly touching these objects. The CityCell system can be installed in a public space such as a park, and any person present in the vicinity of the system can use it. Information from services designed in a similar manner can be accessed by virtually everyone.

On the other hand, a service is said to target a community if it is meant to be used by a specific group of people, such as a company or family. An example of such a system is ClassBeacons [1], which attempts to provide real-time feedback to a teacher in a classroom. It illuminates specific light bulbs depending on the group of students that the teacher approaches. Specifically, while a group task is being performed in the class, the system senses the distance between the bulbs and the teacher, and changes the colors of the lights based on the distance. Therefore, the teacher would be able to determine if he or she is providing a fair distribution of attention toward the student groups. Only the teacher would know the colors of the lights and the groups that he or she may not be providing with enough attention. Because the service targets a certain community only, the system should also change according to the context. For example, in the case of ClassBeacons, the classes may be conducted in different classrooms, or the group sizes, academic advisors, and/or times of use may change. Regardless of the classroom situation, the system should still be usable.

In contrast with services that target specific communities, services targeting the public are made available in places that can be accessed by anyone who needs the information delivered by these services. Instead of focusing on certain users, services that target the public focus on certain places and situations. If service designers want to make such services more pervasive, they can simply assign these services to other places where these services are required. On the other hand, with regard to services that target specific communities, if the designers want to make these services more pervasive, they should also consider the context of the places where they wish to assign these services. Services that target specific communities are not required by everyone located at a given place. The designers must therefore consider privacy if they are using sensitive information and assign a higher value for information conversion level.

A service targeting an individual is a system that displays information for a specific individual. An example of this system is Calm Automation, which can be customized by the user based on the content that he or she wants to display and how he or she wants it to be displayed. Another example of a service that targets specific individuals are smartphone notifications. Such a system is designed for individual use. Some of these services have fairly low information conversion levels, where people, in general, can easily understand the information being displayed by these systems. As a result, few people have to acquire information from services that target specific individuals; they can, in some cases, avail of these services for their own individual use instead. By our definition, these types of services developed for individual use are also categorized based on their information conversion levels. Because these services are designed for individual use, and are non-public systems similar to services that target specific communities, the service designers should properly consider the context when they make these services more pervasive.

Targeting a community and targeting an individual are connected continuously. Some services are developed as targeting either a community or a person, whereas other services are designed to target both. In Fig. 2, we visualize how services tend toward targeting a community or targeting an individual. In Table 4, we outline a sampling of these services divided into three categories based on target.

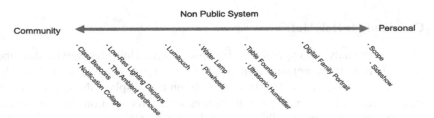

Fig. 2. Classification of services categorized as non-public systems.

Table 4. Classification based on target of service.

Public	Non-public	
CityCell	ClassBeacons	NotifiVR
Information Percolator	Low-res lighting displays	Kiumra
	Ambient Birdhouse	Scope
	Dangling String	Sideshow
	Informative art	What's Happening
	Kandinsky	Ambient Orb
	Lumitouch	My Yahoo! web portal
	Notification Collage	Apple's dashboard
	Table fountain	Water lamp
	Lamp	Pinwheels
		Ultrasonic humidifier

3.4 Summary of Design Space

For the design space obtained from this analysis, five dimensions can be extracted: information acquisition methods, perception relevant to media expression, information provision by device, information conversion level, and target of service. Service designers can better determine the characteristics of their services by examining their services along these dimensions. In addition, this design space may be useful for extracting the elements that restrict these services. By disassembling existing services using the design space, designers can better understand their features and limitations. In Table 1, we present a template for analyzing a service using this design space.

4   Application of Design Space on Case Studies

In this section, we demonstrate through case studies how to use each of the dimensions of the design space proposed in Sect. 3.

4.1   Case Study 1: HoloMoL

For our first case study, we apply the design space on the HoloMoL service described in Sect. 2.1.2, using the template shown in Table 1. First, we review how the HoloMoL system works. Because this system is an application that displays the information the user wants to remember in real space, it requires spatial recognition. This application communicates information visually via a see-through HMD. Because the information to be remembered is placed directly in space, the value of "Information conversion level" is "Low." The "Target of service" is "Individual," because this system focuses on improving individual memory performance. The results of disassembling HoloMoL are outlined in Table 5.

Table 5. Result of disassembling HoloMoL into elements.

Information acquisition method	Display of media			Target of service
	Perception	Information provision by device	Information conversion level	
Spatial recognition (subcategory 2)	Visual	See-through HMD	Low (contents are set by user and are mainly text and picture to remember.)	Individual

Fig. 3. Concept of DESI.

4.2 Case Study 2: DESI

For this case study, we extend a service, namely the distributed embedded sound information (DESI) service, as shown in Fig. 3 [17], to utilize it more pervasively with the proposed design space. By extracting the knowledge obtained in this process, we build a service design framework for smart objects.

Music has enriched people's lives. For example, music is used for emotion control, self-expression, and social combinations [13]. Ambient music is one of the music genres that are easiest to introduce into people's lives. Music of this genre does not actively speak to people; rather, it is similar to natural environmental sounds and does not have clear rhythm or melody. In this case study, we aim to use ubiquitous computing technology to bring music into life in greater degrees than what has been achieved thus far.

We developed DESI as an interactive ambient music prototype system. With this system, a user can assign favorite sounds to the things in his or her environment, to enjoy the sounds that would later be produced by the system. In addition, its interactive ambient music concept is expected to provide alternative reality experiences that would redefine the meaning of real space [15].

This system recognizes the positions of objects via sound localization. Piano sounds are inputted and pasted onto the objects. Because three-dimensional sound processing is performed by the system, the sounds can be heard from these objects. Therefore, when the objects move, the localization of the sound changes. Figure 4 shows an overview of the environment in which an actual prototype is used.

Fig. 4. Prototype of DESI.

DESI can be disassembled based on the template in Table 1. The system is equipped with a MIDI keyboard, to allow the user to create melodies, and a camera, to recognize the objects in the environment. Through open-air headphones, the system uses auditory perception to obtain necessary information. Information conversion level is low, because the system converts sound localization by matching music to object positions. The original music is not converted. The system is designed to be listened to by a single person through headphones.

5   Framework for Increasing Pervasiveness of Service

In this part of the study, we develop a design framework in a format that service designers can use, based on the design space proposed in Sect. 3.

5.1   Procedure to Increase Pervasiveness of DESI

In this part of the study, we attempt to increase the pervasiveness of the DESI service. First, designers must determine which elements are modifiable and unmodifiable among the dimensions in the design space. In one extreme, changing all elements of the service would result in the original service no longer being provided. To properly differentiate between modifiable and unmodifiable elements, we must consider the purpose of the DESI service. The concept of DESI is to attach music to physical objects in the real world, and to incorporate music into daily life. By focusing on this objective, we can unambiguously clarify the factors that are unmodifiable. The DESI service is thus disassembled based on this concept, using the design space defined in Sect. 3. The results of the disassembly are outlined in Table 6.

Table 6. Result of disassembling DESI into elements.

Information acquisition method	Display of media			Target of service
	Perception	Information provision by device	Information conversion level	
MIDI keyboard (subcategory 4) Fixed camera (subcategory 2)	Auditory	Open-air headphone	Low (system converts sound localization by matching music to position. Original music is not deformed.)	Individual

From these, we extract the elements that are expected to increase the pervasiveness of the service. Because DESI is a service based mainly on music, auditory sense, as its mode of perception, is unmodifiable. In addition, because the system is aimed at providing music on a daily basis, it is not possible to change the information conversion level. Otherwise, sounds would have to be added to the physical objects themselves. On the other hand, it is possible to replace the devices used by the system.

The following examples demonstrate how the service can be made more pervasive through changes in these elements:

Example 1: Replacement of Information Acquisition Devices. When the input device is replaced from a MIDI keyboard to a smartphone application, and when the camera is changed from a fixed-point camera to a smart glass camera, DESI can be utilized even in a space recognizable by a device such as HoloLens. As a result, even when the user is not in a special environment that requires a fixed-point camera, he or she can interact with DESI and produce live music anytime.

Example 2: Replacement of Information Provision Device. Users who do not have headphones can also share music experiences by changing the device to be played from a headphone to speakers. As a result, it becomes possible to change the target of the DESI service to another individual, or a community, or the public. However, stereophonic sounds that can be heard only through headphones are not available to other information provision devices. However, because this extension is not largely outside of the DESI concept (which implies changing sound according to real-world objects), it is possible to extend the service in this direction. As a result, users can collaborate with others, and enjoy and discuss the works of others in a given location. This extension opens a possibility for realizing communication through music.

5.2 Revision of Framework to Increase Pervasiveness

In this section, we discuss a design framework for increasing the pervasiveness of smart-object services based on the design process discussed in Sect. 4.2 and illustrated in Fig. 5.

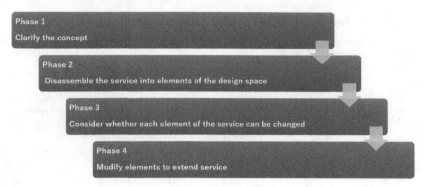

Fig. 5. Overview of framework.

This framework is used to consider changes in the context where services are deployed. By determining applicable changes in the elements in the design space, we aim to clarify the elements by which a service is presently limited, and to extend these elements such that the service can then be used in other contexts. In this framework, designers can deliberate on possible extensions based on the following procedure.

Phase 1: Clarification of Concept. The focus in this phase is the value and information the service provides to the user. A service using a typical smart object presents acquired information to the user. The kind of information that is presented to the user can be the concept of the service. On the other hand, not all services provide information.

DESI is a service that converts information regarding where physical objects are in space. If the concept of this service is to provide information on the positions of objects in the real world, we can extend it using a notification method that does not use sound, provided that the service maintains its ability to detect positions of objects in the real world. By comparison, the actual DESI concept is to incorporate music into the real world. The detection of the positions of objects is merely an implementation for realizing that concept. By examining the extension of the DESI service, we recognize that the concept of service is indispensable for clarifying the elements for the extension.

Phase 2: Disassembly of Service into Elements of Design Space. The designers can then clarify the types of elements the service is composed of by applying the service to each dimension of the design space defined in Sect. 3. However, although Dimensions 1, 2, and 3 can be easily clarified, further discussions may be necessary for Dimensions 4 and 5. As mentioned in Sect. 3, there are cases where Dimension 5 satisfies both personal and community needs. Meanwhile, Dimension 4 is defined by how much of the information is expressed based on the concept of the service defined in Phase 1. For DESI, the information conversion level is low because music is used as the media. However, if DESI is a service that notifies the locations of objects, the information conversion level becomes high because the positions of the objects are converted into music. Designers will have to be aware that the information conversion level depends on the requirements of the service.

Phase 3: Deliberation Regarding Changeable Elements of Service. Based on the service concept, we can then consider whether the services can be deployed elsewhere by extracting things that can be changed among the decomposed elements. We can clarify which elements of the service can be changed against the concept.

Phase 4: Selection of Modifiable Elements for Service Extension. It is possible to increase the pervasiveness of the service by considering changes in modifiable elements to the extent that the requirements of the service concept are satisfied. Designers must be careful that, in this phase, extended services have different contexts. Therefore, it will be necessary to properly change the information conversion level. For example, when a service that delivers personal information is extended to an environment where anyone can see or hear the delivered information, there is a danger that the personal information will be accessed easily. The confidentiality of the information should then be ensured through the use of abstract expressions, and the information conversion level should be raised.

6 Application of Framework to Existing Services

In this part of the study, we use the framework to extend the design of existing services and observe the results.

6.1 Extension of Virtual Aquarium

We extend the Virtual Aquarium service based on the framework procedure. The tasks in each phase are described as follows.

Phase 1: Clarification of Concept. The Virtual Aquarium service provides ambient feedback on toothbrushing to promote correct brushing and toothbrushing habituation. Virtual Aquarium uses immediate feedback and accumulated feedback. The immediate feedback informs the user of the correct brushing methods, whereas accumulated feedback has a role in promoting daily brushing. The reason for providing these feedbacks is to promote proper and habitual toothbrushing. This service expresses the toothbrushing activity using an aquarium metaphor.

Phase 2: Disassembly of Service into Elements of Design Space. Table 7 outlines the elements of the Virtual Aquarium service to realize the service concept.

Table 7. Disassembly of virtual aquarium into elements.

Information acquisition method	Display of media			Target of service
	Perception	Information provision by device	Information conversion level	
Acceleration sensor (subcategory 3)	Visual	Display in front of mirror	High (information received from sensor is converted to aquarium metaphor.)	Individual

Phase 3: Deliberation Regarding Changeable Elements of Service.

Dimension 1 (Information Acquisition Methods). To extract what can be changed among the elements of Virtual Aquarium, we first have to identify the elements of the service. With regard to Dimension 1, we know it is essential for the information acquisition method to be able to sense the movement of the toothbrush. Although it is possible to observe the activities of a toothbrush with image recognition using a camera, it is more difficult to acquire information on the movement of a toothbrush using a camera than using an acceleration sensor. Therefore, the information acquisition device should not be changed.

Dimension 2 (Perception). This service provides feedback only to the visual senses. Because this service uses an aquarium as its main concept, a visual expression of an aquarium is used. Although it is possible to provide immediate feedback using sound and vibration for supplementary effects, feedback via hearing or touch is insufficient for the development of long-term habits because these methods are ineffective at communicating complicated information.

Dimension 3 (Information Provision by Device). People usually brush their teeth in front of a mirror. Therefore, for this service, the display is installed in front of a bathroom sink mirror. However, this display does not have to be fixed to the sink. Therefore, this element can be changed.

Dimension 4 (Information Conversion Level). For this service, it is impossible to change this element because the concept of the service is to convert information acquired by an acceleration sensor into the image of an aquarium.

Dimension 5 (Target of Service). Virtual Aquarium is a service for individual use, but it does not necessarily have to be adapted for individuals only. Usually, people do not brush their teeth in public spaces, and thus it may be impossible to change the target of the service to a public scenario. On the other hand, because people in a community may brush their teeth at a common place, this service can be extended for community use.

Phase 4: Selection of Modifiable Elements for Service Extension. From the results of Phase 3, it becomes clear that the information-providing device and the service target can be changed drastically. Meanwhile, the device for acquiring information can be partially changed. Phase 4 aims to design a more pervasive service based on these modifiable elements.

A problem with this service is that the information is provided only via a display near the bathroom mirror at home. However, according to the results of Phase 3, the device displaying the aquarium does not necessarily have to be fixed. In addition to the existing display, a smartphone can be used as a substitute. The portable device communicates with the acceleration sensor, and the user is able to receive feedback. In addition, because the data received by the smartphone are also reflected in the Virtual Aquarium at home, long-term feedback can be provided correctly. Virtual Aquarium will work even if the user changes his or her location.

Using a smartphone makes it possible to use the service, even if the user is away from home. However, a disadvantage of using a smartphone for this purpose is that the conventional ambient expression is lost. Unlike with the existing Virtual Aquarium, the user will have to actively access the necessary media by setting the smartphone by himself or herself to watch the aquarium. In addition, accumulated feedback is not necessary for the short term. This is because accumulated feedback does not change largely based on short-term information. On the other hand, because it is immediate feedback that is necessary for the short term, the user does not necessarily have to recreate all the expressions used in the original Virtual Aquarium when he or she is away from home. Therefore, in the mobile version used at home, when the activity of the acceleration sensor coincides with the pattern of toothbrushing, the smartphone provides an immediate feedback by music from the built-in speaker of the smartphone. This music increases in volume for correct toothbrushing and decreases for incorrect toothbrushing. It is desirable for this music to be ambient music reminiscent of an aquarium, i.e., using the sound of water. If the music is related to Virtual Aquarium, the user can recognize this music as one of the elements of Virtual Aquarium without any discomfort.

6.2 Extension of Ambient Bot

We also extend the Ambient Bot service based on the framework procedure. The tasks in each phase are described as follows.

Phase 1: Clarification of Concept. The concept of the service is "easy access to information in everyday life through characters." Ambient Bot realizes the ambient conditions and allows information to be accessed easily in everyday life. The service enables user interactions with characters and provides information via see-through HMDs.

Table 8. Disassembly of Ambient Bot into elements.

Information acquisition method	Display of media			Target of service
	Perception	Information provision by device	Information conversion level	
Information retrieved from API (subcategory 1)	Visual and auditory	See-through HMD	High (character is talking information retrieved from web API.)	Individual

Phase 2: Disassembly of Service into Elements of Design Space. Table 8 outlines the elements of Ambient Bot.

Phase 3: Deliberation Regarding Changeable Elements of Service.

Dimension 1 (Information Acquisition Methods). The information presented by Ambient Bot is highly scalable and can be displayed based on whatever content is related to the daily life of the user. Therefore, the user can customize the service.

Dimension 2 (Perception). Because the user interacts with the characters by sight, vision is essential. Hearing is also used to convey information by voice.

Dimension 3 (Information Provision by Device). Ambient Bot displays a character visually and enables the user to access information by looking at and interacting with the character. For that reason, the user needs a device that displays the character in real space. Therefore, a see-through HMD or smart glass is required.

Dimension 4 (Information Conversion Level). The system converts information acquired from the Internet to enable the character to speak information. Because the concept of Ambient Bot is to convey information through the character, this element cannot be changed.

Dimension 5 (Target of Service). Ambient Bot can be used by any audience without any particular limitation. The only requirement related to this element is to show information for everyday use.

Phase 4: Selection of Modifiable Elements for Service Extension. Based on the results of Phase 3, the information to be provided and the target to be displayed can be greatly changed. The original Ambient Bot is already pervasive in that it uses mobile HMD. However, we are looking for ways to use it in a wider variety of contexts.

Individuals using Ambient Bot require information specifically for individuals. However, if the service is to be used to provide information to a specific community, another way of using Ambient Bot will have to be developed. By reconsidering Ambient Bot as an information provision tool for a community, we can arrange the characters for a specific location and reconfigure the character to communicate information regarding the community, rather than concerning an individual, to the person accessing the service. For example, if the designers redesign Ambient Bot to provide information to the residents of an apartment, they can set a character in the lobby to notify residents about the type of garbage discarded on that day and about events in the community. The extended Ambient Bot provides information through characters placed in specific locations. This example is similar to the method of public display. However, this service is different from a general public display in that information can be quickly extracted via interaction through gazes. That is, the designer can apply principles from Ambient Bot to redesign an existing public display into becoming more ambient.

7 Insights

Decisions regarding the service concept are the most important phases in this framework. The reason for these steps is to review the elements that can be changed in the service according to the concept. If the idea of the designers regarding the service concept is incorrect, the foundation of the service is changed, and thereafter the value provided by the service may be lost. For example, in Virtual Aquarium, if the concept is "encourage toothbrushing," the designers can change the display method regardless of the aquarium. In the case of DESI, as we mentioned in Sect. 5, if the concept is to provide information on the positions of objects in the real world, extension using a notification method other than sound can be explored. Different concepts change the parameters for extending the service; therefore, the concept of the service must be carefully decided.

When we first used this framework in the real world, we noticed in some cases that the concepts we decided in Phase 1 were inadequate. When the established concepts were then subjected to Phase 3, there were cases wherein it was not possible to make judgments based on the concepts that were first decided. At that time, we returned to Phase 1 and reviewed the concepts that we have established. We then determined that, to facilitate the process of deciding the concept in Phase 1, it can be effective to remember that the concept will later be referred to in Phase 3. In other words, deliberating on the concept of a service becomes clearer and easier if what is not changed in the service is first considered. From there, it becomes possible to extend the service to enable its use in a wider variety of places and contexts. In addition, it has been suggested that the framework used to extend existing smart-object services can also be utilized as a tool for deciding on clear concepts for new services.

8   Conclusions and Future Research

Through case studies, we developed a service design framework that would allow the handling of more pervasive smart-object services. This framework consists of four phases: Phase 1 is the "Clarification of concept," Phase 2 is the "Disassembly of service into elements of design space," Phase 3 is the "Deliberation regarding changeable elements of service," and Phase 4 is the "Selection of modifiable elements for service extension."

We then extended existing services using the developed framework. As a result, the phase of conceptualization was determined to be the most critical aspect in the extension of services. Furthermore, it was confirmed that the concept can be refined further through repetition of the phase of reviewing whether each element of the service is modifiable and repetition of the phase of thinking about the concept.

Future research may include verification of the practicality of this design framework using services in the real world and understanding of the results through long-term operation. Ambient media often characterize the services to which the framework was applied. Therefore, it is necessary to determine to what extent the extension of the design by the framework is useful. Experimental results regarding the application of the framework on different types of smart objects, such as home electronics and smart furniture, are also desired.

References

1. An, P., Bakker, S., Ordanovski, S., Taconis, R., Eggen, B.: ClassBeacons: designing distributed visualization of teachers' physical proximity in the classroom. In: Proceedings of the Twelfth International Conference on Tangible, Embedded, and Embodied Interaction, pp. 357–367. The Association for Computing Machinery, New York (2018)

2. Cadiz, J., Venolia, G., Janke, G., Gupta, A.: Designing and deploying an information awareness interface. In: Proceedings of the 2002 ACM Conference on Computer Supported Cooperative Work, pp. 314–323. The Association for Computing Machinery, New York (2002)

3. Chang, A., Resner, B., Koerner, B., Wang, X., Ishii, H.: LumiTouch: an emotional communication device. In: Proceedings of the CHI 2001 Extended Abstracts on Human Factors in Computing Systems, pp. 371–372. The Association for Computing Machinery, New York (2001)

4. Cho, M., Saakes, D.: Calm automaton: a DIY toolkit for ambient displays. In: Proceedings of the 2017 CHI Conference Extended Abstracts on Human Factors in Computing Systems, pp. 393–396. The Association for Computing Machinery, New York (2017)

5. Dahley, A., Wisneski, C., Ishii, H.: Water lamp and pinwheels: ambient projection of digital information into architectural space. In: CHI Conference Summary 1998, pp. 269–270. The Association for Computing Machinery, New York (1998)

6. Dantzich, M., Robbins, D., Horvitz, E., Czerwinski, M.: Scope: providing awareness of multiple notifications at a glance. In: Proceedings of the Working Conference on Advanced Visual Interfaces, pp. 267–281. The Association for Computing Machinery, New York (2002)

7. Gellersen, H.W., Schmidt, A., Beigl, M.: Ambient media for peripheral information display. Pers. Technol. 3(4), 199–208 (1999). https://doi.org/10.1007/BF01540553

8. Ghosh, S., et al.: NotifiVR: exploring interruptions and notifications in virtual reality. IEEE Trans. Visual. Comput. Graph. 24(4), 1447–1456 (2018)

9. Greenberg, S., Rounding, M.: The notification collage: posting information to public and personal displays. In: Proceedings of the ACM CHI 2001 Human Factors in Computing Systems Conference, pp. 514–521. The Association for Computing Machinery, New York (2001)

10. Gushima, K., Akasaki, H., Nakajima, T.: Ambient bot: delivering daily casual information through eye contact with an intimate virtual creature. In: Proceedings of the 21st International Academic Mindtrek Conference, pp. 231–234. The Association for Computing Machinery, New York (2017)

11. Gushima, K., Nakajima, T.: A design space for virtuality-introduced Internet of Things. Future Internet 9(4), 60 (2017)

12. Gushima, K., Akasaki, H., Nakajima, T.: A novel interaction design approach for accessing daily casual information through a virtual creature. In: Streitz, N., Konomi, S. (eds.) DAPI 2018. LNCS, vol. 10921, pp. 56–70. Springer, Cham (2018). https://doi.org/10.1007/978-3-319-91125-0_4

13. Hargreaves, J., North, C.: The functions of musician everyday life: redefining the social in music psychology. Psychol. Music 27(1), 71–83 (1999)

14. Hoggenmueller, M., Wiethoff, A., Tomitsch, M.: Designing low-res lighting displays as ambient gateways to smart devices. In: Proceedings of the 7th ACM International Symposium on Pervasive Displays. The Association for Computing Machinery, New York (2018). Article 18

15. Ishizawa, F., Sakamoto, M., Nakajima, T.: Extracting intermediate-level design knowledge for speculating digital–physical hybrid alternate reality experiences. Multimed. Tools Appl. 77(16), 21329–21370 (2018). https://doi.org/10.1007/s11042-017-5595-8

16. Iwata, T., Yamabe, T., Nakajima, T.: Augmented reality go: extending traditional game play with interactive self-learning support. In: Proceedings of 17th International Conference on Embedded and Real-Time Computing Systems and Applications (RTCSA), pp. 105–114. Institute of Electrical and Electronics Engineers (2011)

17. Kinoshita, Y., Nakajima, T.: Making ambient music interactive based on ubiquitous computing technologies. In: Novais, P., et al. (eds.) ISAmI2018 2018. AISC, vol. 806, pp. 199–207. Springer, Cham (2019). https://doi.org/10.1007/978-3-030-01746-0_23

18. Kortuem, G., Kawsar, F., Sundramoorthy, V., Fitton, D.: Smart objects as building blocks for the Internet of things. IEEE Internet Comput. **14**(1), 44–51 (2009)
19. Mao, C., Liu, K., Chiu, W., Lin, C., Chen, C.: CityCell: an interactive OLED lighting system in public space. In: Proceedings of the 3rd International Conference on Communication and Information Processing, pp. 490–494. The Association for Computing Machinery, New York (2017)
20. Mynatt, E.D., Rowan, J., Jacobs, A., Craighill, S.: Digital family portraits: supporting peace of mind for extended family members. In: Proceedings of the ACM CHI 2001 Human Factors in Computing Systems Conference, pp. 333–340. The Association for Computing Machinery, New York (2001)
21. Sakamoto, M., Nakajima, T., Alexandrova, T.: Digital-physical hybrid design: harmonizing the real world and the virtual world. In: Proceedings of the 7th Design and Semantics of Form and Movement, pp. 211–222. Koninklijke Philips Electronics, Amsterdam (2012)
22. Soro, A., Brereton, M., Dema, T., Oliver, J., Chai, M., Ambe, A.: The ambient birdhouse: an IoT device to discover birds and engage with nature. In: Proceedings of the 2018 CHI Conference on Human Factors in Computing Systems. The Association for Computing Machinery, New York (2018). Paper 397
23. Voit, A., Salm, M., Beljaars, M., Kohn, S., Schneegass, S.: Demo of a smart plant system as an exemplary smart home application supporting non-urgent notifications. In: Proceedings of the 10th Nordic Conference on Human-Computer Interaction, pp. 936–939. The Association for Computing Machinery, New York (2018)
24. Weiser, M.: The computer for the 21st century. Sci. Am. **265**(3), 94–104 (1991)
25. Weiser, M., Brown, J.S.: Designing calm technology. PowerGrid J. **1**(1), 75–85 (1996)

Home Appliance Control Using Smartwatches with Continuous Gesture Recognition

Thamer Horbylon Nascimento[1,2] and Fabrizzio Soares[2,3](✉)

[1] Federal Institute Goiano – Campus Iporá, Iporá, GO, Brazil
thamer.nascimento@ifgoiano.edu.br
[2] Instituto de Informática, Universidade Federal de Goiás, Goiânia, GO, Brazil
fabrizzio@ufg.br
[3] Computer Science, Southern Oregon University, Ashland, OR, USA

Abstract. This work proposes the development of a method to control household appliances using smartwatches with continuous gesture recognition and carries out a pilot study to validate the developed method. The devices are controlled by infrared signals. We developed a prototype for smartwatches that allows the user to control the devices by making simple gestures, for this, we define a set of simple gestures made up of lines and curves, which represent commands to the devices. Thus, the method allows the user to send various commands to devices, such as on/off, increase and decrease temperature, increase and decrease volume, among others. We use the method to control the following devices: air conditioner, TV, video player, audio player and lamp. As we use the continuous gesture recognition algorithm, a gesture can be recognized before the user finishes it, allowing for quick interaction. We use the "Broadlink RM Mini 3", an omnidirectional mini infrared controller to send the infrared signals. After performing a gesture by the user, we use the continuous gesture recognition algorithm to recognize the gestures, then the command code corresponding to the gesture is sent to the "Broadlink RM Mini 3" that emits the infrared signal to be received by the device. The pilot study showed that it was possible to control the devices using the proposed method and that the commands were correctly sent to the devices with satisfactory response time.

Keywords: Smartwatch · Home appliances · Infrared · Continuous gesture recognition · Controller

1 Introduction

In the last years, we have witnessed the rise of technology, in which smartphones have been in the leadership. Many other technologies emerged as a tremendous ally to smartphones in the same fashion, improving personal connectivity and interaction, such as smartwatches or convenience to home, such as home technologies. A smartwatch is a wearable device that is attached to the user's wrist

N. Streitz and S. Konomi (Eds.): HCII 2021, LNCS 12782, pp. 122–134, 2021.
https://doi.org/10.1007/978-3-030-77015-0_9

and its use is constantly growing [10,14]. Therefore, creating fast and efficient interaction methods for smartwatches has become an important topic to the researcher community. In the other hand, home technology, in general, refers to any technology developed for the purpose of home use, such as home appliances. It is important to note that, various home devices, such as air conditioner, TV, lamp, music video players, or even washer and dryers, have technologies to connect to the internet and have become part of people's daily lives and are used for various purposes [12,19].

Considering that the automation of home appliances is on the rise and that the use of smartwatches is also on the rise, it becomes interesting to use the smartwatch to control these devices. Considering that several devices cannot be connected to a home network, as they do not have a network connection, this work will use infrared as a means of communication with the devices.

In this way, we will use the "Broadlink RM Mini 3" to send infrared signals to the devices. It is an omnidirectional infrared mini controller, with a range of 12 m and has a compact size (5.5 × 5.5 × 6.45 cm) and weighs only 135 g. Because it is omnidirectional, it does not need to be in the direction of the appliance, so a single controller can be used for all devices in the environment up to 12 m away. Figure 1 shows an example of setting up an environment with the "Broadlink RM Mini 3".

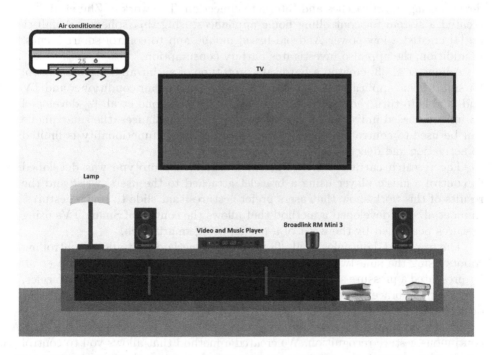

Fig. 1. Example of an environment with TV, air conditioner, lamp, video and music player and the controller "Broadlink RM Mini 3".

This work aims to develop a method that allows to control household appliances using smartwatches with continuous gesture recognition. For this it will be necessary specifically: to define a set of gestures and their respective actions on the devices, to establish communication between the smartwatch and the appliance and, finally, to send commands to the appliances.

Thus, this article presents the first results of the research to control home appliances using continuous gesture recognition on smartwatches and infrared communication using the Broadlink RM Mini 3 device.

The next sections present contents that are relevant to the understanding of the results obtained. The next section presents the related works, then we will explain the prototype developed and how the communication is made between the smartwatch and the home appliances. In sequence, we will approach the evaluation with specialists, right after, the results and finally, the final considerations.

2   Related Work

The work by Kronbauer et al. [12] developed a universal remote control for residential environments, they developed a platform that uses an application installed on a smartphone to control home appliances. Sulayman et al. [1] developed a home automation system using Arduino, it allows the user to control devices using smartwatches and Internet connection. The work of Zhu et al. [21] created a system for controlling home appliances using smartphones. Afifah et al. [4] created a low-power Android-based mobile app to control smart homes, in addition, the app also investigates battery consumption.

Adiono et al. [3] created a hardware prototype of an infrared remote control for smart home applications, the prototype was tested on air conditioner and TV and is able to turn the devices on and off. In 2018, Adiono et al. [2] developed an infrared-based universal remote control for home appliances, the smartphone can be used to control appliances using a central host, functionality is limited to activation and deactivation.

The research carried out by Speier et al. [20] a prototype was developed to control a music player using a bracelet attached to the users' wrist and the results of this work show that users prefer gestures that slide to touch gestures. Luna et al. [13], developed a method that allows the control of Smart TVs using gestures performed by the wrist of a person using smartwatch.

The work by Gkournelos et al. [9] proposed a method that allows controlling robots using the smartwatch as a control mechanism. The work of Ahn et al. [5] presented a pressure sensitive multitouch interaction technique on a bracelet, for using the bracelet for interaction the technique allows interaction without occlusion of the screen.

In our previous works, we presented methods that use smartwatches with continuous gesture recognition. We created a method that allows you to control the Netflix player and interactive movies using smartwatches and continuous gesture recognition [16,18]. In another work we present a method that allows you to control platform games using smartwatch with continuous gesture recognition [17]. We also developed a method that allows text entry on smartwatches using continuous gesture recognition [15]. The continuous gesture recognition algorithm [11] is able to predict partial gestures, so it can recognize a gesture before it is finished with high precision.

The results of these studies show that users were receptive to methods that use continuous gesture recognition on smartwatches, just as it is possible to use the smartwatch to control other devices.

As can be seen in this section, several researches are developed for the creation of new methods of interaction with smartwatches using gesture recognition, as well as research to control appliances using infrared.

However, none of these studies addressed the use of continuous gesture recognition in smartwatches to control household appliances. In this way, this work uses smartwatches and continuous gesture recognition to develop a method that allows controlling household appliances using simple and intuitive gestures.

3   Prototype

We developed a prototype that allows the user to control appliances using smartwatch. The interaction of the user with the smartwatch is performed through gestures, so we created a set of simple and intuitive gestures made up of lines and curves that allow the user to control the devices. The devices that the prototype is capable of controlling are: air conditioner (AC), lamp, TV, video player and audio player. Figure 2, displays the gestures and their actions on the devices.

As can be seen in Fig. 2, some gestures represent more than one action, depending on the device. We can also observe that the gesture to perform the on/off actions is the same for all devices. The actions related to the gestures were thought to be intuitive and easy for the user to remember.

Considering that the method is capable of controlling several devices, the user can select the device to be controlled by sliding his finger up and down. Figure 3 shows the gestures used to select a device.

We use the gestures shown in Fig. 2 and in Fig. 3 for having been validated in our previous work [16,17].

We developed an application for the "Android Wear" system, which was installed on the "Fossil Gen 4" smartwatch to perform the evaluation with specialists. Figure 4 illustrates a user using the prototype on a smartwatch to control an air conditioner.

3.1   Continuous Gesture Recognition

We use the continuous gesture recognition algorithm proposed by (Kristensson and Denby) [11], to recognize the gestures performed by the user. This algorithm can recognize a gesture before it is finished with high precision.

Gesture	AC	TV	Video player	Music player	Lamp
●	On/Off	On/Off	On/Off	On/Off	On/Off
 ↻	Increase Temp.	Increase Volume	Increase Volume	Increase Volume	--
 ↺	Decrease Temp.	Decrease Volume	Decrease Volume	Decrease Volume	--
→	--	Change Channel	Forward Playback	Forward Playback	--
←	--	Change Channel	Rewind Playback	Rewind Playback	--

Fig. 2. Set of gestures and their respective actions on home appliances.

Gestures   Action

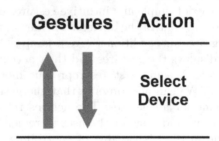

Select Device

Fig. 3. Gestures used to select a device.

Because it is capable of predicting partial gestures, it is not necessary for the user to complete the gesture for it to be recognized, and it is possible to quickly perform the action desired by the user. The prototype was designed to send the action to the device when the user makes a gesture of at least 2 cm and with a minimum recognition accuracy of 80%.

Fig. 4. Illustration of a user using the prototype to perform the actions: select the device, turn on the air conditioner and increase the temperature.

The algorithm uses a technique that considers a gesture as a model and divides it into several segments. Therefore, the segments describe the partial sections of the model in an increasing way [11]. Figure 5, illustrates this technique.

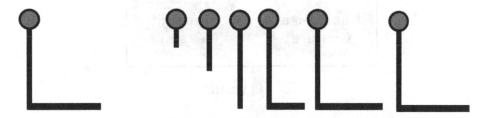

Fig. 5. Full model to the left and segments of the gesture to the right. Adapted from [11].

In Fig. 5, the beginning of a gesture is represented by a circle. A complete gesture, that is, a model, presented on the left with its partial segments on the right.

A model can be considered to be a vector of ordered points in relation to time, that is, a vector of ordered points related to the way the movement should be produced, a gesture is segmented in several parts and in increasing movements.

$$S = [s_1, s_2, ..., s_n]^T \tag{1}$$

A model is represented by w is a pair (l, S), where l is the description of the model and S is a set of segments that describes the complete model. Equation 1, describes a complete model ordered in relation to time T [11].

The continuous gesture recognition algorithm considers each gesture a pattern to be recognized, so it is necessary to calculate the probability of the gesture in execution being each gesture in the set. To reduce the recognition time, we use a parallelization technique of multithreading gesture recognition proposed in [17], to compare n gestures simultaneously, with n being the capacity of threads that the smartwatch can execute in parallel.

3.2 Communication Between Smartwatch and Device

Considering that several devices cannot be connected to a home network, as they do not have a network connection, this work uses infrared as a means of communication with the devices. In this way, we use the "Broadlink RM Mini 3" to send infrared signals to devices, it is an omnidirectional mini controller with a range of up to 12 m, as it is omnidirectional, it is not necessary that it is directed to the appliance, in this way, only one "Brodalink RM Mini 3" is capable of controlling multiple appliances.

To control a device, the user performs the gestures shown in Fig. 2, in sequence the gesture is recognized using the continuous gesture recognition algorithm. After recognition, the command related to the gesture is sent to the "Broadlink RM Mini 3" which sends the infrared signal to the appliance. These steps are represented in Fig. 6.

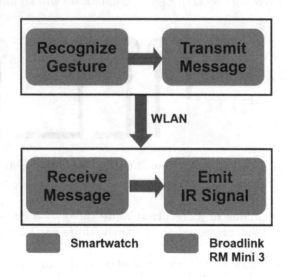

Fig. 6. Steps to emit an infrared signal after performing a gesture.

As can be seen in Fig. 6, the communication between the smartwatch and the "Broadlink RM Mini 3" is carried out over a WLAN network, in this way, the user can control the appliances of several rooms in the house, just needing to be connected to the WLAN network.

We created a database containing the infrared codes of the devices used, so when the user performs a gesture related to this command, the code is sent by the WLAN to the "Broadlink RM Mini 3" which is responsible for emitting the infrared signal. That will be received by the device.

4   Expert Evaluation

Com o objetivo de validar o método proposto, o aplicativo foi instalado no smartwatch *"Fossil Gen 4"*, com as seguintes especificações: 1.4 in. round screen, 454×454 pixels, 4GB RAM memory, Qualcomm's Snapdragon 2100 processor with 1.2 GHz ARM Cortex A7 4-core.

The method was tested and evaluated in an exploratory study by 5 volunteer specialists, during the experiment, the specialists selected the device to be controlled using the gestures shown in Fig. 3 and then controlled the device using the gestures shown in Fig. 2. The specialists controlled all devices supported by the method in the following sequence: Air conditioner, TV, video player, music player and lamp. Table 1 shows the sequence of commands that experts have tested for each device.

Table 1. Devices controlled by specialists and the commands sequence performed.

Device	Commands sequence
Air conditioner	– On – Increase temperature – Decrease temperature – Off
TV	– On – Increase volume – Decrease volume – Change channel – Off
Video player	– On – Increase volume – Decrease volume – Forward video – Rewind video – Off
Music player	– On – Increasae volume – Decrease volume – Forward playback – Rewind playback – Off
Lamp	– On – Off

4.1 System Usability Evaluation

After the end of the experiment, we applied a questionnaire to the experts to verify the usability of the method. In the usability test, we verified the efficiency and effectiveness of the method, as well as the satisfaction of the specialists when using the method. The experience test explored the experts' perception with the developed method.

To create the questionnaire, we adapted the System Usability Scale (SUS) [7] questionnaire. The SUS questionnaire was used because it allows the evaluation of a wide variety of products and services and is independent of technology. It has 10 questions, which the user answers using the Likert scale, from 1 to 5, where 1 means "strongly disagree" and 5 means "strongly agree". Table 2, shows the questionnaire questions.

Table 2. Usability questionnaire. Adapted from [7]

Q1.	I would use this system to control home appliances in my daily life	↑
Q2.	I find the system unnecessarily complex	↓
Q3.	I found the system intuitive and easy to use	↑
Q4.	I think I would need the help of a person with technical knowledge to use the system	↓
Q5.	I think the various functions of the system are very well integrated	↑
Q6.	I think the system is very inconsistent	↓
Q7.	I imagine that people will learn to use this system quickly	↑
Q8.	I found the system very complicated to use	↓
Q9.	I felt confident using the system	↑
Q10.	I had to learn several things before using the system	↓

(↑ - Positive Question, ↓ - Negative Question).

The SUS questionnaire has alternating items in positive and negative statements, in order to avoid bias in answers, in order to make the evaluator read the question and analyze the question and to verify whether he agrees or disagrees with the question. Thus, to calculate the score of the odd answers, one must subtract 1 from 5, from the score assigned by the user $(x - 1)$, where x is the score assigned by the user. For even answers, the user's score must be subtracted from 5, that is, $(5 - x)$, where x is the score assigned by the user. Therefore, all responses will be scored from 0 to 4, with 4 being the best score. Then, you must multiply the score of all answers by 2.5, with this, the score of each question will be in the range 0 to 10 and the sum of the score of questions in the range 0 to 100, it is important to note that it percentage, but a general measure of perceived usability. To be considered a good usability, the score must be at least 68 [7,8].

Bangor et al. [6], defined a scale of descriptive adjectives according to the score of the answers in the SUS questionnaire. Table 3, displays SUS adjectives according to the score of the responses.

Table 3. Descriptive statistics of SUS scores for adjective ratings. Adapted from [6].

Adjective	Mean SUS score
Worst imaginable	12.5
Awful	20.3
Poor	35.7
OK	50.9
Good	71.4
Excellent	85.5
Best imaginable	90.9

The next section presents the results of the evaluation with experts, as well as the result of the usability test.

5   Results and Discussion

The prototype developed was used in an evaluation with specialists and we applied it with a usability and experience test. At the end of the test, experts answered a questionnaire based on the questionnaire adapted SUS exposed in Table 2. Figure 7, displays the average score for each question in the questionnaire.

[] [xlabel=Average Score (×2.5), ylabel = Questions, enlargelimits =0.1 , xbar, legend style = at =(0.5 , -0.18), anchor =north, legend columns = 5 , xtick = 0, 2, 4, 6, 8, 10 , ytick = data, xmin=0, xmax=11, bar width=14pt, y dir=reverse, nodes near coords=[fixed zerofill,
precision=1]" ↑"," ↑"," ↑"," ↑"," ↑"," ↑"," ↑"," ↑"," ↑"[]]
+ [color = frenchblue] plot coordinates(9.0, 1) (10.0, 2) (9.0, 3) (10, 4) (7.5, 5) (8.0, 6) (8.5, 7) (8.0, 8) (9.5, 9) (9.0, 10) ;

Fig. 7. Normalized average score for each statement in the questionnaire.

Analyzing the score of each question individually, we can verify the strengths of the prototype, as well as, in what aspects it can improve. Question 1, scored 9, so there is strong evidence that users would use the method developed in their daily lives to control household appliances. Analyzing the scores of questions 2 to 4, we concluded that the evaluators found the prototype simple, easy to use and that it is not necessary to have training or help from a person with experience in the area to use the prototype.

Checking the scores of questions 5 and 6, we realized that the prototype can do better in relation to the integration of functions for easier use. During the test we verified that the evaluators considered it important that the prototype could detect the room of the house in which it was to prioritize the selection of the devices present in the place.

Considering questions 7 and 8, the evaluators considered that people will learn to use the system quickly, analyzing together with question number 8, we can consider that the evaluators considered the system simple. With the scores of questions 9 and 10, we can consider that the evaluators felt confident when using the system and did not need training to use the system.

As explained in the previous section, Bangor et al. [6] created a scale of descriptive adjectives according to the sum of the questions. The sum of the average score of the questions was 88.5, which puts the prototype developed in the "Excelent" category.

The evaluation showed that using the developed method it was possible to select the devices and control them using the proposed set of gestures. We observed during the experiment that the commands were correctly sent to the selected device with a satisfactory response time. Experts found it easy and quick to control the devices using the prototype.

Our method allowed the user to control the appliances using a device attached to his wrist without the need to use a remote control for each device, as it proved to be able to control different devices from different brands using a small set of gestures. As the gestures used are simple and based on geometric shapes, the user needs to make only one gesture on the screen to control a device, thus, he does not need to look at the smartwatch to perform an action.

6   Conclusions

This work proposes the development of a method to control home appliances using the smartwatch and continuous gesture recognition. In this way, we present a prototype that allows users to control the devices using simple gestures based on geometric shapes such as straight and curved.

To control the appliances, the user performs the gestures shown in Fig. 2 on the smartwatch and in sequence the gesture is recognized using the continuous gesture recognition algorithm. After recognition, the command related to the gesture is sent to the "Broadlink RM Mini 3" that emits the infrared signal to be received by the appliance.

Using the continuous gesture recognition algorithm it was possible to recognize a gesture without the user having to complete it, thus allowing a quick interaction between the user and the prototype.

The results of the evaluation with specialists showed that the method developed has the potential to be used to control household appliances using smartwatches with continuous gesture recognition. Thus, it is expected that the method provides a new experience for users in their daily lives.

The next step in this research will be to incorporate environment mapping into the method, in sequence, it will be tested on other devices. We also propose to include new gestures to the method and to conduct a study with users to define the best gestures to send commands to devices. It is also proposed to develop a technique that sends feedback to the user that uses vibration or sounds when an infrared signal is emitted.

References

1. Abu Sulayman, I.I.M., Almalki, S.H.A., Soliman, M.S., Dwairi, M.O.: Designing and implementation of home automation system based on remote sensing technique with Arduino Uno microcontroller. In: 2017 9th IEEE-GCC Conference and Exhibition (GCCCE), pp. 1–9 (2017)
2. Adiono, T., Anindya, S.F., Fuada, S., Fathany, M.Y.: Developing of general IrDa remote to wirelessly control IR-based home appliances. In: 2018 IEEE 7th Global Conference on Consumer Electronics (GCCE), pp. 461–463 (2018)
3. Adiono, T., et al.: Prototyping design of IR remote controller for smart home applications. In: TENCON 2017–2017 IEEE Region 10 Conference, pp. 1304–1308 (2017)
4. Afifah, K., Fuada, S., Putra, R.V.W., Adiono, T., Fathany, M.Y.: Design of low power mobile application for smart home. In: 2016 International Symposium on Electronics and Smart Devices (ISESD), pp. 127–131 (2016)
5. Ahn, Y., Hwang, S., Yoon, H., Gim, J., Ryu, J.: BandSense: pressure-sensitive multi-touch interaction on a wristband. In Proceedings of the 33rd Annual ACM Conference Extended Abstracts on Human Factors in Computing Systems, CHI EA 2015, pp. 251–254 (2015). ISBN 978-1-4503-3146-3
6. Bangor, A., Kortum, P., Miller, J.: Determining what individual SUS scores mean: adding an adjective rating scale. J. Usability Stud. 4(3), 114–123 (2009). ISSN 1931-3357
7. Brooke, J.: SUS: a 'quick and dirty' usability scale. In: Usability Evaluation In Industry, 1st edn., pp. 189–194. Taylor and Francis, London (1996)
8. Brooke, J.: SUS: a retrospective. J. Usability Stud. 8(2), 29–40 (2013). ISSN 1931-3357
9. Gkournelos, C., Karagiannis, P., Kousi, N., Michalos, G., Koukas, S., Makris, S.: Application of wearable devices for supporting operators in human-robot cooperative assembly tasks. Procedia CIRP 76, 177–182, 2018. ISSN 2212-8271. https://doi.org/10.1016/j.procir.2018.01.019. http://www.sciencedirect.com/science/article/pii/S2212827118300325. 7th CIRP Conference on Assembly Technologies and Systems (CATS 2018)
10. Horbylon Nascimento, T., et al.: Using smartwatches as an interactive movie controller: a case study with the Bandersnatch movie. In: 2019 IEEE 43rd Annual Computer Software and Applications Conference (COMPSAC), vol. 2, pp. 263–268, July 2019. https://doi.org/10.1109/COMPSAC.2019.10217

11. Kristensson, P.O., Denby, L.C.: Continuous recognition and visualization of pen strokes and touch-screen gestures. In: EUROGRAPHICS Symposium on Sketch-Based Interfaces and Modeling (2011)
12. Kronbauer, A.H., Gomes, F.F., Araujo, B.B.: Remote home: a universal control for residential environments. In: Proceedings of the 21st Brazilian Symposium on Multimedia and the Web, WebMedia 2015, pp. 213–216. Association for Computing Machinery, New York (2015). ISBN 978-1-4503-3959-9. https://doi.org/10.1145/2820426.2820451
13. Luna, M.M., Carvalho, T.P., Soares, F.A.A.M.N., Nascimento, H.A.D., Costa, R.M.: Wrist player: a smartwatch gesture controller for smart TVs. In: 2017 IEEE 41st Annual Computer Software and Applications Conference (COMPSAC), vol. 2 (2017)
14. Lutze, R., Waldhör, K.: Personal health assistance for elderly people via smartwatch based motion analysis. In: 2017 IEEE International Conference on Healthcare Informatics (ICHI), pp. 124–133, August 2017. https://doi.org/10.1109/ICHI.2017.79
15. Nascimento, T.H., Soares, F.A.A.M.N., Irani, P.P., de Oliveira, L.L.G., Soares, A.D.S.: Method for text entry in smartwatches using continuous gesture recognition. In: 2017 IEEE 41st Annual Computer Software and Applications Conference (COMPSAC), vol. 2, pp. 549–554, July 2017. https://doi.org/10.1109/COMPSAC.2017.168
16. Nascimento, T.H., Soares, F.A.A.M.N., Nascimento, H.A.D., Vieira, M.A., Carvalho, T.P., de Miranda, W.F.: Netflix control method using smartwatches and continuous gesture recognition. In: 2019 IEEE Canadian Conference of Electrical and Computer Engineering (CCECE), pp. 1–4 (2019)
17. Nascimento, T.H., et al.: Interaction with platform games using smartwatches and continuous gesture recognition: a case study. In: 2018 IEEE 42nd Annual Computer Software and Applications Conference (COMPSAC), vol. 02, pp. 253–258, July 2018. https://doi.org/10.1109/COMPSAC.2018.10239
18. Nascimento, T.H., SoaresSoares, F.: WatchControl: a control for interactive movie using continuous gesture recognition in smartwatches. J. Inf. Process. **28**, 643–649 (2020). https://doi.org/10.2197/ipsjjip.28.643
19. Seklou, K., Kokkinos, P., Tselikas, N.D., Boukouvalas, A.C.: Monitoring and management of home appliances with NETCONF and YANG. In: Proceedings of the 23rd Pan-Hellenic Conference on Informatics, PCI 2019, pp. 25–32. Association for Computing Machinery, New York (2019). ISBN 978-1-4503-7292-3. https://doi.org/10.1145/3368640.3368643
20. Speir, J., Ansara, R.R., Killby, C., Walpole, E., Girouard, A.: Wearable remote control of a mobile device: comparing one- and two-handed interaction. In: Proceedings of the 16th International Conference on Human-computer Interaction with Mobile Devices & Services, MobileHCI 2014, pp. 489–494. ACM, New York (2014). ISBN 978-1-4503-3004-6. https://doi.org/10.1145/2628363.2634221
21. Zhu, A., Lin, P., Cheng, S.: Design and realization of home appliances control system based on the android smartphone. In: 2012 International Conference on Control Engineering and Communication Technology, pp. 56–59 (2012)

Towards a Semantic Classification of Possible Human-to-Environment Interactions in IoT

Pavandeep Kataria[✉]

University of Wollongong College Hong Kong, FW402, 4th Floor, Festival Walk Tower,
80 Tat Chee Avenue, Kowloon Tong, Hong Kong
pahuja@uow.edu.au

Abstract. When looking at the way in which humans choose to participate in and interact with cyber physical-embedded environments such as Internet of Things (IoT), one could assume that such environments are permeated with 'ad hoc', 'heterogeneous' and 'dynamic' interactions in them. Existing literature on human to computer interactions, their types and definitions fail to provide a concrete understanding of these dimensions in cyber physical-embedded environments. Therefore, this paper presents the results of investigating existing categories of Human Computer Interaction (HCI) to make sense of these interactions and the inherent heterogeneity they carry. An integrative literature review using the PRISMA model to locate, select, and include 120 relevant articles has been carried out. The main finding of this review is a semantic classification of possible Human-to-Environment Interactions (HEI). The classification plays an important role as a starting point when looking at the current and future offerings of the HEI in the IoT. The classification also serves input as formal knowledge representations, such as Ontology Web Language (OWL) ontologies, which could assist in creating explicit representations of interaction.

Keywords: Interaction · HCI · IoT · Ontology

1 Introduction

At present, pervasive computing spaces [1] comprise of several objects[1] connected via the Internet, and associated software artefacts that implement their functionality and provide seamless interoperability of them. These spaces have paved the way for the IoT and cyber physical-embedded environments with an increasing emphasis on computational and networked life experiences. Cyber physical-embedded environments, their autonomous and unobtrusive characteristics[2], and constituent Artificial Intelligent (AI) tools and applications further lead to highly dynamic pervasive IoT spaces.

---

[1] where objects denote sensors, actuators, phones, devices, tablets, computers and smart wearables, to name but a few.
[2] which may be needed for their implementation and/or acceptance.

© Springer Nature Switzerland AG 2021
N. Streitz and S. Konomi (Eds.): HCII 2021, LNCS 12782, pp. 135–152, 2021.
https://doi.org/10.1007/978-3-030-77015-0_10

These pervasive spaces enable a variety of HEI to take place and are going to enable new interaction possibilities and experience flow. These new forms of human interactions will no doubt move away from the traditional HCI surrounding single computational objects/devices, or even interaction based on mere user interface functionality and technological entanglement. Instead, they will move towards interactions and experiences based on a variety of elements such as the number of IoT, computing devices, and software artefacts, alongside a user's location, posture, emotion, habit, and intention (both at conscious and subconscious levels) [2–6]. Such interactions will be inherently accommodating to the environment in which they reside and may take place one after another in clear sequential flows, or even in simultaneous concurrent flows of interactions. Such flows of interactions naturally pose increased interactivity and further promote intelligence in such spaces [7].

Subsequently, when looking deeper into this not so distance visioning of pervasive IoT spaces we should remind ourselves that these new 'flows' of interaction and associated user experiences are just beginning to emerge. Their continued functioning reliance in relation to data selection, and data processing in such spaces, give rise to the importance of having such interactions in the first place. And one could continue to assume that without HEI, pervasive IoT spaces (or 'instances' of them) would cease to exist [7–10]. The need for interaction/s to support key triggers in performing 'actions' within/upon different IoT, and call computational functions in associated software artefacts, result in their types and definitions being key to understanding cyber physical-embedded environments.

Furthermore, looking to the way in which users themselves choose to participate in, and interact with, also leads towards IoT spaces that are permeated with 'ad hoc', 'heterogenous' and 'dynamic' interactions in them. Viewing interaction within an 'instance' of IoT, carries a more chaotic tone in terms of not knowing where, why and with what interaction/computation happens in pervasive spaces. And to add further tumult, when looking to heterogeneities concerning the intention, modalities, and degrees of technological entanglement in user experience supported by a variety of visible and invisible Artificial Intelligence (AI) embedded into the environment, current human experience linked to interactions, their types and definitions fail to provide a concrete understanding of these dimensions. Subsequently, the amorphous questioning of such HEI, and the anticipation of them, is the starting point when looking at the current and future offerings of the IoT and Internet of Everything (IoE). Therefore, in this paper we explore possible HEI in pervasive IoT spaces.

2   Modelling HEI Interactions

In order to come close to making sense of HEI interactions in pervasive IoT spaces, we need to understand the semantic dimensions to possible interactions that may or may not take place within an instance of the space. The reasons for introducing a semantic classification of HEI and pervasive IoT spaces is thus as follows.

There are not so many related works that look at the semantics of interactions in IoT, let alone HEI. A semantic classification of such possible interactions could help us to model human experience and the computational content we intend to build, use and call IoT.

IoT and the pervasive spaces in which they live are inherently changeable. So too are the interactions that take place within them, which may include interaction between objects, devices and people, as well as the number of required Machine to Machine communication (M2M). It would be difficult to imagine that a fixed set of interactions will hold true for every instance of IoT spaces. Therefore, a semantic classification of interactions can grasp exactly which semantics would be relevant for the functionality(ies) expected to be delivered by an instance of an IoT pervasive space.

It would also somewhat ease the over burgeoning dependency on understanding interaction as simply human engagement with the user interface of an object in IoT alone, and focus on 'flows of interaction/s', which may change whenever necessary.

Categorization of HEI would help in understanding the nature of, and relationships between human and interactions within pervasive spaces [11–15]. Semantic reasoning could bring more intelligence to potentially complex and constantly changing flows of interaction/s and enable us to perceive IoT as intelligent environments. Finally, in terms of automation in IoT, software artefacts could either use the classification to:

i.   reason upon interaction semantics in order to offer/support interaction flow/s and/or computation control, or
ii. manipulate semantics to create new inferences of interactions, i.e., to support AI in future changing or unknown instances of pervasive IoT.

Consequently, there is also a current need to design interaction for intensive user experiences that are not invasive and that blend the physical with the digital. A semantic classification of such possible interactions could help assist in making everyday objects intuitively interactive.

3 Related Works

There are not so many explicit examples of modelling HEI in cyber physical-embedded environments, let alone which are machine interpretable. The closest that we find to understanding HEI pertain to related works in the broad field of HCI (which include the few works addressing interaction design itself), User Interface (UI) design, and User Experience (UX). We present a short overview of some of the important concepts and research derivatives that bear relation to the purpose of this paper, and to consider when thinking about re-visiting their classifications for future pervasive IOT spaces.

3.1 HCI and Categorising 'Interactions'

When inspecting HCI one may find a number of related works that aim to explicitly describe interaction between human and computer and reach a degree of agreement about concepts describing it. Some notable works that provide the most comprehensive list of tangible concepts pertaining to the HCI field are listed in [16–20]. And although each categorization offers a somewhat number of concepts that help understanding what interaction is, the schematization of interaction, their types and definitions are often overlapping and likely to be User Interface (UI) specific.

As a result, the direct relationship between interaction and UI design can also be seen as the core of major HCI studies till date. These works most certainly always align with user purpose and intention, but for the sake of re-visiting these concepts for IoT, these concepts may also, at the same time, be deemed inexplicit in nature [21]. They quite often are under-defined in terms of interaction boundaries and suggested flow/s of interactions (i.e. when does one interaction end/begin, the sequence/s of flow, interaction relationship to the computer/object). Thus, the quite often end up focusing on bi-directional relationships between concepts on interaction. Concepts that constitute understanding of 'fixed', boundary-defined static interactions, and not towards interactions.

3.2 Shift from HCI to HEI

In contrast to the above, other minority streams of HCI studies may surround themselves around the abandonment of the overused term interaction itself. Arguing for the term to be discounted from the perspective of achieving clearer conceptual constraints of interaction, a new emphasis on interaction as part of human experience (i.e. UX) has also been offered. Works advocating for connected objects that are intertwined with human experience, provide a more enriched and holistic perspective on: conceptualizing UX [22, 23], pleasure and hedonic value [24], and ludic value [25], and entanglement [26] of interactions.

Such 'new' dimensions of understanding UX lead towards the shift from HCI to HEI. There comes a clear use of the term when talking about a future in which people increasingly become confronted with collections of devices constituting smart environments. The emphasis on the 'plural' use of devices and the implication that they come in 'collections' bring attention to new interaction affordances. Affordances that are formed through the constant interaction with both physical and digital worlds that form and characterize UX/s. In turn, this has triggered numerous works defining user interfaces from the perspectives of 'technological entanglement' enriched materials for user interfaces design [27] and increased human centric interactivity [28]. Furthermore, repeated use of the term HEI appears in [3], once again, promoting and justifying interaction design as human experience and technological entanglement, one that is far away from the traditional realms of UI design and UX.

All of the above-mentioned conceptions of interaction as part of experience, one way or another drive forward the various trajectories of HCI research. Many of which lead to innovative and 'natural' interactions, adding to intertwined nature of human experience and technological entanglement. All producing more concepts of interaction that carry forward elements of the non-physical world and the many constellation of meanings attached to the very notion of experience.

3.3 Understanding 'Interaction' in IoT

Lastly, with recent developments in AI, in particular speech based interaction, it can also be seen that more recently, HCI studies have been somewhat dominated by AI engineers designing interactions between person and machine [29–31]. Using AI to add 'intelligence' through embedded machine learning in future cyber physical-embedded environments raise questions as to how such software functionality may also contribute to or even be part of human experience [7]. From the perspective of providing seamless connectivity and hence, triggering automation, within HCI, the issue of software artefact placements (which user or what object triggers some type of 'action'), is constantly evolving as AI redefines the boundaries of what is better done manually or automatically. Therefore, changing complexity in software modalities and the role reversal of software artefacts becoming 'actors' that also have associated interaction flows, promotes for interaction concepts to be re-visited.

To that end, when truly understanding the dynamicity of cyber physical-embedded environments, and taking into account the primary building blocks that serve the IoT (i.e. how such physical objects, their associated embedded sensors facilitate interaction, communication and integration of the surrounding environment), one could argue that just re-modelling interaction concepts will not suffice to really help understand the intricacies AI, cyber things and UX bring to interaction in such environments. We do note the works [32–35] that provide taxonomies of cyber-physical smart objects. However, they do not explicitly talk about interaction.

4   Methodology for Literature Review

There are not so many explicit examples of modelling HEI in cyber physical-embedded environments, let alone which are machine interpretable. In order to further strengthen our understanding of possible HEI interactions, which by their very nature have been agreed to be vast ranging, intangible and heterogeneous, an integrative literature review is also presented in this paper. The results of the literature review is specifically aimed at looking at HCI and interaction concepts applied to the IoT. The sources of the articles have been selected from two digital libraries: ACM Digital Library and Science Direct. A first query aimed at locating any article containing keywords "human computer interaction", "user experience", and "internet of things" was made. Owing to the synonymous nature of the words "classification" and "taxonomy", and previous works under the category of "smart objects", we included in the search also articles containing "smart object" and "taxonomy" (Q1). Performing the queries on the full text of the two aforementioned databases, we obtained 1960 distinct results for Science Direct and 2231 distinct results for ACM Digital Library through Q1. No duplicate records were found, and we obtained 4191 distinct papers. A total of 3447 papers, were excluded, in order to keep only articles with enough relevant content, bringing the total number of eligible papers to 744 (Journal of Human Computer interaction (34), and ACM Transactions of Computer Human Interactions (710).

Finally, to select only papers dealing with specific content, the keywords "interaction" or "experience" and "communication", "connection", "taxonomy", "framework" or "characteristics" were searched and analyzed in the full text. After the screening phase, 444 papers were retained. The eligibility phase aimed at individuating relevant papers. The eligibility criteria was defined as follows. The article is (i) set in a domain which includes the use of cyber physical-embedded objects connected to other objects/people through a form of network technology (e.g. WiFi, NFC, RFID), and (ii) talks about modality, interaction type/s and/or UX elements which are part of HCI, and (iii) resents an explicit classification of (i) and (ii) above. After the full articles were assessed for eligibility, a total of 120 papers were declared as eligible, 300 as not eligible. This process has been conducted following a lightened version of the PRISMA review protocol [36]. The process is summarized in Fig. 1 below.

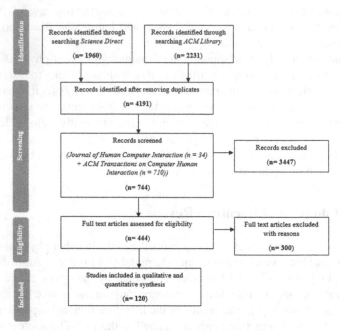

Fig. 1. PRISMA flow diagram of the review process.

5   Results of the Meta-analysis

Owing to the presentation of (a) domain specific IoT applications (11 papers), (b) user experience evaluations (15 papers), (c) AI, Virtual Reality (VR) or augmented reality in application/system design (14 papers), 40 papers were deemed out of the scope of locating interaction concepts. The importance of understanding interaction in IoT design was found in 21 papers, and 5 papers posed similar questions as that of the purpose of this paper. The analyzed articles covered domains pertaining to IoT, Internet of Vehicle (IoV), Internet of Health Things (IoHT) and smart/connected objects in general. Three key interaction types were individuated and Tables 1, 2 and 3 resumes the results of the meta-analysis for the 54 selected papers.

From the Tables 1, 2 and 3, it is possible to notice that the most distinct division in grouping of interaction types is between modalities carried by: HCI and/or M2M interaction, just HCI or just M2M. Although this seems like an obvious division, the differences are key to understanding the ad hoc and dynamic nature of pervasive IoT spaces. And this distinction will help build taxonomic categories in our semantic classification further in Sect. 8. However, for the purpose of this section we concentrate on the three key concepts that generalize main interactions in the IoT.

5.1 Physical Interaction Type

Table 1 below lists the first and most commonly referenced interaction type is in the form of physical interaction which may take place in both HCI and M2M modalities. Presented in terms of either initiating physical interaction through haptic and tactile sensations, (through sense of touch or perception), the implicit boundaries of these definitions make it difficult to understand which initiates action first, touch or sense.

Table 1. Results of the meta-analysis: physical interaction.

Human to Computer + Machine to Machine Interaction		
Interaction type: Physical interaction		
Haptic/tactile sensations		
Hand/motion gesture [37–47]	Gaze [48]	Speech [49–51]
Kinesthetic		
Body engagement [52]	Neuro imaging [53–55]	
Spatial		
Environment [56–59]		

From this perspective we move towards a generalized concept of physical interaction, whose main purpose is to manipulate objects (user interface or device elements) through gesture, gaze and speech. This generalization allows for the accommodation of actions related to both touch and sense, and maybe be considered ontologically intrinsic to each other for the purposes of taxonomic categorization. For example, actions such as a tap or swipe of one finger, relies on our body exploiting a number of sensorimotor skills, both for interpretation (using gaze) and execution (motion). Similarly, actions such as sending a voice command also exploits understanding (using speech) and execution (motion), whereby both interpretation and understanding signal links to perception.

As forms of physical interaction are situated in the physical world, with many sub-interactions constrained behind a screen, (not in the case of kinesthetics through neuroimaging), interactions lean towards physical affordances directly related to peripheral based actions and body engagement (also referred to as technological entanglement). Spatial interactions, similar in nature, are also inherently tangible since they exploit the physical environment to support interaction with multiple IoT objects (which include some form of spatial reasoning).

5.2 Perception/Cognition-Based Interaction Type

The second type of interaction is that of the perception/cognition-based interaction as listed in Table 2 below. This interaction is solely related to HCI and can be seen to have extrinsic connections to the physical interaction type. Driven by either (a) performing physical interactions (usually connected to the interface), or (b) the result of performing physical interactions, this interaction concerns sub concepts about mental action (intention) and experience (feelings and emotions), both past, present and future. With the close ties between perception and cognition, one may argue that this concept may be related to technological entanglement as part of physical interaction. However, we draw a line between physical affordances that entail technological entanglements needed to 'initiate action' by a user (or machine), versus the user's intention (human only) of using the cyber physical-embedded environment.

Table 2. Results of the meta-analysis: perception/cognition-based interaction.

Human to Computer Interaction
Interaction type: Perception/Cognition
Intentions
Interface [60–62]
Experience
Feelings [63–65]

5.3 Object Interaction Type

The third type of interaction is the object interaction listed in Table 3 below. This interaction is specific to M2M modality only and associates with all the concerning cross interactions needed to perform tasks and functionality embedded in underlying software artefact logic. This also includes feedback as part of AI (if any) and communication for message passing and software interoperability purposes. As a means of supporting complex object connections, several everyday physical objects or software artefacts can be programmed with any number of cross interactions, in order to bring physical objects to different functions or behaviors of IoT. Therefore, this interaction type is core to the functioning of IoT, as well as for physical and perception and cognition-based interactions to actually take place.

By observing this important feature of interaction as core to the functioning purpose of IoT, what must be highlighted is the interdependency of HCI and object interactions. Object interactions are key to initiating action through intention. Action which is purposefully in-built part of physical interactions. This becomes an important design element when re-visiting existing HCI categories for the sake of HEI.

In fact, when we take a closer look at each interaction type, which include their subconcepts, one may find that all three sets of interaction types are driven entirely by the notion of 'action'. When considering 'action' as the forefront of driving flow of experience and physical navigation forward with all is reliant underlying cross interactions, it becomes irrelevant as to whom the interaction is between, i.e. whether it is driven by user or machine. It no longer matters when HCI or M2M is the modality of interaction. Therefore, it is this very notion of action that we should bring focus to for the purposes of providing a taxonomy of possible HEI.

Table 3. Results of the meta-analysis: object interaction.

Machine to Machine Interaction
Interaction type: Object interaction
Task/functionality
Learn user data/respond to inputs [67–77]
Feedback
Predict/suggest [78–85]
Communicate
Interoperate/message [86–88]

6   Taxonomy of HEI in the IoT

We present a taxonomy of possible HEI interactions in IoT. Each concept, and the varying instances they carry draws semantics from four distinctive taxonomic categories: Physical Things, Interaction Types, Action, Users and Cyber Artefacts. Selection of instances from these concepts would make up a 'flow of interaction' that would be equivocal to an instance of a pervasive IoT space. The semantics drawn from interaction types that are initiated through a set of actions by either the users or cyber physical artefacts. Figure 2 shows a conceptual model of taxonomic categories for creating a 'flow of interaction'. There is a division between the cyber and physical world (denoted by the black dashed line) to mirror the clear distinction between interactions derived from either HCI and M2M communication.

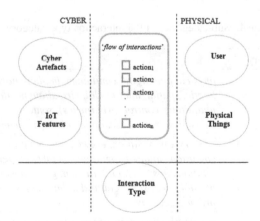

Fig. 2. Conceptual model of taxonomical categories for creating instances of 'flow of interactions'

We start with the classification of **Physical Things**. We would like to include mobile devices (hand-held, wearable), laptop, tablets mobile devices and objects (wearable, sensors, actuators, robots, drones), as well as their associated interface (GUI elements) or environment (which include both movable elements and obstacles (static and movable)). The categorization can further be extended to include semantics from the IoT Lite Ontology as proposed by [89].

In the classification of **Users,** we look at the various groups of users and the environment in which they reside. This includes individuals (the user), goals/purpose of interaction, personal requirements, roles in the environment, skills, choice, and a wide ranging of associated emotions. These users and their environments are most likely going to trigger 'action' via the Physical Things for user intention and experience purposes.

When moving forward towards the cyber part of Fig. 2, we look at **Cyber Artefacts** which are the abstractions of the functioning purpose of the interaction (from software perspective). This includes communication, software as a service, software as a service, software technology and infrastructure, specific software applications, software models, and data. [7] have extensively elaborated upon cyber artefacts and their semantic model can also be included into this concept.

When addressing the semantic of **IoT Features,** we can describe them as the features that support management of the interaction (again, from a software perspective). These features may be categorized as: success or failure of task, accuracy of IoT services, reliability and scalability of services and application, and trust and quality of service, and can be further extended through the concepts of the Semantic Sensor Network Ontology [90].

The **Interaction Type** taxonomic category is vast (compared to others). This category not only accommodates our interaction types as identified in Tables 1., 2. and 3. above, but it also extends to accommodate a wide range of semantics that strengthen its understanding. Table 4 below. above gives a snapshot of the concepts but acknowledges that it is not complete. Due to sheer amount of literature available on the various sub concepts related to this concept, we reinforce the importance of interaction in IoT spaces.

Table 4. Sub-categories of the interaction type category.

Interaction type category	
Physical interaction	*physical and digital continuum, implicit, novel and escalated, haptic, spatial, multimodal, virtual/augmented reality, ubiquitous, control (cybernetics), sonic, dialogue, transmission, tool use, optimal behavior, embodiment, control*
Perception/cognition-based Interaction	*sensory, appreciation, ergonomics, reciprocal, distributed cognition, situated cognition, social (interpersonal relationships, social interaction, group dynamics emotional, physiological state, cultural habits/convention, ownership, privacy, security*
Object interaction	*communication, software as a service, software as a service, software technology and infrastructure, specific software applications, software models, and data*

7   The Power of the Semantic Web

In order to classify possible HEI we must exploit Semantic Web technologies. The classification should be an input into formal knowledge representations such as OWL ontologies which could assist in creating explicit representations of interaction and provide expressive querying, and flexible reasoning for how interaction flow/s are formed or affected by human experience.

7.1   Ontological Characteristics of the Model

When we look to an ontological version of the conceptual taxonomy listed in Fig. 3. below, it is questionable as to whether the same taxonomical structure ceases to exist in the ontological world. It does not. Figure 3. depicts how the taxonomical structure would look through ontological concepts and their relationship properties. Most notably, we can see that **Physical Things** and **IoT Features** become part of the ENVIRONMENT ontological class, and **Users** and **Cyber Artefacts** become part of the ACTORS ontological class. The grouping of the categories seem relatively straightforward in terms of denoting which categories make up constituent parts to the cyber physical-embedded environments, and which categories participate in them through some type of active role (even if not constant).

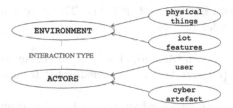

Fig. 3. Ontological model of taxonomic categories for creating instances of 'flow of interactions'

Both the ENVIRONMENT and ACTORS class can list semantics at instance level, as that drawn from Table 2. Interaction Types can now be modelled as relationship property/ies between the ENVIRONMENT and ACTORS class. The reason for this modelling choice is twofold. Firstly, we have extensively discussed the heterogeneous nature of interaction types, plus their degree of overlap when moving to and from the cyber to physical world and vice versa. Secondly, the reason for using the OWL ontology is the freedom and expressivity it offers to exploit triples that provide tri-directional relationships between concepts that otherwise could only be confined to binary relationships. In other words, modelling interaction types as a property relationship allows any number of interaction types to be associated to any number of ontological concepts, at both class and instance level. This extra expressivity is just what we need to understand the extent of semantic overlap and understand HEI concepts from different functioning versions of pervasive IoT spaces.

7.2 Possible Semantic Reasoning

Figure 4 below shows the purpose of the ontological model in terms of possible inferences based on the content of the ACTOR class.

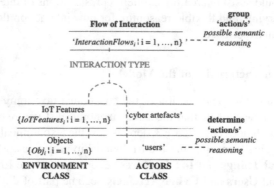

Fig. 4. Possible semantic reasoning upon taxonomical categories for creating instances of 'flow of interactions'

Inferences may be made upon the semantic of the instance the class holds, in order to model the actor's intention of action, and to deduce the set of actions as part of a 'flow of interaction' based on the ENVIRONMENT class. Therefore, semantic reasoning may very well be needed in order to:

a) determine the actor's action $\{Actions_i \mid i = 1, \ldots, n\}$ (i.e. intentions), plus the set of needed IoT objects $\{Objects_i \mid i = 1, \ldots, n\}$ and/or IoT features $\{IOTFeatures_i \mid i = 1, \ldots, n\}$, and

b) group a set of actions $\{InteractionFlows_i \mid i = 1, \ldots, n\}$ from the selection of IoT objects $\{Objects_i \mid i = 1, \ldots, n\}$ and/or IoT features $\{IOTFeatures_i \mid i = 1, \ldots, n\}$.

The inference, as a result of a) and b) above, guarantees correct semantics behind a **flow of interactions**, because it deduces which $Actions_j$ (plus associate interaction types), and which $IoTFeatures_j$ from these IoT $Object_i$ contribute to an instance of a pervasive IoT space.

8 Conclusion

In this paper we propose taxonomical categories of possible HEI which are generic enough fit any cyber physical-embedded environments such as IoT. The taxonomical categories have been derived from an integrative literature review using the PRISMA model and further define ontological concepts for inferring a flow of interactions that make up a specific instance of IoT. The literature review and taxonomy has been derived with having this in mind. To:

- accommodate a variety of heterogenous concepts of interaction, without comprising their given definitions, boundaries, scope or role of importance (also to preserve their presence in literature);
- reveal closer relationships between interaction in modalities of HCI and M2M;
- ensure that interactions in IoT and intention of users (both human and machine) fit and harmonize in the functioning of a space.

The applicability of using semantic web technologies allows the taxonomical categories to become a starting point, especially when visualisng and developing future IoT computational spaces. The core means of inferring 'a flow of interaction' aims to ease the burden on making sense and predicating interactions that deem 'ad hoc' and 'uncertain/unpredictable' in such spaces. Furthermore, the taxonomy alos aims to present an understanding of the environment from interaction as a driving force of future happenings and instances of spaces. Hence, brining developers closer to creating more efficient and useful spaces that accommodate functioning relevant to the interaction type.

Future works include elaborating upon the sub-concepts (instances) contained within major ontological classes. Specifically, the interaction types and computational elements (what new intentions can be achieved with reasons AI affords) should be extended further.

We should also look forward to role of cyber physical artefacts - can they truly hold true accountability for interaction, same as human users of future pervasive IoT spaces, or is their purpose just specific to hard wiring of algorithm rules and functions.

Finally, it would also be useful to explore the way in which the taxonomy could be quantified (if possible) in order to understand and evaluate the effective of interaction IoT applications.

References

1. Weiser, M.: The computer for the 21st century. Sci. Am. **265**(3), 94–104 (1991)
2. Frauenberger, C.: Entanglement HCI the next wave? ACM Trans. Comput. -Hum. Interact. **27**(1), 2:1–2:27 (2019)
3. Stephanidis, C., et al.: Seven HCI grand challenges. Int. J. Hum. Comput. Interaction. **35**(14), 1229–1269 (2019)
4. Harper, R.H.R.: The role of HCI in the age of AI. Int. J. Hum. Comput. Interact. **35**(15), 1331–1344 (2019)
5. Dix, A.: Human-computer interaction, foundations and new paradigms. J. Vis. Lang. Comput. **42**, 122–134 (2017)
6. Earnshaw, R.A., De Silva, M., Excell, P.S.: Ten unsolved problems with the internet of things. In: International Conference on Cyber Worlds 2015 Proceedings, pp. 1–7. IEEE, Sweden (2015)
7. Juric, R., McClenaghan, K.M.: Towards the semantic classification of constituent parts of the internet-of-vehicles. In: 24th International Conference for the Society for Design and Process Science Transformative Research and Education through Transdisciplinary Means Proceedings pp. 17–22, SDPS, Taiwan (2019)
8. Gheisar, M., Wang, G., Chen, S.: An edge computing-enhanced internet of things framework for privacy-preserving in Smart City. J. Comput. Electr. Eng. **81**, (2020)
9. Gulati, N., Kaur, P.D.: Towards socially enabled internet of industrial things: architecture, semantic model and relationship management. J. Ad Hoc Netw. **91**, (2019)

10. Zhu, T., Dhelim, S., Zhou, Z., Yang, S., Ning, H.: An architecture for aggregating information from distributed data nodes for industrial internet of things. J. Comput. Electr. Eng. **58**, 337–349 (2017)

11. Kataria, P., Juric, R., Mandani, K.: Go-CID: generic ontology for context-aware, interoperable and data sharing applications. In: Smith, J.E, (eds.), SEA 2007, pp. 439–444. ACTA Press (2007)

12. Gomez, J., Oviedo, B., Fernandez, A., Sanchez, M.A.Z., Viteri, J.T.M., Leon, A.R.E.: Semantic representation models of sensor data for monitoring agricultural crops. In: Botto-Tobar, M., León-Acurio, J., Díaz Cadena, A., Montiel Díaz, P. (eds.) Advances in Emerging Trends and Technologies (ICAETT 2019). Advances in Intelligent Systems and Computing, vol. 1066, pp. 33–41. Springer, Cham (2019)

13. Ning, H., Shi, F., Zhu, T., Li, Q., Chen, L.: A novel ontology consistent with acknowledged standards in smart homes. J. Comput. Netw. **148**, 101–107 (2019)

14. Pahal, N., Mallik, A., Chaudhury, S.: An ontology- based context-aware IoT framework for smart surveillance. In: Mohamed, B., Abdelhakim, B.A., Ali, Y. (eds.) International Conference on Smart City applications 2018, pp. 1–7. Association for Computer Machinery (2018)

15. Veiga, E.F., Arruda, M.K., Neto, J.A.B., Bulcão-Neto, R.: An ontology-based representation service of context information for the internet of things. In: Roesler, V., Valdeni de Lima, J., (eds.) Webmedia 2017. 23rd Brazillian Symposium on Multimedia and the Web, 2017, pp. 301–308. Association for Computer Machinery (2017)

16. Horbaek, K., Oulasvirta, A.: What is interaction? In: 2017 CHI Conference of Human Factors in Computing Systems Proceedings, pp. 5040–5052. Association for Computer Machinery, New York (2017)

17. Kim, K.J.: Interacting socially with the internet of things (IoT): effects of source attribution and specialisation in human - IoT interaction. J. Comput. Mediated Commun. **21**(6), 420–435 (2016)

18. Bakker, S., Niemantsverdriet, K.: The interaction-attention continuum: considering various levels of human attention in interaction design. Int. J. Des. **10**(2), 1–14 (2016)

19. Kostakos, V., Musolesi, M.: Introduction to the special issue on social networks and ubiquitous interactions. Int. J. Hum. Comput Stud. **71**(9), 859–861 (2013)

20. Reeves, D., Serafin, S.: Sonic interaction design. Int. J. Hum. Comput. Interact. Stud. **6**(9), 905–906 (2009)

21. Reeves, S., Beck, J.: Talking about interaction. Int. J. Hum. Comput. Interact. Stud. **131**, 144–151 (2019)

22. Mechant, P., All, A., De Marez, L.: Evaluating user experience in smart home contexts: a methodological framework. In: Streitz, N., Konomi, S. (eds.) Distributed, Ambient and Pervasive Interactions: Understanding Humans (DAPI 2018). LNCS, vol. 10921, pp. 91–102. Springer, Cham (2018)

23. Pallot, M. Pawar, K.: A holistic model of user experience for living lab experimental design. In: Katzy, B., Holzmann, T., Sailer, K., Thobens, K.D. (eds.) 18th International Conference on Engineering, Technology and Innovation, pp. 1–15. IEEE (2012)

24. Jordan, P.: Designing Pleasurable Products. An Introduction to the New Human Factors, 1st edn. Taylor and Francis, London, New York (2000)

25. Gaver, W.W., Martin, H.: Alternatives: exploring information appliances through conceptual design proposals. In: SIGCHI 2000 Conference on Human factors in Computing Systems, pp. 209–216. Association for Computer Machinery, New York (2000)

26. Stumpf, T., Califf, C.B., Frye, J.J.: The conceptualisation and uses of technological meta-worlds in travel. In: 52nd Hawaii International Conference on Systems Sciences Proceedings, pp. 6937–6946, HICSS, Hawaii (2019)

27. Janlert, L.E., Stolterman, E.: Faceless interaction - a conceptual examination of the notion of interface: past, present, and future. J. Hum. Comput. Interact. **30**(6), 507–539 (2015)
28. Bibri, S.E.: The human face of ambient intelligence: cognitive, emotional, affective, behavioral and conversational aspects. In: Atlantis Ambient and Pervasive Intelligence, vol. 9. Atlantis Press, Paris (2015)
29. Harper, R.H.R.: The role of HCI in the age of AI. Int. J. Hum. Comput. Interact. **35**(15), 1331–1344 (2019)
30. Patterson, R.E.: Intuitive cognition and models of human-automation interaction. J. Hum. –Autom. Interact. **59**(1), 101–115 (2017)
31. Glodek, M., et al.: Fusion paradigms in cognitive technical systems for human-computer interaction. J. Neurocomput. **161**, 17–32 (2015)
32. Dorsemaine, B., Gaulier, J.P., Wary, J.P., Kheir, K., Urien, P.: Internet of things: a definition & taxonomy. In: 9th International Conference on Next Generation Mobile Applications, Services and Technologies Proceedings, pp. 9–11, NGMAST, Cambridge (2015)
33. Barker, L., et al.: Taxonomy for internet of things: tools for monitoring personal effects. In: International Conference on Pervasive and Embedded Computing and Communication Systems Proceedings (PECCS 2014), Portugal, vol. 1 (2014)
34. Fortino, G., Rovella, A., Russo, W., Savaglio, C.: On the classification of cyber physical smart objects in the internet of things. In: International Workshop on Networks of Cooperating Objects for Smart Cities, vol. 1156, pp. 86–94, UBICITEC, Germany (2014)
35. Mamo, K., Nieto, J.I., Leon, M.D.C., Vazquez, M., López, J.D.S., Buenrostro, R.: Major existing classification matrices and future directions for internet of things. J. Adv. Internet of Things **07**(04), 112–120 (2017)
36. Liberati, A., et al.: The prisma statement for reporting systematic reviews and meta-analyses of studies that evaluate health care interventions: explanation and elaboration. PLoS Med. **6**(7), (2009)
37. Popovici, I., Schipor, O.A., Vatavu, R.D.: Hover: exploring cognitive maps and mid-air pointing for television control. Int. J. Hum. Comput. Stud. **129**, 95–107 (2019)
38. Ardito, C., Buono, P., Desolda, G., Matera, M.: From Smart objects to smart experiences: an end user development approach. Int. J. Hum. Comput. Stud. **114**, 52–68 (2018)
39. Xiang, A.C., Li, Y.: Improv: an input framework for improvising cross-device interaction by demonstration. ACM Trans. Comput. Hum. Interact. **24**(2), 15 (2017)
40. Sutcliffe, A., Hart, J.: Analysing the role of interactivity in user experience. Int. J. Hum. Comput. Interact. **33**(3), 229–240 (2017)
41. Loke, L., Robertson, T.: Moving and making strange: an embodied approach to movement-based interaction design. ACM Trans. Comput. Hum. Interact. **20**(1), 7 (2013)
42. Bilandzic, M., Foth, M.: A review of locative media, mobile and embodied spatial interaction. Int. J. Hum. Comput. Stud. **70**(1), 66–71 (2012)
43. McGrenere, J., Baecker, R.M., Booth, K.S.: A field evaluation of an adaptable two-interface design of feature-rich software. ACM Trans. Comput. Hum. Interact. **14**(1), 3 (2007)
44. Benford, S., et al.: Expected, sensed and desired: a framework for designing sensing-based interaction. ACM Trans. Comput. Hum. Interact. **12**(1), 3–30 (2005)
45. Zhai, S., Bellotti, V.: Introduction to sensing-based interaction. ACM Trans. Comput. Hum. Interact. **12**(1), 1–2 (2005)
46. Quek, F., et al.: Multimodal human discourse: gesture and speech. ACM Trans. Comput. Hum. Interact. **9**(3), 171–193 (2002)
47. Benford, S., Dourish, P., Rodden, T.: Introduction to the special issue on human-computer interaction and collaborative virtual environments. ACM Trans. Comput. Hum. Interact. **7**(4), 439–441 (2000)

48. Velloso, E., Carter, M., Newn, J., Esteves, A., Clarke, C., Gellersen, H.: Motion correlation: selecting objects by matching their movement. ACM Trans. Comput. Hum. Interact. **24**(3), 22 (2017)

49. Hornbaek, K., Mottelson, A., Knibbe, J., Vogel, D.: What do we mean by "Interaction"? an analysis of 35 years of CHI. ACM Trans. Comput. Hum. Interact. **26**(4), 27 (2019)

50. Oviatt, S., Seneff, S.: Introduction to mobile and adaptive conversational interfaces. ACM Trans. Comput. Hum. Interact. **11**(3), 237–240 (2004)

51. Truschin, S., Schermann, M., Goswami, S., Krcmar, H.: Designing interfaces for multiple-goal environments: experimental insights from in-vehicle speech interfaces. ACM Trans. Comput. Hum. Interact. **21**(1), 7 (2014)

52. Nansen, B., Vetere, F., Robertson, T., Downs, J., Brereton, M., Durick, J.: Reciprocal habituation: a study of older people and the Kinect. ACM Trans. Comput. Hum. Interact. **21**(3), 18 (2014)

53. Kosmyna, N., Tarpin-Bernard, F., Rivet, B.: Adding human learning in brain-computer interfaces (BCIs): towards a practical control modality. ACM Trans. Comput. Hum. Interact. **22**(3), 12 (2015)

54. Solovey, E.T., Afergan, D., Peck, E.M., Hincks, S.W., Jacob, R.J.K.: Designing Implicit Interfaces for psychological computing: guidelines and lessons learned using fNIRS. ACM Trans. Comput. Hum. Interact. **21**(6), 35 (2015)

55. Kirsh, D.: Embodied cognition and the magical future of interaction design. ACM Trans. Comput. Hum. Interact. **20**(1), 3 (2013)

56. Benford, S., Calder, M., Rodden, T., Sevegnani, M.: On Lions, Impala, and Bigraphs: modelling interactions and physical virtual spaces. ACM Trans. Comput. Hum. Interact. **23**(2), 9 (2016)

57. Vasquez-Alverez, Y., Aylett, M.P., Brewster, R., Von Jungenfeld, S.A., Virolainen, A.: Designing interactions with multilevel auditory displays in mobile audio-augmented reality. ACM Trans. Comput. Hum. Interact. **23**(1), 3 (2015)

58. Mehra, S., Werkhoven, P., Worring, M.: Navigating on handheld displays: dynamic versus static peephole navigation. ACM Trans. Comput. Hum. Interact. **13**(4), 448–457 (2006)

59. Benford, S., GreenHalgh, C., Reynard, G., Brown, C., Koleva, B.: Understanding and constructing shared spaces with mixed reality boundaries. ACM Trans. Comput. Hum. Interact. **5**(3), 185–223 (1998)

60. Hornbaek, K., Hertzum, M.: Technology acceptance and user experience: a review of experiential components in HCI. ACM Trans. Comput. Hum. Interact. **24**(5), 33 (2017)

61. Paik, J., Kim, J.W., Ritter, F.E., Reitter, D.: Predicting user performance and learning in human-computer interaction with the herbal compiler. ACM Trans. Comput. Hum. Interact. **22**(5), 25 (2015)

62. Borsci, S., Macredie, R.D., Barnett, J., Martin, J., Kuljis, J., Young, T.: Reviewing and extending the five-user assumption: a grounded procedure for interaction evaluation. ACM Trans. Comput. Hum. Interact. **20**(5), 29 (2013)

63. Rapp, A., Tirassa, M., Tirabeni, L.: Rethinking technologies for behaviour change: a view from the inside of human change. ACM Trans. Comput. Hum. Interact. **26**(4), 22 (2019)

64. Rozendaal, M.C., Boon, B., Kaptelinin, V.: Objects with intent: designing everyday things as collaborative partners. ACM Trans. Comput. Hum. Interact. **26**(4), 26 (2019)

65. Dalsgaard, P., Hansen, L.K.: Performing perception - staging aesthetics of interaction. ACM Trans. Comput. Hum. Interact. **15**(3), 13 (2008)

66. Raisamo, R., Rakkolainen, I., Majaranta, P., Salminen, K., Rantala, J., Farooq, A.: Human augmentation: past, present and future. Int. J. Hum Comput Stud. **131**, 131–143 (2019)

67. Rhiu, I., Hwan Yun, M.: Exploring user experience of smartphones in social media: a mixed-method analysis. Int. J. Hum. Comput. Interact. **34**(10), 960–969 (2018)

68. Mealla Cincuegrani, S., Jorda, S., Valjamae, A.: Physiopucks: increasing user motivation by combining tangible and implicit physiological interaction. ACM Trans. Comput. Hum. Interact. **23**(1), 4 (2016)

69. Poor, G.M., et al.: Applying the Norman 1986 user-centered model to post-WIMP UIs: theoretical predictions and empirical outcomes. ACM Trans. Comput. Hum. Interact. **23**(5), 30 (2016)

70. Bilandzic, M., Foth, M.: Embedded, embodied and situated contexts in interaction with technologies. Int. J. Hum. Comput. Stud. **70**(1), 66–71 (2012)

71. Kjeldskov, J., Paay, J.: Indexicality: understanding mobile human-computer interaction in context. ACM Trans. Comput. Hum. Interact. **17**(4), 14 (2010)

72. Blackwell, A.F., Rode, J.A., Toye, E.F.: How do we program the home? Gender, attention investment, and the psychology of programming at home. Int. J. Hum. Comput. Stud. **67**(4), 324–341 (2009)

73. Hinckley, K., Pierce, J., Horvitz, E., Sinclair, M.: Foreground and background interaction with sensor-enhanced mobile devices. ACM Trans. Comput. Hum. Interact. **12**(1), 31–52 (2005)

74. Liu, Y., Feyen, R., Tsimhoni, O.: Queueing network-model human processor (QN-MHP): a computational architecture for multitask performance in human-machine systems. ACM Trans. Comput. Hum. Interact. **13**(1), 37–90 (2006)

75. Ruddle, R.A., Savage, J.C.D., Jones, D.M.: Symmetric and asymmetric action integration during cooperative object manipulation in virtual environments. ACM Trans. Comput. Hum. Interact. **9**(4), 285–308 (2002)

76. Zanden, B.V., Myers, B.A.: Demonstrational and constraint-based techniques for pictorially specifying application objects and behaviours. ACM Trans. Comput. Hum. Interact. **2**(4), 308–356 (1995)

77. Jacob, R.J.K., Sibert, L.E., McFarlane, D.C., Mullen, M.P.: Integrality and separability of input devices. ACM Trans. Comput. Hum. Interact. **1**(1), 3–26 (1994)

78. Kang, H., Kim, K.J.: Feeling connected to smart objects? A moderated mediation model of locus of agency, anthropomorphism, and sense of connectedness. Int. J. Hum. Comput. Stud. **133**, 45–55 (2020)

79. Janssen, C.P., Boyle, L.N., Kun, A.L., Ju, W., Chuang, L.L.: A hidden Markov framework to capture human machine interaction in automated vehicles. Int. J. Hum. Comput. Interact. **35**(11), 947–955 (2019)

80. Victorelli, E.Z., Reis, J.C.D., Hornung, H., Prado, A.B.: Understanding human-data interaction: literature review and recommendations for design. Int. J. Hum. Comput. Stud. **134**, 13–21 (2019)

81. Alan, A.T., Costanza, E., Ramchurn, S.D., Fischer, J., Rodden, T., Jennings, N.R.: Tariff agent: interacting with a future smart energy system at home. ACM Trans. Comput. Hum. Interact. **23**(4), 25 (2016)

82. Baljko, M., Tenhaaf, N.: The Aesthetics of emergence: co-constructed interactions. ACM Trans. Comput. Hum. Interact. **15**(3), 11 (2008)

83. McGuffic, M.J., Balakrishnan, R.: Fitts' law and expanding targets: experimental studies and designs for user interfaces. ACM Trans. Comput. Hum. Interact. **12**(4), 388–422 (2005)

84. Abowd, G.D., Mynatt, E.D.: Charting past, present, and future research in ubiquitous computing. ACM Trans. Comput. Hum. Interact. **7**(1), 3–28 (2000)

85. Kieras, D.E., Wood, S.D., Meyer, D.E.: Predictive engineering models based on the EPIC architecture for a multimodal high-performance human computer interaction task. ACM Trans. Comput. Hum. Interact. **4**(3), 230–275 (1997)

86. Dix, A., Rodden, T., Davies, N., Trevor, J., Friday, A., Palfreyman, K.: Exploiting space and location as a design framework for interactive mobile systems. ACM Trans. Comput. Hum. Interact. **7**(3), 285–321 (2000)

87. Lee, M.: An empirical study of home IoT services in South Korea: the moderating effect of the usage experience. Int. J. Hum. Comput. Interact. **35**(7), 535–547 (2019)
88. Bickmore, T.W., Picard, R.W.: Establishing and maintaining long-term human-computer relationships. ACM Trans. Comput. Hum. Interact. **12**(2), 293–327 (2005)
89. Bermudez-Edo, M., Elsaleh, T., Barnaghi, P., Taylor, K.: IoT-Lite: a lightweight semantic model for the internet of things. J. Pers. Ubiquit. Comput. **21**(3), 475–487 (2017)
90. Compton, M., et al.: The SSN ontology of the W3C semantic sensor network incubator group. J. Web Semant. Sci. Serv. Agents World Wide Web **17**(C), 25–32 (2012)

Touchless Interaction on Mobile Devices Using Embedded Ambient Light Sensor

Alen Salkanovic and Sandi Ljubic[✉]

Faculty of Engineering, University of Rijeka, Vukovarska 58, 51000 Rijeka, Croatia
{alen.salkanovic,sandi.ljubic}@riteh.hr

Abstract. In this paper, we introduce and evaluate a mobile application service that allows contact-free interaction with a mobile device by utilizing only an ambient light sensor. The proposed solution enables single-handed UI navigation without touching the smartphone screen. The advantage of implemented service is the use of an embedded light sensor, which the majority of manufactures presently integrate into mobile devices. Hence, the use of any additional accessories or external sensing hardware is not required. The service itself is designed as a floating widget that can be attached to the target mobile application, thus augmenting it with Around Device Interaction (ADI) support. Two different navigation patterns (manual and automatic) can be utilized to control the widget position on the screen and activate target UI elements. A controlled experiment involving 20 participants was conducted in order to evaluate and comparatively assess the performances of the implemented solution. We present and discuss the findings of this empirical research.

Keywords: Touchless interaction · Ambient light sensor · Around device interaction · Mobile devices

1 Introduction

Around Device Interaction (ADI) is a distinguished research topic in the field of mobile device interaction. ADI techniques try to overcome the issues related to small screens, such as the fat-finger syndrome [1] and different scenarios of occlusion [2], which continue to cause difficulties with touchscreen interaction. Namely, the pointing accuracy on a touch-enabled surface is inherently constrained since virtual targets are often smaller than a fingertip. Additionally, occlusion by the finger or forearm prevents visual feedback [3]. ADI concept allows interaction commands to be invoked by gestures made in the space around the device, as well as by making use of changes detected in the surrounding environment. Hence, limitations of touch interaction can be addressed and tackled by enabling alternative mobile interaction modalities that rely on sensory input.

Contemporary mobile devices are equipped with multiple sensors for monitoring various environmental properties. Common hardware-based sensors refer to the gyroscope, gravity sensor (accelerometer), and magnetometer. In addition, other sensors may be used to monitor relative ambient humidity, ambient pressure, ambient temperature,

N. Streitz and S. Konomi (Eds.): HCII 2021, LNCS 12782, pp. 153–163, 2021.
https://doi.org/10.1007/978-3-030-77015-0_11

illuminance, etc. While not all sensors are consistently present on mobile devices, most manufacturers are embedding luminosity sensors to control screen brightness. The light sensor on Android-powered devices measures ambient light level (illumination) in *lux* units. The obtained values correspond to the intensity of light as perceived by the human eye. Unlike most proximity sensors, which return binary values that indicate *near* or *far*, the light sensors generally return a series of values. This feature could be exploited to control and navigate through the user interface on mobile applications without any physical contact with the touchscreen.

2 Related Work

Numerous solutions have been developed to facilitate around-device input methods that do not involve interacting with the touchscreen directly. However, most research efforts have focused on equipping either devices or users with additional sensors/accessories.

SideSight [4] and *Hoverflow* [5] propose equipping a mobile device with external infrared proximity sensors to support multi-touch or hand gestures interaction. *SideSwipe* [6] enables in-air gestures both above and around a mobile device using the unmodified GSM signal. An additional antenna array is required to capture amplitude-modulated GSM signals for hand gesture detection around the phone.

Abracadabra [7], *MagiTact* [8], *MagGetz* [9], and *MagiThings* [10] utilize integrated magnetic field sensor for ADI. However, users need to handle an additional object(s) to interact with the device. Namely, the movement of the external magnetic source can affect the Earth's magnetic field sensed by the sensor. Thus, a properly shaped magnet (e.g. in the shape of a rod, pen, or ring) can be utilized for augmenting interaction space.

Finger in Air [11], *GlassHands* [12], and *Maestro* [13] use the built-in smartphone camera to detect users' in-air gestures or estimate specific hand postures.

Okuli [14] is a prototype peripheral module for an Android device that extends its interaction workspace to any nearby surface area. It consists of one light source and two light sensors and uses a light propagation/reflection model for finger localization. Finally, *UbiTouch* [15] extends smartphones with virtual touchpads using built-in sensors (proximity and ambient light sensor). It supports general touch actions, including tapping and dragging, on a virtual touch area (such as a wooden desktop). A patch must be applied to the OS kernel, to bypass the Android framework and access the raw readings from the hardware directly.

In this paper, we propose a mobile application service that enables touchless interaction by utilizing an ambient light sensor embedded in a mobile device. Instead of holding the device and using tap-based selections, users can interact with UI components single-handedly, without touching the screen. Unlike solutions from related work, the proposed method does not require external sensing hardware. Also, to interact with the device, the users do not have to use or wear any additional accessories. Hence, the interaction with the mobile device is entirely based on the manipulation of the light sensor readings.

3 UI Navigation Based on Light Sensor Utilization

The main concept of the proposed solution is illustrated in Fig. 1. The service is designed as a floating widget that could be placed on top of any existing mobile application.

This semi-transparent widget is used to interact with various UI components, such as buttons, checkboxes, radio-buttons, spinners, etc. To interact with these components, we implemented two navigation techniques for controlling the widget position and activating target elements. Both techniques function similarly, with the only distinction being in widget control modality (manual or automatic).

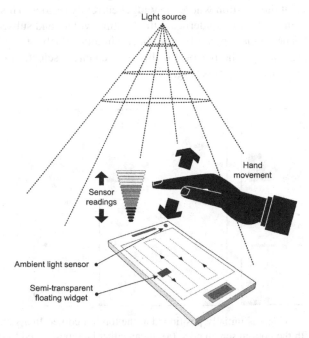

Fig. 1. The concept of touchless interaction based on ambient light sensor utilization.

The first navigation design refers to controlling the floating widget position manually. Initially, the widget is hidden and can be activated by placing the hand above the device's screen. When the ambient light sensor detects a corresponding light level change, the floating widget is activated and visualized on a predefined location (top left corner of the screen) – Fig. 2a. The widget movement is constrained only along the Y-axis, i.e. from top to bottom or vice versa. Sensor readings differ depending on the hand distance from the screen. For instance, the light intensity is lower when the hand is positioned closer to the screen. Thus, the floating widget position is determined by the current sensor reading. When the user moves her/his hand closer to the display, the widget gradually shifts its position downwards, towards the bottom edge of the screen. Similarly, as the user's hand is moving away from the screen, the widget is repositioned upwards, to the top screen margin. To cover the whole screen area, that is, to make each UI component accessible, the screen is divided into several vertical sections. To move the widget between different screen sections, a predefined dwell time value has been utilized. If the widget is held at the top or the bottom edge of the screen for a certain amount of time (2 s), it will be moved to the corresponding section. This way, in a situation when the widget collides with the bottom screen margin and the dwell time has passed, its position is transposed to the nearest right-hand segment of the screen (Fig. 2b). Similarly, if the widget reaches the top screen margin (Fig. 3a), it is automatically relocated to the available vertical section on the left, immediately after the dwell time has elapsed (Fig. 3b).

Regarding the selection of UI elements, it depends on the current widget position. When the widget is not moving for 2 s (and not being at the top or the bottom), the tap action is simulated at the position where the widget currently resides. This immediately activates the UI element located underneath the floating widget and subsequently hides the widget itself. The single tap can be simulated simultaneously at the left and right half of the floating widget. The reason for this is to enable a selection of small-sized elements in high-density UI layouts (Fig. 2c).

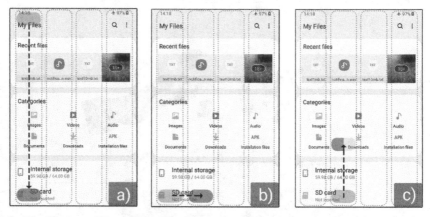

Fig. 2. The floating widget is initially positioned at the top left corner. In a situation when the widget collides with the bottom screen edge (a), it can either be repositioned to the right screen section (b) (in a case when dwell time has elapsed) or moved upwards (if the users' hand is moving away from the screen). The single tap can be simulated at the current widget location on the screen. To select the target element (e.g. *Downloads*), the single tap should be simulated at the right half of the floating widget (highlighted in green) (c). Taps at both widget halves are simulated simultaneously, which allows the selection of small-sized UI elements.

If the widget is kept at the initial position for a predefined period, it will be transposed to the upper right part of the screen (Fig. 4a). On the other hand, when the widget reaches the bottom right corner of the screen and dwell time elapses, it is automatically relocated to the bottom left screen edge (Fig. 4b). These features facilitate faster navigation through the user interface while the widget is controlled manually.

In the second proposed navigation design, users are not able to manually control the floating widget movement. Instead, the widget automatically changes its position at a certain pace, following the corresponding pattern depicted in Fig. 2. The target UI element can be activated simply by positioning the hand above the luminosity sensor at a particular moment. When this happens, the sensor detects abrupt variations in light intensity and the widget ceases to change its position. The underlying UI element is then activated by simulating the single tap event simultaneously at the left and right half

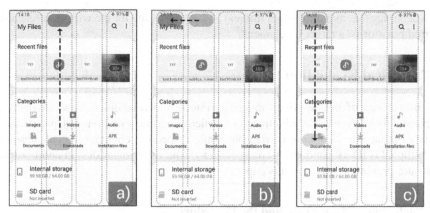

Fig. 3. In case when the widget collides with the top screen margin and is held for a specific amount of time (2 s) at the same position (a), it will automatically be repositioned to the left vertical section of the screen (b). However, if the users' hand is approaching the screen while the widget is positioned at the top of the screen, it will start to move downwards (c). In this example, the target UI element (*Documents*) is wide enough for a single tap to be simulated either at the left or right half of the floating widget.

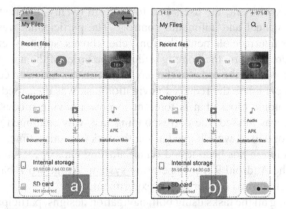

Fig. 4. When the widget reaches its initial position (a), the widget is either transposed to the upper right corner of the screen (if dwell time has passed) or moved downwards (if the users' hand is approaching the screen). When the rightmost screen section is reached (b) and the widget is held at the bottom screen margin for 2 s, it is transposed to the bottom left part of the screen. At this point, the widget can either start moving towards its initial position (by moving the hand away from the light sensor) or be transposed to the next available right section of the screen (in a case when the dwell time has elapsed).

of the floating widget. Subsequently, the light sensor proceeds to wait for changes in ambient light level, so the described interaction patterns can be repeated at any time.

It is important to notice that the widget scroll speed (that is, the period after which the widget automatically changes its position) has been predefined and programmatically set to 850 ms. This was considered to be the optimal value that compensates for the user's accuracy (i.e. avoiding target misses) and waiting time for the widget to reach the required position of a target UI element.

4   Empirical Evaluation

Implementations of the described touchless interaction modalities are evaluated and comparatively analyzed by conducting a controlled experiment involving 20 participants. All experiment activities were carried out while respecting epidemiological measures due to the COVID-19 pandemic. The specifics of the experiment design and obtained results are presented further in this paper.

4.1   Participants, Apparatus, and the Procedure

Twenty subjects (5 of which females) have been engaged in the empirical research. The participants' age varied from 20 to 26 years, with an average of 24.9 years (SD = 1.7). To get acquainted with the two different navigation designs, as well as with the light sensor sensitivity, the participants were engaged in a short practice session before the actual experiment. It should be noticed that no data were collected during this initial testing of introduced solution.

In the actual experiment, the users had to perform twenty different tasks for each navigation style (manual and automatic control). The participants were instructed to select various user interface elements (buttons, checkboxes, spinners, etc.), at different positions on the screen, using the floating widget. The order of the navigation tasks in a given sequence, as well as the order of the navigation styles, has been counterbalanced. The time taken to complete the required navigation task was measured by making use of a built-in monotonic clock that is tolerant to power saving modes. In case when target UI element was missed, the corresponding task was continued until successful execution, and error details were logged along the task execution time. Implementation of the proposed solution has been tested on a Samsung Galaxy S9+ smartphone (SM-G965F) running the Android 9 (*Pie*) operating system. All network-based services on the smartphone were turned off during the experiment.

After completing all the tasks using both navigation designs, participants were asked to complete a post-study questionnaire based on the rating part of the NASA-TLX (Raw-TLX format). To qualitatively assess both manual and automatic widget control, individual opinions about perceived workload had to be estimated on a 21-point Likert scales for five TLX factors.

4.2   Results and Discussion

Average times taken to complete a single navigation task, by utilizing provided interaction modalities, are shown in Fig. 5. It can be observed that the participants accomplished tasks faster when controlling the widget manually, compared to the case when widget automatic repositioning took place.

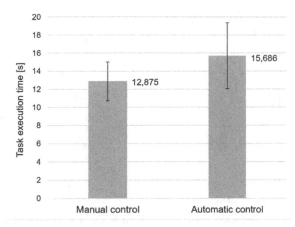

Fig. 5. Task execution times (mean values and standard deviations), obtained while controlling the floating widget either manually or automatically – by utilizing hand gestures above the light sensor.

To analyze the dataset obtained via conducted experiment, the dependent t-test (paired-samples t-test) was utilized. The aim was to formally compare task execution times between the two utilized navigation techniques (i.e. manual and automatic widget control). The t-test revealed a statistically significant difference in task completion time between the two conditions: $t(19) = -2.818$, $p < .05$.

The explanation for the obtained difference may be found in the inherent constraint of automated widget control. Namely, within the automatic control modality, the widget scrolling tempo is programmatically determined in a way it incrementally changes its position every 850 ms. Consequently, the user has to spend a certain amount of time waiting for the widget to reach the position of the element to be activated. In case the user accidentally misses the opportunity to activate the target UI element, it is necessary to wait for the whole cycle for the widget to return to the desired position. In this sense, further research efforts may be focused on studying how different values of widget scroll time affect the speed of task completion when automatic control is utilized.

When it comes to errors being made while using the proposed solution, log records revealed that fewer navigation mistakes (i.e. incorrect selections) were made when the widget was repositioned manually via continuous hand gestures. Figure 6 indicates the number of selection errors being made during the complete task sequence, using both manual and automatic navigation techniques.

Paired-samples t-test was utilized once again, this time to formally compare the number of errors between the two conditions. It revealed a statistically significant difference – the number of errors is considerably higher if automatic control is utilized: $t(19) = -6.144$, $p < .001$.

The observed difference in the number of errors can be explained on the grounds of the user's misjudgment of the moment at which it is appropriate to position a hand above the screen to activate the target UI element. The problem could be specifically related to the predefined speed of the automated widget scrolling. Slower scrolling of the widget would likely result in a fewer number of errors. However, this would prolong the time

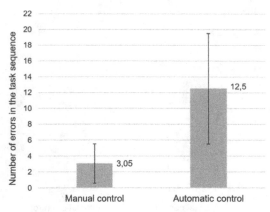

Fig. 6. Number of errors (incorrect selections) within navigation task sequence (mean values and standard deviations), obtained while controlling the floating widget either manually or automatically – by utilizing hand gestures above the light sensor.

required for the widget to reach the position of the target UI element, thus making the task execution slower.

Regarding the qualitative data obtained via Raw-TLX questionnaires, comparative ratings of perceived workload between manual and automatic navigation techniques are presented in Fig. 7. The Wilcoxon signed-rank tests were used to statistically analyze obtained TLX scores for each considered factor: mental and physical demands, level of frustration, perceived performance, and overall effort invested in experiment tasks. When compared to manual widget control, it was confirmed that automatic control implies significantly lower physical demand ($Z = -3.791$, p < .001). In addition, overall effort was found to be significantly lower when automatic navigation design was utilized ($Z = -2.279$, p < .05). The majority of participants assumed they achieved better performance when utilizing manual navigation; however, the corresponding difference can be considered only as marginally (non)significant ($Z = -1.877$, p = .061). For other TLX factors, no significant difference was revealed.

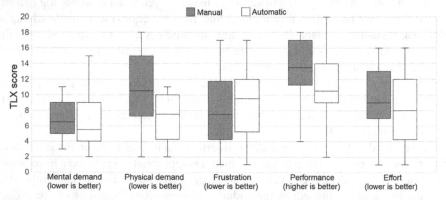

Fig. 7. Users' comparative ratings on perceived workload between different navigation techniques (manual and automatic widget control) implemented within the proposed solution.

It comes as no surprise that both physical demand and overall effort are considerably higher in the case when the floating widget is controlled manually. Namely, a manual control requires continuous hand gestures to be made above the light sensor, in order to fine-tune the target position of the widget before making a final selection. Contrariwise, automatic control assumes programmatically invoked widget repositioning, allowing users to make suitable hand gestures only when target selection is needed.

5   Conclusion

In this paper, we introduced a mobile service that provides touchless UI navigation by utilizing an embedded ambient light sensor. The solution is implemented as a floating widget that could be placed on top of any existing mobile application, thus allowing the introduction of ADI support. Unlike some similar solutions, this service does not require any external sensing hardware or equipping the user with additional accessories.

To navigate the UI, two different navigation patterns were developed within the proposed solution: the manual and automatic design. The manual control depends on the hand distance from the screen (i.e. the luminosity sensor). Namely, the floating widget position is determined according to the current sensor reading. In case when the user's hand is approaching the screen, the sensor reads a lower value of light intensity. Accordingly, the widget gradually shifts its position downwards, to the bottom edge of the screen. Similarly, when the hand is moving away from the screen, the sensor reads higher light intensity values, consequently repositioning the widget to the top screen margin. If the floating widget dwells for 2 s (as the user's hand is at a constant distance from the sensor), a tap-selection is simulated at the current widget position.

The automatic navigation, however, does not allow manual repositioning of a floating widget. Instead, this technique refers to automatically changing the widget position at a certain pace. To activate the target UI element, the user simply needs to position the hand above the luminosity sensor at a particular moment. This immediately prevents the widget from scrolling further, allowing a tap-selection to be simulated at the position where the widget currently resides.

The results obtained from a conducted experiment involving twenty participants have shown that the manual navigation technique was the significantly faster option. Namely, when compared to the automatic navigation design, participants completed given tasks more rapidly when controlling the widget manually. In addition, the study revealed a significant difference in the total number of incorrect selections between the two conditions. Specifically, more selection errors have been made when the automatic control was utilized. As discussed before, these differences may be partially attributed to the predefined pace of the widget automated scrolling.

The qualitative data analysis, based on the obtained TLX scores, revealed that controlling the widget manually implies significantly higher physical demand, as well as significantly higher overall effort. This can be easily explained by taking into account hand gestures that, within the manual navigation, have to be constantly performed for both the widget movement and the target selections. Nonetheless, by utilizing manual widget repositioning, users were able to accomplish given navigation tasks faster and with fewer errors, despite the higher perceived workload.

Further research efforts may be focused on analyzing how different dwell time values and widget scrolling tempo affect the speed of task execution and the number of incorrect selections within navigation tasks.

References

1. Siek, K., Rogers, Y., Connelly, K.: Fat finger worries: how older and younger users physically interact with PDAs. In: Proceedings of the 2005 IFIP TC13 International Conference on Human-Computer Interaction (INTERACT 2005), pp. 267–280. ACM Press, New York (2005)
2. Widgor, D., Forlines, C., Baudisch, P., Barnwell J., Shen C.: LucidTouch: a see-through mobile device. In: Proceedings of the 20th Annual ACM Symposium on User Interface Software and Technology (UIST 2007), pp. 269–278. ACM Press, New York (2007)
3. Huber, P.: Inaccurate input on touch devices relating to the fingertip. In: Media Informatics Proseminar (2015)
4. Butler, A., Izadi, S., Hodges, S.: SideSight: Multi-"touch" interaction around small devices. In: Proceedings of the 21st Annual ACM Symposium on User Interface Software and Technology (UIST 2008), pp. 201–204. ACM Press, New York (2008)
5. Kratz, S., Rohs, M.: Hoverflow: exploring around-device interaction with IR distance sensors. In: Proceedings of the 11th Conference on Human-Computer Interaction with Mobile Devices and Services (MobileHCI 2009), pp. 42:1–42:4. ACM Press, New York (2009)
6. Zhao, C., Chen, K-Y., Aumi, M.T.I., Patel, S., Reynolds, M.S.: SideSwipe: detecting in-air gestures around mobile devices using actual GSM signal. In: Proceedings of the 27th Annual ACM Symposium on User Interface Software and Technology (UIST 2014), pp. 527–534. ACM Press, New York (2014)
7. Harrison, C., Hudson, S.E.: Abracadabra: wireless, high-precision, and unpowered finger input for very small mobile devices. In: Proceedings of the 22nd Annual ACM Symposium on User Interface Software and Technology (UIST 2009), pp. 121–124. ACM Press, New York (2009)
8. Ketabdar, H., Ali Yüksel, K., Roshandel, M.: MagiTact: interaction with mobile devices based on compass (magnetic) sensor. In: Proceedings of the 2010 International Conference on Intelligent User Interfaces (IUI 2010), pp. 413–414. ACM Press, New York (2010)
9. Hwang, S., Ahn, M., Wohn, K.: MagGetz: customizable passive tangible controllers on and around conventional mobile devices. In: Proceedings of the 26th Annual ACM Symposium on User Interface Software and Technology (UIST 2013), pp. 411–416. ACM Press, New York (2013)
10. Ketabdar, H., Haji-Abolhassani, A., Roshandel, M.: MagiThings: gestural interaction with mobile devices based on using embedded compass magnetic field sensor. Int. J. Mob. Hum. Comput. Interact. 5(3), 23–41 (2013)
11. Lv, Z., Halawani, A., Khan, M.S.L., Rehman, S.U.: Finger in air: touch-less interaction on smartphone. In: Proceedings of the 12th International Conference on Mobile and Ubiquitous Multimedia (MUM 2013), pp. 16:1–16:4. ACM Press, New York (2013)
12. Grubert, J., Ofer, E., Pahud, M., Kranz, M., Schmalstieg, D.: GlassHands: interaction around unmodified mobile devices using sunglasses. In: Proceedings of the 2016 ACM International Conference on Interactive Surfaces and Spaces (ISS 2016), pp. 215–224. ACM Press, New York (2016)
13. Dell, N., Dsilva, K., Borriello, G.: Mobile touch-free interaction for global health. In: Proceedings of the 16th International Workshop on Mobile Computing Systems and Applications (HotMobile 2015), pp. 15–20. ACM Press, New York (2015)

14. Zhang, C., Tabor, J., Zhang, J., Zhang, X.: Extending mobile interaction through near-field visible light sensing. In: Proceedings of the 21st Annual International Conference on Mobile Computing and Networking (MobiCom 2015), pp. 345–357. ACM Press, New York (2015)
15. Wen, E., Seah, W., Ng, B., Liu, X., Cao, J.: UbiTouch: ubiquitous smartphone touchpads using built-in proximity and ambient light sensors. In: Proceedings of 2016 ACM International Joint Conference on Pervasive and Ubiquitous Computing (UbiComp 2016), pp. 286–297. ACM Press, New York (2016)

Comparison Between Manual and Automated Annotations of Eco-Acoustic Recordings Collected in Fukushima Restricted Zone

Daisuké Shimotoku[1]([⊠]) [iD], Junya Kawase[1] [iD], Hervé Glotin[2] [iD],
and Hill Hiroki Kobayashi[1] [iD]

[1] Information Technology Center, University of Tokyo, Tokyo, Japan
{shimotoku,kawase,kobayashi}@ds.itc.u-tokyo.ac.jp
[2] Université de Toulon, Aix Marseille Univ, CNRS, LIS, DYNI, Marseille, France
herve.glotin@univ-tln.fr

Abstract. Since 2016, long-term ecological recordings have been conducted in the Fukushima restricted zone to monitor biodiversity. In this paper, we use the simple Dice index to compare the human annotations of bird activities with automatic bird-detection recordings. The results show strong differences with respect to the types of soundscapes. On average, human and automatic annotations matched well at sunrise. In fact, they matched better at sunrise at the start of summer than at sunset at the end of the summer. This effect may be due to the quality of the bird songs that vary with the season and time of the day. To the best of our knowledge, this is the first time that this effect has been investigated by considering the estimation of bird activities in long-term surveys of specific areas, such as the Fukushima restricted zone.

Keywords: Human computation · Eco-Acoustics · Fukushima exclusion zone

1 Introduction

A report published by the International Atomic Energy Agency [3] describing the Chernobyl tragedy discusses the importance of assessing radiation levels and continuously monitoring wildlife in the contaminated zone for several generations. Following the Fukushima nuclear accident, researchers from the University of Tokyo commenced a regular ecological survey of wild animals in the northern Abukuma mountains [17,20], where high levels of radioactive contamination were detected. In [15], the researchers described placing automatic recording devices in the form of portable digital recorders at more than 500 points to collect and survey the vocalizations of the Japanese bush warbler. An effective method for monitoring these birds involves the counting of recorded bird sounds by experts. Auditory communication and auditory ranging and location (echolocation) are

© Springer Nature Switzerland AG 2021
N. Streitz and S. Konomi (Eds.): HCII 2021, LNCS 12782, pp. 164–177, 2021.
https://doi.org/10.1007/978-3-030-77015-0_12

commonly used by various animals, including mammals, amphibians, insects, and birds [5]; this method covers a wide range of animals. Complemented by visual counts, this method is an effective means for investigating the habitats of birds. However, recorded data are often difficult to analyze for the training data sets of artificial intelligence (AI); multiple playbacks are required even for professionals to identify and count the species. The life histories and experiences of professionals are different; therefore, even professionals differed in their identification of the sounds of bush warblers and their sizes, colors, and the kinds of woods. Therefore, if training data are created for the singing voices of a single warbler by multiple experts, the quality of the data set will vary. This variability in the quality of the data set poses a major problem in wildlife monitoring within the contaminated zone. This is because the wildlife singing surveys are not just about what we hear but also about how those singing voices have changed over the decades. Therefore, to efficiently conduct long-term wildlife surveys using AI, it is important to create high-quality datasets.

Kobayashi *et al.* [18] presented an automated audio retrieval system in the Fukushima restricted zone, which has been in operation since 2016; however, the analytical method has yet to be discussed. The radiation effects in the aftermath of the disaster will persist for decades; therefore, the study needs to be continued for as long period. Therefore, we need to use a sustainable analytical method. Related ornithological studies have encouraged the use of professional efforts. However, involving professionals for prolonged studies is not financially viable. In this study, we demonstrate the applicability of human computation in ecoacoustic research.

2   Background

Acoustic data retrieval requires more computational resources and uses advanced signal processing [13, 29]. Neuroscientists and computer scientists have attempted to separate the syllables of bird sounds. A syllable was defined as a continuous vocalization split by a silence of 5 ms or longer [1, 6, 26]. For instance, bush warbler songs can be denoted as "ho-ho-ke-kyo," "ho-ho-ho-ke-kyo," or "ho-ho-ke-kyo-kyo-kyo-kyo," where a syllable would be a chunk separated by a hyphen. To analyze the variations in the vocalizations of a species, it is important to split a song into syllables and to determine the transition probability from one syllable to another [23]. This process assumes that the system is a type of state machine or automaton, and the syllables correspond to specific states of the automaton. The transition probability between the states was then determined according to Chomsky's formal language system [10]. Without knowledge of the transitional probability and by assuming that the future states depend solely on the current state, this process can be easily modeled using a Markov chain [4].

There is a method for eliminating noise and identifying syllables from a stream. For instance, median filtering is a classical and computationally efficient noise filter [21]. Somervuo *et al.* [25, 26] and Harma *et al.* [14] applied sinusoidal modeling of signal processing for syllable recognition.

Other triggering methods are also presented in previous studies. Methodological comparisons are yet to be performed; however, they are not addressed in this paper.

It is known that songbirds can improve their singing abilities by imitating the vocalizations of an elder demonstrative bird. In addition, the singing abilities of female birds are also influenced by the sexual attraction of male birds [31]. Thus, the vocalizations of songbirds are very variable depending on the history and current environment of the birds. Consequently, it is necessary to collect enough samples to determine a bird's species from a stream. To reduce this effort, techniques from natural language processing, such as n-gram, are applied. Somervuo describes how a pair of bigrams can be used to efficiently characterize the types of birds; this can be an example of connecting formal linguistics to natural events [25,26].

Clearly, increasing sample numbers requires additional effort. At present, this effort is almost paid by professional ornithologists. For an improved recognition rate using machine learning, the vocalization must be distinguished from the background to the order of 1 msec. It is difficult, however, for amateur workers to meet such stringent criteria. Nevertheless, it would be too expensive and unrealistic to hire professional ornithologists because the number of recording stations has been increasing, which has led to enormous data streaming sizes. To monitor an entire evacuation zone (approximately $1,150 \, \text{km}^2$ as of August 2013), 500 monitoring stations are necessary, and these stations are expected to be in use for over 30 years [16]. It is unfeasible to get all this work done by professionals; therefore, collective intelligence or human computation must be employed [7,22,28,30,32]. An event with a large sociological impact is more likely to attract public interest; therefore, a higher participation rate in human computation trials is expected.

Public surveys are common in the field of ornithology [9,11]. A systematic study, called the e-Bird project, was conducted by the ornithology department of Cornell University [27]. This project requested ornithology enthusiasts to offer their observational records of birds on a website. The website (http://www.birds.cornell.edu) provided photographs and ecological descriptions of the observed birds. This helped scientists to collect bird migration data; it also helped participants to contribute. Amateur workers are not as reliable as professional workers; therefore, their behaviors needed to be analyzed, and their performances needed to be evaluated. For this evaluation, we drew a comparison between the ground truths and then computed similarities using the Sorensen-Dice coefficient. However, in this study, the availability of the ground truth (or supervisor) is limited. Therefore, we use machine learning results for comparison.

In Sect. 2, we show that a citizen science–based method is necessary to continue performing surveys; however, the quality control by amateur volunteers is a matter of concern. Although professional assistance may be required in the final step to obtain the truth, volunteers can assist in the process by screening and reducing the large amount of data. This study aims to contribute to this screening process.

To achieve this target, we examined the performances of volunteers by providing a natural soundscape, and we evaluated a signal-detecting AI system.

3 Preparation

The Omaru district in Namie Town, Fukushima (37°28′14″N, 140°55′12″E), was the target site; it is one of the most radioactively contaminated areas in the exclusion zone. This district is located 10 km NE of the Fukushima Daiichi nuclear power plant. The nearest monitoring site of the radiation dose levels, which is located 200 m from the target site, detected radiation levels of 10–20 µSv/h as of August 2018, which is 1,000 times the normal level. In this area, there is limited electricity, network, and information infrastructure. We selected the target site to demonstrate the capacity of field surveys in such difficult areas. The area lacks power and traffic infrastructure, and sensing methods were not available on the surface. When field surveys are done, the number of workable hours is strictly limited to decrease the workers' health concerns regarding radiation exposure.

We developed an acoustic data retrieval system from nature called Cyberforest [24]. This system was designed to function in highly remote areas, and it had two key components: an audio component and a transmission block. An omnidirectional weather-durable microphone (Sony F-115B) was connected to an amplifier (Xenyx 802, Behlinger) as the audio component. An audio encoder (Instreamer 100, Barix), which converted the analog signal provided by the audio components to the mpeg-3 format, was used to provide subsequent audio transmission. The audio was collected by the microphones and livestreamed to a broadcast server located at the University of Tokyo in quasi–real-time. In addition to broadcasting the live sound, the sound was recorded and archived automatically.

To ensure that the sounds were publicly reachable, we opened the website http://radioactivelivesoundscape.net/ for asynchronous listening. The sound was compressed in the common mpeg-3 format; therefore, users could access the audio using mpeg-based software. The site was hosted on a server in our laboratory using Linux Fedora 14, and the sound delivery software was implemented in IceCast 2. The sound archives were located primarily in Dropbox and then automatically synchronized to the network-attached storage provided by Synology RS816. This setup avoided the technical difficulties that occurred during remote data download and transmission loss (Figs. 1 and 2).

4 Methods

4.1 Data Collection

The recordings were done from June 2016 in the exclusion zone of Fukushima, Japan (UTC + 9) (Figs. 1 and 2). The summer and winter seasons of the site span from June to September and from December to March, respectively. The mean average temperature is highest in August (23.0 °C) and lowest in January

Fig. 1. Locality map of collection site [12].

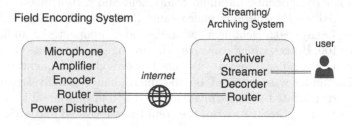

Fig. 2. System diagram of collection site [18].

(2.0 °C). The annual rain precipitation is 1,511 mm at the Namie Meteorological Station, Japan Meteorological Agency, as of 2017 [2].

Audio data were collected live and saved in split mpeg-3 files. The recording began every 6 min, and the maximum length of the files was 1 h. In other words, streaming events were recorded in the duration of 00:06–01:05, 01:06–02:05, and so on in successive hours throughout the day. During collection, we sampled the files with the intention of selecting the maximum acoustic activity of the birds. It is known that bird activity was highest near sunrise or sunset; therefore, we applied a sampling strategy to select only the first 30 min or the last 30 min of a file, depending on which half contained the period corresponding to the sunrise or sunset. This procedure is additionally discussed in Kobayashi *et al.* [18] and Saito *et al.* [24].

As discussed in [18], to reduce the task of manual annotation, only the files from the first day of each month between July 1, 2016, and June 1, 2017, were used. We performed peak normalization of the audio files and high-pass filtering 500 Hz with 20 dB/decade to attenuate the humming noises. Thus, we prepared 24 files (12 months × 2 times/day), each 30 min long.

4.2   Manual Annotation

Japanese nightingales vocalize two kinds of sounds. One kind of sound is called a song and is intended to attract female birds. The other kind of sound is called a call and is intended for a bird to announce itself or to warn others of the presence of a threat. Participants were expected to identify these two sound types because nightingales are quite common in Japan. The participants were familiarized with the typical calls and songs using a public addressing speaker and then asked to work individually using their headphones. The participants were provided with the Audacity software, which depicted the Fourier frequency–time transformation spectrogram of a sound file and were instructed to describe songs or calls. They were instructed to answer questionnaire sheet 3, which included the following four questions: (i) sound start times, (ii) sound end times, (iii) sound type (i.e., song, call, or environmental noise [rain or wind, which was expected to be automatically recognized]), and (iv) sound quality or signal level.

Japanese nightingales vocalize two kinds of sounds. One, called a song, is intended to attract female birds, and the other, called a call, is intended for a bird to announce itself or to warn others of the presence of a threat. Participants were expected to identify these two sound types, as nightingales are very common in Japan. The participants were familiarized with typical calls and songs using a public addressing speaker and then asked to work individually using their headphones. Provided with the Audacity software, which depicts the Fourier frequency-time transformation spectrogram of a sound file, participants were instructed to describe songs or calls. They were instructed to answer questionnaire sheet 3, which included four questions: i) sound start times; ii) sound end times; iii) sound type (i.e., song, call, or environmental noise [rain or wind, which was expected to be automatically recognized]); and iv) sound quality or signal level. As Audacity presents time in milliseconds, participants could copy the times onto the sheet. The types of sounds and the quality had to be answered subjectively, however.

As Audacity presents time in milliseconds, the participants could copy their observations onto the sheet. However, the types of sounds and the quality had to be answered subjectively.

To reduce the workload and increase the participants' concentration levels, 30-min audio files were split into two parts. To reduce human error, each file was evaluated at least a few times by different participants, who worked for 4 h on this task; they were asked to evaluate as many files as possible (Fig. 3).

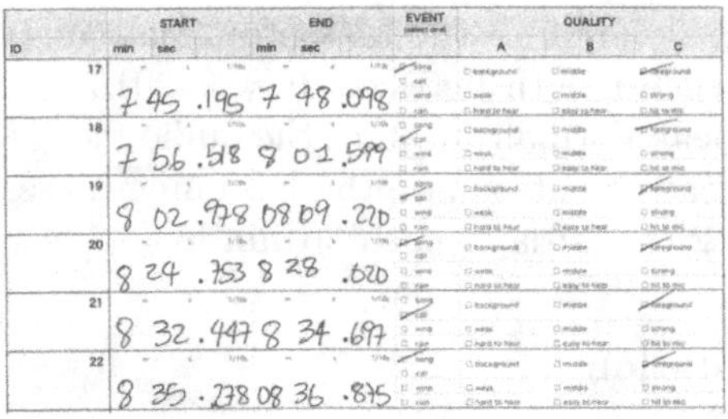

ID	START min	sec	END min	sec	EVENT	A	B	C
17	7 45	.195	7 48	.098				
18	7 56	.518	8 01	.599				
19	8 02	.978	08 09	.220				
20	8 24	.753	8 28	.620				
21	8 32	.947	8 34	.697				
22	8 35	.278	08 36	.875				

Fig. 3. Example of answered questionnaire

4.3 Automatic Detection

This automation detected all the signals from the sound file. A median filter was applied to the original sound file for noise reduction, and binarization was applied to the sound file. The regime and box bound were increased. We hypothesized that the background noise was constant during a 1-min interval, and 30-min audio files were split into 1-min intervals for parallel processing.

The first step was to set a filter bandwidth (500–15,000 Hz) and then to extract all calls from the recordings using a basic adaptive time–frequency filter [19]. Then, we obtained a spectrogram with a Tukey window (1,024 samples). Next, we obtained a binary image using median clipping per time frame and frequency band (3 × median + 3 × standard). If the pixel was superior to this mask, we set the pixel to 1; otherwise, the pixel was set to 0. Then, we used closing and dilation on the boxes and applied a label for each box. Finally, we removed the small objects. For each box, the duration, the minimum and maximum frequency, and the mean and maximum dB were selected.

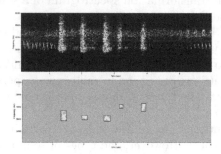

Fig. 4. Sonograms of six bird calls with a filter bandwidth of 500–15,000 Hz and an associated detector

4.4 Evaluation

We calculate the similarity between manual annotation and automated detection using the Dice index D, which is formulated as follows (Fig. 4):

$$D = \sum_j \frac{|A \cap B_j|}{|A| + |B_j|}, \tag{1}$$

where A and B_j are the time ranges designated as positive by manual annotation and automated detection, respectively. The index j represents the participant. A file is scanned by three or more participants; therefore, the Dice index is calculated for each file, and the summation is performed with respect to the participants who annotated a file.

The value of D ranges from 0 to 1. A high D value shows that the manual annotation is similar to the automated process.

5 Results

In June 2018, we conducted a manual annotation experiment in which 21 undergraduate students were recruited to count 711 calls and 571 songs. The most prolific participant detected 196 events with 119 calls and 77 songs, whereas the least prolific participant detected only two events, including two calls (Fig. 5). Warbling events are not uniformly distributed; therefore, these performance differences cannot be attributed to the participants alone. However, automated analysis is necessary for determining the aspects for which humans are responsible.

The automated analysis detected 18,598 signals. We compared the signal durations determined by the automated system and by manual annotation. The automatic analysis provided a specific box for each detected signal; therefore, subtracting the signal start from the end times yielded the signal duration. In manual annotation, both the start and end times of a signal are also available on a questionnaire sheet, and the duration of a warbling can be obtained by subtracting the end time from the start time. The signal durations of the automated system and manual annotations are compared in the histogram shown in Fig. 6. In this figure, the horizontal axis represents the signal duration in seconds, whereas the vertical axis represents the number of boxes that indicate the automatically detected signals or the number of signals annotated manually. Figure 6 shows that more signals were detected by automated analysis than by manual analysis, and almost all the detection occurred in less than 1 s.

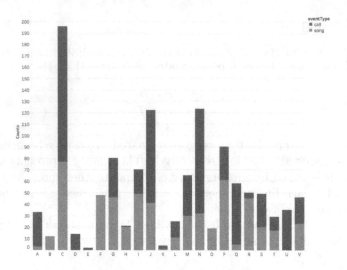

Fig. 5. Number of annotations per user

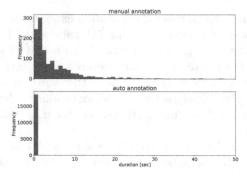

Fig. 6. Duration comparison between automated and manual annotations.

In contrast, human annotation had a peak time at 2 s, which indicated that the participants recognized the warbling sequence as a melody. The automated system separated the sequence into several split syllables. We calculated the similarity between automated detection and manual annotation by using the Dice index given in Eq. (1).

Figure 7 presents the Dice index distribution for the files. The three groups from Fig. 7 are classified. In the highest group with $D > 0.9$, the participants annotating the files were assumed to successfully detect signals. We could not determine how accurately they collected the warbling sounds; however, by comparing their results with those from automated detection, we determined that the participants successfully selected and designated signals from the sound stream. Thus, we considered them high-performance participants. In the same way, we designated participants with $1.5 < D < 0.8$ as middle-performance participants, and participants with $D < 0.4$ as low-performance participants. In the latter group, the participants selected nearly random areas with respect to the signal pattern. Note that these participant classifications depended on the files. Participant performances varied with different sound streams, which might have impact the difficulty of sound annotation.

We determined the transition of participant performances (see Fig. 8). Of the 22 participants, 17 were classified as high-performance participants. Of these, five participants always performed well regardless of the stream, whereas 12 participants displayed middle or low performance for some types of sounds. The remaining five participants were classified as middle performance. Of these, two participants consistently performed at a middle level regardless of the stream. No participants were classified as low-performance participants for all the streams.

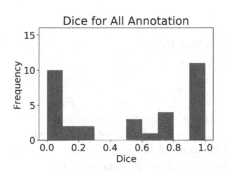

Fig. 7. Dice index over files   **Fig. 8.** User performance comparison.

The minimum and maximum frequencies of the detected signals and the minimum and maximum signal strengths (in decibels) were obtained from the automated system. We performed principal component analysis (PCA) of the above components to determine whether there was a correlation between the signal type and participant performance. The PCA summarizes signals by the types of sound sources in a detected signal box; that is, it illustrates the bird species. The results of the PCA analysis are shown in Fig. 9. The vertical and horizontal axes represent the principal components 1 and 2, and the color represents the Dice index, which corresponds to the participant performance. Figure 9 reveals that there are only local correlations between the Dice index and the principal components that summarize the time–frequency acoustic content. Thus, there is no correlation between the participant performance and bird species represented in the file.

The participants performed significantly better for songs than for calls. The average Dice index was 0.887 and 0.843 for songs and calls, respectively ($p < 0.005$).

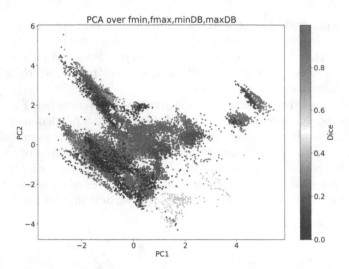

Fig. 9. PCA analysis vs dice index

6   Discussions

In this study, the participants were not informed about the origins of the data or the ways in which the study contributed to the redevelopment of the Fukushima region. As mentioned in the previous section, manual listening requires intense focus whether or not there is a signal. In fact, there is generally much less signal than noise, and the work may become less interesting to the participants. As time progresses and the participants become tired, their performances may decrease if ample motivation is not provided. In this study, files were randomly assigned to the participants; however, this did not guarantee that the signals were uniformly distributed to the participants. Therefore, Fig. 5 only partially explains the effort and performance of the participants. The participants were selected from a group of undergraduate foreign students in Japan; however, there was no detailed background information survey, such as nationality or natural experiences. Additional investigation was required to determine the relationship between the backgrounds of the participants and their performances.

As discussed in the previous section, to cope with an increasing amount of environmental data, it is necessary to have a system that connects participants to an automated system. Participants cannot always be trusted; therefore, an evaluation scheme is helpful for describing how the participants work with the data. In this study, we achieved this evaluation by comparing the annotations between the participants and an automated system. The difficulty of this scheme lies in the fact that both participant annotation and automated annotation are not completely reliable. In the field of human computation, the comparisons between the two have already been discussed in [8, 29]; therefore, it is not being repeated in this paper. This study provides an example using ecoacoustic sounds. In addition, we clarify human perception by using a signal detector. Because the soundscape originates in the Fukushima exclusion zone, the understanding of human perception of nature can help inform the acoustic environmental surveys.

Songbirds have various types of vocalizations; therefore, efficient methods are required to determine their species. In this context, detecting a syllable to find a pattern is a common method. This study is only suitable for syllable detection; additional contributions are yet to be made regarding creating n-gram models for producing bird sound patterns. In this context, syllable detection is a basic technology to support model creation. This study used syllable detection using a natural sound stream with large limitations because of the specifications of the Fukushima restricted zone. The stream contained only 192 kbps of bandwidth, which is small as compared with the environmental ecoacoustic monitoring records used in previous studies. The actual operation of the software was made possible because of the robustness of the signal processing software.

7   Conclusions

We analyzed the performances of the participants using the Dice index computed between human annotations and data obtained from automatic bird-activity detection. Only 23% of the participants always performed well regardless of the type of soundscape.

Large differences were found in the performances of participants with respect to the types of soundscape. In general, human and automatic annotations have a higher congruity at sunrise. In particular, these annotations have higher congruity at sunrise at the beginning of summer and at sunset at the end of summer. This congruity may be related to the quality of the bird calls, which vary with the season and time of day. To the best of our knowledge, this is the first study that describes these congruous effects in detail, and this information can be applied in long-term studies.

Acknowledgement. This study is supported by the following grants: KAKENHI Grant-in-Aid for Challenging Research (Exploratory) 19K22839, Grant-in-Aid for Scientific Research on Innovative Areas 17H05969, Grant-in-Aid for Challenging Exploratory Research 16K12666. We also thank to the Telecommunications Advancement Foundation, and the Tateisi Science and Technology Foundation Research Grant for supporting this study. We thanks the Chaire Intelligence Artificielle ADSIL ANR-20-CHIA-0014, ANR-18-CE40-0014 SMILES, MI CNRS MASTODONS SABIOD.org and EADM MADICS CNRS scaled bioacoustic research groups, and SEAMED Region Sud project.

References

1. Abe, K., Watanabe, D.: Songbirds possess the spontaneous ability to discriminate syntactic rules. Nat. Neurosci. **14**(8), 1067–1074 (2011). https://doi.org/10.1038/nn.2869

2. Agency, J.M.: Japan meteorological agency: namie automated meteorological data acquisition system (2013). https://www.jma.go.jp/jp/amedas/

3. Alexakhin, R., et al.: Environmental consequences of the Chernobyl accident and their remediation: twenty years of experience. Report of the Chernobyl Forum Expert group "Environment". International Atomic Energy Agency (2006)
4. Bartcus, M., Chamroukhi, F., Glotin, H.: Hierarchical dirichlet process hidden Markov model for unsupervised bioacoustic analysis. In: 2015 International Joint Conference on Neural Networks (IJCNN), pp. 1–7. IEEE (2015)
5. Begon, M., Harper, J., Townsend, C.: Ecology: Individuals, Populations and Communities. Blackwell Science Ltd. (December 1997)
6. Berwick, R.C., Chomsky, N.: Birdsong, Speech, and Language: Exploring the Evolution of Mind and Brain. MIT Press (2013)
7. Brady, E., Morris, M.R., Bigham, J.P.: Gauging receptiveness to social microvolunteering. In: Proceedings of the 33rd Annual ACM Conference on Human Factors in Computing Systems, CHI 2015, pp. 1055–1064. ACM, New York (2015). https://doi.org/10.1145/2702123.2702329
8. Branson, S., et al.: Visual recognition with humans in the loop. In: Daniilidis, K., Maragos, P., Paragios, N. (eds.) ECCV 2010. LNCS, vol. 6314, pp. 438–451. Springer, Heidelberg (2010). https://doi.org/10.1007/978-3-642-15561-1_32
9. Cappadonna, J.L., Brereton, M., Watson, D.M., Roe, P.: Calls from the wild: engaging citizen scientist with animal sounds. In: Proceedings of the 2016 ACM Conference Companion Publication on Designing Interactive Systems, pp. 157–160. ACM (2016)
10. Chomsky, N.: On certain formal properties of grammars. Inf. Control 2(2), 137–167 (1959)
11. Cottman-Fields, M., Brereton, M., Roe, P.: Virtual birding: extending an environmental pastime into the virtual world for citizen science. In: Proceedings of the SIGCHI Conference on Human Factors in Computing Systems, pp. 2029–2032. ACM (2013)
12. ESRI: Arcgis version 10.4.1 (2015)
13. Fagerlund, S.: Bird species recognition using support vector machines. EURASIP J. Appl. Sig. Process. 2007(1), 64 (2007)
14. Harma, A.: Automatic identification of bird species based on sinusoidal modeling of syllables. In: 2003 Proceedings of the IEEE International Conference on Acoustics, Speech, and Signal Processing, ICASSP 2003, vol. 5, p. V-545. IEEE (2003)
15. Ishida, K.: Contamination of wild animals: effects on wildlife in high radioactivity areas of the agricultural and forest landscape. In: Nakanishi, T.M., Tanoi, K. (eds.) Agricultural Implications of the Fukushima Nuclear Accident, pp. 119–129. Springer, Tokyo (2013). https://doi.org/10.1007/978-4-431-54328-2_12
16. Ishida, K., Tanoi, K., Nakanishi, T.M.: Monitoring free-living Japanese Bush Warblers (Cettia diphone) in a most highly radiocontaminated area of Fukushima Prefecture. Japan. J. Radiat. Res. 56, i24–i28 (2015). https://doi.org/10.1093/jrr/rrv087
17. Kasten, E.P., Gage, S.H., Fox, J., Joo, W.: The remote environmental assessment laboratory's acoustic library: an archive for studying soundscape ecology. Eco. Inform. 12, 50–67 (2012)
18. Kobayashi, H.H., et al.: A real-time streaming and detection system for bioacoustic ecological studies after the Fukushima accident. In: Joly, A., Vrochidis, S., Karatzas, K., Karppinen, A., Bonnet, P. (eds.) Multimedia Tools and Applications for Environmental & Biodiversity Informatics. MSA, pp. 53–66. Springer, Cham (2018). https://doi.org/10.1007/978-3-319-76445-0_4
19. Lasseck, M.: Large-scale identification of birds in audio recordings. In: CLEF (Working Notes), pp. 643–653 (2014)

20. Lin, T.H., Fang, S.H., Tsao, Y.: Improving biodiversity assessment via unsupervised separation of biological sounds from long-duration recordings. Sci. Rep. **7**(1), 4547 (2017)
21. Poupard, M., De Montgolfier, B., Roger, V., Lohani, D., Glotin, H.: EthoAcoustics: a model based on t-SNE & clustering, applied on pantropical spotted dolphin during whale watching. In: 8th International DCLDE (Detection, Classification, Localization, and Density Estimation) Workshop (2018)
22. Quinn, A.J., Bederson, B.B.: Human computation: a survey and taxonomy of a growing field. In: Proceedings of the SIGCHI Conference on Human Factors in Computing Systems, pp. 1403–1412. ACM (2011)
23. Roger, V., Bartcus, M., Chamroukhi, F., Glotin, H.: Unsupervised bioacoustic segmentation by hierarchical dirichlet process hidden Markov Model. In: Joly, A., Vrochidis, S., Karatzas, K., Karppinen, A., Bonnet, P. (eds.) Multimedia Tools and Applications for Environmental & Biodiversity Informatics. MSA, pp. 113–130. Springer, Cham (2018). https://doi.org/10.1007/978-3-319-76445-0_7
24. Saito, K., Nakamura, K., Ueta, M., Kurosawa, R., Fujiwara, A., Kobayashi, H.H., Nakayama, M., Toko, A., Nagahama, K.: Utilizing the Cyberforest live sound system with social media to remotely conduct woodland bird censuses in Central Japan. Ambio **44**(Suppl. 4), 572–583 (2015). https://doi.org/10.1007/s13280-015-0708-y
25. Somervuo, P., Harma, A.: Bird song recognition based on syllable pair histograms. In: 2004 Proceedings of the IEEE International Conference on Acoustics, Speech, and Signal Processing, ICASSP 2004, vol. 5, p. V-825. IEEE (2004)
26. Somervuo, P., Harma, A., Fagerlund, S.: Parametric representations of bird sounds for automatic species recognition. IEEE Trans. Audio Speech Lang. Process. **14**(6), 2252–2263 (2006)
27. Sullivan, B.L., Wood, C.L., Iliff, M.J., Bonney, R.E., Fink, D., Kelling, S.: eBird: a citizen-based bird observation network in the biological sciences. Biol. Conserv. **142**(10), 2282–2292 (2009). https://doi.org/10.1016/j.biocon.2009.05.006
28. Voida, A., Harmon, E., Al-Ani, B.: Bridging between organizations and the public: volunteer coordinators' uneasy relationship with social computing. In: Proceedings of the SIGCHI Conference on Human Factors in Computing Systems, pp. 1967–1976. ACM (2012)
29. Wah, C., Branson, S., Perona, P., Belongie, S.: Multiclass recognition and part localization with humans in the loop. In: 2011 IEEE International Conference on Computer Vision (ICCV), pp. 2524–2531. IEEE (2011)
30. Wang, F.Y., Carley, K.M., Zeng, D., Mao, W.: Social computing: from social informatics to social intelligence. IEEE Intell. Syst. **22**(2), 79–83 (2007)
31. Wheatcroft, D., Qvarnström, A.: Genetic divergence of early song discrimination between two young songbird species. Nat. Ecol. Evol. **1**(7), 192 (2017). https://www.nature.com/articles/s41559-017-0192
32. Wiggins, A., Newman, G., Stevenson, R.D., Crowston, K.: Mechanisms for data quality and validation in citizen science. In: 2011 IEEE 7th International Conference on e-Science Workshops (eScienceW), pp. 14–19. IEEE (2011)

Towards Infectious Disease Risk Assessment in Taxis Using Environmental Sensors

Hidenaga Ushijima[1]($\boxtimes$), Shota Ono[1], Yuuki Nishiyama[1](iD),
and Kaoru Sezaki[1,2](iD)

[1] Institute of Industrial Science, The University of Tokyo,
4-6-1 Komaba, Meguro-ku, Tokyo, Japan
{hidenaga.ushijima,shota}@mcl.iis.u-tokyo.ac.jp,
{yuukin,kaoru}@iis.u-tokyo.ac.jp
[2] Center for Spatial Information Science, The University of Tokyo,
5-1-5 Kashiwano-ha, Kashiwa-shi, Chiba, Japan
https://www.mcl.iis.u-tokyo.ac.jp

Abstract. The spread of Coronavirus disease of 2019 (COVID-19) has reaffirmed the importance of ventilation in enclosed public spaces. Studies on air quality in public spaces such as classrooms, hospitals, and trains have been conducted in the past. However, the interior of a taxi, where an extremely small space is shared with an unspecified number of people, has not been sufficiently studied. This is a unique environment where ventilation is important. This study compared ventilation methods focusing on the CO_2 concentration in the cabin, and evaluated the frequency of ventilation in an actual taxi using sensing technology.

Keywords: Mobile sensing · COVID-19 · CO_2 · Public transportation

1 Introduction

The emergence and spread of the Coronavirus disease of 2019 (COVID-19) around the world has created a new global public health crisis; it has affected our lives severely. The World Health Organization (WHO) reported that as of October 30, 2020, COVID-19 have infected over 40 million people and killed over 1 million people, worldwide.

COVID-19 is an infectious disease caused by the new coronavirus, SARS-CoV-2, which is spread through direct contact with infected individuals or inhaling airborne particles. The WHO and the Ministry of Health, Labor and Welfare (Japan) strongly recommend wearing masks, washing hands, disinfecting, and avoiding "three-dense" environments where an unspecified number of people are crowded within an enclosed space.

Airborne infections, like COVID-19, spread when a person absorbs microparticles, called aerosols [5, 12], that float in the air and contain the virus. Aerosols can be suspended in the air for several minutes up to several hours, posing a

N. Streitz and S. Konomi (Eds.): HCII 2021, LNCS 12782, pp. 178–188, 2021.
https://doi.org/10.1007/978-3-030-77015-0_13

major challenge to the prevention of airborne, infectious diseases. Public transport, such as trains, buses, and taxis, are particularly high-risk environments when it comes to the spread of airborne diseases. Even though taxis are not strictly a three-dense environment, many different people share the same space, in turn [8]. The risk assessment and prevention of infections in indoor spaces, including car interiors, is a challenging research topic because there is a limited amount of air in the space and virus-containing aerosols may be present.

The regular ventilation of indoor air is necessary to prevent aerosol stagnation. Existing research [3,9] used $CO2$ levels as an indicator of air quality in a space. However, these studies did not assess the ventilation effect in in-vehicle environments such as taxis. Taxi interiors are relatively small, enclosed spaces; moreover, taxis are a frequently used mode of transportation that many people use in turn. Thus, this can be a prime space for the transmission of airborne diseases. Measuring and quantitatively evaluating air exchange in taxis will contribute to future countermeasures against airborne, infectious diseases. In this study, we measured the air quality in the enclosed public space of a taxi using a sensing device and quantitatively analyzed the risk for the spread of airborne, infectious diseases.

In order to measure the unique environment of a taxi, this research was conducted in two stages. First, the air quality inside a stationary vehicle using four different ventilation methods was compared. Second, we measured the $CO2$ concentration in a running taxi vehicle, which allowed us to investigate the air environment inside a taxi. We then compared it with the measurements taken in the stationary vehicle.

2   Related Work

This section describes related work on infectious disease risk assessment in public transportation using environmental sensors.

2.1   Infectious Disease Risk Assessment

Infectious diseases such as tuberculosis and influenza are transmitted through *droplets* and *aerosols*. The infection risk of these diseases is increased especially in enclosed spaces [11]. *Fluesense* [1] is a system for calculating the risk of influenza infection in an enclosed space such as a hospital waiting room. The system monitored the number of people and coughs of each person in the waiting room using an infrared camera and microphone. In addition, the system was able to classify the characteristics of various infectious diseases based on the sound of coughs and present indicators for each area. The system could monitor the infection risk in a room, but could not detect asymptomatic, infected people with no fever or coughs.

2.2   Enclosed Space Detection

CO_2 concentration has been used as an index for room ventilation [2,6,10] because high CO_2 concentration can lead to serious side effects such as fatigue, and headache; it might even cause suffocation. CO_2 concentration outdoors is approximately 400 ppm, and people can start to feel effects like sleepiness at 1000–1500 ppm. At levels above 2500 ppm, people will feel fatigued, have headaches, and could suffocate. Therefore, the Japanese building standards law stipulates that indoor CO_2 concentration should be kept under 1000 ppm.

The cabin of a car is a unique space environment because many people may spend a long time in this small space. Owing to the amount of time spent inside the car for activities such as commuting to and from work, business use, and driving, it can be seen as a living space. Therefore, the air environment inside the car is required to be the same level as that of a building, and vehicle manufacturers are working toward raising their internal standards to meet the standards of the Ministry of Health, Labor, and Welfare's sick house guidelines.

Several researchers [4,7,8] have collected air condition data in the cabin using environmental sensors and evaluated the quality of air from the collected data. Moreno et al. investigated the air quality in diesel and non-diesel taxis in Spain and found that diesel taxis had higher carbon monoxide concentrations than non-diesel taxis. They also found an accumulation of volatile organic matter from brakes [8]. Barnes et al. measured the air quality of private cars in Hong Kong, focusing on PM2.5, CO_2, and volatile organic compounds. They found that the concentration of volatile organic compounds (VOCs) tended to increase in proportion to the age of the vehicle. They also claimed that 96% of the vehicles exceeded the indoor air quality levels specified by the Hong Kong Environmental Protection Department [4]. Grady et al. reported that it was possible to maintain the CO_2 concentration in the vehicle below the target value of 2000 ppm by controlling the operating conditions, i.e., the speed of the air conditioning fan, and the air conditioning recirculation settings [7]. In general, vehicles have two air-control functions, external air introduction and internal air circulation, and vehicle manufacturers recommend using external air introduction.

3   Research Question

There have been many studies that have evaluated the risk of transmission of airborne, infectious diseases in enclosed spaces, and many of them have used CO_2 concentration for environmental monitoring. However, most of these studies focused on buildings, such as classrooms in schools; few focused on taxis, which are enclosed spaces used by an unspecified number of people and where the environment is constantly changing.

The COVID-19 pandemic has been ongoing since the beginning of 2020, and although reducing the risk of infection is necessary, economic activities need to continue. Although there have been studies on monitoring the risk of infection using images and audio and environmental sensors [1,9], they are not sufficient. There is a need for a simple and low-cost method to assess the risk of infection in places where many people gather, such as restaurants and events, or that many people use, such as public transport.

CO_2 sensors are usually used as an air quality index in a room, and we hypothesized that a CO_2 sensor could also be used for detecting the ventilation conditions in a car. Therefore, we investigated whether a CO_2 sensor can be used to detect ventilation conditions, one of the factors that increase the risk of infection, in the actual cabin and throughout the service shift of a taxi.

In this study, we propose a low-cost and simple index to monitor the risk of infection from diseases such as COVID-19 in taxis, which is considered to be a widely-used mode of public transportation.

4 Experiment

To investigate the CO_2 conditions in a car, we collected CO_2 data and drive recorder information (see Sect. 4.1) under two conditions (see Sect. 4.2).

4.1 Sensors and Setup

We used the DFRobot's Gravity series CO_2 sensor, which uses non-dispersive infrared (NDIR) technology (Fig. 1), to collect CO_2 data. This sensor is capable of measuring the concentration of CO_2 in the atmosphere in the range of 0–5000 ppm and has a temperature compensation function so that readings will not be effected by temperature. As shown in Fig. 1, the CO_2 sensor is connected with a M5Stack Gray[1] that had a mobile network (3G) module; power was supplied by a cigar socket through an inverter. The sensor collected CO_2 data every 30 s, and uploaded it to cloud storage[2] through the mobile network.

In addition to the CO_2 sensor, we used a drive recorder (DENSO TEN G500 series[3]) in the taxi. This was used to monitor actual events in the car (e.g., opening of doors, windows, and recording the number of people in the car) to gain a deeper understanding of the events in a taxi while in service. To collect the events, the drive recorder provided video from three angles: the forward direction of the car, from the dashboard to the rear seat, and a view of the driver from the passenger-seat side.

4.2 Study Conditions

CO_2 concentrations were measured in a vehicle while it was stationary and while running.

First, for a control measure, we collected CO_2 concentration data in the stationary condition that is described in Sect. 4.2. After the stationary condition study, we collected CO_2 concentration data and drive recorder data in a taxi that was in service (Sect. 4.2).

---

[1] https://m5stack.com/.

[2] https://ambidata.io/.

[3] https://www.denso-ten.com/jp/biz-recorder/g500/products/function01/index.html.

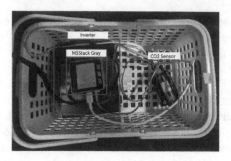

Fig. 1. CO2 sensor

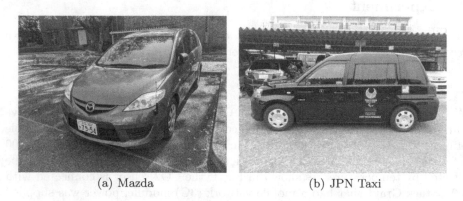

(a) Mazda   (b) JPN Taxi

Fig. 2. Experiment cabin

Stationary Condition: Comparison of Ventilation Methods. The CO2 concentration was measured in a stationary vehicle under the following conditions:

- Vehicle used: 2010 Mazda Premacy
- Subjects: 2 males in their 20s, 2 females in their 20s
- Location: Parking lot, Institute of Industrial Science, University of Tokyo
- Period: November 17th, 11:00–18:00
- Atmospheric CO2 concentration: 620 ppm

In this experiment, the sensor module was placed on the dashboard of the car to compare four ventilation conditions in the car. All participants sat on the left side of the backseat, wore a mask, and conversed with each other using a telephone.

Before the start of each measurement, all the doors were opened so that the CO2 concentration inside the car would equalize with the atmospheric concentration.

The four ventilation conditions during which the measurements were taken are described next.

`Normal`: In the first experiment, the CO2 concentration was measured for five minutes with all windows closed. In this study, we used this measurement as the standard measurement for comparison.

`Open window`: In the second experiment, the CO2 concentration was measured for five minutes with only the front, right window open. The front, right window was assumed to be the most frequently opened window as it is next to the driver.

`Circulation`: In the third experiment, the CO2 concentration was measured with all windows closed and the vehicle's air conditioning was set to the internal circulation mode. This experiment was conducted to measure the CO2 concentration when the air inside the vehicle was circulated and to compare it with the normal condition.

`Intake air`: In the last experiment, CO2 measurements were performed with all windows closed and the vehicle's air conditioning set to the external introduction mode. This experiment was conducted to measure the change in CO2 concentration when the vehicle was ventilated by bringing in external air without opening the windows.

Running Condition: CO2 Concentration in the Real Environment. Next, an experiment was conducted using a taxi while in operation. The experimental conditions were as follows.

- Vehicle used: 2019 Toyota JPN Taxi
- Driving area: Saga City, Saga Prefecture
- Period: 11:00–22:00 on June 25
- Atmospheric concentration: 611 ppm
- Driver: Male

In this experiment, no special instructions were given to the driver to accurately measure the actual real-life air quality of a taxi during operation. The sensor module was installed near the dashboard, and measurements were taken constantly from 11:00, start of business, to 22:00, close of business. By linking the CO2 data with the video from the drive recorder, we labeled the timing when the passengers boarded and when the driver opened the door. Customers boarded the train a total of eight times. In addition, the doors were opened and closed 48 times.

5   Results and Discussion

5.1   CO2 in a Stationary Vehicle Condition

The CO2 concentration of a male who stayed in a closed car for 80 min is shown in Fig. 3. As can be seen from the figure, the CO2 concentration increase is linear. The concentration increased at a rate of 0.92 ppm/s, and it was clear that without ventilation, the concentration would reach 2,500 ppm in a short period. CO2 concentrations at that level can cause a decline in cognitive ability.

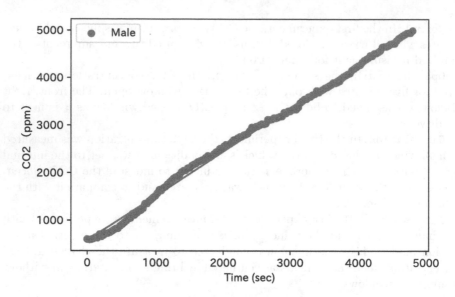

Fig. 3. CO2 concentration

Figure 4 shows CO2 concentration in a car using four different ventilation methods.

Under the **normal** condition Fig. 4(a), the participants did not do anything. We compared the measurements of the men and women and found that the CO2 concentration increased at 0.61 ppm/s and 0.02 ppm/s for men and women, respectively. The slower rate of increase in CO2 concentration for women compared to men can be attributed to CO2 emissions that differ based on body size and lung capacity and that CO2 concentration is noticeably higher in a confined space.

Figure 4(b) shows the CO2 concentration under the **open window** condition. The rate of increase in concentration was lower for both men and women when compared to the normal condition. In men, the rate of increase was approximately 50%. The ventilation effect was observed even when only one window was open.

The results under the **circulation** condition is shown in Fig. 4(c). The results showed that the CO2 concentration increased by 0.77 ppm/s and 0.43 ppm/s for men and women, respectively. During internal circulation, the speed of increase in CO2 concentration increased compared to normal conditions. As the air was circulated inside the car, the concentration was no longer biased.

In the case of the **intake air** condition, the concentration increased at 0.16 ppm/s for males and decreased at 0.05 ppm/s for females. When air was introduced from outside, the CO2 concentration fluctuations were extremely small for both men and women.

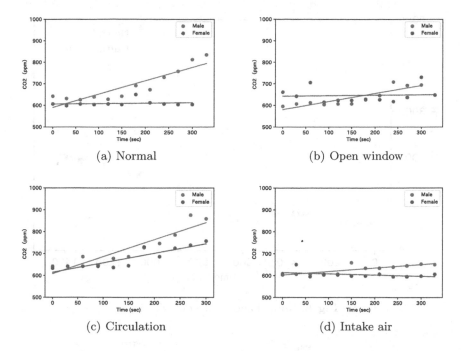

Fig. 4. Ventilation methods

To further verify the effect of external air introduction, a 1500-s measurement was conducted to compare with the normal condition. Figure 5 shows the results. When measurements were taken over a long time, the CO_2 concentration did not change under normal conditions; however, the external air introduction maintained a CO_2 concentration almost equal to that of the atmosphere. These results showed that CO_2 continues to accumulate inside a car if no ventilation is provided, but sufficient ventilation can be achieved by introducing external air without opening the windows.

5.2   CO2 in a Running Vehicle Condition

We measured the degree of ventilation in a taxi, where an enclosed space was shared by an unspecified number of people, by measuring the CO_2 concentration during the taxi's operation. The driver was a man in his 50s, and the CO_2 concentration in the air was 611 ppm.

The results are shown in Fig. 6. As shown in the figure, the CO_2 concentration was found to be higher than the recommended standard concentration for 51% of the business hours. Notably, the increase in CO_2 concentration due to passengers boarding was limited. This can be attributed to the fact that passengers on average ride for 15 min or less, and the doors are opened and closed before and after boarding, which has a certain ventilation effect.

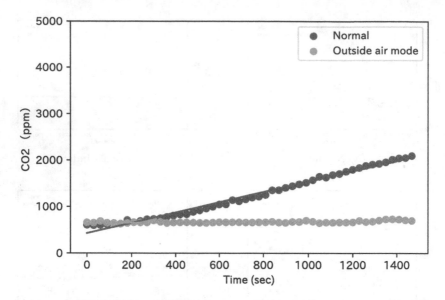

Fig. 5. Normal and intake outside air

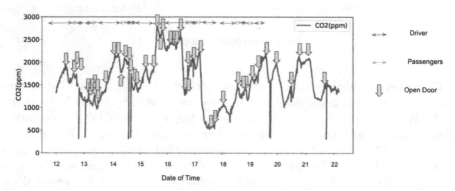

Fig. 6. Daily change in CO2 concentration

By measuring and comparing the CO2 concentrations of stationary and running taxi vehicles, we were able to verify several ventilation methods and investigated the air environment inside a taxi while it was running.

6   Conclusion

In this study, we used CO2 concentration to measure the ventilation status of a taxi, wherein an unspecified number of people shares an enclosed space. From the comparison results of several ventilation experiments, it was found that the CO2 concentration inside a car will increase linearly, that the introduction of outside air could maintain a CO2 concentration almost equal to the atmospheric concentration, and that internal circulation spread the CO_2 concentration inside the vehicle faster than usual. Comparing the increase in CO_2 concentration between males and females, we found that in a small, enclosed space such as the interior of a car, there was a significant difference in the speed of increase in concentration between males and females. In the test conducted in an actual taxi, it was found that the CO_2 concentration exceeded the standard value of 1500 ppm for as much as 51% of the business hours, and exceeded 2500 ppm [10], which is said to affect cognitive ability, for as much as 4% of the time. In addition, passengers were actually in the car for less than 10% of the time, so the effect of the increase in CO_2 concentration was extremely limited. In the future, we aim to construct a recommender system that warns drivers and users and asks them to take appropriate actions when the risk of infection increases

Acknowledgment. This research was partially supported by AMED under Grant Number JP20he0622042 and Institute of Industrial Science through IIS special funding to support COVID-19 related research.

References

1. Al Hossain, F., Lover, A.A., Corey, G.A., Reich, N.G., Rahman, T.: FluSense: a contactless syndromic surveillance platform for Influenza-Like illness in hospital waiting areas. Proc. ACM Interact. Mob. Wearable Ubiquitous Technol. **4**(1), 1–28 (2020)
2. Andrews, J.R., Morrow, C., Wood, R.: Modeling the role of public transportation in sustaining tuberculosis transmission in south Africa. Am. J. Epidemiol. **177**(6), 556–561 (2013)
3. Angelova, R.A., Markov, D.G., Simova, I., Velichkova, R., Stankov, P.: Accumulation of metabolic carbon dioxide (CO_2) in a vehicle cabin. IOP Conf. Ser. Mater. Sci. Eng. **664**(1), 012010 (2019)
4. Barnes, N.M., Ng, T.W., Ma, K.K., Lai, K.M.: In-Cabin air quality during driving and engine idling in Air-Conditioned private vehicles in Hong Kong. Int. J. Environ. Res. Public Health **15**(4) (2018)
5. van Doremalen, N., et al.: Aerosol and surface stability of SARS-CoV-2 as compared with SARS-CoV-1. N. Engl. J. Med. **382**(16), 1564–1567 (2020)
6. Du, B., Tandoc, M.C., Mack, M.L., Siegel, J.A.: Indoor CO_2 concentrations and cognitive function: a critical review. Indoor Air **30**(6), 1067–1082 (2020)
7. Grady, M.L., Jung, H., Chul Kim, Y., Park, J.K., Lee, B.C.: Vehicle cabin air quality with fractional air recirculation. Technical Report, SAE Technical Paper (2013)
8. Moreno, T., et al.: Vehicle interior air quality conditions when travelling by taxi. Environ. Res. **172**, 529–542 (2019)
9. Peng, Z., Jimenez, J.L.: Exhaled CO_2 as COVID-19 infection risk proxy for different indoor environments and activities. MedRxiv (2020). https://doi.org/10.1101/2020.09.09.20191676, https://www.medrxiv.org/content/early/2020/09/10/2020.09.09.20191676
10. Satish, U., et al.: Is CO_2 an indoor pollutant? direct effects of low-to-moderate CO_2 concentrations on human decision-making performance. Environ. Health Perspect. **120**(12), 1671–1677 (2012)

11. Workman, A.D., et al.: Endonasal instrumentation and aerosolization risk in the era of COVID-19: simulation, literature review, and proposed mitigation strategies. In: International Forum of Allergy and Rhinology. Wiley Online Library (2020)
12. Zhang, R., Li, Y., Zhang, A.L., Wang, Y., Molina, M.J.: Identifying airborne transmission as the dominant route for the spread of COVID-19. Proc. Nat. Acad. Sci. USA **117**(26), 14857–14863 (2020)

The Value of the User Evaluation Process in the European IoT Large-Scale Pilot for Smart Living

Reiner Wichert[1]([⊠]), Saied Tazari[2], Axel Albrecht[1], and Monika Wichert[3]

[1] Assisted Home Solutions, Freiherr-vom-Stein-Straße 10, 64331 Weiterstadt, Germany
{r.wichert,a.albrecht}@assistedhome.de
[2] Fraunhofer IGD, Fraunhoferstr. 5, 64283 Darmstadt, Germany
saied.tazari@igd.fraunhofer.de
[3] SageLiving, Borngartenstr. 10, 64319 Pfungstadt, Germany
monika.wichert@sageliving.de

Abstract. Within the EU ACTIVAGE [1] project, a multi-centric IoT-Large Scale Pilot on smart living environments for aging well, we enrolled our smart living solutions in Germany with 184 older adults and a number of their formal and informal caregivers as end users and performed in the last year of the project an evaluation of our deployments. This paper presents the results of this evaluation. The main goal of the assessment was to find an optimal set of devices and functions to increase the users' wellbeing based on IoT activity monitoring and detection of emergencies. The evaluation used information from sensors installed in homes and nursing rooms, combined with surveys on demographic data of users, user satisfaction survey, and a marketing survey to assess other features that the system should have to offer an attractive solution on the market. After an overview of the piloting setup and a focused discussion of the evaluation results, the paper concludes with further development, which resulted in a new system.

Keywords: Ambient assisted living (AAL) · Activity sensing · Field studies and deployments · Healthcare and well-being · Impact of ambient intelligence and IoT on society · Internet of Things (IoT)

1 Introduction

The IoT Large-Scale Pilots Programme of the EU [2] funded five large-scale pilots. Here, ACTIVAGE was the multi-centric IoT-LSP on smart living environments for ageing well that started in 2017 by reusing several IoT platforms, technologies and standards at scale and eventually managed to build the first European IoT ecosystem across 12 Deployment Sites (DS) in nine European countries with over 7200 users. The DSes extend the independent living of older adults in their living environments and respond to real needs of older adults, their caregivers, related service providers and public authorities. As the German DS in ACTIVAGE, our main goal was to increase the health situation of our users and evaluate the usefulness of the prototypes of our solution, called **uLive**, within

© Springer Nature Switzerland AG 2021
N. Streitz and S. Konomi (Eds.): HCII 2021, LNCS 12782, pp. 189–209, 2021.
https://doi.org/10.1007/978-3-030-77015-0_14

an experimental process. We consider this as part of our path-to-market strategy with a focus to find an optimal set of devices and functions for uLive to increase our users' wellbeing – by passive indoor monitoring towards IoT-based detection of emergency situations in the life of older adults – and evaluate its usefulness in real-life experiments. After several months of study and analysis of the data and information obtained through surveys and interviews, we are able to summarize the outcome of our experimental journey.

The evaluation process has been of high importance for our DS since it was planned from the beginning to take the results of the project for a product placement in the coming months after the project. Therefor our DS has seen this evaluation process not only to get direct feedback on the prototype as a passive indoor monitoring system for the detection of emergency cases through sensors in the involved homes, but also to continuously identify the weak points and improve the systems, as well as to know how to address which customer. The 184 older adults at the German DS either live independently in residential complexes in Weiterstadt, Rodgau and Türkheim, or are residents of care centres in Weiterstadt and Treuchtlingen with 24/7 stationary care; around one-third of the latter ones may not leave the bed alone.

Using different questionnaires and interviews with older adults, we collected our data within three evaluation phases. After each phase, the data was uploaded to the ACTIVAGE DS evaluation LSP dashboard and the data analysis was carried out so that the results could be included in a continuous improvement process for a future business.

2 Market Analysis

According to the Federal Statistical Office, there are 14,500 nursing homes, 14,100 outpatient nursing services and 3.4 million people in need of care in Germany. Hospitals and care centres usually make use of a "nurse call system" without any voice connection. About 1 Mio of people in need of care use the classic emergency call systems at their own homes. Not least due to the challenges of the aging society, this industry is currently on the threshold of the renewal of the systems and has high hopes for digitization. So far, however, there is a lack of effectively beneficial solutions that are practical and go beyond laboratory and model apartment installations.

The dominant product on this market is certainly the classic home emergency call, which consists of a call button and a base station as a hands-free speakerphone. The system connects individual people in their apartments with the so-called "call centers", which receive calls for help and initiate any assistance that may be required. Home emergency call systems are offered in Germany mainly by the DRK/BRK, the Johanniter, ASB and Malteser. The technology for home emergency call systems (with the base station as the main component) has been manufactured in Germany since 1980. For about 10 years there has been increasing criticism of home emergency call systems, especially with regard to the following points:

- The fixed emergency buttons can be out of reach at the time needed; the wearable version, on the other hand, is hardly compatible with forgetfulness.
- The more sensitive people in need feel stigmatized by wearing an emergency button and try to hide it from visitors and later forget to wear it again.

- The number of emergencies that go unnoticed is not negligibly small, be it for the above reasons or because of black-out in the accident or losing the call button in the course of falling. Hence, the requirement for passive detection of emergencies (compared to active calls for help) are getting stronger.
- The dominance by few manufacturers on this market has resulted in reselling almost the same technology for 30 years without special investment in improvement.

However, the demographic change in an aging society has increased the pressure on service providers in this industry to improve the efficiency of their services with the help of digital technologies. After few years of waiting for the old vendors to replace the technologies, it showed how complex the implementation of the passive detection of emergency situations can be, which led to evaluating new vendors' innovative offers.

But as a matter of fact, none of the new systems has passed the tests so far because

- many sensors don't have the necessary quality for the provision of critical data,
- the situation recognition has not been realized in several stages of semantic abstraction but rather directly on the basis of sensor reports, and
- the result of the situation recognition is not verified before the action is initiated.

As a result, they end up with very weak assumptions with too many false positives and therefore again cause unnecessary costs. Some system providers try to circumvent this problem through monitoring: instead of generating an alarm directly, they send a notification for a manual checking of the plausibility in an app (rejected by caregivers) and possibly clarifying the situation directly with the monitored person by phone.

Since the derivation of situations from the analysis of the sensor data has proven to be rather complicated, there is also the approach of developing more complex specialized sensors, especially for the purpose of reliable fall detection, which make sense as participants in a larger distributed compound system. Attempts to push such devices to become the controller for smart living often fail because of the resulting complexity.

2.1 Competition

Our customers compare only few products with uLive, which we explore here:

- *Climax* [3] acts primarily as the vendor of modern home emergency call devices. The equipment of Climax controllers is considerable in some models, e.g. with integrated microphone and loudspeaker and support for Bluetooth/BLE, ZigBee, ZWave, SIP and a kind of speech recognition. They do not come with any reasoning module for recognizing situations and reacting to them. Only the handling of an active emergency call via panic button or by voice is pre-programmed as a useful function. In addition, Climax offers (Web) similar to classic smart home systems. Hence, Climax is not a real competitor to uLive as a software solution, but rather a potential partner for hosting uLive and maturing as a real controller for IoT based assistance systems.
- *Dosch & Amand* [4] is a DECT specialist. The award-winning DECT Pendant product functions as a home emergency call device: beyond an emergency button, the small companion device integrates a fully configurable DECT speakerphone with voice

recognition. It detects falling of the device and via acoustics also smoke alarms with on-device processing. In emergency cases, individually configured contact persons are called who can directly speak to the monitored person via speakerphone. The device supports also voice commands for normal telephony. The main weakness of the device is the high charging frequency as a usability problem for the target users. Despite the successful realisation of the concept, D&A DECT Pendants are no real competitors for uLive due to the underlying utility-device-centric approach, limited capacity for extensibility and lack of situation recognition capabilities.

- *easierLife* [5] follows the vision of early detection of danger based on monitoring using a Climax device as base station. Only active help request with the armband is reliable enough to be accepted by the home emergency call centres and covered by the care insurance. Therefore, data planned for passive emergency detection is now sent to registered family members in an app for further elaboration. In the background, easierLife saves all data on an own server in the Cloud with pattern recognition algorithms for detecting anomalies that generate still more notifications. Thus, real dangers are recognized only by chance and dealing with the multitude of messages requires a lot of patience from the formal and informal caregivers.

- The solution provided by *ahs.digital* [6] has been used as an alternative solution in our DS since 2018, in parallel to the development of own prototypes. It recognizes pre-defined situations at homes, but cannot verify the guesswork in the system, which led to some false alarms. Therefore, the company has organized manual alarm management for filtering out false positives by own staff. In addition, alarms are based on a single-number central telephony service so that no differentiation based on the caller number is possible; an obstacle for integration with emergency call centres. Also, the system is closed despite the underlying openHAB [7], which causes risks in system extensibility.

2.2   Concluding the State-of-the-Art

Many new systems do not have any passive mechanism for recognizing emergency situations, but invest on other features, such as benefiting from new communication technologies. The GSM emergency call devices, for example, can also locate the device by GPS, but must be charged daily. As a wearable connected to mobile network, however, they are not bound to a fixed place, as opposed to home emergency call systems.

All others try to expand their features by integrating new types of sensors and/or eHealth products. In the end, however, they have too many false positives, which is not acceptable for caregivers. Often poor quality is masked by low system prices. Therefore, so far there are no solutions that manage to prevail, only ideas and attempts. This shows that the pressure to offer something new is increasing.

Cell phones, wearables and voice assistants are succeeding more easily because they have many synergies in daily life, letting emergency calls look like a simple add-on. But, dealing with people's lives based on typifying as well as the careless handling of privacy is increasingly confronted with acceptance problems, even rather insurmountable for professional service providers. Cloud providers like *Verklizan*, who connect many devices to home emergency call service providers via their platform, have potential for improving emergency call systems and reducing false alarms. But, apart from privacy concerning, they remain limited to monitoring instead of recognizing the specific situation. In the end, only systems that can recognize the specific verified emergency cases will succeed to prevail – at this point.

3 The German Deployment Site

The ACTIVAGE DS in Germany, known as WoQuaZ or LiNeCs[1], has been piloted in 102 homes and 71 nursing rooms and 10 other environments with 261 users: 184 older adults, 42 informal carers, 29 formal carers and 6 other users. The installation of 4253 sensors and other devices, has led to the creation of one of the first socio-health ecosystems in the society, in Weiterstadt and further locations in Germany. WoQuaZ has been evaluating the impact of the new model incorporated in our deployment site in ACTIVAGE, for the provision of social, health services and nursing houses and it has very successfully developed the following areas in ACTIVAGE based on the monitoring in assisted living:

- The passive alarm in assisted living (opposed to active help request via panic button)
- The verification of alarms by the user in the house emergency call
- The evaluation of call systems in the stationary area through differentiated forwarding of alarm situations to the nursing staff

    These developments were targeted to

- capture and transfer of specific alarm situation: no monitoring, no alarm suspicions, no wasting time on interpretations, while verifying system behaviour retrospectively.
- relieve and support the staff, relatives, neighbours and house emergency services.
- give a high level of security to the user through direct communication by the system (except in the nursing home and in the dementia shared apartment where this kind of communication does not make much sense).

Assistance, as we understand and develop, is characterized by the recognition of a defined and concrete situation, on which a previously configured action takes place, beside the involvement of the user. In the nursing home and the dementia shared apartment, the user was not involved, but the staff was immediately informed. uLive has impressed and convinced the people particularly in the nursing home through its simplicity and real work relief. Flexibility and acceptance are the other essential goals of our programme. That is the reason that early failure in Türkheim was an important point in our new development.

Our valuable experience led us to the fact that optimized communication and alarm management in the nursing home are the essential parts of the success. Through involving more and more users and operators, now we have created a system, which can be accepted even by home emergency call service providers, the ones that we didn't consider in the first steps of our project. Today we know that we can significantly improve and simplify

---

[1] From German "**Wo**hn- und **Qua**rtierszentren", meaning "**Li**ving and **Ne**ighbourhood **C**entres".

the processes in the nursing home and in the emergency call system for the operator, as shown in Sect. 4. During the development of uLive in ACTIVAGE, we tried and tested a large number of devices, sensors and wireless protocols. We tested the interchangeability and, of course, the improvement of the sensors. Today we can offer even more individual systems in terms of price and scope. Today we have systems that can detect a fall within a few seconds, or in another situation, react after 3–5 h in order not to constantly recognize the "normal case" as an emergency. It is important that we supervise without monitoring by workforce. Nobody should worry about the systems - it works completely unnoticed in the background and becomes noticeable only when it reacts to the recognized situations, like turning a nightlight on and off or announcing the assumption of a critical situation to be verified by the inhabitant.

3.1 The DS Users

Our users are older adults who live independently in residential complexes, such as in Weiterstadt, Rodgau or Türkheim. Some of these residential complexes are supervised like in Rodgau, others completely unsupervised like in Türkheim or partly supervised like in Weiterstadt have been. The residents of the dementia shared flats and the residents of the nursing home in Treuchtlingen are taken care 24 h a day; in some cases, around one third of them are in bed all the time.

Together 261 users have been involved in our deployments, but not all have participated in the evaluation: 184 elderly, 42 relatives, 29 formal carers and 6 administrators. Some of them did not want to make interviews or fill out the questionnaires. As a basis for the evaluation, first some socio-demographic data on age, gender and technological knowledge was requested from the users. The average age of the participants in all sites is 81.8 years, where most of the participants are between 80 and 90 (39.2%), followed by the age between 70 and 80 (31.4%), where 38.6% of them are living in care centres. At the group beyond 90 we had 20.3% and only a few younger below 70 (9.2%). The average age in the care centre is around 5 years higher than in independent living, while around 2/3 of the 90+ people are in the care centre. The oldest participant is celebrated her 100th birthday in 2020; the youngest is 51 years old. Thus, the physical and social health state was very different between the end users.

At the four pilot locations (from five) that stayed with the project, the distribution of gender is in the normal range, which is 66,7% women and 33,3% men, due to the higher life expectation of women which is very similar in the care centre and the flats (Fig. 1).

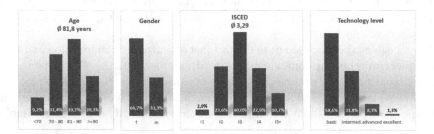

Fig. 1. Overview of the socio-demographic profiles of WoQuaZ users

Most of the participants have an education at ISCED level 3 (40.0%). Only 2.9% are in ISCED level 1. The highest degree of education has been a PhD of one participant and 7 have a master degree. The education level at the care centre is much lower than in the flats. The reason might lay in the years of the second world war and after, since the age in the care centre is higher (see above) and there had been less possibilities to get a good education in those years. The technology knowledge is also in average of the 60+ population: 58.6% have only basic and only 1.3% excellent knowledge. In the care centre is the technology level a bit lower, which also may be caused by the higher age.

3.2 The DS Installations and Services

A total of 1853 installations were carried out: 102 flats (22 in Weiterstadt, 48 in Rodgau, 6 in Treuchtlingen, 26 in Türkheim), 71 care rooms (11 in Weiterstadt, 60 in Treuchtlingen), 3 shared room in senior facility and 7 other spaces participated at the four locations of the German DS.

Actual available handling of alarm situations:

#	Situation recognised	Announcement and control call	Action in the home
1	Active Emergency Call	The emergency call button was pressed	--
2	Suspicion of a fall	Unusual lying position discovered	--
3	Unusually long periods of inactivity (including bathroom)	No physical activity for a long time	--
4	Leaving bed	if defined in care centres as alarm: Resident in room xx leaves the bed	Night light is switched on
5	No return to bed	The bed stayed empty for an unusually long time	--
6	Not getting up in the morning	No physical activity for a long time	Light is switched on
7	Not going to bed in the evening	You are up for an unusually long time	--
8	Smoke alarm	Smoke detected	Electricity / stove will be turned off, but lights will be turned on / the shutters are raised and the door is opened
9	Entrance door open	The entrance door is open for an unusually long time	--
10	Unusually long water consumption	The water has been running for an unusually long time	The water was therefore turned off
11	Window is open	The window is open for an unusually long time	--
12	High humidity / CO_2 values	--	Fan turns on
13	The apartment is heated by the sun	--	The roller shutter goes down - but only when nobody is in the apartment or on the balcony
14	Reminder function	Announcement text freely selectable	--
15	Problematic blood sugar level	Your blood sugar is out of the desired range	--
16	Problematic blood pressure value	Your blood pressure is outside the desired range	--
17	Oxygen saturation problematic	Your oxygen saturation is outside the desired range	--
18	Incoming calls from the inhabitant's (or an authorized carer's) phone	This is your apartment speaking	Press zero: alarms are reset / Press one: door can be opened / Press five: you can speak into the home through the speakerphone / ... further actions are possible

realized functions	in development	available soon

Fig. 2. uLive features

If the multi-sensor devices are counted as four sensors, altogether 4253 sensors have been installed at the four sites: 773 Motion sensors, 668 Temperature sensors, 668 Humidity sensors, 668 Light sensors, 233 Controllers (Raspberry Pis), 203 Door contacts, 178 Panic buttons, 152 Bed sensors, 148 Light Relays, 114 Relays roller shutter, 92 Switches and router for SIP, 88 Sockets, 82 Smoke Sensors, 58 Switches, 55 Speakerphones, 48 fall detection sensors, 27 Motor Locks for doors. In Weiterstadt 765 other devices already installed before ACTIVAGE, which have also been used to collect information, derive behaviour from them and provide assistance services to the end users.

During ACTIVAGE piloting 33,321,578 events from movement detectors, 7,887,965 room changes, 344,311 absence and presence interpretations, 335,005 bed occupancy detections, 57,695 cases of absence longer than two hours and 642 alarms had been sent. In Weiterstadt with all the additional sensors installed before project start, 179,791,226 events detected including 418,296 water flow events, 1,899,064 CO2 events or 3,153,952 humidity measurements. If a critical situation was detected an alarm was sent to the phones into an escalating alarm chain.

Figure 3 illustrates the project outcome in terms of the product getting ready for entering the market with uLive as its operating system. It readily comes with 12 main features, all implemented and evaluated during ACTIVAGE in the flats and care rooms mentioned above, three others are in development at the moment and three more will follow in near future (see Fig. 2).

Fig. 3. The first controller with uLive as operating system and the set of supported protocols for binding off-the-shelf components

4   Evaluation

The primary goal of WoQuaZ was to prepare the pathway for a product placement after the project. Consequently, we strived to demonstrate the need and feasibility for smart living environments based on Internet of Things (IoT) technologies during the project, and to show positive effects in the quality of life of people over 60. To this end, the gaol was to reach the following outcomes for our secondary goals:

- The use of uLive as an IoT solution for monitoring can provide substantial support to people over 60 years, enhancing their quality of life by feeling safer at home and to allow older people to stay longer at home
- The use of the system brings great advantages for formal caregivers with regard to the management of emergency situations and monitoring the status of the users, and leads to time and monetary savings
- The use of the system helps to ease the care for caregivers can have a positive impact on the overwork and overburdening perceived by them
- uLive respects the privacy and security of user by storing and processing all data in the user's private network and by refraining from uncontrolled data transfer to external entities
- The system is able to link various sensors and components from different manufacturers by numerous communication channels and protocols to enable a flexible interplay between the components
- The passive emergency call is being revolutionised by intelligent sets of rules and verification of situations to convert computed conjecture to higher levels of certitude

This evaluation phase also made a number of recommendations aimed at finding a marketing solution that primarily increases the length of stay at home with sustainable quality of life. Furthermore, the business model could be specified more precisely. This also resulted in recommendations for the composition of the hardware and the setting of the rules, installation, maintenance and ongoing operation. Finally, a more specific way was found how new customers can be addressed.

4.1 Local Evaluation Procedure

To measure the impact of the assessment an experimental method has been used, which compares the effects of the situation before and after the test phase at the four German pilot sites. The evaluation focuses on the impacts for older people and their informal carers. The implementation process of the evaluation observes where the barriers are and what the margin for improvement is towards upscaling and replication in future sites.

For this reason, information has been collected from the different questionnaires of the three phases and in parallel by evaluating the data from different sensors, actuators and devices, as well as further analysis of the data at higher levels towards behavioural reasoning to support the objectives (KPIs) mentioned above. To achieve this, the local evaluation procedure in WoQuaZ was as follows:

Since the users in Weiterstadt had previously participated in the ReAAL project [8], WoQuaZ started with the initial system at this site. During the project duration further sites had been acquired and the rollout of the system tested in Weiterstadt to the other sites had been possible. After joining ACTIVAGE, each pilot had to make sure that the participants filled out the consent forms and a questionnaire for finding the appropriate parameters needed for individualizing the system behaviour. During the project runtime the users had always some time (3–6 months) to experience the latest system release between each phase of evaluation, to find the advantages or the weak points by using it 24/7. In the end of each phase, the users had been interviewed personally in their apartments while filling the questionnaires. In case of Treuchtlingen the care persons filled out the questionnaires due to the bad health conditions of the end users (most of them suffering from dementia).

Following data has been collected: (1) Demographic data, (2) Quality of Live Questionnaire for formal and informal caregiver (QoL-7D), (3) Global KPIs as defined in ACTIVAGE equally for all deployment sites, (4) Quality of Life Questionnaire for elderly (EQ-5D-3L), and (5) Local KPIs on the satisfaction changes over time.

For the further product development, additional questions had been asked in the final evaluation about the strengths and weaknesses of the system in the areas, that we use to evaluate uLive chances on the market: (1) privacy, (2) IT protection, (3) inconspicuousness, (4) maintainability, (5) costs, (6) interoperability, (7) reusability, (8) expandability, and additional questions on the satisfaction with the system.

Except from Treuchtlingen, all of the 261 end users are participants from assisted living in own homes. Treuchtlingen itself is a care centre for people in need of stationary care, often with dementia. Due to changing health conditions, four persons died and four elderly moved out within the evaluation year. Due to the higer numbers of false positives appeared in the first months, 18 persons denied the further participation in the project. As consequence, the hardware configuration was changed in the next iteration. Due to some expected drop-offs at WoQuaZ, more questionnaires had been planned in the three phases. All questionnaires have been filled by the end users themselves, except for the 59 elderly at Care level 5 in Treuchtlingen, which have been done by the care personnel.

The evaluation started with the definition of the local KPIs and continued with the planning, execution and analysis of the results. The set of KPIs were used to adapt the system in iteration processes according to the needs of the site users and for proofing the sustainability of the health services. The information has been collected using the following procedure: conducting questionnaires in three phases, at the beginning, middle and end of the project. In summery a total of 1,231 questionnaires have been completed in the WoQuaZ for older adults and caregivers:

- 479 sociodemographic data sets have been collected from older adults and caregivers
- 33 questionnaires for quality of life (CarerQoL7D) completed by caregivers
- 423 QOL questionnaires (EQ-5D-3L) have been completed by older adults
- 296 Acceptance and Use of Technology (UTAUT) questionnaires have been filled by users (274 by older adults, 22 by caregivers)

4.2 Analysis of the Results

ACTIVAGE followed a value-driven innovation with the aim to support decision makers' choices, promote sustainability and improve the quality of life of the European aged adults on the evidence of the usage of IoT-AHA (Active and Healthy Ageing) solutions. To compare the results at the DSs, rich key performance indicators (KPIs) have been defined for all three objectives [9, 10]. With the help of the installations at the four pilot sites in Germany, experience with the system was recorded in the three evaluation phases through questionnaires and interviews. In order to achieve the mentioned objectives above many questions had been asked from the end users (elderly, family members and formal carers). The evaluation of these KPIs in WoQuaZ demonstrates the benefits of intelligent living environments with IoT technology, in terms of satisfaction, safety, quality of life and independence among others; here is an excerpt of the evaluation (Fig. 4):

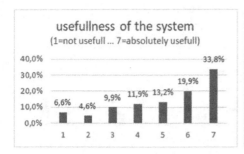
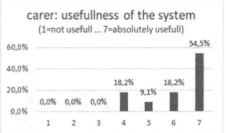

Fig. 4. Usefulness of the system overall (left) and carer alone (right)

Altogether, the participants see the system as useful. More than 50% see it as absolutely useful (33.8%) or very useful (19.9%). Especially for the care personnel, the system helps a lot at their daily work (Fig. 5).

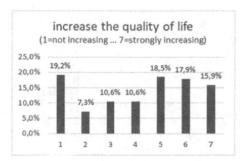
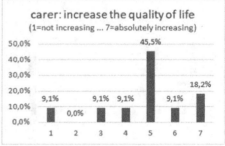

Fig. 5. Increase of quality overall (left) and carer alone (right)

The increase of quality of life is seen very distributed between all users. We hope that users will see more advantage after the rollout of the new system in all four pilots (Fig. 6).

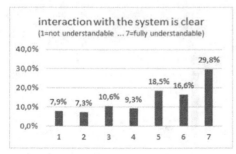
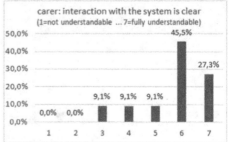

Fig. 6. Interaction with the system overall (left) and carer alone (right)

For most of the participants is fully understandable (or close to it) how the users have to interact with the system. Especially the care personnel finds it very understandable (Fig. 7).

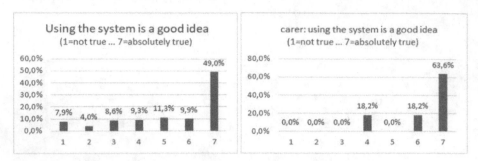

Fig. 7. Idea of the system overall (left) and carer alone (right)

A very good result is that also half of the users see the use of the system as a very good idea. Also here, the care personnel finds the usage as absolutely a good idea (63.6%) (Fig. 8).

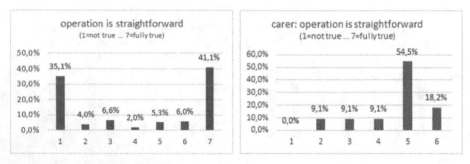

Fig. 8. Operation of the system overall (left) and carer alone (right)

The care personnel understands very well the operation of the system (see right side). The overall view on the straightforwardness of the operation of all users is a bit surprising, but when splitting the result into flats and care rooms it gets explainable (see below) (Fig. 9).

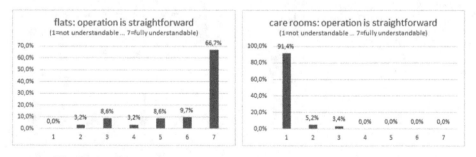

Fig. 9. Operation of the system flats alone (left) and care rooms alone (right)

The users of the flats fully understand the system how it works and what they have to do. The people in care are often suffering from dementia and could no more understand the technology. Therefor we have to address the care centres themselves since the care personnel see the system as very useful (see above). Here we have seen the need of a completely different marketing strategy. Thus, we have now developed different concepts with specific flyers and marketing material for the two different approaches (Fig. 10).

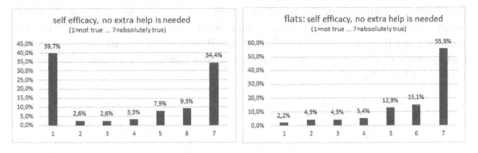

Fig. 10. Self efficacy of the system overall (left) and carer alone (right)

The same situation appeared when asking the end users if they can handle the system without outside help. Here 55.9% the end users of the flats absolutely agree and additional 15.1% fully and 12.9% slightly agree with it. Here, the objective of an "easy to use system, self-explanatory where no outside help is required" was vastly met (Fig. 11).

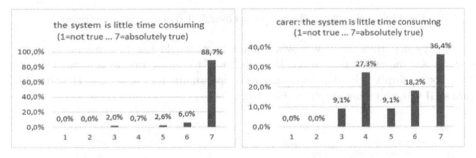

Fig. 11. Expenditure of time overall (left) and carer alone (right)

The end users have the opinion, that the system is very little time consuming (88.7%). For the care personnel a bit time is needed to control the state of the users every morning, but on the other hand, time is saved due to less inspection routines (Fig. 12).

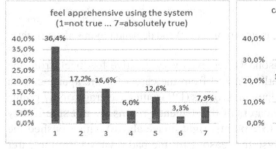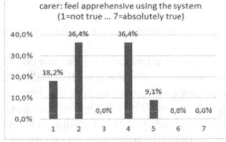

Fig. 12. Concern overall (left) and carer alone (right)

Another positive outcome of the evaluation had been, if the users feel apprehensive about using the system. Here answered more than half of the participants with "not true" or "almost not". Since the picture of the care personnel is a bit more skeptical, we asked further questions from the carer: the result is, that they are not afraid to use the system and make un-correctable mistakes, and also not feel intimidated/unsettled by the technology, but they are afraid that information will be lost through incorrect operation. Therefor we will have to put more emphasis on the graphical verification features to reduce their fears (Fig. 13).

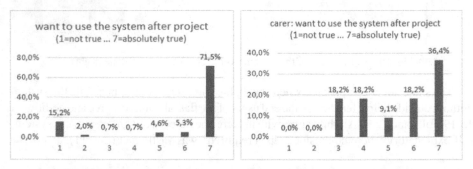

Fig. 13. Continued use after the project overall (left) and carer alone (right)

A very important result was whether the users would like to continue using the system after the end of the project. Here 71.5% of the users want to continue using it. Therefor we firmly believe in a strong market opportunity for our system. Here too, the care staff was a bit more skeptical (Fig. 14).

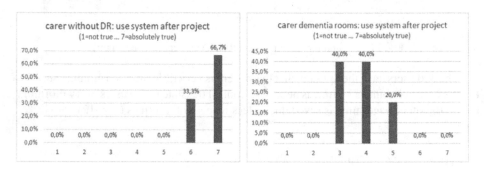

Fig. 14. Continued use carer without dementia rooms (left) and dementia rooms alone (right)

When we asked them for the reason, we received very positive feedback from the care personnel from Rodgau, Treuchtlingen and from the carers for the apartments in Weiter-stadt without the carer of the dementia rooms (DR) with an average of 6.7 points (see left image above). However, the carers of the dementia rooms are not sure if they want to use the system in the future (3.2 points, right image above) which pushed the average down. Here we have to analyse the reasons for the bad review form the carer of the dementia rooms. Also questionnaires with local KPIs have been collected in all three phases of the evaluation. Here, questions on requirements and functionality of the system have been addressed, e.g. if the users reject the system completely (Fig. 15):

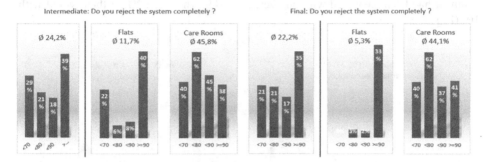

Fig. 15. Intermediate and Final evaluation: reject the system

The first prototype which was evaluated in the intermediate evaluation had been rejected by 24.2%. After the improvements of the system to get a higher accuracy, the rejection rate went down to 22.2%. A very positive result was that the rejection rate of residents at the apartments decreased strongly from 11.7% in the intermediate phase to 5.3% in the final evaluation (see below). Here especially the younger residents see the system very positive (0% rejection rate at the age of younger than 70). However, there is still the group of beyond 90 years where we and their relatives have to put on more emphasis to convince them. Thus, the reimplementation of the system had very positive effects for the acceptance. Our focus for marketing of the system should lay especially for people below 90 years living independently in own home.

Due to the high rejection rate of assisted persons in care rooms (44.1%) we have to address the care personnel instead of the people in need of help. Here, the care personal answered this question with 0% rejecting rate (see below LKPI Care Personnel Q2.4)! Here the objectives "reach an increased acceptance and low rejection rate by the end users" have been achieved in a very good manner.

OUR DS also made a marketing questionnaire in parallel to the final evaluation (Fig. 16).

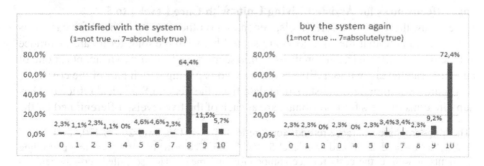

Fig. 16. Satisfaction with the system (left) and willingness to purchase (right)

In this context, we asked questions about the satisfaction with the system. In a range from 0 to 10 the end users answered this question with an average of 7.52 (64.4% of them with 8). Even better was the result of the question, if they want to buy the system again. It had been answered with an average of 8.91 (here, 72.4% of them voted with 10) (Fig. 17).

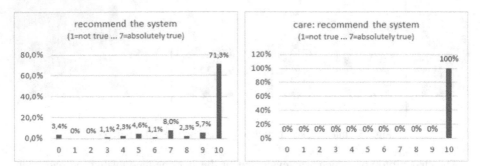

Fig. 17. Recommendation overall (left) and carer alone (right)

The recommendation of the system to others was rated with an average of 8.82 where 71.3% see it as absolutely recommendable (10). In the care sector, it even laid at 100% with 10. Consequently, the objective to "get a highly satisfaction, an increased level of approval for use and a high recommendation rate to other people" was very successfully fulfilled.

4.3 Cost Effectiveness

The WoQuaZ partnership planned from the beginning of ACTIVAGE to conclude the project with a marketable product. Therefore, it was necessary to compare the cost of our solution with the costs of the current traditional care systems. Without this data, it is difficult to approach potential customers, be it the relatives of the people in need of care or organizations, such as the German Red Cross or Johanniter, that operate assisted living sites, emergency call centres or care centres. This analysis is also very important to show the value for the public social system.

Cost Effectiveness for Assisted Living Units with Care Level 1 to 5
In Germany, there are five care levels, depending on the severity of need for care. It is also worth to note that the care costs are shared between the long-term care insurance and the persons affected[2]. The analysis in this section applies only to residents at one of these five care levels, without differentiating who is paying which part of the costs.

Figure 18 summarizes the statistical data from the Federal Statistical Office of Germany in terms of costs for traditional care at each of the five levels, differentiated by the

---

[2] The long-term care insurance refunds for care level 1 = € 125, level 2 = € 770, level 3 = € 1,262, level 4 = € 1,775 and care level 5 = € 2,005. The resident hat to bear any exceeding amounts as well as the costs for accommodation and meals. This so-called "co-payment" is usually between € 1,800 and € 2,600 per month, regardless of the care level. For economically weak people, the social system may take over the co-payment fully or partially.

care type. The chart on the left illustrates costs in EUR per person and day, and the table on the right lists the same costs in EUR per person and month. These numbers do not include the monthly allowance for room/flat and meals, so that the same living style with regard to, e.g., room size or specific eating habits are assumed throughout this analysis.

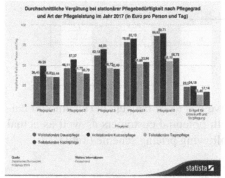

Alternative Service		Average monthly cost per user	
Level 5	Public Nursing Home (full-time permanent care)	2635 € (2017)	=86,62*365/12
	Public Nursing Home (full-time temporary care)	2728 € (2017)	=89,71*365/12
	Day Care Center (semi-stationary day care)	1679 € (2017)	=55,19*365/12
	Night Care Center (semi-stationary night care)	1786 € (2017)	=58,73*365/12
Level 4	Public Nursing Home (full-time permanent care)	2401 € (2017)	=78,95*365/12
	Public Nursing Home (full-time temporary care)	2528 € (2017)	=83,13*365/12
	Day Care Center (semi-stationary day care)	1571 € (2017)	=51,66*365/12
	Night Care Center (semi-stationary night care)	1641 € (2017)	=53,94*365/12
Level 3	Public Nursing Home (full-time permanent care)	1891 € (2017)	=62,18*365/12
	Public Nursing Home (full-time temporary care)	2129 € (2017)	=69,98*365/12
	Day Care Center (semi-stationary day care)	1421 € (2017)	=46,73*365/12
	Night Care Center (semi-stationary night care)	1384 € (2017)	=45,49*365/12
Level 2	Public Nursing Home (full-time permanent care)	1402 € (2017)	=46,11*365/12
	Public Nursing Home (full-time temporary care)	1745 € (2017)	=57,37*365/12
	Day Care Center (semi-stationary day care)	1269 € (2017)	=41,72*365/12
	Night Care Center (semi-stationary night care)	1210 € (2017)	=39,79*365/12
Level 1	Public Nursing Home (full-time permanent care)	1107 € (2017)	=36,41*365/12
	Public Nursing Home (full-time temporary care)	1502 € (2017)	=49,39*365/12
	Day Care Center (semi-stationary day care)	1090 € (2017)	=35,83*365/12
	Night Care Center (semi-stationary night care)	1078 € (2017)	=35,44*365/12
Costs Formal caregiver (everage costs employer gros		2568 € (Weiterstadt)	

Fig. 18. Statistical data: average daily costs for traditional care

This analysis uses the numbers in Fig. 18 for nursing homes as the only reference, because there is no similar statistics for other sectors, such as the supervised living sector. There are also further costs, such as facility management, cooking, cleaning and other costs, that could not be taken into consideration. Therefore, the analysis is done with approximation and contains uncertainties in the calculation.

Despite the above inaccuracy, the actual care-related costs in the WoQuaZ pilots for people at care level 2 in the baseline (I.e., before starting to use any assistance system) come relatively close to the related numbers in Fig. 18. The higher the care level, the greater the deviation is among the actual versus the reference numbers.

Apart from the doubt, whether someone with care level 1 or 2 really has to go to a nursing home at all, our analysis shows that economically, it is clearly more beneficial when people below level 3 use uLive and with that continue living in own homes, instead of changing to a nursing home.

The remaining of this section focuses therefore on data for **care level 2 with reference costs per month and elderly person for traditional care in a nursing home amounting to € 1,402.** The study presented here compares this reference cost with the care costs for a similar person living independently in our pilot in Weiterstadt. The first element for calculating the care costs in the assisted living units in this pilot building is the difference of the amount of monthly rent paid in the pilot compared to similar homes in the same town. In average, the apartments in our pilot are ca. € 100 more expensive; in case of the care rooms, this difference is € 50. The difference is mostly linked with characteristics, such as barrier-free building and costs for two lifts.

The next element to consider is the **gross employee costs of 2568 € for one care person in Weiterstadt** (this is the average costs for carers of the Federal Statistical Office of Germany). Considering that one experienced caregiver can in average look after 15 people at care level 2 who use our assistance system, this type of costs can be estimated at € 171.20 per inhabitant per month (Table 1):

Table 1. Direct monthly caregiving costs per end user, depending on the number of inhabitants one caregiver can look after

Level 5: 1 experienced Care person per 5 elderly	513,60 €	=2568/5
Level 4: 1 experienced Care person per 7 elderly	366,86 €	=2568/7
Level 3: 1 experienced Care person per 10 elderly	256,80 €	=2568/10
Level 2: 1 experienced Care person per 15 elderly	171,20 €	=2568/15
Level 1: 1 experienced Care person per 30 elderly	85,60 €	=2568/30

As the last element, the direct costs of uLive has to be budgeted. The amount calculated here is based on price negotiations with potential customers as well as actual signed contracts achieved so far, namely the following pricing scheme (Table 2):

Table 2. uLive pricing per unit, depending on number of ordered units, also per month

For the purchase we have a graduation depending on the number of systems ordered (net price):	Tax	SUM	Return of invest after 48 months
for 10 to 25 systems for 4,000 euros per system	760,00 €	4.760,00 €	99,17 €
for 26 to 50 systems for 3,000 euros per system	570,00 €	3.570,00 €	74,38 €
for 50 to 100 systems for 2,500 euros per system	475,00 €	2.975,00 €	61,98 €
for more than 100 systems for 2,000 euros per system	380,00 €	2.380,00 €	49,58 €

In average, the potential customers are interested in around 20–25 units. For such a contract the costs for one system would be 4.760 € including tax. We are calculating a return of invest after 48 months which brings us to € 99.17 on a monthly basis. Since the system includes one alarm server per building for € 2,500, with the same return of invest after 48 months, we must also budget € 2.60 per month and unit (2500 €/48 months/20 units). Finally, we end up with a monthly system costs per unit amounting to € 111.77 after adding costs for 1st, 2nd and 3rd level support (Table 3):

Table 3. Resulted total costs per unit and month for enabling independent living in Weiterstadt

Cost item	Operative
Service infrastructure costs (leasing monthly)	99,17 €
Alarm server cost	2,60 €
1st level support	3,00 €
2nd level support	3,00 €
3rd level support	4,00 €
SUM (montly rate)	111,77 €
Level 2: --> 1 experienced Care person per 15 elderly	171,20 €
Additional costs for barrier-free in comparison to rent	100,00 €
In Total per months and unit	382,97 €

Together with the costs for the carer and the additional costs of the barrier-free flats, the total care costs for independent living in own homes with uLive help will be €

382.97 per month and unit at this pilot in Weiterstadt. Compared to the € 1,402 costs for traditional care at level two, this results in € 1,019.03 or 72.68% saving per month and unit.

Table 4 shows the savings for all the five care levels in analogy, while reminding the uncertainties in the calculation, namely (1) missing statistical information for the additional costs, and (2) validity only for residents with one of the five care levels. In addition, uLive offers a much faster response time than the traditional care and in consequence, it offers a higher personal safety level and an increase in the quality of life. Therefore, the piloted solution is of very high personal benefit for those affected and at the same time offers considerable benefit for the society. In every emergency situation, every minute is important until help really comes, as the state of health worsens with every minute. uLive, on the other hand, gives an alarm message very quickly, so that deterioration can usually be prevented and you can quickly return to your previous state of health. This is also shown by the experiences in Weiterstadt and Rodgau (our other ACTIVAGE pilot) in different emergency situations. On the other hand, if help comes late, this can lead to death or lead to an increase in the care level due to deterioration in health. Therefore, depending on how many care levels would have been increased without uLive, additional costs arise from the change to other care levels (Table 5):

Table 4. uLive saving potential for each care level

	Comparison full-time permanent care traditional and the uCore system				
Care level	uLive usage costs	Pilot solution (additional 111,77 + 100)	Tradititionl Care	Cost savings €	Cost savings %
Level 5	513,60 €	725,37 €	2.635,00 €	1.909,63 €	72,47%
Level 4	366,86 €	578,62 €	2.401,00 €	1.822,38 €	75,90%
Level 3	256,80 €	468,57 €	1.891,00 €	1.422,43 €	75,22%
Level 2	171,20 €	382,97 €	1.402,00 €	1.019,03 €	72,68%
Level 1	85,60 €	297,37 €	1.107,00 €	809,63 €	73,14%

Table 5. Additional cost savings by changes in care levels

	Pilot	traditional	Savings by change in care levels					
Level 5	725,37 €	2.635,00 €	2.523,23 €	2.337,63 €	2.252,03 €	2.166,43 €	2.056,38 €	1.909,63 €
Level 4	578,62 €	2.401,00 €	2.289,23 €	2.103,63 €	2.018,03 €	1.932,43 €	1.822,38 €	
Level 3	468,57 €	1.891,00 €	1.779,23 €	1.593,63 €	1.508,03 €	1.422,43 €		
Level 2	382,97 €	1.402,00 €	1.290,23 €	1.104,63 €	1.019,03 €			
Level 1	297,37 €	1.107,00 €	995,23 €	809,63 €				
Level 0	111,77 €	---	- €					
			Level 0	Level 1	Level 2	Level 3	Level 4	Level 5

· Example: if without uLive the state of health worsens to such an extent that the care level would increase from care level 2 to care level 4, the monthly savings with uLive due to preventing such dramatic change would additionally increase by € 999 for the difference of traditional care costs between the assumed two levels. On top of this, there will be a high benefit in the quality of life for both caregivers and subjects of care.

We believe that a more comprehensive cost effectiveness study based on full comparative data could provide a more profound evidence of cost savings as one of the means for boosting the uptake of smart living solutions for ageing well. Policy makers should consider that only a joint research project could tackle such complicated study.

5 Conclusion

The evaluation and the analysis performed within ACTIVAGE enabled WoQuaZ to improve its prototype, reach a high readiness level with uLive and bring an evidence of usefulness and effectiveness both on the side of cost savings and on the side of the improvement of the QoL: older citizens feel safer at home and caregivers can do their job with less stress and with a higher quality. After having been able to conclude the project successfully and reach the goal of preparing a product pathway, the WoQuaZ partnership plans to place the results as product onto the market within 2021, together with its specific variant tailored to the work processes at care centres, named uCare. Both lines, uLive and uCare brings the realms of building technology, IP telephony, and the general IoT together. By using the telephony system as the main user interface, existing resources such as emergency call centres and alarm servers can continue to be operated as usual. Despite the complexity resulted from such vast integration of different worlds, uLive remains true to the protection of user privacy: By local data storage and processing within the living unit, uLive avoids uncontrolled data transfer and limits communication with external entities to audio messages via IP telephony, unless the system is explicitly configured differently by the data owner.

With support for an increasing number of the most important device networking and communication protocols and for a large set of component types, uLive enables a flexible interplay of sensors and devices from different vendors and remains openly extensible at both levels of integration and orchestration even after deployment. In addition to privacy protection and system openness [11], uLive include (1) real-time data analysis towards on-the-fly recognition of situations of interest and automatic reaction to them in an adaptive way at both levels of recognition and reaction, and (2) minimizing false positives by verifying emergency situations with the inhabitants before going to the alarm chain.

Nevertheless, thanks to the evidences resulted from the evaluation process in ACTIVAGE, uLive has become an applicable innovation with a clear business chance and plan. This has brought us in a close contact with new clients, such as a service provider in Bavaria with planned installations for 100 users and a framework agreement for 1000 users in discussion, a city in the Rhein-Main area with a signed contract for 18 apartments and 132 further flats in negotiation, as well as a town in the same area negotiating the equipment of 5 blocks with at least 40 apartments. Our goal is to improve the quality of life for as many people as possible

References

1. ACTIVAGE project webpage. http://activageproject.eu/
2. IoT Large-Scale Pilots Programme. https://european-iot-pilots.eu/
3. Climax Technology Co., Ltd. https://climax-deutschland.com
4. Dosch & Amand Products GmbH. https://www.da-products.de/

5. easierLife webpage. https://www.easierlife.de/
6. ahs.digital webpage. https://ahs.digital/
7. OpenHAB webpage. https://www.openhab.org/
8. ReAAL project webpage. https://cordis.europa.eu/project/id/325189
9. Fico, G., et al: Tools and processes for the implementation of the evaluation methodology. ACTIVAGE project deliverable D6.2, October 2017 (2017)
10. ACTIVAGE evidence at https://evidence.activage.lst.tfo.upm.es/global-results/
11. Open systems definition at https://www.universaal.info/blog/post/3487/

Learning and Culture in Intelligent Environments

Technology Probes to Explore How Children Learn About Gender Stereotypes

Weilin Jiang[1]([⊠]), Yujie Su[1], Shijia Liu[2], Fangtian Ying[3], and Cheng Yao[1]

[1] College of Software Technology, Zhejiang University, Hangzhou, China
{21951221,21951229,yaoch}@zju.edu.cn
[2] College of Insurance, Central University of Finance and Economics, Beijing, China
[3] College of Design, Hubei University of Technology, Hubei, China

Abstract. There are widespread gender stereotypes in society that would influence children's physical and mental cognitive development and future career choices. Gender equality education for children is critical. However, few studies have explored how technology can be used to promote gender equality education and developed educational tools to help children learning gender equality. To explore the HCI form of learning gender stereotypes for children in early adolescence, this paper introduced three technology probes to test with children and drew several conclusions.

Keywords: Gender stereotypes · Gender equality · Digital technology and gender · Technology in education

1 Introduction

In recent years, although some achievements have been made in the development of gender equality, there are still many challenges. Some laws and social norms of gender discrimination and gender stereotypes still exist in society, which might have negative impacts on children. Gender stereotypes are widely held beliefs about the characteristics and behavior of women and men [1]. Children's perception of gender is more or less affected by the widespread stereotypes of gender in society. Without proper education and guidance, their gender stereotypes would lead to distortion of gender values and become the shackles of thought. We can find the negative effects of gender stereotypes on children from past research. Cimpian et al. pointed out that gender through stereotypes would affect children's perception of themselves and aspiration of future career [2]. Aina and Cameron argued that young children's negative stereotype would influence their self-esteem and future career path [3]. Moreover, children would grow up one day and their cognition of gender would finally influence the social balance of gender equality.

In the field of HCI, many studies focus on finding children's gender bias and solving gender disparity in a certain discipline. While few studies developed educational tools and explored how technology can be used to promote gender equality awareness education. Our purpose is to explore the educational techniques that could efficiently

© Springer Nature Switzerland AG 2021
N. Streitz and S. Konomi (Eds.): HCII 2021, LNCS 12782, pp. 213–223, 2021.
https://doi.org/10.1007/978-3-030-77015-0_15

make children aware of the existence of gender stereotypes and then establish positive attitudes and values toward gender.

In this study, we chose gender roles as an important component of the content of gender equality education. Through gender-role education, we inspired children to be aware of the existence of gender stereotypes. To explore interactive forms that correspond to educational content, we designed three technology probes to guide children to guess the gender of characters, watch videos of celebrities who behaved in ways that break gender stereotypes, create their gender roles, and then self-expression to convey their ideas on gender equality and gender stereotypes. After the experiments of these probes, we drew several conclusions and technical suggestions on the development of HCI educational tools for children.

2 Related Work

2.1 Social Psychological Theories

According to gender schema theory [4] and social cognitive theory [5], children's cognitive development combined with social influences greatly affects the thinking mode that determines the characteristics of "male" and "female".

Social learning theory [6] points out that the social environment has a great influence on shaping and strengthening learners' gender roles. For example, learners can observe and imitate the role models around them to form an understanding of gender [7]. And Bandura [8] indicated that these role models that influence learners include those in family, school, peer, book, and media.

The knowledge of gender stereotypes about personal-social attributes appears around the age of 5 and grows steadily throughout childhood [9]. Huston [10], largely based on a review of studies that allowed children to classify items as equally suitable for both sexes, concluded that after about 7 years old, children's knowledge of stereotypes continued to increase, but their rigid acceptance of stereotypes that were fixed or morally correct begins to decline. Newly acquired knowledge on gender issues is fixed in a rigid either-or way and reach the most rigid level in 5–7 years.

However, early adolescence is related to gender intensification [11]. At this age, long-term gender bias will have a far-reaching impact on children [12]. Rubegni et al. pointed out this period is a key window, during which it is necessary to encourage children to think about gender-related issues [13]. Therefore, this study chooses children aged 10–11 as the target and explores how to arouse them to realize the existence of gender stereotypes.

Most existing related studies are based on gender binary [13]. And for practicality, this study adopts the same theory to interpret gender, which will be improved on this basis in the future.

2.2 HCI Studies

At present, gender equality research in the field of HCI is mainly divided into two types. One centers on the use of HCI means to dig out children's own gender bias.

Rubegni et al. [13] mainly focus on children's gender bias exposed in Digital Storytelling (DST) and intend to detect these gender stereotypes, they have established a set of methodology with five lenses. By analyzing the digital stories created by children, they can understand children's ideas with each lens revealing different aspects. Subsequently, Rubegni et al. conducted three workshops to explore how DST could support children in their awareness of negative gender stereotypes, and then put forward nine concepts to guide the design of a DST tool [14]. Besides, Jamal et al. developed interactive tangible tools for children aged 7–9, which integrated storytelling into board games, elicited children's sociological mindset in the process of storytelling, and assessed their hidden socio-economic and gender bias level [15].

The other focuses on finding and solving the gender disparity in a certain discipline through HCI tools. Carnegie Mellon University's Alice (www.Alice.org) [16] is used by teachers at all levels from middle schools (and sometimes even younger) to universities, in school classrooms and in after school and out of school programming, and in subjects ranging from visual arts and language arts to the fundamentals of programming and introduction to java courses. Invent-abling [17] is a girl-centered design toolkit for children aged 5–15. With a variety of smart materials and electronic components for interactive craft projects, the toolkit is aimed to promote creativity and freethinking and solve gender inequality in STEM learning tools by exploring how aesthetics, materials, applications, and learning styles impact girls' engagement with educational materials. In the Bots for Tots project [18], researchers encouraged children from different communities to use high-tech tools and technologies to make toys for young children in their schools. And interviews with girls participating in the project show how these girls' low self-perceptions of competencies with technology do not match their actual high capabilities.

However, most related work is devoted to finding the gender equality problems that are unfavorable to children in the HCI field, and few tools are designed directly to help children complete gender equality education. Therefore, from the perspective of education and awareness, we designed technology probes to help children realize gender stereotypes and cultivate gender equality values.

3 Technology Probes

In this study, we do experiments with the method of technology probes [19]. Hutchinson et al. introduced technology probes as a method for use in the process of codesigning technologies with users [19]. We designed technology probes to explore which techniques are more appropriate to use, and do not consider them prototypes for our future system.

To explore the interaction forms in different educational themes of gender stereotypes, we created three technology probes. The content of the probes is based on *A guide to gender equality education in primary and secondary schools* [20], including "Gender roles perception", "Gender equality celebrities cases", "Gender role creation" and "Self-story expression". These technology probes also detected children's learning interest, efficiency, and outcomes when using different media. We chose an iPad as our primary digital interaction medium and explored the possibility of combining physical and digital interfaces.

One ethics teacher was invited and six children aged 10–11 years in early adolescence were selected and grouped to participate in our experiments. We recorded the experimental results through questionnaires and semi-structured interviews (Table 1).

Table 1. Breakdown of themes, choice of mediums, and participants for Probes 1, 2, and 3.

	Probe 1	Probe 2	Probe 3
Theme	Gender roles perception	Gender equality celebrities cases	Gender role creation & Self-story expression
Choice of medium(s)	iPad vs Human voice + notes	iPad(AR) + Double-sided stand-up vs Digital screen only	iPad + Apple Pencil vs iPad (AR) + Card painting
Participants	Group 1 2 female & 1 males Group 2 1 female & 2 males	Group 1 2 female & 1 males Group 2 1 female & 2 males	Group 1 2 female & 1 males Group 2 1 female & 2 males

3.1 Probe 1: Gender Roles Perception Based on Interest Patterns and Personality Labels vs Notes

To be aware of gender stereotypes, it is important to understand "gender role" first. In this experiment we made children perceive gender roles by describing the personalities and interests of the characters.

As shown in Fig. 1 (Top left & Top right), Group 1 used an iPad as the interactive medium, in which the software application announced several characters' stories by digital voice. After each story, children were asked to select the interest patterns and personality labels of the character according to the content of the announcement, and finally discuss to guess the gender of the character. These interest patterns and personality labels are based on our study on the interests and personalities of children aged 10–11 years.

The interaction media for Group 2 were the human voice and sticky notes. The character stories were narrated by the ethics teacher. After listening to each story, each child was asked to write down the character's interests and personalities on a sticky note. Finally, children were asked to guess the gender of the character and post their notes in the appropriate area of the whiteboard.

Results

- Children in both groups guessed the gender of the characters exactly the same.
- The choice of the personalities of the characters between children in both groups differed somewhat but were generally the same.
- Group 1 (Digital group) finished earlier than Group 2 (Paper group).

Fig. 1. (Top left) Interest patterns selection. (Top right) Personality labels selection. (Bottom left) The teacher reads the story and the children write the cards. (Bottom left) The result of gender selection.

- In the semi-structured interview, A boy in Group 1 said, "The patterns and labels helped me summarize the characteristics of the person more quickly and left a strong impression in my mind." When asked why she guessed a character's gender to be female, a 10-year-old girl in Group 2 said, "Because this person likes pink, she must be a girl."

3.2 Probe 2: Celebrities Video Cases Through AR Double-Sided Stand-Up vs Screen Only

After children were aware of the existence of gender stereotypes, we need to use cases of gender-equitable celebrities to guide them towards equality values.

Group 1 used an iPad to scan AR double-sided stand-up to identify the video messages. As is shown in Fig. 2 (The first and second picture), the children were given a double-sided stand-up sign of the same shape, with "male" on one side and "female" on the other. Then they were asked to choose an interest pattern sticker and put it on each side of the sign. For example, in the case of the basketball player, one side of the stand-up sign was a male character with a "basketball" interest pattern, and the other side was a female character with the same "basketball" pattern. Children scanned the male side of the stand-up sign through our iPad application to see the male basketball player case. After watching the male case, children were asked to reverse the side of the sign, and scan it to watch the female basketball player case on the flip side. The aim was to explore whether the children could have a deeper understanding and reflection on gender stereotypes through the process of gender transposition.

Fig. 2. The process of using iPad scanning AR double-sided stand-ups to watch a video.

While the children in Group 2 only watch the celebrities' video cases on a digital screen without the process of AR scanning the two sides of the stand-up sign.

Results

- AR technology was very appealing to children and they were interested to interact in this way.
- The children in Group 1 (AR group) were prompted to think differently by the inter-action with the double-sided stand-up, and all of them talked about "gender disparity" or "stereotypes" in the semi-structured interview.
- In Group 2 (Screen group), only one girl mentioned "gender disparity", while the other two children understood the video as "following your heart and chasing your dream".

3.3   Probe 3: Digital Painting and Story Expression vs Card Painting and AR Performance

To explore the impact of gender stereotypes on self-awareness and perception, each child needs to create their own character image and self-express. Probe 3 aims to explore which technique can better help children show themselves while triggering their interest.

As is shown in Fig. 3, during the character creation stage, children in Group 1 were arranged to use the apple pencil to design and paint their own character in the specified area of the iPad software interface, and then to score the personality attributes (ranging from 1–5). The attributes include Courage, Intelligence, Beauty, Consideration, Honesty (All these terms are translated from Chinese). In the self-expression stage, children were asked to select a scene from a library of environmental scenes, and see the keywords provided in the scene and tell a story based on the keywords. The sequence and manner of interaction: select the created character to place it in the scene; drag the character during storytelling to adjust his/her position in the scene; click the record button to record the character's lines; adjust the voice tone after recording. The interaction method for adjusting the tone: long press on the speech bubble to slide up to raise the tone; long press on the speech bubble to slide down to lower the tone.

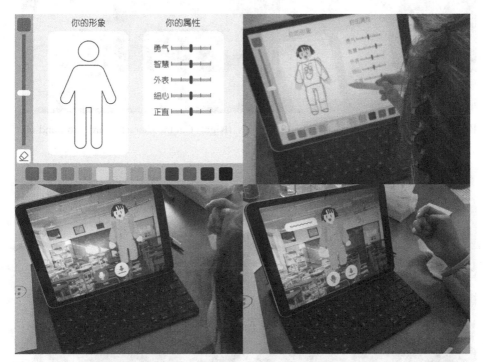

Fig. 3. (Top left) Self-character setting UI interface. (Top right) Paint the character with an Apple pencil. (Bottom left) The created character in the selected scene. (Bottom left) Adjust the tone of the recording.

In the experiment of Group 2, during the card painting stage, children were arranged to design their own character on white cardboard and subsequently cut it into stand-up as is shown in Fig. 4. Meanwhile, set the attribute values of the character attribute table with the same content as Group 1.

In the performance stage, children were asked to select a scene card from the scene card set, scan it using an iPad and see the scene keywords, and then insert the stand-up card in front of the scene card. As is shown in Fig. 5, After our AR software on iPad recognized the character stand-up, children could click on the button to record the character's lines, also could adjust the tone of the voice. In this interaction mode, children have to manually adjust the position of the character in the physical world.

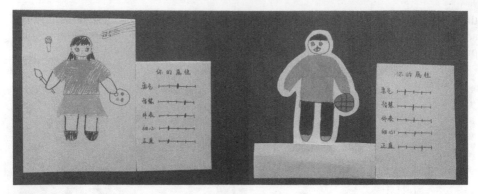

Fig. 4. (Left) Card painting & Attributes Settings. (Right) Cut the character card into stand-up.

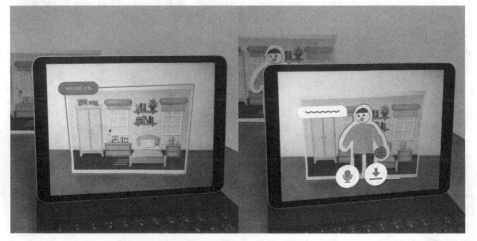

Fig. 5. (Left) Scan the scene card and see the keyword(s). (Right) Put the character in the scene and record voice to perform.

Results

- Digital painting and paper painting appeal to children to about the same degree.
- The interactive mode of combining physical and digital interactions was appealing to children, with one girl in Group 2 saying, "It's like making a movie when I move my character in front of the iPad's camera and record my voice."
- Keyword guidance and step-by-step guidance were important for inspiring children to express themselves. One boy in Group 2 stated, "I'm not good at expressing myself, but with this step-by-step manipulation, I was able to say it."
- The result of the character attribute settings revealed a different trend in boys and girls. For example, the value of the attribute "Appearance" was set higher by girls than boys, and the value of the attribute "Courage" was set higher by boys than girls.

4 Discussion and Future Work

In this study, three technology probes were designed to explore which techniques and interactions can better help children in early adolescence to learn "gender stereotypes". Group experiments were conducted across the three technology probes, and comparative experiments revealed that different techniques and interactions appealed to children differently and led to different learning outcomes and efficiencies.

4.1 Findings from Probe 1 (Gender Roles Perception)

- Gender stereotypes are already common among children in their early adolescence.
- The digital user interface is more attractive to children and helps them complete the task more efficiently.
- With the help of the interest patterns and personality labels, children can develop a more tangible perception of gender role after being told the character's gender.
- The Voice + Card interaction mode better facilitates gender discussions among children.

4.2 Findings from Probe 2 (Gender Equality Celebrities Cases)

- The double-sided stand-up sign allows children to think more visually about male and female transposition.
- The double-sided stand-up sign is better for children's understanding of video content.
- Children can have a deeper understanding and reflection on gender stereotypes through the process of gender transposition.

4.3 Findings from Probe 3 (Gender Role Creation and Self-story Expression)

- The combination of the physical and digital interactive interface is most attractive to children.
- Keywords based on the character's personality and the environment the character is in can help children express themselves well.

Based on the results of the three probes, we get good feedback based on gender role interaction education. We concluded that the combination of physical and digital interaction form is more engaging for children to learn gender stereotypes. Meanwhile, in Probe 3 a child mentioned that the AR interaction interface is like making a movie, which gives us a good inspiration. In the future, we intend to develop an HCI tool for gender equality education based on these findings.

5 Conclusion

The contribution of this study is the design of three technology probes to explore which techniques and interactions can better help children in early adolescence to learn about gender stereotypes. This paper describes the details of the three technology probes, presents the results of group experiments with the probes, and draws several conclusions about children's learning of gender stereotypes. The results show that visualization and labeling of gender roles can help children to improve their knowledge of gender stereotypes when learning. At the same time, the combination of physical and digital interaction is more appealing to children when learning gender stereotypes.

Acknowledgment. This research was funded by the Engineering Research Center of Computer Aided Product Innovation Design, Ministry of Education, National Natural Science Foundation of China (52075478), Major Project of Zhejiang Social Science Foundation (21XXJC01ZD).

References

1. Manstead, A.S.R., Hewstone, M.: The Blackwell Encyclopedia of Social Psychology, 1st edn. Blackwell, Oxford/Cambridge (1995)
2. Cimpian, A., Mu, Y., Erickson, L.C.: Who is good at this game? Linking an activity to a social category undermines children's achievement. Psychol. Sci. **23**(5), 533–541 (2012)
3. Aina, O.E., Cameron, P.A.: Why does gender matter? Counteracting stereotypes with young children. Dimens. Early Child. **39**, 11–20 (2011)
4. Liben, L.S., Bigler, R.S., Ruble, D.N., Martin, C.L., Powlishta, K.K.: The developmental course of gender differentiation: conceptualizing, measuring, and evaluating constructs and pathways. Monogr. Soc. Res. Child Dev. **67**(2), i–183 (2002)
5. Bandura, A.: Social cognitive theory. In: Vasta, R. (ed.) Annals of Child Development: Annals of child development, vol. 6, pp. 1–60. JAI, Greenwich (1989)
6. Bussey, K., Bandura, A.: Social cognitive theory of gender development and functioning. In: The Psychology of Gender, pp. 92–119 (2004)
7. Mischel, W.: A social-learning view of sex differences in behavior. In: Maccoby, E.E. (ed.) The Development of Sex Differences, pp. 56–81. Stanford University Press, Stanford (1966)
8. Bandura, A.: Social foundations of thought and action: a social cognitive theory. J. Appl. Psychol. **12**(1), 169 (1986)
9. Martin, C.L., Ruble, D.: Children's search for gender cues. Curr. Dir. Psychol. Sci. **13**(2), 67–70 (2016)
10. Huston, A.C.: Sex-typing. In: Hetherington, E.M. (ed.) Handbook of Child Psychology: Socialization, Personality, and Social Development, vol. 4, pp. 387–467. Wiley, New York (1983)
11. Galambos, N.L., Almeida, D.M., Petersen, A.C.: Masculinity, femininity, and sex role attitudes in early adolescence: exploring gender intensification. Child Dev. **61**(6), 1905–1914 (1990)
12. Carlson, E.A., Sroufe, L.A., Egeland, B.: The construction of experience: a longitudinal study of representation and behavior. Child Dev. **75**(1), 66–83 (2004)
13. Rubegni, E., Landoni, M., De Angeli, A., Jaccheri, L.: Detecting gender stereotypes in children digital storytelling. In: Proceedings of the 18th ACM International Conference on Interaction Design and Children, pp. 386–393. Association for Computing Machinery, New York (2019)
14. Rubegni, E., Landoni, M., Jaccheri, L.: Design for change with and for children: how to design digital StoryTelling tool to raise stereotypes awareness. In: Proceedings of the 2020 ACM Designing Interactive Systems Conference, pp. 505–518. Association for Computing Machinery, New York (2020)

15. Jamal, S., Zaidi, M., Shahid, S., Kitchlew, M.: Eliciting social biases in children using tangible games. In: Proceedings of the 17th ACM Conference on Interaction Design and Children, pp. 632–637. Association for Computing Machinery, New York (2018)
16. Alice Homepage. http://www.Alice.org. Accessed 17 Nov 2021
17. Guler, S., Rule, M.: Invent-abling: enabling inventiveness through craft, pp. 368–371. Association for Computing Machinery, New York (2013)
18. Thanapornsangsuth, S., Holbert, N.: Bots for tots: girls' perceived versus actual competency in technology and making. In: Proceedings of the 2017 Conference on Interaction Design and Children, pp. 458–465. Association for Computing Machinery, New York (2017)
19. Hutchinson, H., et al.: Technology probes: inspiring design for and with families. In: Proceedings of the SIGCHI Conference on Human Factors in Computing Systems, CHI 2003, pp. 17–24. Association for Computing Machinery, New York (2003)
20. Feng, J.: A Guide to Gender Equality Education in Primary and Secondary Schools, 1st edn. South China University of Technology Press, Guangzhou (2015)

Collectively Sharing Human Hearing in Artful CollectiveEars

Risa Kimura$^{(\boxtimes)}$ and Tatsuo Nakajima

Department of Computer Science and Engineering, Waseda University, Tokyo, Japan
{r.kimura,tatsuo}@dcl.cs.waseda.ac.jp

Abstract. Our world is filled with a variety of beautiful and artistic sounds, and we consciously or unconsciously hear the sounds in our everyday lives. We are hearing the songs of birds, the sounds of bells and so on every moment in the places where we are. These sounds may influence our daily attitude and behavior, but it is hard to imagine the effects of the sounds that other people are hearing if those sounds become available for us anytime and anywhere. This study has developed Artful CollectiveEars which is a digital platform to share collective human hearing. This paper explores the opportunities and pitfalls of Artful CollectiveEars.

Keywords: Sharing collective human hearing · Head gesture · Sharing economy · 3D sound · Artful sound listening · Artful experience

1 Introduction

Our lives have changed dramatically with the recent popularization of a variety of smart devices. The smart devices have powerful computational capabilities and allow easy access to a variety of information in the world. In the near future, we will see the wearable smart devices such as smart glasses [13] and smart earphones [14]. Such wearable smart devices should be able to gather information around us more easily. Having access to the sight and hearing of others will allow you to be flexible in your thinking and think more deeply.

Our world is filled with a variety of beautiful sounds, both natural and artificial, and we consciously or unconsciously hear the sounds in our everyday lives. We are hearing the songs of birds, the sounds of bells and so on every moment in the places where we are. If the beautiful sounds are easily available anytime anywhere through the wearable smart devices, our daily lives are becoming more mindful and calm. Also, these sounds stimulate our artistic senses to explore the philosophic foundations in our daily lives.

In this paper, we propose Artful CollectiveEars which is a digital platform that allows human hearing to be shared more easily. The platform is based on smart earbuds and provides an experience where a user can make others' hearing his/her own. The digital platform enables us to listen to what people are currently hearing, allowing us to enhance our imagination about our world.

The remainder of this paper presents an overview of the Artful CollectiveEars platform and shows several interactive methods to present and navigate the sounds that are

© Springer Nature Switzerland AG 2021
N. Streitz and S. Konomi (Eds.): HCII 2021, LNCS 12782, pp. 224–234, 2021.
https://doi.org/10.1007/978-3-030-77015-0_16

heard by other people in a user's personal listening space. Then, we show an experiment that was conducted to explore some opportunities and pitfalls to share people's hearing.

2 Artful CollectiveEars

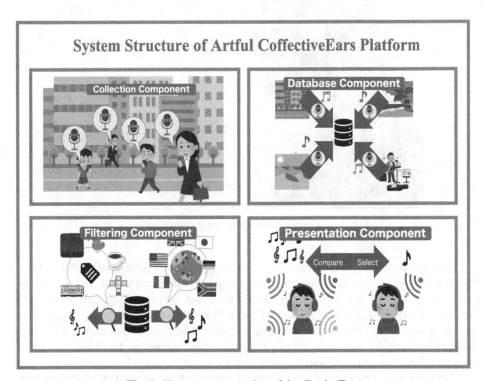

Fig. 1. Four components in artful collectiveEars

The current Artful CollectiveEars consists of the following four components as shown in Fig. 1. The first component is Collection Component (CC). It collects the heard sounds captured through people's hearing capabilities around the world. The current component assumes that the people use wearable microphones such as the eSense device [2] to share their hearing. The second component is Database Component (DC). It stores all hearing sounds gathered in Collection Component. The third component is Filtering Component (FC). It selects the stored sounds from the shared database based on the selected theme channel. The last component is Presentation Component (PC). It shows multiple sounds selected by the theme channel.

We adopt Unity to present multiple sounds in a user's 3D listening space. An end-user of the Artful CollectiveEars wears a headphone equipped with the Nintendo JoyCon device [10], as shown in Fig. 2. The device contains an acceleration sensor for detecting the user's head gesture and transmits the sensor data through Bluetooth.

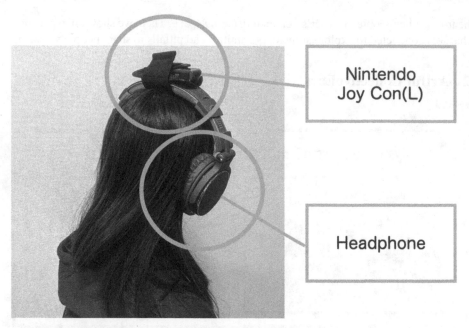

Fig. 2. Listening to sounds in artful collectiveEars

The purpose of the current research is to investigate the feasibility of Artful CollectiveEars in which we would like to present the opportunities and pitfalls in terms of an end-user's point of view. Artful CollectiveEars focuses on presenting multiple sounds that directly offer a user experience to end-users. However, we do not focus on gathering and recording a large number of collective human hearing in the current Artful CollectiveEars because the current research's focus is to investigate the feasibility of Artful CollectiveEars from the end-user's point of view.

The following subsections focus on Artful CollectiveEars's main three characteristics that are essential for the end-user experience when using Artful CollectiveEars.

2.1 Multiple Sounds Presentation in a 3D Space

Artful CollectiveEars offers a novel method to present multiple sounds. The method is called as the spatial presentation method. In the spatial presentation method, sound sources are placed around a user, and multiple sounds are presented simultaneously. Here, we used the Unity's 3D sound function and prepared one Listener object as a user's listening position and multiple Audio Source objects as each sound source. All Audio Source objects were placed equidistant from the Listener object so that all sound sources could be heard at about the same size by the Listener object. Figure 3 shows the arrangement for the eight sound sources in Artful CollectiveEars. In the figure, the Listener object at the listening position is represented by a square, and the Audio Source object at the sound source is represented by a circle.

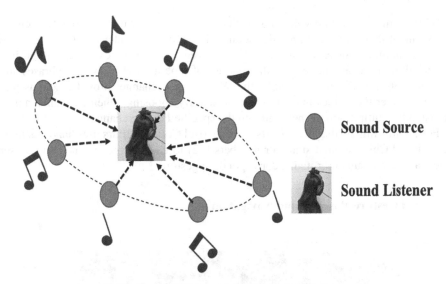

Fig. 3. Spatially presenting multiple sounds

2.2 Theme Channel Abstraction for Choosing Sounds

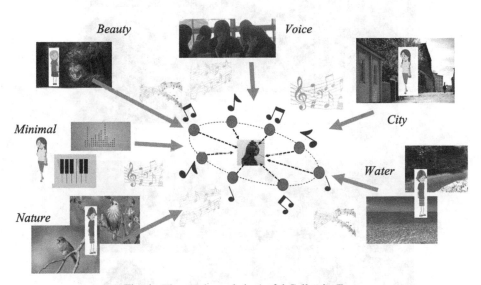

Fig. 4. Theme channels in Artful CollectiveEars

A user specifies a theme channel to choose multiple sounds that are presented around the user, such as selecting a TV channel from the stored sounds in the database. Artful CollectiveEars that offers six theme channels as shown in Fig. 4. The Beauty theme channel provides sounds that people feel that the sounds are beautiful. The Voice theme channel provides sounds that people feel that the sounds include people's conversation. The Nature theme channel provides sounds that people consider the sounds in the nature.

The City theme channel provides sounds that people consider that the sounds in cities. The Minimal theme channel provides sounds that people consider that the sounds are similar to minimal music, which is a musical movement based on extremely simplified, prolonged, rhythms and patterns with great use of repetition of individual phrases and avoidance of embellishment. Finally, the Water theme channel provides sounds that people consider the sounds in the river or the sea. By choosing a theme channel, a user can listen to multiple sounds belonging to the specified theme channel.

For identifying the theme channels easily, Artful CollectiveEars uses hand gestures. We assigned Chinese hand signs for numbers [12] to each theme channel, and a user selects a theme channel through a corresponding gesture.

2.3 Head Gesture-Based Sound Navigation

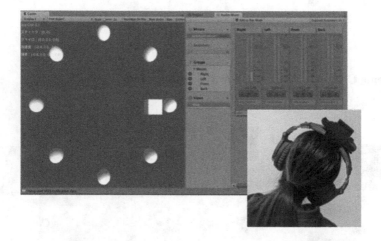

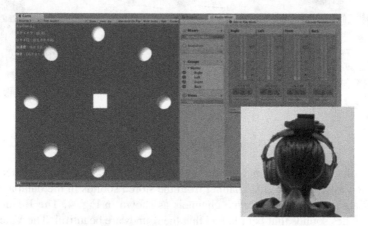

Fig. 5. Head gesture based sound navigation

When using the spatial presentation method, the sound focusing (SF) function was implemented, where the SF function makes it possible to loudly hear sounds in the direction of a head tilt. For example, if a user tilts his/her head to the right, the sound of the Audio Source object located on the right side of the Listener object in the Unity's 3D space will be heard loudly; if he/she keeps listening for a few seconds, the sound will be selected. The upper part of Fig. 5 shows the arrangement and loudness of each object when the head is not tilted. Each volume bar in the Audio Mixer indicates that the sounds in all directions are about the same loudness. The lower part of Fig. 5 shows the arrangement of each object and the loudness when the head is tilted to the right. By tilting the head, the Listener object moves to the right, and the sound to the right becomes louder.

2.4 Tagging Sounds, Collective Hearing, and Novel Use Cases

One key design issue is how to classify sounds in each theme channel. The current Artful CollectiveEars adopts the manual tagging of respective sounds into the six theme channels. A user who hears sounds inserts tags represented as hash tags indicating the name of each theme channel into respective sounds before registering the sounds in Artful CollectiveEars. If the user considers that the sounds are not classified into the six theme channel, the sounds are not stored in Artful CollectiveEars, and are discarded.

A typical use case of Artful CollectiveEars is to unconsciously hear sounds in the world as artful experiences. A user typically cannot distinguish similar sounds well so he/she hears that these sounds are almost the same, but he/she is aware of the small changes in the sounds. Therefore, he/she feels that the sounds are heard like music. One essential issue of the current design is caused by the manual tagging to sounds because the tagging may be wrong or be cheated. The issue may cause awful experiences that break comfortable artful experiences and solving the issue is very essential for offering better artful experiences in the next step.

When choosing a theme channel at the first time in Artful CollectiveEars, a user listens to eight sounds with the spatial presentation method. Artful CollectiveEars chooses the eight sounds categorized by the specified theme channel. One important aspect of Artful CollectiveEars is to present the sounds to all users, so they hear the same sounds. If someone changes one of sounds, all users hear the change. Presented sounds in the same theme channel are similar so the change may not be so significant without causing uncomfortable feeling. The approach offers users a feeling of collective hearing.

Another novel functionality of Artful CollectiveEars is to offer an innovative walking experience in a 3D sound space. When a user of Artful CollectiveEars walks in a room, presenting sounds are changed. When going forward, the user feels that he/she is closing to something that making a sound categorized in a specified theme channel. The sound may be associated with a real physical object in the room, where the same object is owned by a person capture the sound. Thus, he/she can also feel a sense of the person who captures the sound. The direction also may be used for notifying the agency of sounds ambiently.

3   A Preliminary Experiment of Artful CollectiveEars

The purpose of this preliminary experiment is to investigate the opportunities and pitfalls of current Artful CollectiveEars in terms of the end-user experience perspective to share people's hearing and to navigate multiple sounds with head gestures. We conducted the experiment focuses on the usability of the head gesture-based sound navigation to manage multiple sounds offered by current Artful CollectiveEars.

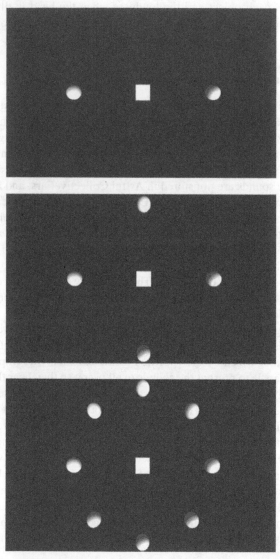

Fig. 6. Sound sources (Top: 2 sound sources configuration, Middle: 4 sound sources configuration, and Bottom: 8 sound sources configuration)

In the experiment, we investigated several insights on the multiple sounds presentation and the head gesture based sound navigation in current Artful CollectiveEars. In each trial, each participant used the system with the following two modes. The first mode adopts the spatial presentation method with the SF function, and the second mode adopts the spatial presentation method without the SF function. We also changed the number of sound sources to 2, 4 and 8, as shown in Fig. 6 when adopting the first and second modes. Then, we interviewed the participants to ask about their experiences using head gestures in Artful CollectiveEars.

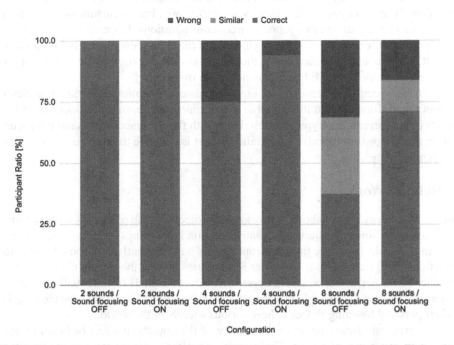

Fig. 7. The results of the experiment in terms of the number of sound sources and the SF function

We hired sixteen participants who were asked to complete a listening test using the spatial and temporal presentation methods, and their correct response rates were investigated. In the experiment, 15 tests were conducted, including 5 for each configuration of the different number of sound sources presented. To simulate the sounds heard by people in various locations around the world for the theme channels of Artful CollectiveEars, sounds were selected from Cities and Memory [9]. We expected that the rate of correct answers would decrease as the sounds became more similar and difficult to distinguish, which is why we categorized them in this way. Figure 7 shows the results of this experiment when participants used the first and second modes. Each column shows the percentages of correct, similar and wrong answers. Similar answers mean that people chose the sound source located next to the "target sound" in the question where the number of sound sources was eight. For example, if the "target sound" is located on the "right", the person answered "right oblique front" or "right oblique back".

When looking at Fig. 7, the correct answer rate for the two sound sources configuration was 100%. Therefore, it is possible to distinguish between left and right sounds whether the SF function is turned on or off. In the case of listening to the four sound sources configuration, the correct answer rate was approximately 75% when the SF function is turned off, while it improved to approximately 90% when the SF function is turned on. The result indicates that the SF function is more appropriate than without the function in the case of the four sound sources configuration.

Regarding the case of the eight sound sources configuration, the rate of correct answers is extremely low in the case without the SF function. When the SF function is turned on, the correct answer rate increases significantly, but it remains low compared to the cases of the four and two sound sources configurations. If we sum up the similar answer rate and the correct answer rate in the case of the eight sound sources configuration without the SF function, we can see that the correct answer rate for the four sound sources configuration without the SF function is not much different.

Therefore, accurate listening in the eight sounds configuration is extremely difficult without the SF function, but it is possible to determine the approximate location of the sounds in the current prototype platform. Even with the SF function, it is more difficult than in the two or four sounds configuration, but it is possible to improve the accuracy of listening.

4   Related Work

Cities and Memory is a collaborative worldwide project for field recordists, sound artists, musicians and sound enthusiasts who contribute sound recordings collected from various cities in the world [9]. More than 500 contributors have currently contributed to record more than 2,000 audio sounds from over 80 countries around the world on the Web. On the other hand, Artful CollectiveEars presents multiple sounds from around the world, which are collected from people who use it simultaneously, and users navigate the sounds in their personal listening spaces to hear various sounds in the world.

The term soundscape refers to the totality of the sounds that can be heard at any moment in any given place [7]. The soundscape offers only what an individual can listen to and not what a collection of people hear. However, using artistic sounds in the world as collective sharing resources has not been well investigated in future smart urban environments.

Audio augmented reality is another direction to enhance the use of sounds. For example, NavigaTone integrates the needed navigational cues into the regular stream of music in an unobtrusive way [1]. Instead of moving the entire track around in stereo panorama, we only move a single voice, instrument, or instrument group. Artful CollectiveEars is also considered to enhance our real world in terms of sounds.

A user interface to music repositories called nepTune creates a virtual landscape for the arbitrary collection of digital music files, letting users freely navigate the collection [3]. Automatically extracting features from the audio signal and clustering the music pieces accomplishes this. The clustering helps generate a 3D island landscape. The interface projects multiple sounds only in a spatial way. In contrast, Artful CollectiveEars offers both spatial and temporal ways to project multiple sounds in a user's 3D listening space.

Adaptive walk on a fitness soundscape is a new kind of interactive evolutionary computation for musical works [8]. It provides a virtual two-dimensional grid in which each grid point corresponds to a listening point that generates a sound environment. People's localization and selective listening abilities make them walk toward the grid points that generate more favorable sounds.

360 Reality Audio offers a new music experience that uses an object-based spatial audio technology [11]. Individual sounds such as vocals, chorus, piano, guitar, bass and even sounds of the live audience can be placed in a 360° spherical sound field, giving sound artists and creators a new way to express their creativity. Listeners can be immersed in a field of sound exactly as intended by sound artists and creators. The approach will offer Artful CollectiveEars future directions to locate sounds in a more immersive way in a 3D space.

A digital platform to share collective human eye sights, CollectiveEyes has been proposed [4]. CollectiveEyes offers spatial and temporal multiple view modes similar to Artful CollectiveEars, and the views can be navigated through gaze-based gestures. CollectiveEyes is enhanced for achieving various purposes. For example, In [5], it is enhanced to increase position emotions in our daily life. Also, in [6], it is enhanced as a social watching infrastructure for a citizen science game to help new combinations of protein-protein docking.

5 Conclusion and Future Direction

This paper presented Artful CollectiveEars, which is a digital platform for developing services that uses humans' collective hearing. The preliminary study conducted an experiment and an exploration about Artful CollectiveEars and showed the some opportunities and potential pitfalls of sharing human hearing.

Current Artful CollectiveEars used a simple 3D audio interface to locate multiple sounds in a 3D space. The approach has limitations in recognizing a large number of sounds, but a new technology such as that in [11] will offer new opportunities to locate sounds in a 3D space in a more immersive way.

References

1. Heller, F., Schöning, J.: NavigaTone: seamlessly embedding navigation cues in mobile music listening. In: Proceedings of the 2018 CHI Conference on Human Factors in Computing Systems (2018)
2. Kawsar, F., Min, C., Mathur, A., Montanari, A.: Earables for personal-scale behavior analytics. IEEE Pervasive Comput. 17(3), 83–89 (2018)
3. Knees, P., Schedl, M., Pohle, T., Widmer, G.: Exploring music collections in virtual landscapes. IEEE Multimedia 14(3), 46–54 (2007)
4. Kimura, R., Nakajima, T.: Collectively sharing people's visual and auditory capabilities: exploring opportunities and pitfalls. SN Comput. Sci. 1(5), 298 (2020)
5. Kimura, R., Jiang, K., Zhang, D., Nakajima, T.: Society of "citizen science through dancing". In: Novais, P., Vercelli, G., Larriba-Pey, J.L., Herrera, F., Chamoso, P. (eds.) ISAmI 2020. AISC, vol. 1239, pp. 13–23. Springer, Cham (2021). https://doi.org/10.1007/978-3-030-583 56-9_2

6. Kimura, R., Nakajima, T.: Gathering people's happy moments from collective human eyes and ears for a wellbeing and mindful society. In: Schmorrow, D., Fidopiastis, C. (eds.) HCII 2020. LNCS (LNAI), vol. 12197, pp. 207–222. Springer, Cham (2020). https://doi.org/10.1007/978-3-030-50439-7_14

7. Rudi, J.: Soundscape and listening. In: Rudi, J. (ed.) Soundscape in the Arts, NOTAM (2011)

8. Suzuki, R., Arita, T.: Adaptive walk on fitness soundscape. In: Kampis, G., Karsai, I., Szathmáry, E. (eds.) Advances in Artificial Life. Darwin Meets von Neumann. ECAL 2009. LNCS, vol. 5778. Springer, Berlin, Heidelberg (2011). https://doi.org/10.1007/978-3-642-21314-4_12

9. Cities and Memory. https://citiesandmemory.com/ Accessed 10 Jan 2021

10. McWhertor, M.: Nintendo Switch Joy-Con controller does some amazing things. https://www.polygon.com/2017/1/12/14260790/nintendo-switch-joy-con-controller-features Accessed 10 Jan 2021

11. Reality Audio. https://www.sony.com/electronics/360-reality-audio Accessed 10 Jan 2021

12. Chinese Number Hand Gesture. https://www.thatsmags.com/shanghai/post/17604/if-you-didn-t-already-know-china-uses-hand-signs-to-express-numbers Accessed 10 Jan 2021

13. Google Glass. https://www.google.com/glass/ Accessed 10 Jan 2021

14. eSense. https://www.esense.io/ Accessed 10 Jan 2021

What are we Supposed to be Learning? Motivation and Autonomy in Smart Learning Environments

Pen Lister[(⊠)] [iD]

University of Malta, Msida MSD 2080, Malta

Abstract. This paper responds to participant interview comments made in the author's research into experiencing smart learning from pedagogical analysis perspectives. Interviewees remarked on what was supposed to be learned as oppose to what they might have actually been interested in, motivated by or simply doing in the smart learning journey activities being investigated. Through analysis of data, it appeared that structures of relevance formed strong reasoning in the minds of learners that subsequently substantially affected their depth and type of experience, beginning before they participated in an activity. This paper explores and develops thinking around pedagogical approaches to enhance and support some significant motivating factors for autonomous participation in smart learning activities.

Just-in-time learning forms part of the ambient and pervasive interactions 'ubiquitous computing' landscape of digitally connected learning cities, already a future-present representation of what may become commonplace in ad-hoc 'smart enough' cities in the near future. Smart learning environments can only be considered smart if effective learning can take place, therefore designing learning activities for smart environments requires considerable reflection of intended aims and measurement of what may constitute learning effectiveness. Understanding potential for learning in these contexts can enhance pedagogical design and approach to support engaging and effective smart learning activities within this unfolding future learning terrain.

Keywords: Motivation · Autonomy · Digital skills · Smart learning · Smart learning environments · Smart pedagogy

1 Introduction

This paper discusses concepts of pedagogical approach to support motivation and autonomy in smart learning activities. For the purposes of discussion in this paper, smart learning activities are generally conceptualised as journeys in real world urbanised digitally connected spaces, formed from several hyperlocal locations [9] related by topic of activity, with digitally mediated participant interactions.

Smart learning activities are often intended as autonomous with voluntary participation, and learner participants may be requested to engage in them not always knowing why participation is of value or where value resides. Participant learner demographics

© Springer Nature Switzerland AG 2021
N. Streitz and S. Konomi (Eds.): HCII 2021, LNCS 12782, pp. 235–249, 2021.
https://doi.org/10.1007/978-3-030-77015-0_17

may vary widely according to activity type and purpose, from citizen learners in informal activities through to formal learners participating in summatively assessed work. This makes planning and designing activities that have value for learning as part of desired outcomes a potentially problematic and tangled challenge. Citizen participants might not be expecting (or even desiring) to learn yet may be learning implicitly as a result of participating in an activity [30] if the activity topic is of interest to them or for other reasons that offer value such as community networking. Formal learners, for example students in undergraduate or postgraduate degrees, may not estimate value in partici-pation of smart learning activities unless they are obligatory and formally assessed and may regard formative voluntary participation as 'not worth it'. Autonomous learning activities that request participation with no explicit reasons of value or relevance for the participant may therefore not be considered as important or worthwhile (for any type of participant), and value may be associated with aspects other than credentialised or explicitly measured learning outcomes. How the expectations of different participants might be absorbed into more flexible hybrid pedagogical approaches for these kinds of learning activities are explored and reflected on in light of findings from recent research by the author.

Using the methodology of phenomenography [36, 38], participants of two separate yet similar smart learning journey activities were interviewed using a semi-scripted responsive emergent approach. Categories of experience variation were discovered from these interviews that shed light on some of the issues surrounding autonomy, motivation and the situated relevance structures of autonomous participatory learning activities [31, 32]. In this research (and this paper) the 'ubiquitous computing' immersive learning [13] of smart learning journeys using ad-hoc mobile apps is regarded as a future-present [22, 23] representation of what may become commonplace in ad-hoc 'smart enough' [19] cities in the near future. Learning as and when need or curiosity necessitates may be part of the ambient and pervasive interactions landscape of future connected learning cities, promoting some of the lifelong learning ideals of Sustainable Development Goal 4[1] and related national policies for citizen 21st century skills and competences support [7, 8, 30]. Understanding potential learning in these contexts, if and how learning might be taking place and what that learning might actually constitute can further enable pedagogical design and approach being refined to flexibly support participant engagement more effectively in smart learning activities within this unfolding future learning terrain.

2 Smart Learning and Smart Learning Environments

Smart learning activities are generally conceptualised in this paper as journeys in real world urbanised digitally connected spaces, formed from several hyperlocal locations [9] related by topic of activity, supported by digitally mediated participant interactions. Technology forms a part of participation interaction but is not regarded as of greater significance than any face-to-face or personal reflective inter and intra-actions with place and location.

Smart learning might be a term more commonly associated with technologically mediated 'personalised' learning using artificial intelligence and detailed learner profile

---

[1] Unesco SDG 4: https://sdgs.un.org/goals/goal4.

ontologies, e.g. [47], however the significance of citizens and their quality of life is increasingly placed at the centre of discussions about what may constitute smart cities and smart learning as a concept, e.g. [16, 42, 55]. The ongoing emphasis of the role and importance of technology in smart cities [17] may therefore be misplaced within educational paradigms of the learning city.

Smart learning environments can be considered smart if effective learning is possible [12, 54], therefore necessitates considerable reflection of what may constitute learning effectiveness. Learning effectiveness can be usefully summarised in the context of smart learning within hybrid urban settings as "learning to learn, learning to do and learning to self realisation" [34, p. 209]. By adopting this open interpretation, a flexible approach to pedagogical considerations within the design of an activity might be better achieved, with additional awareness being focused on what participants themselves may consider as learning.

3 Effective Learning in Smart Environments

Learning to learn may be the most relevant aspect of Liu et al.'s [34, p. 209] description in context of what makes learning smart in a smart learning environment, as an integral part of the "induction into the global dialogue of humanity" in the Internet Age [57, p. 107]. To examine learning effectiveness is therefore an important debate when considering motivation, autonomy, and understanding what effective learning might be from the perspective of the learner, and what they think they are supposed to be learning, or might be learning without being consciously aware of it.

Learning to learn has been at the forefront of relevant epistemological discussion for some time, with noticeable complementary ideas and useful examples. Utilising conversation theory as a basis for cybernetic learning system design, Boyd advises to "(a)nswer *(a learner's)* questions; explain why you are answering that way" and to "(a)sk the learners why they are asking (those) questions, in order to evoke metacognitive consciousness of how they are learning to learn" [2, p. 191]. Pask, the author of conversation theory, discusses 'teaching people to learn', inducing 'learning to learn' [44, p. 139], and noting that "gaining versatility" as a general aptitude of learning, transferred from one subject matter to another, is a sign of the skill of learning. Pask asks "(c)an 'gaining versatility' be equated with 'learning to learn'? And as a practical consequence, can 'conversational experience' thus be regarded as 'training the skill of learning'?" [44, p. 144]. This somewhat echoes Wegerif's comments that 'Education for the Internet Age' is dialogic, "and characterises education as learning to learn, think and thrive in the context of working with multiple perspectives and ultimate uncertainty" [57, preface]. Learning to learn, think and play are the focus of Papert's "art of learning" [43, p. 82]. He bemoans that "school children are taught more about numbers and grammar than about thinking" [43, p. 85], then quoting his earlier work: "we tell them about numbers, grammar and the French Revolution; somehow hoping that from this disorder the really important things will emerge all by themselves..." (p. 85). Reflecting on Polya's [45] heuristic problem solving techniques, Papert particularly highlights taking time as being a key requisite to create conditions of effective learning: "spending relaxed time with a problem leads to getting to know it, and through this, to improving one's ability to deal with other problems like it" [43, p. 87]. This appears to reiterate ideas about flexibility in adapting one's learning approach to the problem at hand.

Engeström [15] cites Brown, Campione and Day's [4] idea of "metacognition as the basis of 'learning to learn'", and list the learner's own cognitive characteristics, available learning strategies, demands of various learning tasks and inherent structure of the material as being 'competing demands', that a learner must "tailor their activities finely" in order to become "flexible and effective learners" [4, pp. 16, 17] in [15, p. 137]. Again this emphasises the need for versatility making for more effective learning. Brown et al. state that "students must develop some of the same insights as the psychologist into the demands of the learning situation" [in 15, p. 137]. This chimes with the phenomenographic 'therapeutic session' interview approach [38, p. 130], reflecting phenomenographic debate regarding the learner's awareness of their own learning, that "there is a consciousness of (the learner) being conscious of "the learner's experience of the act of learning" [40, pp. 473, 474]; also citing [50]. The 'demand structure' of a learning activity [38, pp. 169, 170] referred to by Brown et al. as the 'demands of the learning situation' is of pertinent relevance to this paper, as relevance and demand structures as perceived by learners appear to have significant impact on any learning that might be potentially going on.

The meta-awareness of learner participants for what they might be learning or interpret as of value is further reflected on in subsequent sections in relation to surrounding context of the emergence of relevant pedagogical considerations. Further, referring to the authors own research examining smart learning activity participant experiences, it was noted that within the activities that were investigated participants expressed value and learning in a range of ways that were unintended by the instructor, perhaps indicating the need for a more flexible acknowledgement of what is possible to learn in a smart learning activity.

4 Motivation and Autonomy

Tangible, substantive, explicit as well as implicit, abstract and affective motivational factors in autonomous learning contexts might all be considered as key significant aspects of an engaged participation in smart learning, e.g. [27, pp. 363, 364]. Awareness and planning for the expectations, benefits and value to the participant might therefore usefully form core principles of flexible hybrid pedagogical approaches for learning and engagement.

In discussing the meta-awareness of learning to learn, it may be that factors of motivation and autonomous agency are defining influencers for how awareness about learning is perceived and interpreted by participants of smart learning activities. In light of much smart city learning literature orientating toward technologically supported personalisation of learning in one form or another, it may be logical to assume that personalised learning implies autonomy and an individual empowerment toward self-directed learning and participation. Citing Zimmerman [58], Maina and González provide a succinct summary, stating: "(a)utonomous learning supposes some forms of self-regulation. Self-regulated learning is demanding since it assumes that people are 'meta-cognitively, motivationally and behaviourally active' in their own learning process" [35, p. 89]. In this it is clear that a participant needs to be aware of what might be of interest (intrinsically motivating), possible to learn, and be positively empowered toward activities involving some kind of learning. At heart, these are the challenges of autonomous smart learning, not only in fully considering the potential hurdles manifested by absence of these factors, but in how to overcome them.

Both intrinsic and extrinsic motivation are significant in relation to smart learning activities. If an activity is obligatory for participants, perhaps it may only be valued in extrinsic reward terms, yet if an activity is not obligatory, perhaps motivation is absent to participate at all. Intrinsic motivation [12, 48] is adversely affected by extrinsic factors of reward and assessment, and may additionally be negatively impacted by other types of imposed goals. For example, assessed achievements such as badged awards, qualification credits or community tokens that act as extrinsic mechanisms for increasing motivation to participate erode intrinsic motivation due to loss of personal control. Ryan and Deci refer to this as the locus of causality, that "not only tangible rewards but also threats, deadlines, directives, pressured evaluations, and imposed goals diminish intrinsic motivation because, like tangible rewards, they conduce toward an external perceived locus of causality" [48, p. 70]. Marton and Booth refer to 'technification' as the process of over instructing in task design, giving examples of studies showing increased instructional design results in less being learned [38, p. 169] as learners feel obligated to complete what is being specifically required - to jump through the hoops. This results in a surface approach to learning in order to pass the test, rather than exploration for a deeper engagement with the topic. Dron emphasises that intrinsic motivation cannot emerge unless a person has a sense of autonomy, "against which the traditional classroom model thus actively militates" [12, p. 11]. In smart learning activities however, the classroom has been removed, and this may position these types of potential learning experiences at a greater advantage in fostering and maintaining intrinsic motivation.

Larson reflects on relevant motivational factors in his youth work research. He notes that youths 'taking part in high-quality programs' are 'super-motivated' and deeply engaged, the 'arc of work' they were involved in offered opportunity to develop purpose and that "youth in project-based programs might be voluntarily and intensely engaged in powerful processes of self-creation" [28, p. 75]. Youths said their "projects had become connected to personal goals, including to future school and work goals", and further "noble goals that are 'beyond the self'" [28, p. 75]. These goals reflect varying concepts of the "global aspects of learning" of possible futures and the individual's place in the world [38, p. 141]. Additionally, Larson notes the significance of interpersonal co-constituted meaning and purpose in being part of an activity with others, that youth were "invested not just as individuals, but often as members of teams working toward shared project goals" [28, p. 75]. Maina and González support this, stating "there is also a crucial role played by others (teachers, peers, experts, etc.) in the successful development of self-regulation" [35, p. 89]. As earlier implied by Brown et al. in Engeström [15, p. 137], self regulation requires that learners must "tailor their activities finely" in order to become "flexible and effective learners" is reiterated in this context of teamwork and shared objectives.

5 The Research

The research on which discussion in this paper has been inspired is briefly outlined here. Research was carried out to investigate two different yet similar smart learning activities conceptualised as real-world journeys, formed by several hyperlocal [9] points of interest related by topic in a locality that together formed a journey. Points of interest were augmented with digital interactions using ad-hoc free smartphone apps and technologies, to permit participant access to context aware content. Apps used were HP Reveal[2], Edmodo[3] and Google MyMaps[4]. Original knowledge content, hosted on a custom website[5], was supplemented by related WikiPedia, WikiMedia and other digital knowledge commons content. Participants additionally were requested to create their own content relating to their participation in the journey and upload to Edmodo group areas. Activity participants took part voluntarily in their own time, and did as much or as little of the journey as they chose. Often, though not always, participants took part in small groups.

5.1 Sample and Method

Twenty-four participants agreed to take part in the research, drawn from two universities in two countries, London Metropolitan University, UK and the University of Malta. The sample was purposeful and convenience [46, p. 6, 14, p. 22] as all participant interviews were voluntary. Students were studying BEd. and MA education related degrees, with one other subject discipline represented, BA English Literature and Creative Writing. A wide international demographic was represented across cohorts in both countries, with age range approximately twenty to thirty five years old. A potential limit of the study was gender balance, with nineteen female and six male students represented.

5.2 Methodology

Phenomenography [36] was selected as the methodology suitable for the research as learner experience is at the heart of the investigation and phenomenography examines experience variation using an emergent interview approach. Additionally, qualitative research work related to relevant fields of technology enhanced learning use phenomenography, e.g. [11, 53], and user experience, e.g. [26, 59]. Phenomenography draws on Gurwitsch's [21] ideas about theme, thematic field and margin to analyse experience using a 'structure of awareness' analytical framework [10]. Known as a second order perspective [36, p. 2, 37, p. 183, 51, p. 340], phenomenography is non-dualist [38, p. 122] in nature, making an epistemological assumption that there is only one world as experienced by the learner, "where there is an internal relation between the inner world and the outer world" [24]. Here we are not concerned with ontological discussions of reality, or of the essence of a phenomenon [38, p. 117], but rather only the reality concerning phenomena of interest to the research as experienced by individuals being researched.

---

[2] https://hpreveal.com (defunct).

[3] https://edmodo.com.

[4] https://google.com/mymaps.

[5] https://smartlearning.netfarms.eu.

5.3 Analysis

Phenomenography analyses learner experience looking for experience commonality and variation at collective level rather than the individual context, though context is retained. Using an interpretation of the structure of awareness analytical framework [10], a phenomenographic outcome space (e.g. [39, 46, p. 8]) of 'experiencing a smart learning journey' was formed, with four categories of experience variation, each with four layers of complexity, see Table 1.

Table 1. Understanding experience complexity of a smart learning journey

	Category A Doing the tasks	Category B Discussing	Category C Being there	Category D Knowledge and place as value
Level 4	Research tasks and topic beforehand, take time doing and reflecting on tasks	Share tasks, content, do additional learning, discuss related experience and knowledge	Live it, being in the picture, live the atmosphere, take more time, seeing the whole and related parts	Knowing, seeing knowledge and place as valuable, personal experience, deeper engagement, 'possibilities'
Level 3	Tasks indirectly related to coursework or assessment	Discuss tasks and topic in relation to time and place	Experience place relating to other people, aspects, memories, connections between places and knowledge	Engage further with knowledge in topics, create upload content for tasks and at locations
Level 2	Do the tasks of interest, directly related to coursework or assessment	Discuss the tasks, help each other with tasks and tech	Locations are of some interest, potential for learning, creativity or inspiration	Click a few content links, save links 'for later', make screenshots of augmentations or tasks
Level 1	Do the tasks, go home	Discuss who does the tasks, how technology works	Go to locations, do tasks, go home	No engagement with content or knowledge, don't create or upload content

Descriptive guidelines were noted to outline the emergent differentiating factors of meaning for these categories and levels of experience complexity, to assist and support interpretation of utterances in interviews. Using the descriptive guidelines summary of the table of experience complexity as a foundation, a model of pedagogical considerations for smart learning was formed that came to be known as the Pedagogy Of Experience Complexity For Smart Learning (PECSL), further outlined in Lister [31, 32].

The categories and levels of experience complexity indicated possible interpretations of intrinsic motivation and relevance, perhaps providing glimpses of how to anticipate areas of potential experience that participants may have, dependent on the nature and location of a smart learning activity.

6 Structures of Experience Variation

The categories and levels of experience variation discovered by the research may serve as potential signifiers of participant motivational factors from an experience perception perspective. They may further act as indicators of the significance of participant reflection (either prior to, or more especially after taking part in an activity) in relation to self-awareness and meta-cognition for learning, e.g. [33]. In the activities investigated by the research, participants referred to a wide variety of aspects in the activities that may have impacted their forming of structures of relevance for motivational factors and contexts. The categories of experience variation that the study discovered from participant interviews offered insight into how these structures of experience variation, and any wider context of awareness, together formed these relevance structures. Brief summaries of topics of conversation provided in Table 2 show aspects of significance in the activity as related by participants, demonstrating multiple topics and depth of interest. Extrinsic motivators such as 'doing the tasks' or 'doing the locations' are omitted, provided here is a glimpse of the richer, deeper scope of intrinsic motivational experience as mentioned in interviews by participants, showing areas of interest, motivation and value to them.

The activity significance of 'meaning' [39] that was attributed during analysis to the experience variation quotes of participants (and formed each participant's structure of awareness), may be interpreted and understood as types and areas of intrinsic motivation. The significance of these aspects to participants are often not in connection with any perceived 'demand structure' of the instructional design, but were aspects of experience complexity that were more informally influenced by peers, friends, or for personal relationships and agency connected to places and knowledge, separate from any 'intended objects of learning' [41, pp. 4, 5]. These might have been somewhat 'triggered' by general aspects of intended objects of learning but were distinct from those, existing in personal spheres of memory, observations or peer discussion, appearing to be the embodiment of learners' 'vital objects of interest' as described by Greeno and Engeström [20, p. 134]. Perhaps these vital objects of interest, being so varied and flexible in the context of a smart learning activity out in the real world are themselves forming as well as being formed by, structures of relevance as experienced by learners. These structures are continuously reconstituted as intersubjective lifeworlds [49], building reflective understanding. This can be micro or macro in scope of topic, and intra- and inter-understanding and reflection.

Table 2. Aspects of significance of the activity as related by participants (summarized by the researcher)

Personal motivation for learning and taking part
- Value of being there for creativity and authenticity in written work
- The novelty of the digital assistant
- The wow factor and sci-fi experience of using the (AR) app
- A natural sparking of interest while using the (AR) app
- Appreciating potential for SL activity in other scenarios for own future practice

Value in place and being there
- Getting to know the detail and atmosphere of a place
- Being outside away from the classroom
- Appreciating global cultural value differences
- Sharing memories related to location and topic of activity
- Learning more about local surroundings than would normally be noticed
- Becoming like a tourist in one's own locality

Being with friends and helping each other
- Being able to ask questions of each other outside of classroom pressure
- Meeting others who might usually be only online or names in another similar class
- Helping others to achieve shared goals
- Sharing (discussing) cultural differences related to topics and locations
- Comparing experiences of the activity with peers

7 Structures of Relevance

Participant learners form relevance structures related to learning activities either as explicit relevance, by making decisions about value and relevance of task for their grades or future working life, or implicitly, by making decisions about whether they are interested in a task or topic, whether it relates to other useful aspects of their lives, and how much of an activity to take part in as a result of their intrinsic interest. Much of this value estimation may occur in ways not obviously consciously aware to the learner. The 'metacognitive consciousness' of what participants interpret as of significance and value to them may highlight where areas of learning are potentially present and could be supported, either implicitly or explicitly. This may hint at support for structure making, as an aspect of learning to learn. Returning to Pask, who outlines the connotation of learning to learn as the ability to structure and make sense of disordered experience:

> *"The usual connotation of 'learning to learn' also comprehends an ability to structure and make sense of otherwise unordered experience. For this, more than versatility is required. What is required is the skill of building up an approximation to a personalised conversational domain. Understood in this way 'learning to learn' could have great practical value in education."* [44, p. 144].

This considers each single act of learning in the context of the versatility required to move between subject domains and experiences to learn effectively, building a 'personalised conversational domain'. The personalised conversational domain might be described as internal reflections on interpretations of value and structure for making sense of an 'otherwise unordered experience' in relation to other experiences. Making connections between aspects of relevance is essential to creating useful transferrable skill and understanding. Bransford, Brown and Cocking [3] argue that relevant knowledge "helps people organize information in ways that support their abilities to remember [...] to go beyond the information given and to think in problem representations, to engage in the mental work of making inferences, and to relate various kinds of information for the purpose of drawing conclusions" [3, p. 237]. This latter aspect of making inferences and relating various kinds of information to enable drawing conclusions seems especially relevant to smart learning as echoes utterances made by participants in research interviews that involved discussing cultural or social differences between participants' prior experiences and memories. These mental inferences are notably connectivist in nature, as Siemens states "the learning that happens in our heads is an internal network [...]" [52, p. 29]. Perhaps these internal connections are fluid relationships being continually reconstituted, dependent on the situation that a learner finds themselves in relation to the stimuli and relevance available to them as they become aware of it in their experience.

Marton and Booth refer to relevance structures [38, pp. 143, 144], demand structures [38, pp. 169, 170] and global aspects of learning [38, p. 141] as all potentially impacting the structure of awareness for a learner as they participate in a learning activity, and the subsequent effectiveness of any learning in it. The relevance structure of the learning situation is discussed in terms of the immediate context of a task or action required of learners. The demand structure is a way of describing how the learning instructions and requirements might be designed (that define the relevance structure). The global aspects of learning are the wider context surrounding that which a learner may perceive as part of the learning activity.

8 Relevance Structure Influencing Factors

A smart learning activity may or may not be considered as a learning activity by a participant in some circumstances. As the author's research with degree students indicates, sometimes in voluntary non-assessed learning the sub-conscious global aspects of learning may outweigh the direct explicit relevance and demand structure of the activity within a participant's own awareness. Additionally, value and benefit for participants may not be clear within their own perceived global aspects of learning (consciously or not). The question arises, how to alert the awareness of the participant toward aspects they find of interest to develop further insight and gain greater depth of engagement and value. In turn to then reflect on this, expanding their awareness and ideally gaining useful learning that they themselves uncover and acknowledge.

8.1 Reflection with Peers

Motivation is potentially fostered by active dialogue and reflection, both between tutor and learner and between peers in more social learning contexts. This is echoed in various texts and past research, for example previously cited work from Larson in youth projects [28] and Wegerif's expansion of the dialogic space, of "learning to learn, think and thrive in the context of working with multiple perspectives and ultimate uncertainty" [57]. The art of reflection then, both individually and in groups, may perhaps be key to unlocking participant motivation and awareness. Lin, Galloway and Lee outline how "action learning is performed in groups so individuals can learn from each other ... there should be a task designed or assigned for action and participation (and) reflection is the end product", continuing "(f)rom reflection, they can generalise their learning to other situations. As a result, the learning cycle through experience is formed" [29, p. 55]. The author's work in classroom practice further acknowledges the power of group reflection to uncover learning and awareness in participants [33]. Marton and Booth refer to this as figure ground reversal [38, p. 149], reflection with peers brings about the consciousness of the act of learning itself [40, pp. 473, 474], what the learner perceives as having been learned, or when learning took place. Further reflecting together on activities that everyone took part in fosters articulated awareness together, then creating deeper and more complex ideas and learning as conversation develops.

8.2 Context and Awareness

Context can be interpreted and impact experience awareness in multiple ways. Physical and virtual presence [56, p. 197], socio-cultural contexts of place [6] and pedagogy of place [25] all play a part to influence interpretations of learning in the authentic real-world environments in which smart learning activities are often situated. The complex learning environments that are formed by these elements are described by Goodyear and Carvalho as a three architecture terrain of material, social and epistemic factors, with interactions involving fast (automatic) and slow (subjective agency) thinking [18, p. 55]. This helps to illustrate how a smart learning activity and environment can potentially impact each learner in distinct ways and is therefore useful for participants to explore these differences, highlighting to each other in emergent conversation how they have interpreted aspects of the activity. This builds individual intra-contextual [39, p. 344] interpretations, and supports a wider understanding of possible application and useful-ness, encouraging transferability and hence "a personalised conversational domain" to make sense of otherwise unordered experience [44].

8.3 Twenty-First Century Skills, Autonomy and Self-directed Learning

Maina and González further highlight that "distinctive characteristics of autonomy in learning are congruent with the twenty-first century competency framework, particularly those related to "self-direction, adaptability, flexibility, and collaboration" [35, p. 89]. Further, Blaschke and Hase suggest "the skills required to be an effective learner in the twenty-first century have changed dramatically, as the learner evolves from passive recipient to analyst and synthesizer" [1, p. 26]. Describing heutagogy, the learner is seen as "the major agent in their own learning, which occurs as a result of personal experiences" [1, p. 27], they are outlining what Breunig describes as "transformational learning", that "(n)on-formal education embeds learning content in activities across an array of settings providing wide latitude for self-direction and interpretation on the part of learners" [5, p. 3]. Smart learning should seek for learning strategies to be in the hands of the learners themselves, to find and construct learning either individually or in groups, building total immersion and engagement with knowledge and associated relationships to place [32].

9 Conclusions

Autonomous self-directed learning in complex learning environments is impacted by motivation, and motivation is impacted by perceived experience and awareness. Understanding more about participant experience structures of awareness and factors defining relevance and significance of activity as perceived by learners themselves can aid in supporting the design of smart learning activities and environments to offer more adaptable, flexible, efficient and effective learning opportunities. By considering experience possibilities as a multilayered context of relevance and awareness, the significance of motivational factors and impact of peer reflection can be emphasised, enabling self-directed learners to foster "metacognitive consciousness of how they are learning to learn" [2]. This can bring about the 'personal conversational domain' [44] that Wegerif describes as learning to learn, think and thrive for learning in the Internet Age [57].

References

1. Blaschke, L.M., Hase, S.: Heutagogy: a holistic framework for creating twenty-first-century self-determined learners. In: Gros, B., Kinshuk, Marcelo, M. (eds.) The Future of Ubiquitous Learning, LNET, pp. 25–40. Springer, Heidelberg (2016). https://doi.org/10.1007/978-3-662-47724-3_2
2. Boyd, G.M.: Conversation theory. In: Jonassen, D.H. (ed.) Handbook of Research on Educational Communications and Technology, 2nd edn., pp. 179–197. Lawrence Erlbaum Mahwah, New Jersey (2004)
3. Bransford, J.D., Brown, A.L., Cocking, R.R. (eds.): How people learn, brain, mind, experience and school (Expanded Edition). National Academy Press, Washington, DC (2004)
4. Brown, A.L., Campione, J.C., Day, J.D.: Learning to learn: on training students to learn from texts. Educ. Res. **10**(2), 14–21 (1981)
5. Breunig, M.: Experientially learning and teaching in a student-directed classroom. J. Exp. Educ. **40**(3), 213–230 (2017)
6. Buell, L.: Space, place, and imagination from local to global. In: Buell, L. (ed.) The Future of Environmental Criticism: Environmental Crisis and Literary Imagination, pp. 62–96. Blackwell, Malden, MA (2005)
7. Bughin, J., Hazan, E., Lund, S., Dählström, P., Wiesinger, A., Subramaniam, A.: Skill Shift: Automation and the Future of the Workforce. McKinsey, San Francisco (2018)
8. Carretero, S., Vuorikari, R., Punie, Y.: DigComp 2.1: The Digital Competence Framework for Citizens with eight proficiency levels and examples of use. European Commission, Publications Office of the European Union (2017)
9. Carroll, J.M., Shih, P.C., Kropczynski, J., Cai, G., Rosson, M.B., Han, K.: The internet of places at community-scale: design scenarios for hyperlocal neighborhood. In: Konomi, S., Roussos, G. (eds.) Enriching Urban Spaces with Ambient Computing, the Internet of Things, and Smart City Design, pp. 1–24. IGI Global (2017)
10. Cope, C.: Ensuring validity and reliability in phenomenographic research using the analytical framework of a structure of awareness. Qual. Res. J. **4**(2), 5–18 (2004)

11. Cutajar, M.: The student experience of learning using networked technologies: an emergent progression of expanding awareness. Technol. Pedag. Educ. **26**(4), 485–499 (2017)
12. Dron, J.: Smart learning environments, and not so smart learning environments: a systems view. Smart Learn. Environ. **5**, 25 (2018)
13. Dunleavy, M., Dede, C., Mitchell, R.: Affordances and limitations of immersive participatory augmented reality simulations for teaching and learning. J. Sci. Educ. Technol. **18**(1), 7–22 (2009)
14. Edwards, S.: Panning for gold: Influencing the experience of web-based information searching. Doctoral Dissertation, Queensland University of Technology, QUT ePrints, Queensland (2005)
15. Engeström.,Y.: Learning by Expanding: An Activity-Theoretical Approach to Developmental Research. Orienta-Konsultit, Helsinki (1987)
16. Giovannella, C., Martens, A., Zualkernan, I.: Grand challenge problem 1: people centered smart "cities" through smart city learning. In: Eberle, J., Lund, K., Tchounikine, P., Fischer, F. (eds.) Grand Challenge Problems in Technology-Enhanced Learning II: MOOCs and Beyond. SE, pp. 7–12. Springer, Cham (2016). https://doi.org/10.1007/978-3-319-12562-6_2
17. Goodspeed, R.: Smart cities: moving beyond urban cybernetics to tackle wicked problems. Camb. J. Reg. Econ. Soc. **8**(1), 79–92 (2015)
18. Goodyear, P., Carvalho, L.: The analysis of complex learning. In: Beetham, H., Sharpe, R. (eds.) Rethinking Pedagogy for a Digital Age: Designing for 21st Century Learning, pp. 49–63, 2nd edn. Routledge, New York (2012)
19. Green, B.: The Smart Enough City, Putting Technology in its Place to Reclaim our Urban Future. Strong Ideas. MIT Press, Cambridge (2019)
20. Greeno, J.G., Engeström, Y.: Learning in activity. In: Sawyer, R.K. (ed.) The Cambridge Handbook of the Learning Sciences, pp. 128–147, 2nd edn. Cambridge University Press, Cambridge (2014)
21. Gurwitsch, A.: The Field of Consciousness. Duquense University Press, Pittsburgh (1964)
22. Husman, J., Lens, W.: The role of the future in student motivation. Educ. Psychol. **34**, 113–125 (1999)
23. Ireland, C., Johnson, B.: Exploring the FUTURE in the PRESENT. Des. Manage. Inst. Rev. **6**(2), 57–64 (1995)
24. Ireland, J., Tambyah, M.M., Neofa, Z., Harding, T.: The tale of four researchers: trials and triumphs from the phenomenographic research specialization. In: Jeffery, P. (ed.) Proceedings of the Australian Association for Research in Education (AARE) 2008 International Research Conference. Changing Climates: Education for Sustainable Futures, pp. 1–15. The Australian Association for Research in Education (2009)
25. Jayanandhan, S.R.: John Dewey and a pedagogy of place. Philos. Stud. Educ. **40**, 104–112 (2009)
26. Kaapu, T., Tiainen, T.: User experience: consumer understandings of virtual product prototypes. In: Kautz, K., Nielsen, P.A. (eds.) SCIS 2010. LNBIP, vol. 60, pp. 18–33. Springer, Heidelberg (2010). https://doi.org/10.1007/978-3-642-14874-3_2
27. Krivova, L., Imas, O., Moldovanova, E., Mitchell, P.J., Sulaymanova, V., Zolnikov, K.: Towards smart education and lifelong learning in Russia. In: Uskov, V.L., Bakken, J.P., Howlett, R.J., Jain, L.C. (eds.) SEEL 2017. SIST, vol. 70, pp. 357–383. Springer, Cham (2018). https://doi.org/10.1007/978-3-319-59454-5_12
28. Larson, Reed W.: Discovering the Possible: How Youth Programs Provide Apprenticeships in Purpose. In: Burrow, Anthony L., Hill, Patrick L. (eds.) The Ecology of Purposeful Living Across the Lifespan, pp. 73–92. Springer, Cham (2020). https://doi.org/10.1007/978-3-030-52078-6_5

29. Lin, T.C.Y.W., Galloway, D., Lee, W.O.: The Effectiveness of Action Learning in the Teaching of Citizenship Education: A Hong Kong Case Study. In: Kennedy, K.J., Lee, W.O., Grossman, D.L. (eds.) Citizenship Pedagogies in Asia and the Pacific, CERC Studies in Comparative Education, pp. 53–80. Springer, Dordrecht (2011). https://doi.org/10.1007/978-94-007-074 4-3_4

30. Lister, P.: Smart learning in the community: supporting citizen digital skills and literacies. In: Streitz, N., Konomi, S. (eds.) HCII 2020. LNCS, vol. 12203, pp. 533–547. Springer, Cham (2020). https://doi.org/10.1007/978-3-030-50344-4_38

31. Lister, P.: Understanding experience complexity in a smart learning journey. SN Soc. Sci. 1, 42 (2021a)

32. Lister, P.: Experiencing the smart learning journey: a pedagogical inquiry. Doctoral Dissertation, University of Malta, Malta (2021b)

33. Lister, P.: Future-present learning and teaching: a case study in smart learning. In: Sengupta, E., Blessinger, P. (eds.) Changing the Conventional Classroom, Innovations in Higher Education Teaching and Learning (IHETL). Emerald Publishing (2022, in Press)

34. Liu, D., Huang, R., Wosinski, M.: Future trends of smart learning: Chinese perspective. Smart Learning in Smart Cities. LNET, pp. 185–215. Springer, Singapore (2017). https://doi.org/10.1007/978-981-10-4343-7_8

35. Maina, M.F., González, I.G.: Articulating personal pedagogies through learning ecologies. In: Gros, B., Kinshuk, Maina, M. (eds.) The Future of Ubiquitous Learning, LNET, pp. 73–94. Springer, Heidelberg (2016). https://doi.org/10.1007/978-3-662-47724-3_5

36. Marton, F.: Phenomenography - describing conceptions of the world around us. Instr. Sci. 10, 177–200 (1981)

37. Marton, F.: Cognoso ergo sum – reflections on reflections. In: Dall'Alba, G., Hasselgren, B. (eds.) Reflections on phenomenography: Toward a methodology?, pp. 163–187. Acta Universitatis Gothoburgensis, Gothenburg (1996)

38. Marton, F., Booth, S.: Learning and Awareness. Lawrence Erlbaum Associates, Mahwah, NJ (1997)

39. Marton, F., Pong, W.P.: On the unit of description in phenomenography. High. Educ. Res. Dev. 24(4), 335–348 (2005)

40. Marton, F., Svensson, L.: Conceptions of research student learning. High. Educ. 8, 471–486 (1979)

41. Marton, F., Tsui, A.: Classroom Discourse and the Space of Learning. Lawrence Erlbaum Associates, Mahwah, NJ (2004)

42. McKenna, H.P.: Human-smart environment interactions in smart cities: exploring dimensionalities of smartness. Future Internet 12(5), 79 (2020)

43. Papert, S.: The Children's Machine: Rethinking School in the Age of the Computer. Basic Books, New York (1993)

44. Pask, G.: Styles and strategies of learning. Br. J. Educ. Psychol. 46, 128–148 (1976)

45. Polya, G.: How to solve it: A New Aspect of Mathematical Method. Princeton University Press, Princeton, NJ (1945)

46. Reed, B.: Phenomenography as a way to research the understanding by students of technical concepts. In: Núcleo de Pesquisa em Tecnologia da Arquitetura e Urbanismo (NUTAU): Technological Innovation and Sustainability, São Paulo, Brazil, pp. 1–11 (2006)

47. Rezgui, K., Mhiri, H., Ghédira, K.: An ontology-based profile for learner representation in learning networks. Int. J. Emerg. Technol. Learn. (iJET) 9(3), 16 (2014)

48. Ryan, R.M., Deci, E.L.: Self-determination theory and the facilitation of intrinsic motivation, social development, and well-being. Am. Psychol. 55(1), 68–78 (2000)

49. Sandberg, J.: How do we justify knowledge produced within interpretive approaches? Organ. Res. Methods 8(1), 41–68 (2005)

50. Säljö, R.: Learning about learning. High. Educ. **8**, 443–451 (1979)
51. Sjöström, B., Dahlgren, L.O.: Applying phenomenography in nursing research. J. Adv. Nurs. **40**(3), 339–345 (2002)
52. Siemens, G.: Knowing knowledge. Internet Archive. https://web.archive.org/web/200612062 14545/http://www.knowingknowledge.com/book.php (2006). Accessed 20 Jan 2021
53. Souleles, N., Savva, S., Watters, H., Annesley, A., Bull, B.: A phenomenographic investigation on the use of iPads among undergraduate art and design students. Br. J. Educ. Technol. **46**(1), 131–141 (2014)
54. Spector, J.M.: Conceptualizing the emerging field of smart learning environments. Smart Learn. Environ. **1**, 2 (2014)
55. Thomas, V., Wang, D., Mullagh, L., Dunn, N.: Where's wally? In search of citizen perspectives on the smart city. Sustainability **8**(3), 207 (2016)
56. Traxler, J.: Context reconsidered. In: Traxler, J., Kukulska-Hulme, A. (eds.) Mobile Learning: The Next Generation, pp. 190–207. Routledge, London (2015)
57. Wegerif, R.: Dialogic: Education for the Internet Age. Routledge, London (2013)
58. Zimmerman, B.J.: A social cognitive view of self-regulated academic learning. J. Educ. Psychol. **81**(3), 329–339 (1989)
59. Zoltowski, C.B., Oakes, W.C., Cardella, M.E.: Students' ways of experiencing human-centered design. J. Eng. Educ. **101**(1), 28–59 (2012)

Design Inspired by Intangible Cultural Heritage of Taoyuan Woodcarving Craft Platform

Mingxiang Shi[(⊠)] and Chunyi Liu

School of Fine Arts, Hunan Normal University, 36, Lushan Street,
Changsha 410081, Hunan, People's Republic of China

Abstract. The intangible cultural heritage (ICH) of the Taoyuan woodcarving craft (TWC) platform provides designers with a source of culture and creativity. Designers can retrieve, find and download resources that inspire product creativity from the platform's portal to improve design efficiency. The woodcarving material library is an essential part of the knowledge platform. With 3D scanning and other technologies, we have restored the woodcarving patterns wholly and vividly. Standardize the size, proportion and style of the pattern to keep the woodcarving materials consistent with the original style when the design is reused. With the help of CAM technology, the materials can be directly used in production, which will help the ICH of TWC be transformed into products to promote culture's market dissemination. This paper is one of the ICH of TWC series of research. Based on the previous results, this paper studies the practical functions and art forms related to TWC furniture and interior furnishings explores the extraction methods of auspicious culture and carries out auspicious elements modelling features are transformed and applied to new furniture product design.

Keywords: Taoyuan woodcarving craft · Intangible cultural heritage · Knowledge platform · Furniture product design

1 Introduction

Taoyuan woodcarving craft (TWC) is the intangible cultural heritage of Hunan Province. However, the current traditional woodcarving industry model has limited development space. The shortcomings are mainly reflected in the fact that the innovative development mechanism from handicrafts-traditional arts and crafts products-contemporary innovative design products has not been formed [1]; A service platform for the internationalization and industrialization of intangible cultural heritage protection and innovative design; the independent innovation and market expansion capabilities of woodcarving artisans are limited, and they have failed to form an influential brand and production base. The Taoyuan woodcarving intangible cultural heritage knowledge platform is guided by the woodcarving industry's needs, providing critical information support for digitalization, informatization and product design for related industries, perfecting and enriching the diversified industrial chain, and supporting the development of woodcarving artisans and their brands [2]. Creation and development to cultivate a group of innovative

N. Streitz and S. Konomi (Eds.): HCII 2021, LNCS 12782, pp. 250–259, 2021.
https://doi.org/10.1007/978-3-030-77015-0_18

design and innovative talents for Taoyuan Woodcarving. Through the study and analysis of Taoyuan wood carving intangible cultural heritage knowledge, such as handicraft knowledge, cultural background, utensil function, modelling and decoration, etc., we can deeply understand the stories, connotations and meanings behind regional cultural resources, which can stimulate designers' creative inspiration and increase product design cultural connotation [3]. At the same time, with its unique cultural value, regional culture can enhance the value of design and gain recognition in the global market. In order to preserve the authenticity of intangible cultural heritage, it is necessary to study its cultural characteristics and transform them into modern products. According to product design positioning and the protection strategy of intangible cultural heritage, the design of related cultural and creative products can be divided into two directions [4, 5]. One is to inherit and improve the products related to traditional regional culture, such as the redesign of traditional handicraft products. The other is the design of cultural products that emphasize creativity, which caters to market demand by adding distinctive regional cultural values to available products, mainly embodied in creative tourism products. Based on the TWC knowledge platform, this paper studies the auspicious culture and the extraction methods of auspicious elements, and transforms them into modelling features to guide the redesign of contemporary furniture products.

2 Related Research

Intangible cultural heritage knowledge comes from the understanding, skills and philosophical system developed during the long-term interaction between society and the surrounding environment. This knowledge widely exists in language, entertainment, medicine, architecture, food, social interaction, rituals and spirits, etc. [6]. They are hidden in the lives and wisdom of villagers and provide a basis for daily actions. Intangible cultural heritage knowledge not only promotes cultural diversity and human needs for cultural diversity but also fully reflects its own national wisdom and rich emotions. Adequate intangible heritage knowledge can better establish relationships for various objects in a specific knowledge field. Design knowledge includes a collection of information such as knowledge itself, design method, and design process, which can provide a basis for design output [7]. The main manifestations are drafts, models, process effects, and the designer's ideas and principles for solving problems. Designers learn about intangible cultural heritage to obtain useful knowledge for design.

As the characteristic cultural industry has become an essential strategic asset of the national and regional economy, designers have played an increasingly important role in the process of promoting the development of cultural industries. Design research is a creative activity based on demand realization, including analysis, deconstruction, and synthesis. Many processes, such as evaluation and evaluation, require multi-disciplinary expertise summarization and practice accumulation. Design research is based on intangible cultural heritage knowledge as the source of creativity. It has become an essential way for a contemporary design to solve the cultural identity crisis and revitalize local culture and economy. Faced with substantial local knowledge resources, designers should reconstruct the intangible cultural heritage knowledge system framework according to the principle of demand-driven. Data collection, information sorting, evaluation and comparison, and design reuse are more efficient and convenient [8].

At present, there are different classification methods of knowledge. According to the form of knowledge, it can be divided into tacit knowledge and explicit knowledge. Tacit knowledge exists in the human brain and usually manifests as experience, skills, skills, etc.; explicit knowledge is outside the human brain. Other knowledge that can be clearly expressed [9]. Tacit knowledge is difficult to flow, and needs to be mastered in the context by means of "words and deeds." There is also a method of knowledge classification that is generally accepted), skill knowledge (Know-How), resource knowledge (Know-Who); according to the design requirements in the distributed resource environment, knowledge can be divided into integrated knowledge and unit knowledge. This knowledge comes from local culture, and culture is a comprehensive and complex concept, it is difficult to have a strict and precise classification of it, so the classification of culture is often analyzed from different angles. Structurally, it can be divided into surface touch layer, middle behaviour layer and deep perception layer. The surface touch layer is the culture of visible, tangible, and usable concrete material; the middle behaviour layer is the visible, audible but intangible spiritual and behavioural culture; the deep perception layer is invisible and invisible penetrates the first two layers A philosophical culture of ideas and consciousness in the culture.

Tie Ji, Hui Li and others divided intangible cultural heritage knowledge into material cultural knowledge, behavioural cultural knowledge, and psychological, cultural knowledge. Woodcarving intangible cultural heritage knowledge (ICH) for design innovation can be divided into the following types into specific knowledge [10], as shown in Fig. 1.

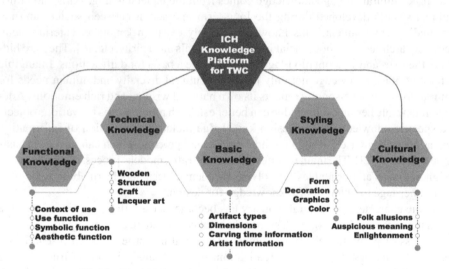

Fig. 1. The ICH knowledge classification framework model

In the previous research, we have studied the practical functions and art forms of Taoyuan woodcarving in furniture, interior furnishings, and architectural components through the investigation of regional culture, customs, and lifestyles; through the structural nature of Taoyuan woodcarving non-genetic people use methods such as unstructured interviews and participatory observations to acquire tacit knowledge such as creative ideas, subject selection, and creative processes [11]. On this basis, build TWC intangible cultural heritage knowledge platform. It mainly includes first, the professional knowledge base of Taoyuan woodcarving culture and carving techniques. Second, the shared woodcarving furniture product database and related design specifications; third, the Taoyuan woodcarving art education and service platform. The following part will be based on the professional knowledge base of Taoyuan woodcarving culture and carving techniques, select "auspicious culture" from creative ideas, extract modelling elements, and apply them to the innovative design of furniture products.

3 Taoyuan Woodcarving Craft and Auspicious Culture

Taoyuan County is located in Changde City, Hunan Province. Since ancient times, the Taoyuan area has been known as a "paradise on earth and a paradise". It is also famous for Tao Yuanming's "Land of Peach Blossoms". "Taoyuan area has simple customs and people are generous and enthusiastic. Taoyuan woodcarving is the product of the unique local concept of creation. Its formation and development are closely related to the regional culture of Taoyuan. The regional culture profoundly affects the cultural connotation of Taoyuan woodcarving. Taoyuan woodcarving According to the purpose, they are divided into three main categories, including architectural wood carving, furniture wood carving and sacrificial wood carving. Whether it is architectural wood carving, furniture wood carving or sacrificial wood carving, they are all related to Taoyuan people's yearning for an auspicious and happy life. Humans have a share of trees themselves. Unique emotion, it not only records the traces of the development of life in the universe, at the same time, its gentleness, colour, smell, and other properties also reflect the affinity with humans [12]. Taoyuan people have always believed that tree planting is a good thing for future generations. They treat nature with gratitude and take wooden objects for their use. Especially the most widely used furniture and woodcarving touch all aspects of life. Highly skilled folk artists use the gifts of nature to carve their own works of art. At the time, it also created people's material homeland and gave people spiritual sustenance.

Taoyuan woodcarving auspicious culture is a kind of yearning for a better life and the psychological needs of the whole body. The themes of wood carving mainly include three categories, characters, animals and flowers and birds. The most walking beasts are followed by flowers and birds. The landscapes are relatively rare because they have too few cultural implications [13]. Traditional Chinese patterns have always had meanings. As the saying goes, patterns must be meaningful, patterns must be written, and they must be auspicious. TWCs often use a variety of expression techniques, such as homophony, symbolism, etc., to express their love for auspicious cultures such as "Fu Lu Shou Xi" and their yearning for a better life. For example, in TWC, animal subjects such as lions, bats, deer, sheep and so on. The lion can demonstrate the status of the master and has the auspicious meaning of fortune [6]. Therefore, in TWC, the shape of the lion is also the richest is also the most common [14]. Because the word "bat" is the same as the word "Fu", the bat means happiness, peace and good fortune. In many cases, the craftsmen will replace the head of the bat with the head of a dragon to make it feel like a beast. Similarly, the homonym of "deer" is "Lu", and "yang" means "Xiang"; these are the embodiment of auspicious culture. There are also plant themes, such as the combination of grapes and squirrels, and the combination of pomegranates and peanuts, which all signify multiple births; the combination of pine trees and cranes signifies health and longevity; the combination of lotus and heron signifies the ancestral family. These symbolic expressions reflect the auspicious culture pursued by local folk customs and show people's beautiful psychological needs.

4   Taoyuan Woodcarving Auspicious Cultural Symbol Extraction

The refinement and determination of the auspicious cultural elements of Taoyuan wood-carving will help form a unified design style as a whole and enhance the recognizability and artistic effect of furniture design. At present, the research on the methods of extracting cultural elements mostly focuses on product design and graphic design. In the refinement of traditional home symbols, Yaoyin Zhang proposed the use of modern design morpho-logical derivation methods to converge the characteristic symbols of traditional furniture into a representative basic form or graphic abstract in a specific communication context [15]. Bingchen Gou and others used the analytic hierarchy process to identify the genes that affect the auspicious cultural style and regarded pattern genes, colour genes, and morphological genes as the most specific genes in the design of cultural products [16]. Based on the Taoyuan woodcarving knowledge platform framework, this article effec-tively extracts cultural genes and provides useful information for the design of cultural products.

TWC forms in furniture products can be divided into round carving, relief carving, open carving, Yin carving, paste carving, and mosaic carving. Round carving is mixed carving, mostly used to express ornaments of independent appreciation and combined decorative furniture or architectural components. Reliefs are carved on the ground. They are sun-carved. They are raised in deep and bas-relief. They are mostly used for hanging screens, beams and pillars, doors and windows. Open carving is hollow carving. It is divided into single and double-sided decorative carving. It is a unique form of carving interspersed with round carving and relief. It is commonly seen in architectural flower covers, hangings, birds, doors and windows. Yin carvings are sinking carvings. They are inscribed in a concave form and are often carved on cabinet doors, couplets and signboards. Paste carving and inlay carving are new forms created by later crafts. Paste carving is about to paste the small pieces that have been carved into larger pieces, such as decals. Inlaid carving is inlaid with other materials, such as the famous inlaid glass painting on TWC bed.

Taoyuan woodcarving is rich in styling patterns, vivid and profound cultural con-notations, and strong contrasting colours. It extracts the most distinctive woodcarving patterns such as stepping on the song, phoenix tail, tic-tac-toe, sun, moon, dragon, fish, etc. The pattern is simplified, abstracted, and reorganized to give it a national cultural spirit and show the essence of national culture with better visual effects. Wood carving patterns are used in design practice, giving furniture design new regional cultural con-notations, and further sublimating the cultural heritage. Colour is the visual information symbol that is most sensitive to visual stimuli and has the fastest response speed among the visual elements of the human body. In the refinement and performance design of regional characteristics, colour elements play a pivotal role. The characteristic colours of auspicious culture are mainly expressed in red, gold, or black interweaving, emphasizing contrast, vividness, and liveliness to achieve the effect of gorgeous, colorful and not vulgar. The color matching of regional characteristics is used to continue the colour style of Taoyuan's regional cultural characteristics. The colour image of the ethnic region is combined with the dynamic graphic design. This colour-matching not only conforms to the regional cultural characteristics of Taoyuan but also has beautiful visual effects.

5 Reconstruction and Application of Auspicious Cultural Symbols in Furniture Design

After the design elements are fully refined, the extracted modelling elements are constructed reasonably. In the process of constructing auspicious cultural elements, it is necessary to recognize the interactive relationship between graphic design and regional cultural elements, not only to follow the principles of formal beauty and furniture modelling design but also to respect the objective laws of the original object, to shape the furniture product symbol. It is more recognizable, communicative and innovative. In the furniture design of Taoyuan's auspicious cultural elements, text and graphics are combined, and colours, textures, and proportions are used to form a composition with formal beauty. Try to combine the refined space with paper-cut elements, deconstruct and reorganize abstract patterns, unify the design of the entire auspicious cultural graphic with line elements, reconstruct according to the rules of point, line, and surface composition, and use auspiciousness cultural element symbols to strengthen innovation.

5.1 Reconstruction and Design of Furniture Product Language Structure

The semantic structure of furniture products is the composition law for the setting, cognition, and the combination of product symbols. The structure of each element of the product and the choice of material technology manifests product language structure. In the furniture product design featuring Taoyuan woodcarving auspicious culture, the reconstruction of the structure layer is firstly reflected in the recombination and editing of the multiple design elements of the furniture; secondly, it is reflected in the extension and innovation of the functional form of the furniture; and again in the choice of select materials on. For example, taking the study room as the design context, refine the combination mode of furniture such as TWC desks, chairs and bookcases to promote the innovative design of new products, as shown in Fig. 2.

5.2 Innovative Design on the Semantic Level of Furniture Products

The product is composed of shape, size, colour, and material, and conveys various information with particular "words". Therefore, the key to furniture product design is to handle the product language to produce the best product information. The application of product semantics to the design process of furniture products is mainly reflected in

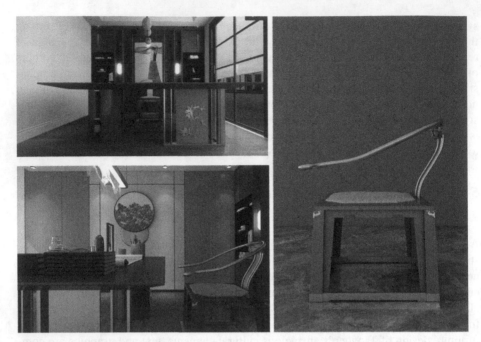

Fig. 2. Refine the combination mode of furniture such as TWC

three levels [17]. The first level is the materialized display of cultural semantics of a specific region. The second level considers human factors and penetrates the consumer's visual, psychological, spiritual, and empirical characteristics. The semantics of product design conforms to people's perception of the product focus on furniture products' compositional ability. The third level is the product's cultural level, which conveys the cultural connotation of the product through its semantic characteristics and reflects the specific cultural value contained in the symbol. For example, in the chair's design, first, use "Wu Fu Peng Shou" inauspicious culture as the design semantics, and then extract the shape of "Wu Fu Peng Shou" TWC veneer and traditional auspicious patterns. Five bats surround the pattern. The words may be composed of peaches, which means more blessing and longevity. Finally, the pattern is integrated with the furniture component design, as shown in Fig. 3.

5.3 Innovative Design at the Product Pragmatic Level

Good product design must comprehensively consider the relationship between product-people-environment. Product pragmatics refers to the relationship between the product, the user, and the environment. The contextual stories related to auspicious culture are mainly the design methods in the context of product use. Combining the user's needs, characteristics, events, and the relationship between the product and the environment imagine the use context of the product from the user's perspective and the use environment. To explore product ideas and design themes. In the furniture design related to auspicious culture, 1 Consider the design and innovation of furniture from the needs of

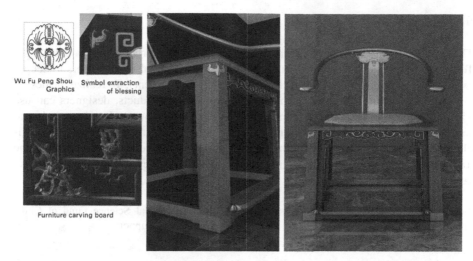

Fig. 3. Use "Wu Fu Peng Shou" inauspicious culture as the design semantics

users in the living room, calligraphy, dining room and other different functional zones. 2 It is necessary to consolidate the lifestyle of modern cities, and carry out superior design according to the use environment of furniture. Also, the modelling symbols of the furniture must convey the use environment of the product. For example, the use of bamboo and wood materials in furniture reflects the concept of human-environmental friendliness. At the same time, bamboo also contains the meaning of safety and prosperity. The design shown in Fig. 4 extracts the bamboo-shaped symbols from the Taoyuan woodcarving furniture panels and uses them in the desk design.

Fig. 4. The bamboo-shaped symbols in the desk design

6 Conclusion

The application of cultural elements is an effective method of product innovation design. To design auspicious cultural furniture products, it is essential for designers to deeply explore and use intangible cultural characteristic design elements. To realize the design innovation of intangible cultural characteristic furniture products, designers can use TWC intangible cultural heritage knowledge system to organize cultural symbols and send Message. Innovation is an essential requirement of design. The pursuit of intangible cultural heritage cannot be on the surface of the basin. Designers should combine traditional cultural elements with innovation to inherit and develop intangible cultural heritage.

Acknowledgement. This research is supported by National Social Science Fund of China program (17BG149). We also gratefully acknowledge the financial support.

References

1. Ji, T., Guo, M.: Social transformation and design participation in rural cultural construction. Zhuangshi **4**(300), 39–43 (2018)
2. Shi, M., Ren, S.: A study on productive preservation and design innovation of Taoyuan wood carving. In: Rau, P.-L.P. (ed.) HCII 2019. LNCS, vol. 11576, pp. 203–214. Springer, Cham (2019). https://doi.org/10.1007/978-3-030-22577-3_14
3. Zhao, X.: The artistic achievements of Taoyuan wood carving. J. Art China **3**(7), 82–90 (2014)
4. Qiu, C.: Productive protection: 'self-hematopoiesis' of intangible cultural heritage. J. China Cult. Daily **2**(21), 15–18 (2012)
5. Zheng, X.: Traditional and modern technology. Zhuangshi **5**(301), 55–59 (2018)
6. Zhang, D., Ji, T.: Collaborative design "Trigger" revival of traditional community. J. Zhuangshi **12**(284), 26–28 (2016)
7. Li, J., Ying, J.: Taoyuan folk wood carving art. J. Central South Univ. (Soc. Sci. Edn.) **4**(2), 84–90 (2003)
8. Luo, S., Dong, Y.: Integration and management method of cultural artifacts knowledge for cultural creative design. Comput. Integr. Manufact. Syst. **4**(24), 964–977 (2018)
9. He, S.: Analysis of intangible heritage digital protection under new media diversification. Cult. J. **5**(10), 86–92 (2018)
10. Shi, M., Zeng, Q.: Designing an interactive platform for intangible cultural heritage knowledge of Taoyuan woodcarving craft. In: Streitz, N., Konomi, S. (eds.) HCII 2020. LNCS, vol. 12203, pp. 636–647. Springer, Cham (2020). https://doi.org/10.1007/978-3-030-50344-4_46
11. Chai, C., Bao, D., Sun, L.: The relative effects of different dimensions of traditional cultural elements on customer product satisfaction. Int. J. Ind. Ergon. **48**(10), 77–88 (2015)
12. Liu, W., Wu, Z.: Cultural creative product made of hongmu and its principle of development design. Pack. Eng. **37**(14), 169–173 (2016)
13. Zhu, Y.: Study on wood carving decoration of folk architecture. J. Interior Des. **1**(10), 35–44 (2014)
14. Manzini, E., Zhong, F.: Design, When Everybody Designs. 1st edn. Electronic Industry Press, Beijing (2016)
15. Liang, P.: Study on the current situation of Taoyuan wood carving artists. J. Mingsu Mingfeng **7**(11), 59–65 (2015)

16. Tang, L., Wen, H., Lei, F.: The application of Taoyuan wood carving art in visual communication design. J. Liter. **2**(4), 170–177 (2012)
17. Sanders, N., Stappers, P.: Co-creation and the new landscapes of design. J. CoDesign **4**(1), 5–18 (2014)

Strategies for Panel Sequence Segmentations in d-Comics

Xinwei Wang[1]([✉]), Jun Hu[2], Bart Hengeveld[2], and Matthias Rauterberg[2]

[1] University of Nottingham Ningbo China, Ningbo, China
`xinwei.wang@nottingham.edu.cn`
[2] Eindhoven University of Technology, Eindhoven, The Netherlands
`{j.hu,b.j.hengeveld,g.w.m.rauterberg}@tue.nl`

Abstract. In contrast with reading a comic book where a reader needs to flip the physical pages, in d-Comics (digital comics) there are no physical pages and no page-flipping interaction. The screen sizes for displaying the comics, as well as the way a reader can interact with the content varies between different electronic devices. The author intended segmentation, used to be well embedded with physical pages, needs to be converted to fit different methods in d-Comics. In a previous experiment, we identified two types of panel sequence segmentations in d-Comics. This article describes a follow-up expert review to justify the detailed panel transition changes for the results collected. Nine categories (character, object, environment, symbol, text, frame, camera angle, drawing style and narrative time) were summarised for analysing the recognised changes for panel sequence segmentation. Besides a confirmation of the earlier results, the outcome of the expert review provided how the segmentations were identified. Based on these results, we argue there are three strategies to be considered by the author when creating panel sequence segmentation in d-Comics – narrative structure, visual space (including visual elements and spatial layout) and interaction.

Keywords: Digital comics · Panel sequence · Segmentation

1 Introduction

Comics as a storytelling medium is constructed by panel sequences [1, 2]. Due to the prevalence and accessibility of electronics devices, d-Comics (Digital Comics) provide a tremendous potential as a popular format for comics. However, many issues are still under discussion [3–5]. For example, whether sound and animation should be introduced in d-Comics? How to migrate panel sequences from printed comics and display them with different electronic devices? How to provide pleasant reading experience with d-Comics?

An obvious difference between printed comics and d-Comics is the physical carrier – whether a panel sequence is printed on physical pages or displayed on electronic screens. This also leads to a difference from the perspective of interaction – a reader flips the physical pages with the printed comics, while the interaction for continue reading d-Comics can be different with different electronic devices. For example, a panel

© Springer Nature Switzerland AG 2021
N. Streitz and S. Konomi (Eds.): HCII 2021, LNCS 12782, pp. 260–272, 2021.
https://doi.org/10.1007/978-3-030-77015-0_19

sequence displayed vertically on a smart phone screen that a reader can use a finger to tap and scroll the screen [6]. And many d-Comics are displayed with web browser on a desktop screen where a reader should interact with a cursor to read [7, 8]. Moreover, as virtual reality, augmented reality and mixed reality technology are becoming more accessible, d-Comics can be visualised in a virtual 3D space and a reader can walk through to read [9, 10].

The page-flipping interaction happens because a panel sequence has been segmented by physical pages. These segmentations can contain various storytelling intentions defined by the author such as curiosity, suspense, surprise, emphasis and storytelling pace (also known as "page-turner" and "cliffhanger"). However, the page structure doesn't exist with d-Comics. Therefore, we started to explore whether there is a unit in d-Comics similar to the page?

In a previous study [11], we conducted an online experiment[1] to investigate how panel sequences are segmented in d-Comics. By analysing the collected data from 80 participants based on examples of 4 panel sequences, two types of segmentation of panels in d-Comics were identified and discussed (Fig. 1). A phasel (created by combining "phase" and "sequel") in d-Comics is represented by one panel or multiple panels that belong to each other. The author cannot decompose these further into smaller phasels. A phasel describes a strong relation among a certain number of panels and a significant difference with other phasels, determined by the author's storytelling intention. A fadel (created by combining "fade" and "sequel") is represented by one panel that the author considers to be part of both the previous phasel and the next phasel. A fadel describes an overlapping transitional relation between two phasels, and it contains both the fading of the previous phasel and the starting of the next phasel determined by the author's storytelling intention.

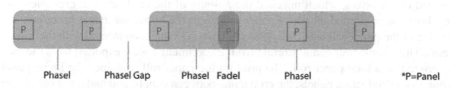

Phasel   Phasel Gap   Phasel Fadel   Phasel   *P=Panel

Fig. 1. Demonstration of phasel, fadel and phasel gap.

After identifying the units in d-Comics for panel grouping, the next question is: What affects the identification of the units? In another word, what influence the decision of segmentation? We adopts mainly from the panel transition types from McCloud [2, 12], combined several other panel transition categorisations through literature review [13–15] and answers in Experiment 1, came up with the following nine categories of changes between two panels: 1) Character (such as a human, a dog, a talking robot, with the difference in action, facial expression, appearance and amount of character); 2) Object (such as an apple, a clock, a sword, with the difference in appearance and movement); 3) Environment (such as a room, a forest, sea, with the different of location and weather); 4) Symbol (such as impact stars and motion lines); 5) Text (such as the

---

[1] We will address that experiment as Experiment 1 in this article.

character's dialogue, narration and sound effect); 6) Frame (such as different sizes and shape of a panel); 7) Camera angle (such as zooming in/out and looking up/down); 8) Drawing style (such as black and white, certain colour combination and abstract or concrete); 9) Narrative time (such as different direction and duration of narrative time). This article further investigates how readers could distinguish segmentations with the listed categories. Then to discuss how these categories could be considered as strategies, when authors want to adapt panel sequences for various electronic devices.

2   Design of the Expert Review

In previous research, a questionnaire was used to investigate what kind of changes have readers recognised when identifying certain panel segmentations. However, due to limitations such as the experiment time as well as the various backgrounds of the participants, it was not possible to allocate the changes for segmentation to unique panels. Therefore, we invited reviewers to provide their detailed understanding and reflection regarding the results received from Experiment 1.

2.1   Materials

Firstly, a card set which visualised and explained the potential nine categories for panel sequence segmentation was created to help improve the reviewers' understanding (Fig. 3). Secondly, a training session was created to introduce the reviewers to how the provided card set should be applied. Four other examples from SIR KEN ROBIN-SON: Full body education [16]— from Gavin Aung Than, the same author of the stories used in Experiment 1—were selected (shown in Fig. 2). The categories were listed with coloured check boxes, which matched the colours of the card set. The examples and checkboxes were printed on a long paper roll (to fit the horizontal linear panel layout). The size of the paper roll was 29.7 × 84 cm (two A3 papers connected with the longer edges). Thirdly, the four comic stories[2] from Experiment 1 were exported from the web and printed on a long paper roll. The print on the paper roll contained the linear panel layout, two introduction panels, the crop icons between panels, and under the panels the complete set of categories with the coloured checkboxes. The length of The Lucky Ones was 29.7 × 84 cm, In Spite of Everything was 29.7 × 126 cm, Because It's There was 29.7 × 252 cm, and Ithaka was 29.7 × 294 cm. The reviewer could indicate on the paper roll — using the checkboxes — the categories for every gap, especially for the identified segmentations. Finally, the result of the segmentation by the participants of Experiment 1 was printed and shown to the reviewers. The goal of this step was to trigger discussion of the reviewers about the segmentations created by the participants of Experiment 1.

---

[2] The four comics stories are from webcomics *Zen Pencils: The Lucky Ones* [18], *In Spite of Everything* [19], *Because It's There* [20] and *Ithaka* [21]. The panel numbers and gaps in-between are not included due to the page limit of this article, yet can be found in Appendix I in [22].

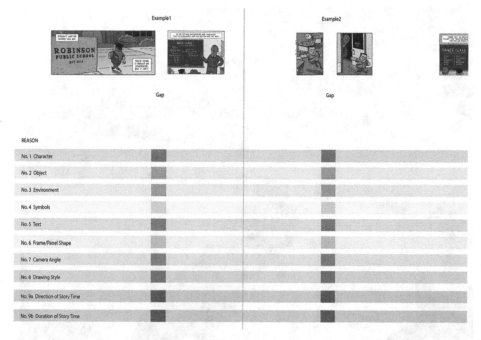

Fig. 2. The layout of the training examples.

2.2 Procedure

Three reviewers were invited, they were all PhD researchers in the field of Industrial Design. One female and two males, with an average age of 29.7. The cultural backgrounds of the reviewers were: one Asian, one European and one American. Each reviewer was invited to an office where the test was conducted. First, the goal of the experiment was introduced, and then the card set with the categories for segmentation was provided and introduced. After the reviewer had confirmed the understanding of the card set, the training session started.

In the training session, the full comic story was presented linearly on a touch-screen tablet (screen size 9.7 in., resolution 1024×768 pixels). Simultaneously, a long paper roll was placed on a table with the same linear story and the coloured checkboxes to mark the categories for segmentation. The reviewer could use the card set as a reference for the training task. As the investigator, the author of this article was involved in this session to confirm the reviewer's opinions regarding the answers.

After the training session, the reviewer was provided, one by one, with each of the four comic stories which were also used in Experiment 1. Besides the interactive version on the tablet, a long paper roll was placed on the table for each story that could be used to fill in the categories for each segmentation (Fig. 3). After the reviewer had finished filling in the segmentation categories for each gap in each comic story, an interview was conducted. The investigator asked the reviewer their opinions about the segmentation data received from Experiment 1. Each reviewer answered the questions for all four comic stories. The conversation was audio-recorded during the whole interview.

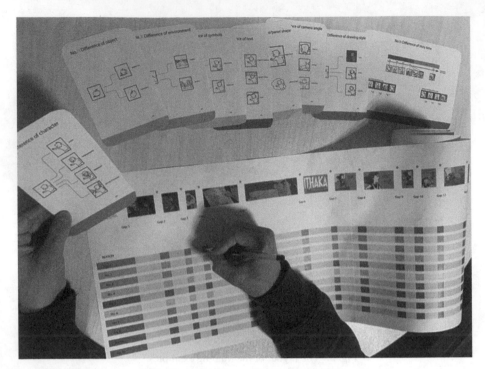

Fig. 3. The settings of the expert review.

3   Results

The aim of this experiment was to investigate which specific elements in the panel sequences can influence the decision of segmentations. In this section, the data that resulted from the questionnaires and interviews from the reviewers will be analysed to find similarities among the reviewers. Two visualisation methods will be applied to inform the analysis. The intersection method will be used to visualise the categories that all the reviewers agreed. The union method will be used to visualise all the categories combined for each gap by all the reviewers, no matter if there was only one reviewer who considered it or all of them. The category and colours in the visualisations match with the colours used in the questionnaire. To provide a clear comparison between the different segmentations in each story, both the intersection and union visualisation will be discussed.

3.1   "The Lucky Ones"

The intersection visualisation based on all of the reviewers' opinions can be found in Fig. 4. The change of character, text and camera angle are considered to be important categories for each gap by all reviewers. Excluding Gaps 1 and 10 (transition between introduction image and story content), the highest number of categories appears in Gap 5, while the lowest in Gap 3.

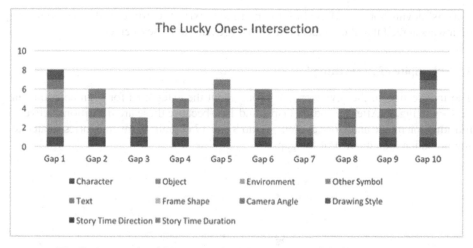

Fig. 4. Intersection of the categories for segmentation of The Lucky Ones.

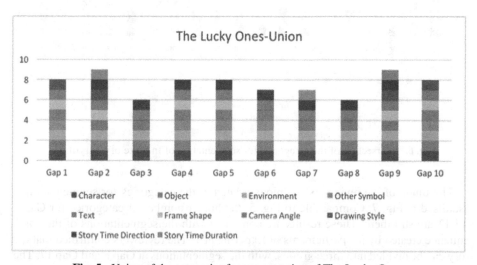

Fig. 5. Union of the categories for segmentation of The Lucky Ones.

The union of all the reviewers' opinions combined is shown in Fig. 5. In this diagram, the differences between the gaps appear to be less obvious compared to Fig. 3. The major difference between the intersection and union is the consideration of narrative time. The reviewers explained that the narrative time is going backward in the panels. It is mainly because of the visual clues, such as the appearance of the characters becoming younger. In other words, the narrative is conveyed through the panels placed in space. The reviewers pointed out during the interview that they didn't consider any segmentations because the time direction was constantly going backward. Additionally, according to the text in the panels, the story happens in the narrator's mind, which meant that, although the memories of the narrator are moving backward in time (based on the images), the actual story is moving forward (based on the narration text). According to the interview, all reviewers agreed that the panels in this story are hard to be segmented.

3.2 "In Spite of Everything"

The intersection of the reviewers' opinions about the categories for segmentation can be seen in Fig. 6. After excluding Gap 1 and 19—because these are transitions between introduction image and story content—Gap 8 and 17 contain more categories related to segmentation than the rest of the gaps.

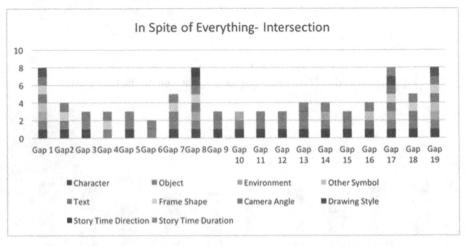

Fig. 6. Intersection of the categories for segmentation of In Spite of Everything.

The union of the reviewers' opinions related to the categories for segmentation is visualised in Fig. 7. Comparable to Fig. 5, the higher number of categories for Gap 8 and 17 are still there. These results are consistent with the segmentations of the panel sequence created by the participants of Experiment 1. The reviewers confirmed that the story can be divided into three groups, with the segmentations at Gap 8 and Gap 17. The most important categories for this segmentation are caused by changes in narrative time and supported by the change of the character's appearance and the change of colour.

3.3 "Because It's There"

The intersection of the reviewers' opinions about the categories for segmentation is described in Fig. 8. The differences between the gaps in this diagram are subtle. Excluding Gap 1 and 36 (transition between introduction image and story content), the highest number of categories appears in Gap 3, 12 and 14, while the lowest is in Gap 32.

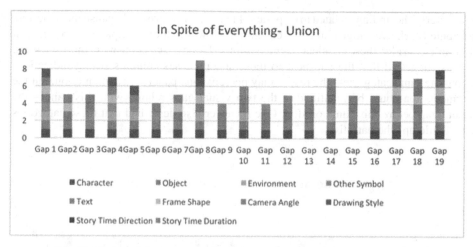

Fig. 7. Union of the categories for segmentation of In Spite of Everything.

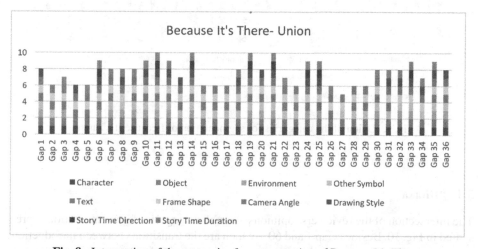

Fig. 8. Intersection of the categories for segmentation of Because It's There.

The union of the reviewers' opinions related to the categories for segmentation is illustrated in Fig. 9. By adding all the individual opinions of the reviewers, Gap 6, 10, 11, 12, 14, 19, 21, 24, 25, 33 and 35 become the gaps with most categories. Gap 3 is not part of this, and Gap 27 replaces Gap 32 to become the lowest one. In Experiment 1, the gaps 3, 7, 12, 14, 19, 21, 24, 25 were considered as important segmentations of the panel sequence. In this story—although less obvious than The Lucky Ones— the identified segmentations of the panel sequence from Experiment 1 can be matched with the categories of the reviewers in this review. During the interview, the reviewers confirmed that there were various categories related to the segmentations in this story. For example, Gap 3 is recognised mainly because of the narrative time duration change and environmental change, while Gap 19, 21, 24 and 25 are more related to the change of characters. The findings related to Gap 6 and 11 are more surprising because the reviewers attributed a relatively high number of categories. However, the participants of Experiment 1 didn't consider these as clear segmentations. Upon discussion with the reviewers, it was suggested that the gap next to these special cases contains strong indications about the same categorie—the reader may perceive one panel for segmentation, but the segmentation could be identified at the two visual gaps related with this panel—the visual gap before this panel or after. One reviewer also described that these categories can "build up" the narrative.

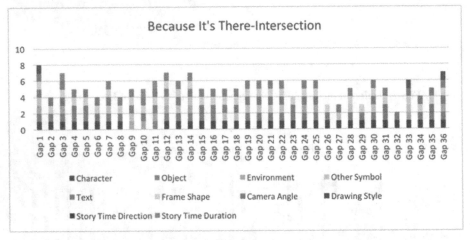

Fig. 9. Union of the categories for segmentation of Because It's There.

3.4 "Ithaka"

The intersection of the reviewers' opinions about the categories for segmentation is presented in Fig. 10. Besides Gap 1 and 60—which are the transitions between introduction image and story content—the highest number of categories for segmentation appear in Gap 6, 43 and 49. The lowest number can be found in Gap 17, 27 and 52.

The union of the reviewers' opinions related to the categories for segmentation is shown in Fig. 11. By adding all the individual opinions of the reviewers, Gap 11, 41, 43 and 54 became the gaps with most categories for segmentations (9 categories). Gap 6, 12, 30, 35, 37, 40, 42, 45, 46, 47, 49, and 59 have the second highest number of categories for segmentation (8 categories). The general pattern of intersection and union matches with the result from Experiment 1. All the gaps that were indicated as segmentations by at least 50% of the participants of previous experiment (Gap 8, 30, 37, 49) also have a high number of categories as suggested by the reviewers in the current experiment.

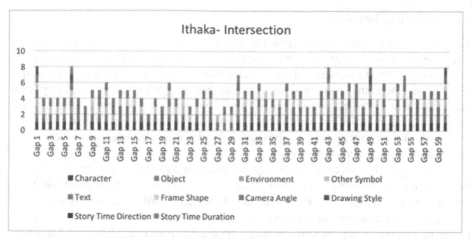

Fig. 10. Intersection of the categories for segmentation of Ithaka.

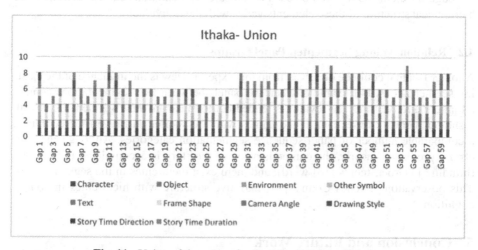

Fig. 11. Union of the categories for segmentation of Ithaka.

4 Discussion

All three reviewers confirmed that the panel segmentation patterns from Experiment 1 were valid and could be interpreted with the materials provided. The categories for panel sequence segmentation in d-Comics are complex. The influence of narrative timeline, narration texts, and other visual elements can be observed from the designed experiments. However, it remains difficult to compare the intensity of the categories for the segmentation. Due to various factors such as age, gender, cultural background, personal experience and evoked emotion by the story of the readers, the focus of identifying segmentation in d-Comics can be different.

4.1 Number vs Intensity

The current measurement of how a panel sequence can be segmented is based on the listed categories such as the narrative time, character and colour. By using the "intersection" and "union" method to describe the categories that the reviewers mentioned, the results matched in general the segmentations from Experiment 1, which is how majority (over fifty percent of the participants) perceive the segmentations. However, there are still exceptions. When reviewers were invited to explain the exceptions, the intensity was increased. This means that the perceived intensity of certain elements could overrule the influence of the number of elements.

However, it is not yet clear how the intensity of visual elements can exactly influence the segmentation. The results of both Experiments 1 and this expert review showed that the text elements and the other visual elements do not necessarily have to be synchronised in the panels. For example, in The Lucky Ones the texts flow forward through the panels. However, the images represent the narrative time going backward. Image and text may have a different influence on how a narrative is understood by the reader. In another word, although the elements that can be used to indicate segmentations can be identified, the hierarchical structure of these elements varies with the individual.

4.2 Relation Among Segmented Panel Groups

Another fact that could be observed from this expert review is the influence of the existing segmentations. For example, when the panels between two segmentations contain a longer narrative time, the reviewers tended not to make any new segmentations with a shorter narrative time, even if the panels with the shorter narrative time contained a comparable number of panel sequence segmentation categories. Although the panels are presented linearly, the comprehension of the story is accumulated in the mind (braiding in Groensteen's [13] word), and there exist hierarchies in the segmentations. This observation matches Cohn's [17] narrative structure with hierarchies in comics cognition.

5   Conclusion and Future Work

This article investigated the strategies of narrative structure (narrative time) and visual elements (character, object, environment, symbol, text, frame, camera angle and drawing style) for panel sequence segmentations in comics. The results of Experiment 1 and this expert review show that the strategies can be used to explain the perceived segmentations. However, individual readers have different understanding of, and preferences for, these strategies. For example, some readers were not that sensitive to changes in duration of the narrative time compared to others. Some of the readers focused more on how the characters change, some used the changes of the environment as a reference, and some were more influenced by the changes in colour tone. Even for the same reader, there was not necessarily a consistency among the influencing factors: a reader could create segmentations based on different strategies.

In printed comics, a segmentation in a panel sequence, aligns with the narrative structure, expressed through visual space, and is connect with the physical page. The existence of the physical page is not only the segmentation of the panel sequence, but also influence the author's decision of layout of the panels in the page/spread, moreover, requires an interaction from the reader which is flipping the page. Since the physical page doesn't exist with d-Comics, we have explored using interaction and visual layout with different electronic devices for expressing segmentation [10]. We plan to include interaction with narrative structure and visual elements for the future study to further establish the strategies for panel sequence segmentation in d-Comics.

Acknowledgements. The authors would like to thank Mr. Gavin Aung Than for kindly giving permission to use his comics for the purpose of this research, and the participants for joining the review.

References

1. Eisner, W.: Comics and Sequential Art: Principles and Practices from the Legendary Cartoonist. WW Norton & Company (2008)
2. McCloud, S.: Understanding Comics: The Invisible Art. Northampton (1993)
3. McCloud, S.: Reinventing Comics: How Imagination and Technology are Revolutionizing an Art Form. Harper Collins (2000)
4. Groensteen, T.: The Impossible Definition. A Comics Stud. Read. **124** (2009)
5. Goodbrey, D.M.: Digital comics–new tools and tropes. Stud. Comics. **4**, 185–197 (2013)
6. Cho, H.: The webtoon: a new form for graphic narrative. Comics J. **18** (2016)
7. Huynh, M.: The Boat. http://www.sbs.com.au/theboat/. Accessed 09 Jan 2021
8. Sutu: These Memories Won't Last. https://www.sutueatsflies.com/art/these-memories-wont-last. Accessed 09 Jan 2021
9. VR Forum: Virtual-Comics - Read Your Comic Books/Graphic Novels in Space!
10. Wang, X., Hu, J., Hengeveld, B., Rauterberg, M.: Expressing segmentation in d-comics. In: Stephanidis, C. (ed.) HCII 2019. CCIS, vol. 1032, pp. 402–409. Springer, Cham (2019). https://doi.org/10.1007/978-3-030-23522-2_52
11. Wang, X., Hu, J., Hengeveld, B., Rauterberg, M.: Segmentation of panels in d-comics. In: Brooks, Anthony L., Brooks, E., Sylla, C. (eds.) ArtsIT/DLI -2018. LNICST, vol. 265, pp. 28–37. Springer, Cham (2019). https://doi.org/10.1007/978-3-030-06134-0_4
12. McCloud, S.: Making Comics: Storytelling Secrets of Comics, Manga and Graphic Novels. Harper, New York (2006)
13. Groensteen, T.: The System of Comics. University Press of Mississippi, Jackson (2007)
14. Tezuka, O.: Creating Manga (マンガの描き方: 似顔絵から長編まで). Kobunsha (1996)
15. Duncan, R., Smith, M.J., Levitz, P.: The Power of Comics: History, Form, and Culture. Bloomsbury Publishing (2015)
16. Than, G.A.: SIR KEN ROBINSON: Full body education. https://www.zenpencils.com/comic/kenrobinson/. Accessed 09 Jan 2021
17. Cohn, N.: The Visual Language of Comics: Introduction to the Structure and Cognition of Sequential Images. A&C Black (2013)
18. Than, G.A.: The Lucky Ones. https://www.zenpencils.com/comic/81-richard-dawkins-the-lucky-ones/. Accessed 09 Jan 2021
19. Than, G.A.: In Spite of Everything. https://www.zenpencils.com/comic/113-vincent-van-gogh-in-spite-of-everything/. Accessed 09 Jan 2021
20. Than, G.A.: Because It's There. https://www.zenpencils.com/comic/mallory/. Accessed 09 Jan 2021

21. Than, G.A.: Ithaka. https://www.zenpencils.com/comic/131-c-p-cavafy-ithaka/. Accessed 09 Jan 2021
22. Wang, X.: Segmentation of Panels in D-Comics, (Doctoral dissertation, Eindhoven University of Technology, Eindhoven, the Netherlands) (2019). https://pure.tue.nl/ws/files/120338362/20190314_Wang.pdf

Papimation: A Symbol System for Children to Animate Their Drawing

Cheng Yao[1](✉), Xinglin Zheng[2], Zhangzhi Wang[2], Yue Hao[2], Xiaoqian Li[2], Yuqi Hu[3], and Fangtian Ying[4]

[1] College of Computer Science and Technology, Zhejiang University, Hangzhou, China
yaoch@zju.edu.cn
[2] College of Software Technology, Zhejiang University, Hangzhou, China
{xinglin_zheng,21951499,21951215,21951505}@zju.edu.cn
[3] International School of Design, Zhejiang University, Ningbo, China
yuqihu@nit.zju.edu.cn
[4] College of Design, Hubei University of Technology, Wuhan, Hubei, China

Abstract. Drawing for children is an intuitive way to express themselves. But the static property of paper drawing and children's shortage of expressive words limit them. Animating children's drawings could break the static state into a dynamic one and help them to convey ideas. However, the complex animation process is difficult for children to understand and correctly use.

So, in this paper, we present Papimation, an animation symbol command system for children to achieve animation effect on their drawing by themselves. We conducted three user studies to design and evaluated it. Progressively we investigated the possible motion that children intent to achieve, generated understandable and accessible animation symbol command vocabularies for children, and evaluated the feasibility and enjoyment of our system. Results show that children achieve high agreement in our system and could learn and use them with ease. Our system gave more play to children compared with only drawing.

Keywords: Drawing · Animation · Symbol command

1 Introduction

Drawing on paper is the most intuitive way for children to express themselves. No matter how messy children's drawings are, there are stories or ideas conveyed. What matters is not the final artwork they draw but the idea or story they express through drawing. The act of drawing is a dynamic process however the end product is static in paper or digital interface, making it hard to convey their idea fully. Animating children's drawings as they wish could largely diminish the static state of drawing, at the same time express children's ideas more clearly and visually dynamic. We think this would help them greatly in imagination, self-expressing, and fun play.

However, there are few opportunities for children to make animation by themselves because of the complexity of animation making. So, we introduce the neo smartpen

© Springer Nature Switzerland AG 2021
N. Streitz and S. Konomi (Eds.): HCII 2021, LNCS 12782, pp. 273–286, 2021.
https://doi.org/10.1007/978-3-030-77015-0_20

technology and augmented paper to our system to achieve drawing on paper while synchronizing the draw in the digital platform to break the traditional static paper drawings while preserve the affordance of paper drawing for children.

In this paper, we conducted three user survey studies to analyze and design the animation symbol command system to help children animate their drawing for better expression and fun play.

The main contributions of our work are:

1. exploring the possible symbol command that is understandable for children to achieve basic animation movement.
2. contributing the Papimation system which was valued by participants for its feasibility and attractive property.

2 Related Work

2.1 Drawing

In this paper, we refer to children's drawings because it is the most intuitive way for children to express their ideas and stories. Einarsdottir J, Dockett S and Perry B [1] stated that children's drawing is a way for them to express their idea and experiences. Malchiodi and Cathy A [2] conclude the children's drawing development, children's drawing become more and more concrete and start development of visual Schemata in their 6–9 years old. In this scope of age, children were stated to have the most willingness and capability to draw to express themselves. That's also why we choose children in this age group as our participants.

One drawback of paper drawing is that the image is static, but the children's expression has its limitation both in words and drawings. Many researches are dedicated to introducing multiple dimensions of expression for children's drawing. Jabberstamp helps evoke children's ability in talking by introducing voice and sound recording in children's drawings [3]. But voice still has its limitation in display children's dynamic idea since not all children are good at vocalizing their imagination out. Jacoby and Buechley [4] use conducted ink for children to draw and enable voice record once conducted ink linked with slots attached on paper. Conducted ink is an intriguing way in children's the drawing. But again, voice is not dynamic enough for children since some children are not expressive enough.

So in this paper, we integrate animation into children's drawing, hoping that the dynamic of animation could help set off drawing's static and thereby help children in learning and better expressing their story.

2.2 Animation

Animation is a broad subject. For children, as we researched in the last section, hand drawing is the most intuitive and ubiquitous way for children to express themselves, so here we mainly focus on animation that drives hand-draw object moving.

Momeni A and Rispoli Z [5] introduce a real-time animation control on drawing or pictures by hand gesture which required a lot more equipment setting and lacked access to the non-expert and younger users. So, they developed a new version that only required a smart tablet [6]. Their method to animate drawing is by hand gesture while ours is by symbol command in the paper interface, the advantage of ours is this may realize multiple objects animate in the same time to form a harmonious animated picture.

Besides the animation achieved by hand gestures, some achieve the animation effects by strokes as well. Motion doodles [8] are the motion sketch that works as a trajectory to direct characters' motion which was quite similar to our intention to use symbol stroke to animate the sketch. While the difference is that their motion trajectories were delicate in differences which are way too difficult for children to control their stroke that precisely. Davis J, Agrawala M, Chuang E, et al. [7] created a rapid 3D figure animation by drawing 2D keyframe poses. which is different from our 2D drawing oriented animation for children. Among all the stroke-driven animation, Yonemoto S's [9] work is the most similar one to ours however. Their work mainly aims for novice animators and it's controlled in a computer which is not fit with children's intuitive preference to drawing on paper and the operation are not very explicit for children.

Besides passive driven animation, Lingens L, Sumner R W, Magnenat S [10] described a system that could automatically animate the drawing however its animation process performs deformation a lot which might frighten children as they mention in their paper. Besides, it is automatic animation so it is not controllable like ours.

There are also many commercial products to help novice users make animation such as stykz [11] pencil 2D [12] and FlipaClip [13]. But these are difficult and time consuming for children in general.

Based on previous research and inspiration, animating children's drawings is a promising field to help children express their idea. So, we present the animation symbol command system which enables children to transform their paper drawing into digital animation themselves.

3   Symbol Command

Inspired by the finding in the research stating that children tend to draw arrows or lines to indicate the direction of their drawing subject's motion [14], we thought about using such indicative symbol in children's drawing and let children's drawing moving like they imagining by themselves.

To accomplish children's usage of the animation symbol system, we need to take children's drawing habits, their ability of learning and understanding, and their anticipation into account. We summarized the following design goals for the system design:

- Easy to understand and use: the system needs to be simple enough to present in front of children so that it costs children little to learning, understanding, and memorizing
- Combine with children's drawing habits: children's drawings are creative and nothing should limit their freestyle in drawing.
- High agreement: the symbols need to obtain children's high agreement while being used by them.

Following these principles listed, we need to solve the following three key questions:

- what kind of animation/motion effect that children want to express in their drawings?
- what type of symbol can children understand and recognize with ease?
- how to achieve the corresponding animations accurately, when children draw the symbols?

To solve the questions above, we carried out three survey studies accordingly through which we extracted the motion that children want to express, explored what kind of symbol children will achieve high agreement, and finally analyzed system accessibility (see Fig. 1).

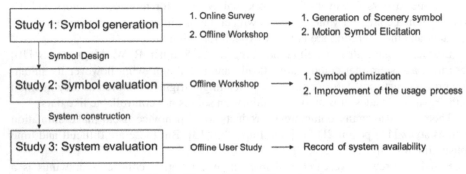

Fig. 1. The workflow of three studies

4   Study1: Symbol Generation

The goal of this study is to solve the first question. We first started online research to analyze drawings of children age 6 to 9. Then we conducted an offline workshop to test which animation operation children would understand and likely to use. Comparing the online and offline analysis, we analyze the most commonly used element in children's drawing, extracted the scenery symbol stroke, and understood what type of animation effect children can understand and have willing to do.

4.1   Generation of Scenery Symbol

To understand what kind of motion children want to express. We collect 435 drawings of children (aged 6 to 9) from the internet. Two researchers analyzed the drawing by looking into what type of motion children has expressed in their drawing and what kind of element they use to express it. Table 1 shows the result.

Table 1. Motion and the element used to express the motion

Motion	Element to express
Fly	Bird, butterfly, balloon, kite, airplane, spaceship
Fall/drop	Snowflake, raindrop, cloud, the trajectory of fallen leaves
Float	Boat, bubble, curvy stroke, cloud
Swim	Fish and bubble
Flow	The wavy line for water/river flow, dot, and lines
Run	Athletic track, running people, multiple lines, curvy line
Drive	Car, multiple lines, the spiral line for gas
Wave	Figure hands up, wavy line
Wiggle	An object that leans to the other side like flowers and tree
Speak	Dialog box
Smile	Smiley faces
Blink	Star, moon, wink eyes, sun

From Table 1 we found that besides different types of lines that children use to express emotion, the property of certain objects is another way to show motion such as sun and star in the sky, raindrop, snowflake, smoke from a chimney, etc. Therefore, we list the most frequently drawn item that can indicate motion (see Fig. 2). We categorized them as scenery symbol which defined as a set of sketch item that has its own motion property and acts as decoration in children's drawings.

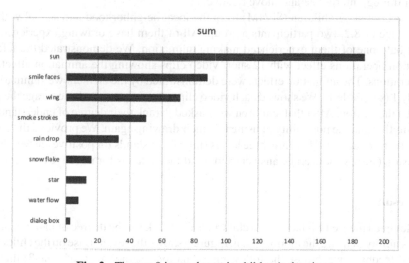

Fig. 2. The top 9 items drawn in children's drawings.

We further conclude the basic stroke that children used in the drawing set we gathered (see Table 2). Besides that, we could not summarize more symbol information because children's stroke is so random and not all of their drawings have motion stroke.

Table 2. Basic element stroke children used in their drawings.

DOT	●
LINE	
SHAPE	○ □ △

4.2 Offline Workshop: Motion Symbol Elicitation

As children at a young age have limited words to express and their drawings are too different to summary the common symbol. We tried to identify what kind of motion children could understand and like to use.

To obtain the possible motion, we refer to 18 animation operations that K-sketch system [15] concluded. Among which, we ruled out 6 that are too difficult for children like set timing, interpolate and move relative, etc.

We recruited 12 children (8F/4M) from the local neighborhood and school with an average age of 8.2, two participants a group. All of them have drawing experiences in school but none of them experienced making animation. We demonstrated the left 12 animation operations effect with 12 short video clips showing the animation effects of the operations. The animation effects were demonstrated by the element we summarized in study 1 (see Table 1). We showed each video clip to participants and encourage them to describe the motion. After that, children were asked to rank their degree of understanding of the motion and the possibility of using it in their drawing again. We provided the emoji to help them valuation. There are three levels smile face (stands for positive answer) none expression (stands for average answer) and a sad face (stands for negative answer).

4.3 Result

We calculated the 3 emoji faces from children's feedback for the degree of understanding and possibility of using the motion again. Figure 3 shows the result. Base on the children's rate and feedback we choose the following animation operations (see Table 3) that are more understandable and likely to be used in children's drawings according to their feedback.

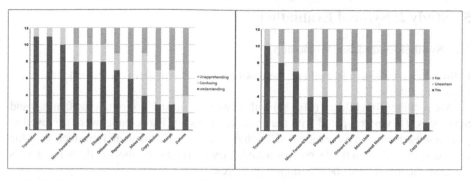

Fig. 3. Understanding of motion feedback (left) and likability of using the motion (right)

Table 3. Motion and the element used to express the motion

Animation operation
Translate, rotate, scale
Appear, disappear
Repeat motion
Move back and forth
Orient to path

4.4 Symbol Design

After the online and offline study, we tried to design the motion symbol by integrating the basic element (see Table 2) to express the motion effect that was proof understandable and possible to be used by children. The design of the motion symbol must be simple and easy to understand by children. Figure 4 shows the design process. All symbols will be listed in the next session after symbol evaluation.

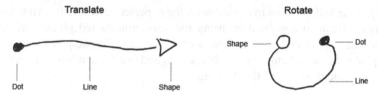

Fig. 4. The design of symbols command.

5 Study 2: Symbol Evaluation

5.1 Symbol Evaluation Workshop

In this study, we aimed to evaluate the motion symbols whether it is understandable for children to use.

We recruited 10 children (5F/5M) with an average age of 7.6 from local families and neighbors. They participated with their parent's consent. Participants were surveyed in pairs and each session were recorded. Each pair were firstly given an introduction of the motion symbols. Then they would be asked to try to use the symbols to draw in pictures we gave them and describe the motion they drew.

In the introduction part, to explicitly explain the function of a symbol without technical involvement yet (we use PowerPoint here to demonstrated). Each motion symbol was shown with an example object. After the symbol applied to the objects, the object would move as the symbol defined (on next slides). To help participants identify drawing stroke and symbol stroke, we use different colors to indicate them, black color for drawing stroke and red color for symbol stroke. The Combination of different drawing objects in the same pictures is also demonstrated in two comparing slides, one was before adding the static symbol, the other was after adding the symbols in which the picture is animated. These example usage of the symbols at the end were working as a guideline and visually extend to show how this symbol would work.

After the introduction of the motion symbols, participants were given several already drew sketches which are all sketches accessible in children's recognition like animals and scenery sketches. They need to use the red pen we provided and draw the symbol stroke on to these semi-construction sketches according to what motion they want to achieve. When participants were drawing, all the symbols drew in square cards were shown in front of them. The intention to do so is what we want to explore is whether children could use the symbol as they wish, while not require them to remember all the symbols. When they finish drawing motion symbols, researchers encouraged them to describe what kind of motion they want to express by using the symbols. We measured whether the symbol is understood by participants by two standards. First, if participants could draw the motion symbols correctly, and Second If they express it with the right motion effect.

Finally, we asked children to comment on the experience to use the symbol strokes. We encourage them to comment by using the semi-constructed phrases, if only, the experience will be perfect. Figure 5 shows a peek of study 2. Participants were welcome to drawing new pictures themselves (in black pen) and use the symbol command (in red pen) to express the dynamic of the drawing.

5.2 Result

In general, the feedback of most group was positive, many children expressed their interests and curiosity in the introduction part and convey a willingness to animate their drawings after the semi-construction session. However, we also found some problems:

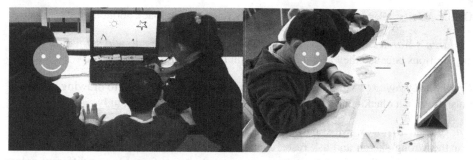

Fig. 5. A pair of participants listening to researches introduction of the symbols (left), and drawn symbols by themselves (right) (Color figure online)

- there are some preferences on certain motion symbols, compared with other symbols, translate is the most used symbol. We assume that is because the symbol is most intuitive and convenient for every drawn object.
- two participants had a confused understanding of "Orient to Path" and translation for its precise differences.
- symbols with more strokes more inclined to evoke error drawing. 3 younger participants misusing the motion symbols with less stroke in.

According to the feedback from the participants, we adjusted and redesigned motion symbols as Fig. 6 shows.

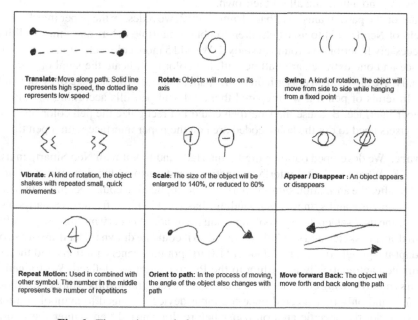

Fig. 6. The motion symbol command we iterated after study 2.

Other Advice. Participants also give us very precious feedback about their experience.

Children's Worries. 4 participants express their unwillingness to add symbol to assign any motions because they afraid it would ruin the drawings

Colors in Drawings. More than 5 kids ask for a more colorful pen to drawing since we only provide a black pen for them to free sketch at the end of the study.

Unexpected Mistakes. Most participants encounter mistake stroke. They unexpectedly star the wrong sketch and ask researchers for help stating that the stroke wasn't their intention. In the other situation, some younger participants forgot to use different color pens to draw the symbols which also drew our attentions.

6 Study 3: System Evaluation

6.1 System Introduction

Hardware. We use Neo Smartpen [16] and augmented paper with special dots pattern (Ncode [17]) as our input devices. With the help of the IR cameral embedded inside the smartpen to trace the sketch in dot patterned paper, users' sketch in the paper could be synchronized to digital display in real-time. Through this way we could preserve the quality and enjoyment of paper drawing for children while accomplishing dynamic animation effects which would fulfill children with a sense of satisfying and accomplishment for drawing and animating all on their own.

Base on the participants' feedback from study 2, we redesign the paper interface with the help of Ncode [17] to assist children to obtain multiple colors and other additional and necessary functions we found in study 2. We add 5 more color selections on the paper interface and one extra square outline with red color to indicate the symbol command used only. We also add an eraser icon on the paper interface for the sake of error symbol input. In terms of pen fill, we prepared them colorful pen fills according to colors on the paper interface. Because the smartpen could not recognize the pen color other than black. Users need to dot the color-coded area on the paper interface with a pen tip.

Software. We developed our own digital interface and link it with Neo Smartpen using their SDK. What the digital interface function was to display the dynamic state of the drawings after the animation symbol marked. The application could recognize two kinds of input (drawing and symbol commanding) base on the input from the Smartpen side (whether the user selects the symbol input square or not). Scenery motions were defined as both drawing sketch and symbol command so it could be drawn under drawing stroke. We adapt the google quick draw dataset [18] to spot the scenery motions and they will be animated automatically according to the Python script we defined. We trained our motion symbol drawing classifier ourselves. And the recognition procedure of the motion symbol would only be triggered once the input devices changed to symbol command mode (pen dot the specific area on paper before drawing). To encounter the multiple objects' animation problem, we introduced the quote stroke which is the corner mark on the diagonal of the target objects. It is also recognized under symbol drawing mode, without which the algorithm would regard the full paper's object as the target to animate by default.

The digital interface could be seen in Fig. 7 which were also explained the procedure of the system.

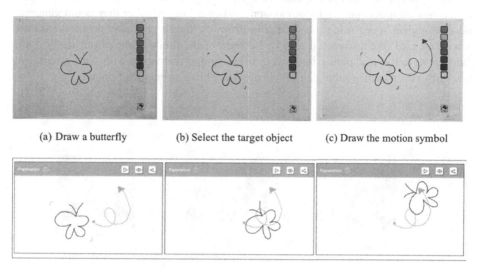

(a) Draw a butterfly   (b) Select the target object   (c) Draw the motion symbol

(d) Animation result on the digital interface

Fig. 7. The process of the system functions.

6.2 System Evaluation Workshop

In the study, we recruited 14 participants (10F/4M) from local neighborhoods and schools with an average age of 8.2. Six of them participated in our second study. At the beginning of this study, we introduced them to the symbol commands and showed participants how to animate the drawing strokes with a few examples. Then participants could draw themselves with one researcher besides to guide them. After they finished their drawing, Researchers will ask them the following 3 questions, and participants were asked to answer with emoji faces we introduced in First study.

- Q1. I feel interested in animating my drawings?
- Q2. I find it easy to use the system?
- Q3. With this system, I will have more ideas when I draw

6.3 Result

In general, participants showed great interest in our systems. Most of them required to do more drawing after they experience it once. Figure 8 shows the children's answers to the question we designed which indicated that the system is promising and interesting for children to use. Over 86% of participants felt over average interesting in the form of animating their own drawings. They express their interests in it not only by the answers but also expressing it during the study. In terms of the accessibility of the system, half of the participants gave positive answers while the other half gave the average or below. We found that those negative answers were given by younger participants whose strokes sometimes are unrecognized by our system. When asking whether they could generate more new ideas when using the system to draw, we didn't get many positive answers as we expected. We analyzed it may be because of the limited time of our study goes, children were too fascinating into trying drawing and animating with our system. So, they didn't even come to the idea of whether they have a new idea or not.

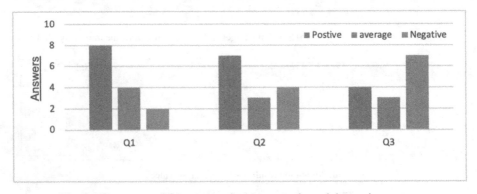

Fig. 8. The answer children gave after they experienced the motion system.

Besides the data we collect, we also found some problems during the process of the study.

- Younger participants whose strokes were broke times during symbol drawing, causing mistake recognition of symbol and no response sometimes. This largely frustrated them while using our system. One of the participants became cranky seeing other counterparts' drawing works while his not.
- Some participants forget the step to quote the targeted objects and failed to animate the drawing. We found that children prefer to draw one object with one symbol command followed instead of finishing the drawing and animated them at last. This causes way more steps to go between drawing and animation commanding.
- The objects in participants' drawings sometimes were too close causing the selection of objects were overlaying. some of our participants are tent to fulfill the whole pictures or draw two objects really close which cause the selection problems and bug the animation process.

7   Discussion

Through three studies, we completed the end-to-end exploration of the animation symbol command design for children, from children's dynamic drawing potential, their preferences in animation effect, symbol command generation, symbol evaluation to the usability study. Base on the result of three studies, we discuss the dynamic intention in children's drawing, understandable and accessible symbol command for children to use and the usability of the Papimation system.

The fundamental design goal of Papimation system was to design the intuitive command that children can use with ease to animate their drawing to better express their ideas. In study 1 we invest what kind of motion children intended to express in their drawing in online research and concluded that other than using line or dots to express speed or trajectory of the objects, there are several common scenery items to express motion appeared in children's drawings which we categorized it as scenery symbol and could animate themselves. However, we also concluded that children's drawings have too many uncontrollable factors we could not distill more drawing symbols from it. Instead, we put our eyes on what kind of animation effect that children could understand and design it with the basic element children use in their drawings.

To evaluated the design of animation symbol we conducted Study 2, the feedback of the participants was shown that some most intuitive commands are commonly used like translating and rotation while some similar command were confused used in the drawing. And comparing with the symbols that have more strokes, less stroke symbols have high accuracy among children. So, we iterated the symbol commands and developed the Papimation system.

The usability of the Papimation system was tested in study 3, participants were taught and encourage to use the system by themselves afterwards. Through the workshop and feedback of participants, the system was understandable and accessible for children which was in line with what we hope in the beginning. However, the current symbol system has several limitations, the tolerate for children's stroke is still low and the multiple-steps like quoting were burdening children's drawing process, and the feedback of the system was not very clear for children when their commands weren't recognized.

Looking into the future, we will iterate the system and hope to bring this system into a broad field. We believe it is promising in children's habiting nurturing and learning for example children's storytelling and expression.

8 Conclusion

Papimation is a system that enables children to use symbol stroke on paper and animated their drawings on the digital screen. Children's drawing is a static way to express their ideas, this paper was dedicated to let children animated their drawings by simple symbol command stroke which could turn the static expression into a dynamic one. We conducted 3 survey studies. From the first study, we concluded scenery symbols from children's drawings on the internet and filter the animation operations effects that could be understood and described by children. Base on that, we design motion symbols and evaluated them among children in study 2. We filter again with children's better understanding of motion symbols and iterated the motion symbols after study 2. Papimation system were developed and applied to study 3. We evaluated the system's usability among participants. As results shows, most participants were like to use the system except for some problems they encounter in the process which we will solve and upgraded the system. We are hoping to use the system in children's education, fun play, and storytelling in the future.

Acknowledgement. This research was funded by the Engineering Research Center of Computer Aided Product Innovation Design, Ministry of Education, National Natural Science Foundation of China (52075478), Major Project of Zhejiang Social Science Foundation (21XXJC01ZD).

References

1. Einarsdottir, J., Dockett, S., Perry, B.: Making meaning: children's perspectives expressed through drawings. Early Child Dev. Care **179**(2), 217–232 (2009)
2. Malchiodi, C.A.: Understanding Children's Drawings. Guilford Press, Newyork (1998)
3. Raffle, H., Vaucelle, C., Wang, R., et al.: Jabberstamp: embedding sound and voice in traditional drawings. In: Proceedings of the 6th International Conference on Interaction Design and Children, pp. 137–144 (2007)
4. Jacoby, S., Buechley, L.: Drawing the electric: storytelling with conductive ink. In: Proceedings of the 12th International Conference on Interaction Design and Children, pp. 265–268 (2013)
5. Momeni, A., Rispoli, Z.: Dranimate: rapid real-time gestural rigging and control of animation. In: Adjunct Proceedings of the 28th Annual ACM Symposium on User Interface Software & Technology, pp. 61–62 (2015)
6. Momeni, A., Rispoli, Z.: Dranimate: paper becomes tablet, drawing becomes animation. In: Proceedings of the 2016 CHI Conference Extended Abstracts on Human Factors in Computing Systems, pp. 3735–3737 (2016)
7. Davis, J., Agrawala, M., Chuang, E., et al.: A sketching interface for articulated figure animation. In: ACM Siggraph 2006 courses, p. 15-es (2006)
8. Thorne, M., Burke, D., van de Panne, M.: Motion doodles: an interface for sketching character motion. ACM Trans. Graph. (TOG) **23**(3), 424–431 (2004)
9. Yonemoto, S.: A sketch-based skeletal figure animation tool for novice users. In: 2012 Ninth International Conference on Computer Graphics, Imaging and Visualization, pp. 37–42. IEEE (2012)
10. Lingens, L., Sumner, R.W., Magnenat, S.: Towards automatic drawing animation using physics-based evolution. In: Proceedings of the 2020 ACM Interaction Design and Children Conference: Extended Abstracts, pp. 314–319 (2020)
11. Stykz. https://www.stykz.net/
12. Pencil2D, Animation. https://www.pencil2d.org/
13. FlipaClip. https://support.flipaclip.com/hc/en-us
14. Mohd Shukri, S.R., Howes, A.: How do children adapt strategies when drawing on a tablet? In: CHI'14 Extended Abstracts on Human Factors in Computing Systems, pp. 1177–1182 (2014)
15. Davis, R.C., Colwell, B., Landay, J.A.: K-sketch: a 'kinetic' sketch pad for novice animators. In: Proceedings of the SIGCHI Conference on Human Factors in Computing Systems, pp. 413–422 (2008)
16. Neo Smartpen Homepage. https://www.neosmartpen.com/en/
17. Neo Smartpen Ncode-SDK2.0. https://github.com/NeoSmartpen/Ncode-SDK2.0
18. Googlecreativelab quickdraw-dataset. https://github.com/googlecreativelab/quickdraw-dataset

TangiLetter: An Interactive Vocabulary System for Children to Learn Words About Wild Animals

Fangtian Ying[1], Pinhao Wang[1]($\boxtimes$), Yuping Zou[2], Xinglin Zheng[2], Muling Huang[2], and Cheng Yao[1]

[1] College of Computer Science and Technology, Zhejiang University, Hangzhou, China
{group318,12021205,yaoch}@zju.edu.cn
[2] College of Software Technology, Zhejiang University, Hangzhou, China
{21951518,xinglin_zheng,21951218}@zju.edu.cn

Abstract. Word-learning is a vital process for children to form language, and it is the fundamentals of people interacting with each other. However, few studies focus on children's experiences during the learning process, and most of them are passive learning. Because of the development of multi-sensory technology and intelligent hardware, we can create TangiLetter, a word-learning system that combines abstract language with the physical world. Through our research on children, we find that children at the age of 3–6 are curious about living things, and they are developing a native framework for them. Inspired by this, we propose TangiLetter, an interactive vocabulary system for children to learn wild animal words. By combining children's language ability, motor ability, and observation ability to balance the physical and digital worlds, children learn wild animal words more intuitively. Children can pronounce the animal's name and find the corresponding letter balls to get a related audiobook as a reward. It creates intriguing experiences when children are learning. In this paper, we detail the system design of TangiLetter and present the design principles of the word-learning system. To explore our system's usability, we conducted studies. The result showed that TangiLetter could facilitate children to learn wild animal words, and there is a high level of engagement and willingness with the system.

Keywords: Word learning · Preschool education · Multi-sensory interaction · Play-based design · Children · Intelligent hardware device

1 Introduction

By age 3, children spontaneously start knowing the physical world and meanwhile categorizing objects in their world. At this vital age, they need to learn the essential words to define the world they see. Learning primary vocabulary at early childhood can develop not only their savvy pre-academic but also social skills. Language is the fundamentals of people interacting with each other, and words are the infrastructure of language. Furthermore, wild animals' sounds and noises appeal to children's attention

© Springer Nature Switzerland AG 2021
N. Streitz and S. Konomi (Eds.): HCII 2021, LNCS 12782, pp. 287–298, 2021.
https://doi.org/10.1007/978-3-030-77015-0_21

to some extent and interest them most, such as cat's sound 'Meow,' 'squeak' from mouse and 'howl' from wolves. It is relatively easy for toddlers to mimic and then try to understand them. By learning wild animal words, children can combine those natural sounds with particular animals. By learning abstract vocabulary, they can connect conceptual language with the physical world. Thus, the category of wild animal words is an ideal start for children to learn vocabulary.

The rapid development of technology and the digital world leads to dramatic growth in interactive applications and children's toys. The percentage of children who own a tablet is 43%, and who has access to a smartphone is 95%. Since 2011, it has increased by 54% [1]. There are thousands of products on the Apple Store or Google Play aimed at young children for preschool vocabulary education. Many of them are not scientific and cannot meet children's needs. It is necessary to design a word learning system by using age-appropriate technologies. It proves that transferring digital information to a tangible realm could benefit children and enhance their informational aspects [2]. Tangible User Interface (TUIs) can also promote children's learning and collaboration, making child-related products more fun and attractive. Multi-sensory design determines how people react to feedback in many aspects, including subtle and obvious ways, consciously and unconsciously ways. The multi-sensory design's main feature uses multi-sensor technology to provide information to different human sense organs, such as sight, smell, taste, and touch. Thus, bring new experiences or enhancement to users and create more fun or productivities. It has more potential to design an appropriate children's word-learning system and combine real-world with digital information that promotes new learning experience for children.

In this paper, we conducted an interview survey of target users (3–6 years old children) and found out that they are interested in seeing animals and even want to touch them. However, wild animals are scarce and impossible for children to feel them in the physical world. Somehow digital technology and a multi-sensory approach could be the bridge between children's learning and wild animals. We tried to find an appropriate connection between these two situations. Therefore, we designed an interactive word system that combines wild animals' information with multi-sensory feedback to promote children's motivation and engagement in learning animals' word-spelling. This system includes two parts: the software part and the hardware part, using voice recognition, natural language processing (NLP), near field communication (NFC), wireless control, motor movement control and other technologies. We conducted user research to study how children reacted to this system and to what extent this system benefits children in learning wild animal words. Our study's main contribution is that we combine children's language ability, motor ability, and observation ability to balance the physical and digital world, which can help children learn wild animal words more intuitively. Furthermore, this study presents the strategy of children's word-learning design.

2   Related Work

2.1   Play-Based Learning

In recent years, play-based learning contributed a lot to the HCI community. It has rich interactions and could form into different kinds of hybrid products for both adults and children. Many researchers have confirmed that play-based learning is a practical approach for children to learn new knowledge. Luiza Superti Pantoja [3] investigated existing design technologies methods aiming at children under the age of 5 and introduced play-based design and method by involving 3–4-year-old children in the design process. Linda de Valk [4], a TU/e Ph.D., designed several open-day prototypes and conducted many kinds of research. The results demonstrated that applying the three stages of play can enrich designs for playful experiences and provide valuable insights. Valentina Andries [5] devoted himself to create child-friendly spaces in a pediatric hospital to meet modernization and involve related stakeholders to explore how social play among 3–5-year old children supported by digital technology.

During playing, preschoolers can focus on design tactile 3D shapes and can construct a specific concept [6]. Tania Rocha [7] paid an effort to enhance the writing and reading activities of children with learning disabilities, and the user tests revealed the success of multimedia interaction. Bodily play and game experiences also contribute to learning Danish Linguistic Connotations through movement-based games [8]. Design age-appropriate game experiences can enhance learning and make it accessible to preschoolers. We create an interactive word learning system with an engaging, interactive experience that involves children in fetching dynamic letter balls in the physical world. Despite previous research, which mostly focuses on play-based design methods and passive learning, our system concentrated on arousing preschoolers' initiative to learn about wild animals' interest and curiosity. Furthermore, involving children in an exploratory learning experience.

2.2 Applications for Word Learning

Many previous studies conducted on vocabulary learning, and there are already plenty of applications on the Apple App Store or Google Play. Berto Gonzalez [9] designed a virtual agent that can embody whole-body behaviors and encourage children to use this kind of expression for better learning language. Using Near Field Communication (NFC) technology, Ivan Sanchez [10] tagged objects in the everyday environment and linked them to mobile devices to create participatory learning applications and enhance foreign language, biology, and physical exercise studies. Many of them focused on word recognition, virtual reality (VR) has been used to develop Autism Spectrum Disorder (ASD) Children's social, cognitive, and literacy skills [10].

Pure software like Energetic Alpha [11] utilized motion and video design to educate preschoolers and focus on creating an educational but entertaining experience. Mei Pu and Zheng Zhong [12] developed an AR-based interaction game in improving preschool English-vocabulary learning. The research result shows that this situational interaction gaming approach improves learning interest significantly meanwhile decrease cognition load. Besides, through augmented reality (AR), Min Fan [13] built an AR PhonoBlocks app for children from low socioeconomic status (SES) schools to better learning of English alphabetic. 'Swipe-N-Tag' and 'Snap-N-Recognize' [14] are lightweight picture-based word-learning applications on the mobile phone. They are flexible and individually adaptable, specially designed for the early language learning of ASD children.

Some researchers are concerned that, on the one hand, these digital applications provide children various opportunities and methods for learning vocabulary and increase digital learning [15]. On the other hand, they decrease physical exploration [16]. So, it reduces the likelihood for children to interact with their surrounding world. The real world is the foundation of our daily lives. Sooner or later, children will engage in this world, and the balance of the virtual world and the real world determines whether children will adapt to society in the future.

2.3 Multi-sensory Design

The design could be intriguing and the experience could be rich by using multi-sensory [17], presenting a perceived affordance [18]. It can also provide numerous opportunities for users to engage with products and even in the educational field. Franca Garzotto and Eleonora Beccaluva [19] present Interactive Multi-Sensory Environments (iMSEs) based on ambient embedded devices and physical materials. It demonstrated that iMSEs could improve children's behavior. However, it is limit to large space and the challenges in real educational contexts. Tangible user interface (TUIs) has become popular in recent years. Due to the improvement of modern technology and physical sensor [20], tangible products could build the bridge that mapping semantics and physical manipulations—for example, the robot as a new technology for children to learn [21]. MIT Lifelong Kindergarten group created educational toys based on digital manipulatives [22, 23]. Zaman B, Xie L believe that tangible products are more interesting than simple digital products and more suitable for children to learn [24, 25]. In this paper, we pay an effort to utilize multi-sensory as a medium to bridge abstract wild animal words and their physical characteristics, such as voice patterns.

3   Learning with TangiLetter

Children learn pronunciation before learning primary vocabulary. Usually, toddlers know how to pronounce 'dad' and 'mama' initially. Then they start to define the world by using the 'word' they absorb from the outside world. In terms of growth, ages 3–6 are crucial for developing executive skills [26], such as selective attention, cognitive flexibility and planning. At this age, curiosity, social play, language and communication also are built as their core foundations [27]. Child growth is a dramatic and high-complex process [28]. Within several years, they master plenty of crucial skills and there is a milestone shift. Three-year-old children can copy the dynamic surrounding behavior and name familiar things or people if they get instructed. Later they understand a simple concept, develop the abstract ability, expressing their interests and feel excited about exploring new things. It is beneficial to engage them in activities that they are willing to participate in and can enjoy.

Based on the above researches and studies, we designed TangiLetter, an interactive vocabulary system for children to learn wild animals' words. It can motivate children's learning interests and cater to their need to explore nature. Despite previous research which focuses on designing learning application on mobile devices based on pure digital method, we concentrated on motivating them and provide them an intriguing but natural experience for engagement and education, thus led to a better understanding of wild animals' words. With interest, learning will be initiative and positive, and children can learn better through play.

We explored new possibilities and interactive forms of children's learning of primary words by mimicking wild animals' natural characteristics in digital and physical ways. Expand the multi-dimensional training of children's word-learning and enhance their engagement by designing the system mechanism. Deepens their understanding of inaccessible natural animals and abstract concepts by presenting a perceived affordance.

4 System Design

4.1 Description of the System

TangiLetter system consists of two parts: the software part and the hardware part (Fig. 1).

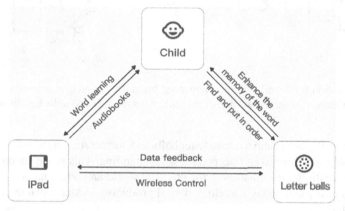

Fig. 1. Interaction framework of TangiLetter.

Software system: this software system offers children a choice of four types of animals, including sea, land, forest and polar. It will listen to the word children pronounced and match the correctness. Then the system instructs children to find the running letter balls by voice. When they bring letter balls back, the software system will tell them to put them together in the correct order. When placed in the right order, the software rewards the child with audiobooks related to the animal. It helps kids strengthen their listening and pronunciation skills and expand their imagination and comprehension skills (Fig. 2).

Hardware system: the system provides children with 26 balls, and each of them corresponds to a letter of the English alphabet. When the child selects an animal and says its name, the corresponding letter ball will move, make the animal's sound, and vibrate slightly, as if awaken a living creature. Thus, offer an educational but entertaining learning experience.

The system provides multi-sensory interactive modes. Children can play and interact with the TangiLetter by selecting one kind of wild animal and pronounce the animal's name. It will actuate letter balls. And the driving force is provided by the motor inside.

Fig. 2. Application for TangiLetter. (a) Homepage interface; (b) pick an animal; (c) follow the instruction to learn wild animal words; (d) put letter balls in order and unlock audiobook.

System voice will guide them to chase letter balls and correct spelling words. And finally, get audiobooks as a reward and deepen the understanding. This mode encourages children to explore digital information in the physical world and retain natural characteristics as far as possible in today's world of digital products—Foster social interaction and engagement.

4.2 Procedure

We classified the TangiLetter system into four steps (Fig. 3). Step 1 is picking an animal. Children can pick up an animal type and select an animal. The visual and graphical user interface consists of easily identifiable cartoon images and simple words, which do not add to children's cognition load. Step 2 is learning the vocabulary of an animal. System voice will instruct and say 'What is This?'. When the child knows it and names the animal in English, it will say, 'Bingo, you are great!'. When the child does not know it, the system will reveal the answer and invite the child to repeat the answer. Step 3 is finding the letter balls. Voice will say 'The animal is lost, could you find them and bring them back?', meanwhile the related letter balls will be driven by the motor inside and make a significant movement. Step 4 is a learning enhancement. The child puts the letter balls in order and deepens understanding of the word. When the system detects the correct placement, it triggers subsequent sound and animation, mapping the letter ball's states to the interface. Finally, play the audiobook story as part of the reward mechanism and provide further learning.

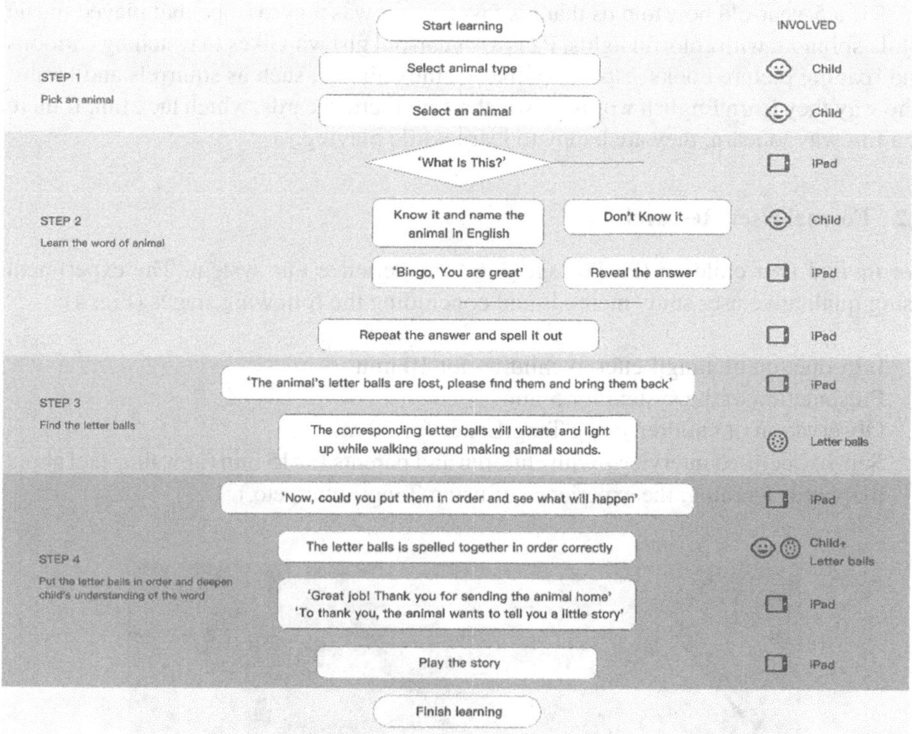

Fig. 3. Workflow of TangiLetter system.

4.3 Feature of Our System

By engaging children in interacting with TangiLetter, the system could teach young kids how to pronounce animal words and their spelling and foster the will of self-directed learning. Once a child learns simple wild animal words, he/she will start to create meaning and crosslinking with other words. More importantly, it establishes building blocks and the foundation for sentences. By knowing 'horse,' they understand 'run like a horse.' Furthermore, the system provides children with a new learning experience and increasing engagement, combining physical exercise and digital learning products. Wild animal words are fun and engaging, making it easy and appropriate for building the TangiLetter system. The multi-sensory design helps build children's vocabulary and expand their view of what an animal is.

5 Studies

5.1 Preliminary User Research

Two children were invited for semi-structured interviews to better understanding what the children were interested in word learning.

P1, a 5-year-old boy, told us that his favorite toy was a gyroscope that played music while spinning with colorful lights. P2 is a 4-year-old girl who likes to watching cartoons and reading picture books, especially likes some animals, such as squirrels and lambs. The way they learn English words now is through literacy cards, which lack fun. If there is a fun way to learn, they are happy to learn while playing.

5.2 Formal User Research

We invited four children (P3-P6) age 3–6 to experience our system. The experiment using qualitative user study methods and concluding the following stages (Fig. 4):

1. Introduction of TangiLetter to children for 10 min
2. Presentation of the system for 5 min
3. Observation of children using TangiLetter for 20 min
4. Semi-structured interviews with children and parents for 15 min (how they feel about the words learning, the experience of using TangiLetter, etc.)

Fig. 4. Children interacting with TangiLetter system in the experiment.

6   Results

The results showed the TangiLetter system was a fun and novel way of learning words about wild animals. All the children were interested in TangiLetter. The engagement of users is high, which shows the accessibility and suitability of the system. Children (age 3–6) can express themselves, including their ideas and feelings, rather than just talking about the world around them, and they can answer simple questions (such as, "What do you feel when you see the letter ball moves?"). They understand what the system voice is saying and have fun with it. When we talk with them, we can understand much of what they said. In this study, to make the results more accurate and reliable, we confirmed their feelings (positive or negative) by observing them interact with the system and then draw a conclusion by asking them simple questions. Questions include "Do you like to play with it?", "Is this funny and interesting?", "Do you like learning words in this way?". All the children were interested in TangiLetter, and some users said they were excited to see the letters come alive. P3 said the system gave her a new way to enjoy learning English words. P4 and P6 said they would like to own such a system.

Interestingly, children would grab the letter balls subconsciously once they saw the balls moving and making animal noises, which successfully captured their attention. P5 said that he likes to chase the light-up ball because of the funny.

Besides, we found that TangiLetter could enhance the connection and understanding of animals' words for children. P3 said she had heard the sound of a chicken before but didn't know how to spell the word chicken. P4 said she didn't know what a squirrel's call sounded like before until learning this vocabulary.

We also encountered some problems during the experiments. For example, P4 needs two letters "R" of the alphabet when learning the word squirrel. And another letter ball, "R," is added, which is a problem that needs to be improved. Besides, there was also a problem that the letter ball ran too far because the children did not find the letter ball in time (P5).

There were some useful feedback and advice from children and parents. P6 suggested that this system could have a multiplayer mode so that he could play with his sister. Some parents suggested that, to some extent, expanding the range of words in the app to include plants, people, sports, flags, etc., can enrich the system and make it more interesting.

7 Suggestions for Designing Systems for Children's Word-Learning System

Word-learning systems can be categorized as several levels for different target users. As discussed earlier, the word-learning system has multiple ways to construct including play-based and multi-sensory. We propose principles based on TangiLetter's design and study feedback for the future design of children word-learning systems:

- When designing such systems, researchers should introduce age-appropriate design methods. Products should meet children's cognitive level at this age, rather than adding plenty of interaction or design elements.
- Moving objects are more attractive to children than static things. Children feel exciting and lively to communicate and play with dynamic objects or place themselves in a dynamic environment.
- Compared with pure software interaction, physical world interaction and spatial cues bring children more thrilling experiences, especially those under six years old.
- Colors, voices and animal sounds enrich the interaction and make objects more vivid. It benefits to learning effectiveness of children and fosters the willingness to learn by themselves.
- The mimicked animal based on multi-sensory triggers curiosity and enhance the exploring motivation. It is easy for children to understand it.

8 Limitation and Future Work

The TangiLetter is welcomed by our target users (children at the age of 3–6), they are very active throughout the experience. However, the current system still has several limitations. First, there is some room for improving the accuracy of speech recognition, sometimes the child names the animal correctly, but the system does not trigger the interaction of congratulations. It reveals the answer, thereby leads to a frustrating experience. Second, letter balls have no obstacle avoidance system, and it is very likely to hit the obstacle in the narrow space, resulting in damage. And each letter ball could present only one kind of letter. When there are repeated words, like goose or squirrel, it becomes difficult to form words. We tried to use the two halves of the ball to represent two words, but it increases children's cognitive load and may confuse them. In the future, we will explore digital screens to replace a particular letter. It could also provide more possibility to generate more interaction. Third, we found that older children (more than six years old) have a faster grasp of the system, and the vocabularies are less complicated. Still, they feel good about the reward audiobook and the dynamic environment created by letter balls' movement, which makes them feel warm, just like a smart companion animal.

In the future, our system will be further improved. We will continue developing the TangiLetter by adding more categories and wild animal species, constructing the knowledge database, and adding optional senior modes to enhance the system's sustainability. Besides, we will make the movement of the letter ball more controllable and stable. We will also pay an effort to develop a guidance mechanism to help children access and explore more knowledge, teach children about empathy, and love and care for animals in the world. In addition, we are about to involve interaction between parents and teachers with children to enhance communication and socialization.

9 Conclusion

In general, this paper presents a novel interactive system for 3–6-year-old children to learn wild animal words and stimulate interest in learning. Compared to the previous system, we concentrated on arousing preschoolers' initiative learning interest and curiosity about wild animals, engaging exploratory learning experience for children. An intriguing mechanism has been designed to motivate children to learn wild animal words in exciting interactive ways. We also present design principles of such a word-learning system according to the experiment of the TangiLetter.

Overall, we believe this study is a ground-breaking experience by appropriately using multi-sensory technology to bridge abstract wild animals' words and their physical characteristics. We created the TangiLetter to enhances children's engagement in learning wild animal words by combining real-world with digital information, promoting new learning experiences for children and facilitating their word-learning exploration.

Acknowledgments. This research was funded by the Engineering Research Center of Computer Aided Product Innovation Design, Ministry of Education, National Natural Science Foundation of China (52075478), Major Project of Zhejiang Social Science Foundation (21XXJC01ZD).

References

1. Washington, D.C: The common sense census: media use by kids age zero to eight. Common Sense Media, 263–283 (2017)
2. Detken, K., Martinez, C., Schrader, A.: The search wall: tangible information searching for children in public libraries. In: Proceedings of the 3rd International Conference on Tangible and Embedded Interaction. TEI 2009, Cambridge, UK, pp. 289–296 (2009)
3. Superti Pantoja, L., Diederich, K., Crawford, L., et al.: Play-based design: giving 3- to 4-year-old children a voice in the design process. In: Proceedings of the 2020 CHI Conference on Human Factors in Computing Systems CHI 2020, Honolulu, HI, USA, pp. 1–14 (2020)
4. De Valk, L.: Designing for emergent play. In: Proceedings of the 11th International Conference on Interaction Design and Children IDC 2012, Bremen, Germany, pp. 335–338 (2012)
5. Andries, V.: Play technology with 3–5-year old children in a hospital setting. In: Proceedings of the 2018 Annual Symposium on Computer-Human Interaction in Play Companion Extended Abstracts CHI PALY 2018, Melbourne, VIC, Australia, pp. 5–8 (2018)
6. Södergren, A.C., Van Mechelen, M.: Towards a child-led design process a pilot study: when pre-schoolers' play becomes designing. In: Proceedings of the 18th ACM International Conference on Interaction Design and Children IDC 2019, Boise, ID, USA, pp. 629–634 (2019)
7. Rocha, T., Nunes, R.R., Barroso, J., et al.: Using game-based technology to enhance learning for children with learning disabilities: a pilot study. In: Proceedings of the 2019 3rd International Conference on Education and E-Learning ICEEL 2019, Barcelona, Spain, pp. 89–94 (2019)
8. Matjeka, L.P., Mueller, F.F.: Designing for bodily play experiences based on danish linguistic connotations of "playing a game". In: Proceedings of the Annual Symposium on Computer-Human Interaction in Play CHI PLAY 2020, Canada, pp. 19–31 (2020)
9. Gonzalez, B., Borland, J., Geraghty, K.: Whole body interaction for child-centered multimodal language learning. In: Proceedings of the 2nd Workshop on Child, Computer and Interaction WOCCI 2009, Cambridge, MA, pp. 1–5 (2009)
10. Winoto, P.: Reflections on the adoption of virtual reality-based application on word recognition for Chinese children with autism. In: Proceedings of the 15th International Conference on Interaction Design and Children DIC 2016, Manchester, UK, pp. 589–594 (2016)
11. Rinnert, G.C., Martens, M., Mooney, A., et al.: Energetic alpha, playful handwriting practice for children. In: Proceedings of the 2017 Conference on Interaction Design and Children DIC 2017, Stanford, CA, USA, pp. 687–691 (2017)
12. Pu, M., Zhong, Z.: Development of a situational interaction game for improving preschool children' performance in English-vocabulary learning. In: Proceedings of the 2018 International Conference on Distance Education and Learning ICDEL 2018, Beijing, China, pp. 88–92 (2018)
13. Fan, M., Antle, A.N.: An English language learning study with rural chinese children using an augmented reality app. In: Proceedings of the Interaction Design and Children Conference IDC 2020, London, UK, pp. 385–397 (2020)
14. Winoto, P., Tang, T.Y.: Poster: two lightweight and customizable picture-based word-learning mobile applications for chinese children with autism. In: Proceedings of the 2018 ACM International Joint Conference and 2018 International Symposium on Pervasive and Ubiquitous Computing and Wearable Computers UbiComp 2018, Singapore, Singapore, pp. 291–294 (2018)
15. Alakärppä, I., Jaakkola, E., Väyrynen, J., Häkkilä, J.: Using nature elements in mobile AR for education with children. In: Proceedings of the 19th International Conference on Human-Computer Interaction with Mobile Devices and Services MobileHCI 2017, Vienna, Austria, pp. 1–13 (2017)

16. Manches, A.: Digital manipulatives: tools to transform early learning experiences. Int. J. Tech. Enhanc. Learn. **3**(6), 608–626 (2011)

17. Schifferstein, H.N.J.: Multi-sensory design. In: Proceedings of the Second Conference on Creativity and Innovation in Design DESIRE 2011, Eindhoven, The Netherlands, pp. 361–362 (2011)

18. Soni, N., Gleaves, S., Neff, H., et al.: Adults' and children's mental models for gestural interactions with interactive spherical displays. In: Proceedings of the 2020 CHI Conference on Human Factors in Computing Systems CHI 2020, Honolulu, HI, USA, pp. 1–12 (2020)

19. Garzotto, F., Beccaluva, E., Gianotti, M., et al.: Interactive multi-sensory environments for primary school children. In: Proceedings of the 2020 CHI Conference on Human Factors in Computing Systems CHI 2020, Honolulu, HI, USA, pp. 1–12 (2020)

20. Zaman, B., Abeele, V.V., Markopoulos, P., et al.: Editorial: the evolving field of tangible interaction for children: the challenge of empirical validation, pp. 367–378 (2012)

21. Druin, A., Hendler, J.A.: Robots for Kids: Exploring New Technologies for Learning. Morgan Kaufmann Publishers Inc., San Francisco (2000)

22. Resnick, M., et al.: Digital manipulatives: new toys to think with. In: Proceedings of the SIGCHI Conference on Human Factors in Computing Systems CHI 1998, New York, NY, USA, pp. 281–287 (1998)

23. Zuckerman, O., Arida, S., Resnick, M.: Extending tangible interfaces for education: digital montessori-inspired manipulatives. In: Proceedings of the SIGCHI Conference on Human Factors in Computing Systems CHI 2005, New York, NY, USA, pp. 859–868 (2005)

24. Zaman, B.: Editorial: the evolving field of tangible interaction for children: the challenge of empirical validation. Pers. Ubiquitous Comput. **16**(4), 367–378 (2012)

25. Xie, L.: Are tangibles more fun? Comparing children's enjoyment and engagement using physical, graphical and tangible user interfaces. In: Proceedings of the 2nd International Conference on Tangible and Embedded Interaction TEI 2008, Boon, Germany, pp. 191–198 (2008)

26. Klenberg, L., Korkman, M., Lahti-Nuuttila, P.: Differential development of attention and executive functions in 3-to 12-year-old Finnish children. Dev. Neuropsychol. **20**(1), 407–428 (2001)

27. Centers for Disease Control and Prevention. Milestone moments (2011)

28. Siegler, R.S.: Cognitive variability. Dev. Sci. **10**(1), 104–109 (2007)

Designing Intelligent Environments

A Gaze-Based Unobstructive Information Selection by Context-Aware Moving UI in Mixed Reality

Nozomi Hayashida[✉], Hitoshi Matsuyama[✉], Shunsuke Aoki[✉], Takuro Yonezawa[✉], and Nobuo Kawaguchi[✉]

Graduate School of Engineering, Nagoya University, Nagoya, Japan
{linda,hitoshi,shunsuka,takuro,kawaguti}@ucl.nuee.nagoya-u.ac.jp

Abstract. Mixed reality (MR) technology has been attracting attention in the automobile industry and logistics industry for work training and remote work support for newcomers. However, work support using MR technology has the problem that displaying too much information obstructs the user's field of vision and rather interferes with the work. Therefore, it is necessary to detect the user's intention and provide only the information that the user wants. In addition, the system should be able to detect naturally from the user's behavior without interrupting the work, which the user explicitly selects. To solve these problems, in this paper, we use the user's gaze to determine whether to display content by estimating whether or not they are looking at information. Another problem with gaze-based research in MR work support is that it is difficult to determine which space you are looking at in a space where virtual space and real space intersect. In order to overcome this problem, in this research, we grasp the user's behavior from the movement of the user's gaze, and we suggest a way to determine make the user interface (UI) the movement of the gaze that is unlikely to occur during that behavior to see if the user is looking at the UI. As a result of the experiment, we were able to promote the movement of gaze that is different from the characteristics of the movement of gaze during work with the proposed UI movement.

Keywords: Mixed reality · Eye tracking · Gaze interaction · Natural user interfaces · Interaction techniques

1 Introduction

Work support using Mixed Reality (MR) technology, which combines the virtual world and the real world, has been attracting attention. For example, Japan Airlines (JAL) in the airline industry has introduced MR technology for flight crew pilot training and mechanic maintenance training. In the automobile industry, Toyota Motor Corporation is using MR technology at its maintenance sites to display work procedures and other information by superimposing 3D images on

© Springer Nature Switzerland AG 2021
N. Streitz and S. Konomi (Eds.): HCII 2021, LNCS 12782, pp. 301–315, 2021.
https://doi.org/10.1007/978-3-030-77015-0_22

the relevant areas. Also, many researchers are conducting research and development in various situations such as the construction industry where workers can work while displaying columns, pipes, ducts, etc. in 3D on-site, and the logistics field using MR technology for navigation and remote support in warehouses.

However, work support using MR technology has the following problems. When information is presented in MR technology, it fills the user's field of view and prevents them from working. The information required by the user depends on the user and the user's situation. Narrowing the information to context awareness is possible, but limited. Therefore, It is necessary to know what the user is looking for (whether they want that information or not). You can make the user make an explicit choice, such as hitting the "delete" button or saying "close", but this causes interruption of the work, which is not good. Therefore, the system must be able to naturally detect whether the user is trying to view the information or not. In addition, although many context-aware user interfaces (UI) using gaze have been studied, gaze-based UI in MR has the problem that it is difficult to determine which space the user is looking at in a space where virtual space and real space intersect.

In this paper, we propose a gaze-based unobstructive information selection by context-aware moving UI in MR. This system moves the information presentation window (UI) and matches it with the movement of the user's line of sight to determine whether the user wants information (Fig. 1). A core idea of the proposed method is to determine whether the user is looking at the information or not by generating movements of the UI that generate eye movements that generate eye movements that are unlikely to occur in normal work. In our preliminary experiment, we measured the directions of the head and the gaze during three different indoor tasks and confirmed that there are tasks in which only the gaze moves, and tasks in which the head and gaze do not move in tandem. Based on this experiment, we designed and implemented a small moving UI for work with moving eyes and a large moving UI for work with moving heads.

As a result of experimenting with our system to five subjects to see if they were looking at the UI during three different tasks, we confirmed that their gaze and the movement of the UI matched when they were looking at the UI, but not when they were looking at the background. According to the user survey conducted after the experiment, most of the participants answered that the movement of the UI was easy to follow, but for all tasks, they said that the movement of the UI was slow and they spent a lot of time gazing at it.

In summary, the contributions of this paper are threefold,

- We provide the basics of the relationship between work content and gaze movement through preliminary experiment in three common indoor tasks.
- Based on preliminary experiments, we consider eye movements that are unlikely to occur during work, and present a gaze-based information selection system by context-aware moving UI.
- We evaluated the usability of the UI through the user survey. As a result, we confirmed that the proposed UI was easy to follow, but the speed of movement should be faster and the dwell time shorter.

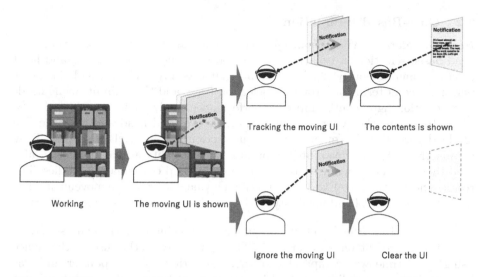

Fig. 1. Eye movement when looking at the moving UI and when not looking at it

2   Related Work

2.1   Activity Recognition Using Gaze

Andreas Bulling et al. devised 90 features based on the main eye movement features for recognizing human activity: saccades, fixations, and blinks [1]. In this study, they verified the method using five activity classes for eight participants in an office environment. Using a person-independent learning scheme, the average accuracy of all classes and participants was 76.1%, achieving a recall of 70.5%. The results showed that eye movement analysis is a rich and promising modality for activity recognition. Javier De Lope et al. proposed a system to recognize action behaviors performed in front of a computer using eye tracking information from low-resolution images captured by a conventional laptop webcam [2]. As a result of the experiment, it was concluded that it is possible to classify the behaviors performed in a typical office for multiple subjects having different physical characteristics such as skin, eye color, and face shape. Rafal Doniec et al. Based on a series of signals of accelerometer, gyroscope, and EMG acquired using smart glasses, a series of signals of accelerometer, gyroscope, and EMG acquired using smart glasses [9]. They predicted the appropriate activity class in about 85% of the cases. However, they concluded that there is insufficient research on the characteristics of specific classes of cognitive activity in this area, and that a more complex classification of activities associated with driving a car would help improve learning outcomes in driver training and testing centers. However, the methods developed in these studies were aimed at recognizing only those activities that are restricted to one specific location. So we extended the scope of our analysis to indoor tasks.

2.2 Gaze-Based Interaction

Head Orientation. Yuan Yuan Qian et al. compared eye-based selection with head-based selection in isolation to selection using both eye tracking and head tracking simultaneously [8]. They found that eye-only selection had the worst performance in terms of error rate, selection time, and throughput, while head-only selection significantly improved performance. Ludwig Sidenmark et al. proposed to exploit the synergistic motion of the eyes and head and used the Eye & Head gaze The design principle of interaction has been clarified [10]. They demonstrated Eye & Head interaction in a virtual reality application and evaluated their technique against baselines in pointing and confirmation studies. The results showed that the Eye & Head technology enables new eye movements that provide more control and flexibility to the user in fast eye pointing and selection.

Dewll Time. Ken Pfeuffer et al. compared three techniques for menu selection: dwell time, gaze button, and cursor [7]. The results showed that user performance using dwell time was comparable to menu selection using a pointer and was less physically demanding. Mishael Fernandez et al. proposed a dwell time gaze input and feedback method [5]. In their method, visual feedback is presented to the user in the form of a filled wheel that, when fully filled, selects where the user is gazing. They compared three ways to respond to the user when they are staring away from the target. They found that the infinite and pause and resume GazeWheel were more error prone than the reset GazeWheel, but significantly faster when using a dwell time of 800–1000 ms.

Motion Match. Eduardo Velloso et al. analyzed motion correlation as an interaction principle for object selection by motion matching [3]. They found that pointing is more effective for fine-grained selection, which is common in desktop interfaces, and therefore not optimal in principle, but that when user motion is directly coupled with the device's motion feedback (i.e., not via a user-controlled input device) We have found motion correlation to be useful and compelling. Augusto Esteves et al. compared clickers and dwellers to implementations of motion matching [4]. Their experiments showed that clickers were the fastest and dwellers the most accurate, but they concluded that motion matching may provide a valuable compromise between these two poles.

As you can see, gaze-based interaction has been studied extensively, but experiments have been conducted with restricted behaviors, and not many have been analyzed for each type of behavior. In addition, in spaces where virtual space and real space intersect, such as MR, there is the question of which space is being looked at.

3 Methodology

In this section, we explain the proposed method for determining whether the user needs the information, the preliminary experiment to confirm whether the hypothesis that eye movements are related to behavior is correct, the system design based on the preliminary experiment, and the equipment used in the experiment.

3.1   Methodology Overview

This paper describes how to determine from the user's behavior whether the user needs or does not need the information presented in front of them while working. There has been a lot of research on UIs that make choices by matching the movement of the target with the movement of the eye [3, 4], however, we do not know how to move the target in a way that is suitable for indoor work. Since eye movements are different for each task as shown by Andreas Bulling et al. and Javier De Lope et al. [1, 2] our proposed method creates UI movements that are different from the eye movements during the task, and when the UI is actively moved and the user's eyes move in sync with the movement, we determine that the user needs the UI. Therefore, we conducted a preliminary experiment to investigate how gaze and behavior can be related. In the next section, we will explain the preliminary experiment.

3.2   Preliminary Experiment

Purpose. The purpose of conducting a pre-experiment is to find out if and how eye movements can be associated with the behavior. Andreas Bulling et al. used eye gaze for behavior recognition [1]. These studies were mainly conducted on desk work for behavior recognition. However, indoor work also includes standing and sitting tasks, which require more head movement. In this study, we measure head orientation and gaze movements for three indoor tasks, and confirm that head and gaze movements are related to behavior.

Experimental Setting.

Details. As a preliminary experiment, we measure head orientation and gaze direction using the HoloLens2 described in Sect. 3.3.1 for three behavior patterns. We measure head and eye directions for three behavioral patterns: "desk work" (reading text on a display), "eating" (eating alone at a desk), and "searching" (searching for a book on a bookshelf). The reason we chose these three behaviors is that desk work is one of the most common indoor tasks. We thought that searching for books from a bookshelf is similar to picking, which is a warehouse task. Also, since eating is not a time to stare at anything, in particular, we want to find out how the gaze of this behavior works.

Subjects. In this experiment, five students are asked to participate as subjects. We ask each student to perform each task for 5 to 10 min, and record their head orientation and eye movements during that time.

Data Contents. The data to be acquired in this experiment is unit vectors that indicate the direction of the user's head and gaze, with the frontal direction of the user on the z-axis, the vertically upward direction on the y-axis, and the rightward direction on the x-axis. For example, it is $(-1,0,0)$ if the user is facing left, and (0,1,0) if the user is facing up. Note that the direction of the head and the direction of the gaze are independent of each other. In other words, if you move only your eyes to the right while keeping your head facing the front, the eye data will be (1,0,0) and the head direction will be (0,0,1), and if you move your head and gaze to the right at the same time, (gaze, head) = (1,0,0).

Results. The data of one subject obtained in the preliminary experiment is shown in Fig. 2 to Fig. 2. Here, the head orientation data has been subtracted from the gaze data to make it easier to understand the difference between head movement and gaze movement. In other words, the gaze here represents the orientation relative to the head orientation. The mean, variance, minimum, and maximum of the data for each task are also summarized in Table 1. From the desk work in Fig. 2 and Table 1, we found that the variance of gaze movement is large and the variance of head movement is small. In other words, the orientation of the head hardly changes during desk work, and only the gaze moves a lot. This means that when we read the text on the display in front of us, we do not move our head but only follow it with our eyes. In addition, since letters are generally read horizontally, eye movements are more active in the horizontal direction than in the vertical direction. From Fig. 2 and Table 1, we can see that most of the time during a meal, people are looking down. Also, most of the time, head movement and eye movement are linked. From the explorations in Fig. 2 and Table 1, in the task of searching for a book, the head orientation was more active in vertical movements and the gaze was more active in horizontal movements. It can be said that when looking for a book on a bookshelf, the orientation of the head determines which shelf the book is on, and the gaze determines where on the shelf the desired book is located.

3.3   System Design and Implementation

System Design

Overview. The system design of this research is outlined in the Fig. 3. The system design consists of four components: an Activity Recognition component that recognizes actions, a Contents management component that determines the contents to be displayed, a UI movement design component that determines the UI movement, and a Focus Status Detection component that determines whether the user is looking at the UI. By repeating these components, the system presents information that is appropriate for the user. The following is a detailed description of each component.

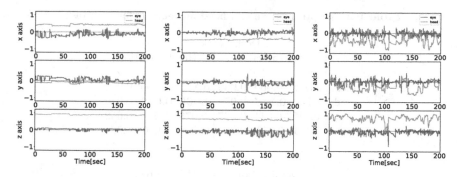

Fig. 2. Eye and head orientation movements using eye tracking and head tracking of HoloLens2: left) during desk work, center) while eating, right) when looking for a book on a bookshelf

Activity Recognition Component. As described in Sect. 3.2, head orientation and eye movement can be associated with behavior, so the current behavior can be inferred from each feature.

Contents Management Component. The Contents management component determines the information to be displayed according to the behavior estimated by the Activity Recognition Component.

UI Movement Design Component. The UI movement design component determines how to move the UI according to the behavior estimated by the Activity Recognition Component.

Focus Status Detection Component. The Focus Status Detection component compares eye movements with UI movements to determine if the user is looking at the UI. If the eye movement and the UI movement match, then the user is looking at the UI, and since the user is interested in this information, more detailed information is displayed. However, if the eye movement and the UI movement do not match, the user is not looking at the UI, and the UI is turned off.

3.4   Implementation

Hardware. This experiment is implemented using Microsoft's HoloLens2, a head-mounted mixed reality display that doubles the viewing angle and resolution of its predecessor, HoloLens1. The device is equipped with sensors such as eye tracking with two infrared cameras, head tracking with four visible light cameras, depth with a 1 MP time-of-flight (ToF) depth sensor, and hand tracking enhanced to five fingers. In this experiment, we use these eye tracking and head tracking features to determine whether the user was looking at the displayed content or the background.

Table 1. Description of eye and head movements for each task

Desk Work

	Eye direction			Head direction		
	x	y	z	x	y	z
mean	0.300	-0.000	0.930	0.403	-0.099	0.906
std	**0.140**	**0.147**	0.054	**0.065**	**0.049**	0.026
min	-0.546	-0.644	0.667	-0.073	-0.721	0.652
max	0.740	0.259	0.999	0.554	0.066	0.988

Eating

	Eye direction			Head direction		
	x	y	z	x	y	z
mean	-0.325	**-0.679**	0.552	-0.372	**-0.571**	0.683
std	0.156	0.256	0.197	0.101	0.220	0.106
min	-0.997	-0.993	-0.409	-0.928	-0.849	0.352
max	0.557	0.207	0.100	0.009	0.536	0.100

Search

	Eye direction			Head direction		
	x	y	z	x	y	z
mean	-0.404	-0.366	0.695	-0.379	-0.356	0.744
std	0.293	0.294	0.220	0.268	0.251	0.200
min	-0.100	-0.942	-0.568	-0.996	-0.917	-0.777
max	0.818	0.596	0.999	0.998	0.413	0.100

Software. In this experiment, we prepare two patterns of notifications to be displayed: "Notice" and "Warning". These two types of notifications are commonly used in various situations. Notifications are displayed in yellow, and warnings are displayed in red, colors that are easy to attract the eyes. Also, Based on the characteristics of the head and eye movements of the three work patterns in the preliminary experiment, we set the UI to make the following movements respectively.

- DeskWork
  When Users was working at their desk, We found that their head hardly moved and only their eyes moved a lot. Therefore, we set the UI to move up and down in small movements within the visible range without moving the head (Fig. 4). The reason for the up and down movement is to distinguish it from the horizontal movement of the gaze when reading the text on the display. Also, since the distance between the display and the person is close, the UI is displayed closer and smaller than the display.
- Eating
  We found that most of the time when Users eat, their head and gaze are looking down. So we created UI that goes upward so that the head looks upward (Fig. 4). Also, the size and distance of the displayed UI were set to the size and distance recommended by Microsoft [6].

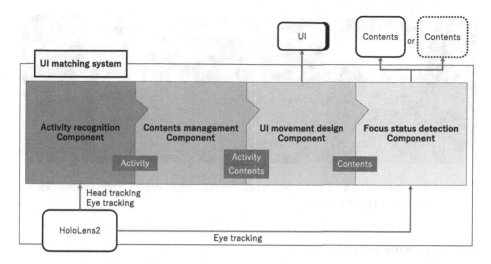

Fig. 3. System design overview: flow from activity recognition to content selection using gaze

– Search

The behavior of searching for a book on a bookshelf tended to be large up and down movements with the head and small horizontal movements with the eyes. So we move the UI horizontally to move the head sideways (Fig. 4). Also, unlike other tasks, the position of the body also changes, so we display it far and large.

Operation. We create a simple menu for experimentation to display the UI. There is a button to select the display method for each task, a start button to display the UI, and a reset button to turn off the display. When the start button is pressed, the UI will be displayed after a random time. Then, once the user looks at the UI, the UI will move in a predetermined way. If the user continues to follow the UI for a total of 5 s, it will display the details. If the user does not make eye contact with the UI after it starts moving, the UI will disappear after 15 s.

4   Experiments

This section describes an experiment using gaze and a moving UI to determine whether a user is looking at the UI, as well as the results and discussion of the experiment.

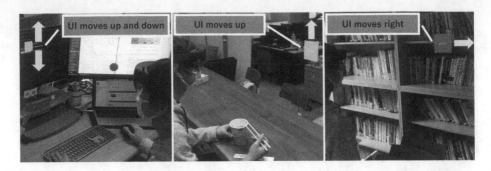

Fig. 4. UI movement: left) during desk work, center) while eating, right) when looking for a book. (Color figure online)

4.1 Experimental Design

Purpose. The purpose of this experiment is to investigate the ability to determine whether the user is looking at the UI by comparing the user's eye movements with the UI movements we devised based on preliminary experiments.

Details. In this experiment, five students who participated in the preliminary experiment are asked to perform the task. As in the preliminary experiment, we have each student wear a HoloLens2 and perform three different tasks. We ask the users to specify in advance whether they want to look at the UI or not, and check whether they can distinguish between them based on their eye movements.

We also ask the users questions after the experiment to evaluate the usability of the UI. For each task, we ask the users to rate the following 7 questions on a 5-point scale: 1) is the UI movement appropriate, 2) is the speed of the UI movement appropriate, 3) to 5) is the position of the UI display appropriate (height, width, depth), 6) is the size of the UI appropriate, and 7) is the time spent staring at the UI appropriate.

4.2 Result

Evaluating Whether the User Is Looking at the UI and Making a Decision. We invited five subjects to participate in the experiment and collected data on eye movements with and without looking at the UI. Figure 5 to Fig. 7 show the eye movements of one subject for each task while looking at the UI and when not looking at it. From Fig. 5, we confirmed that the subject was able to control the user's eye movements well when looking at the UI during desk work. Figure 6 shows that when looking at the UI during a meal, the user raises his face slightly in response to the movement of the UI. Finally, Fig. 7 shows that when looking for a book, the user is looking to the right according to the movement of the UI. From the above, when the user is looking at the UI, the gaze is locked on the UI and the movement corresponds to the movement of the UI.

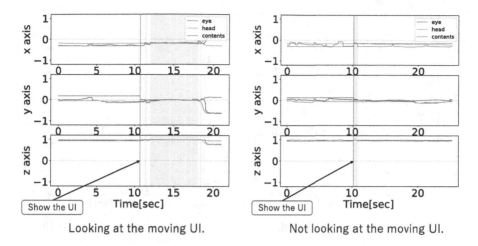

Fig. 5. Differences in eye movements during desk work: left) looking at the UI (yellow-painted area), right) not looking at the UI. (Color figure online)

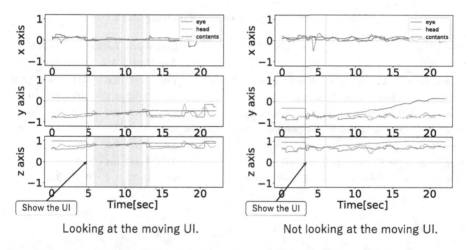

Fig. 6. Differences in eye movements during the meal: left) following the UI (yellow-painted area), right) not following the UI. (Color figure online)

User Survey. Table 2 is the result of the questionnaire about the usability of the UI conducted after the experiment. Table 2 is the average and variance values of the results of the five-point evaluation by five people. For desk work and search, all respondents answered that the movement and speed of the UI were easy to follow and slow, respectively, while for eating, the respondents were divided into those who answered that the UI was easy to follow but slow, and those who answered that the UI was fast and hard to follow. In all tasks, more respondents said they spent a long time staring.

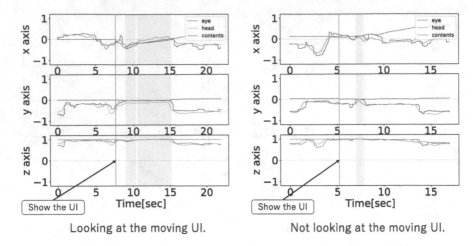

Looking at the moving UI.   Not looking at the moving UI.

Fig. 7. Differences in eye movements while looking for a book: left) following the UI (yellow-colored area), right) not following the UI. (Color figure online)

Table 2. User survey on ease of following the UI

	DeskWork		Eating		Search	
Question	Ave.	Std.	Ave.	Std.	Ave.	Std.
How easy is the movement to follow? 1 easy - 5 difficult	1.6	0.547	2.6	1.341	1.8	1.788
How fast does the UI move? 1 fast to 5 slow	3.6	0.547	3.2	1.095	3.8	0.447
How high is the display position? 1 High - 5 Low	2.2	0.836	2.4	1.673	3.0	0.707
How about the side of the display position? 1 Left - 5 Right	2.6	0.894	3.0	1.224	3.4	0.894
How close is the depth of the display position?	3.2	1.095	3.2	1.095	3.4	0.894
How large is the UI? 1 large to 5 small	2.8	0.447	2.4	0.894	3.2	0.836
How short is the following time? 1 short - 5 long	4.0	0.707	3.4	0.894	3.8	0.447

4.3   Discussion

Accuracy of Gaze-Based Action Recognition. Preliminary experiments have shown that only gaze moves when working at a desk, that we look down most of the time when eating, and that our head moves vertically and our gaze moves horizontally significantly when looking for a book. We think it is possible to recognize behaviors in a limited number of tasks with data on gaze alone, but it is difficult to make judgments based on gaze alone when the scope is expanded to include indoor activities such as standing and sitting. However, by including the orientation of the head, we were able to obtain various behavioral characteristics, such as behaviors in which the head and eyes move in the same way, behaviors in which only the eyes move, and behaviors in which the head and eyes move separately.

Advantages of Moving the UI. By moving the UI, we were able to determine that the user is looking at the UI by encouraging eye movements that differ from the characteristics of eye movements during work. In addition, the determination of looking by moving the gaze is advantageous compared to other methods in that it does not depend on the size of the UI. Modalities such as gaze and hand tracking are in an "always on" state. Therefore, if the size is increased too much, it may cause malfunction. Therefore, the size needs to be adjusted.

Appropriateness of the Way the UI Works. In this experiment, we set up a simple motion that moves in a straight line. Therefore, users found it easy to follow the UI in most cases. However, simple motion is not always good, as we need to be able to robustly discard false positives as well as accurately follow the UI. In this experiment, we also set the speed of the UI to be slower and the gaze time to be longer for accuracy. However, according to the post-experiment questionnaire, most of the users answered that the speed was slow and the staring time was long. Since there is a trade-off between accuracy and speed of operation, we thought it would be necessary to adjust the speed depending on the situation.

In addition, the tasks performed in this experiment do not include actions that significantly change the background, such as walking actions. In such actions, the head direction and gaze are expected to fluctuate significantly. Therefore, it is necessary to consider the movement of the UI in consideration of the movement of the background.

5   Conclusion

In this paper, we investigated whether it is possible to determine whether the user is looking at the UI displayed in the virtual space or the background of the real space based on the user's head direction and eye movement by adding movement to the UI. In this study, five subjects were asked to perform three indoor tasks: working at a desk, eating, and searching for a book from a bookshelf. As a result, during desk work, the subjects' heads did not move, and only their gaze moved minutely. When they were eating, they looked down most of the time, and their head direction and eye movements were linked. When looking for a book, the head moved up and down, and the gaze moved left and right. From this experiment, it was found that the type of indoor task was associated with head orientation and gaze movement.

In addition, by taking into account the characteristics of eye movements for each activity, we proposed UI movements that can induce eye movements that do not appear in the activities. We implemented a UI that makes small up-and-down movements to the extent that the user does not have to move his or her head when working at a desk, climbs upward to turn the head upward when eating, and makes large sideways movements to move the head sideways when searching for a book. As a result of our experiments, we were able to determine that the user was looking at the UI when the gaze and UI movement matched, and looking at the background when they did not.

However, after the experiment, we conducted a questionnaire survey on the viewability of the UI, and found that most of the users answered that the UI movement was easy to follow when they were working at a desk or looking for a book, while they were divided into two groups: easy to follow and hard to follow while eating. On the other hand, in all tasks, the respondents answered that the speed of UI movement was slow and that they spent a lot of time staring at it. In this experiment, we set the parameters to accurately capture what we are looking at, but in the future, we need to investigate various parameters to improve usability. Furthermore, although our approach is quite promising for hands-free task support, the tasks performed in this experiment are only a small part of indoor tasks. Therefore, we need to investigate the relationship between more behaviors and eye movements in order to know how to move the UI better.

Acknowledgement. This research is supported by JST OPERA(JPMJOP1612), CREST(JPMJCR1882), COI-NEXT(JPMJPF2006) and TMI program (WISE graduate program for lifestyle revolution based on transdisciplinary mobility innovation).

References

1. Bulling, A., Ward, J.A., Gellersen, H., Tröster, G.: Eye movement analysis for activity recognition using electrooculography. IEEE Trans. Pattern Anal. Mach. Intell. **33**(4), 741–753 (2010)
2. De Lope, J., Graña Romay, M.M.: Behavioral activity recognition based on gaze ethograms. Int. J. Neural Syst. **30**, 2050025 (2020)
3. Eduardo, V., Marcus, C., Joshua, N., Augusto, E., Christopher, C.: Motion correlation: selecting objects by matching their movement. ACM Trans. Comput. Hum. Interact. **24**(3), 1–35 (2017)
4. Esteves, A., Shin, Y., Oakley, I.: Comparing selection mechanisms for gaze input techniques in head-mounted displays. Int. J. Hum. Comput. Stud. **139**, 102414 (2020)
5. Fernandez, M., Mathis, F., Khamis, M.: GazeWheels: comparing dwell-time feedback and methods for gaze input. In: Proceedings of the 11th Nordic Conference on Human-Computer Interaction: Shaping Experiences, Shaping Society, pp. 1–6 (2020)
6. Microsoft: eye tracking on HoloLens 2. https://docs.microsoft.com/en-us/windows/mixed-reality/design/eye-tracking. Accessed 15 Feb 2021
7. Pfeuffer, K., Mecke, L., Delgado Rodriguez, S., Hassib, M., Maier, H., Alt, F.: Empirical evaluation of gaze-enhanced menus in virtual reality. In: 26th ACM Symposium on Virtual Reality Software and Technology, pp. 1–11 (2020)
8. Qian, Y.Y., Teather, R.J.: The eyes don't have it: an empirical comparison of head-based and eye-based selection in virtual reality. In: Proceedings of the 5th Symposium on Spatial User Interaction, pp. 91–98 (2017)

9. Doniec, R., Sieciński, S., Piaseczna, N., Mocny-Pachońska, K., Lang, M., Szymczyk, J.: The classifier algorithm for recognition of basic driving scenarios. In: Pietka, E., Badura, P., Kawa, J., Wieclawek, W. (eds.) Information Technology in Biomedicine. AISC, vol. 1186, pp. 359–367. Springer, Cham (2021). https://doi.org/10.1007/978-3-030-49666-1_28
10. Sidenmark, L., Gellersen, H.: Eye&head: synergetic eye and head movement for gaze pointing and selection. In: Proceedings of the 32nd Annual ACM Symposium on User Interface Software and Technology, pp. 1161–1174 (2019)

Online Medical Platform Oriented Identification of User Needs Related to Alzheimer's Disease and Ontology Construction

Xinting Liang, Yongxin Kong, and Guochao Peng(✉)

Sun Yat-sen University, Panyu District, Guangzhou 510000, China
liangxt9@mail2.sysu.edu.cn, penggch@mail.sysu.edu.cn

Abstract. Online medical platform is an important means for Alzheimer's disease patients and their families to obtain timely and useful medical information. The establishment of an information service mode centered on user needs is of great significance for improving the information utilization efficiency of patients and their quality of life. In this paper, the text data of questions on Alzheimer's disease on online medical platform is used to fully tap the real information needs of users with the text feature analysis method and content analysis method, and a user needs framework is established, covering four topics of needs including medical treatment, prevention, prognosis and daily management as well as their sub topics. Then, it is integrated with the existing disease ontology to establish a practical ontology model of Alzheimer's disease, which is conducive to providing professional and accurate knowledge services for users.

Keywords: Online medical platform · Alzheimer's disease · User requirements · Ontology

1 Introduction

Alzheimer's disease (AD), also known as senile dementia, is a progressive neurodegenerative disease with hidden onset. Clinically, it is characterized by comprehensive dementia such as memory impairment, aphasia, apraxia, agnosia, visual spatial skill impairment, executive dysfunction, personality and behavior changes, and the etiology is still unknown. At present, AD has become one of the major diseases threatening the health of the elderly. According to statistics, the number of AD patients worldwide reached about 44 million in 2013 and will increase to 150 million in 2050 [1]. In recent years, the increase in the incidence of AD in China has attracted particular attention. The number of AD patients in China has reached 10 million and is still increasing. AD is incurable and irreversible, which not only brings a heavy burden to the patient families, but also brings severe challenges to the aging society.

© Springer Nature Switzerland AG 2021
N. Streitz and S. Konomi (Eds.): HCII 2021, LNCS 12782, pp. 316–330, 2021.
https://doi.org/10.1007/978-3-030-77015-0_23

Among all patients with chronic diseases and disabilities, AD patients have imposed the greatest burden on family caregivers. At present, 75%–80% of AD patients in the world live in the community and are cared for by non-professional caregivers [3, 4], while family caregivers are the cornerstone and main force of the care and support system for AD patients [2]. The slow development of AD and the insufficient understanding of the disease by most caregivers have led to the lag and lack of professional guidance in the process of home care. In this process, various online medical platforms, featuring openness and accessibility, have become the main platforms for patients and their families to exchange and share health information. Their various services have made up for the above gaps to a certain extent and are important sources of professional medical guidance for users facing AD. Therefore, discussing the construction of AD knowledge service model by online medical platform, providing users with disease-related information that truly meets their needs and forming a hospital-family-online medical platform nursing response mechanism are of great significance for delaying the worsening of AD patients, ensuring the quality of care and improving the quality of life of both caregivers and the cared.

However, for one thing, medical guidance services provided by various online medical platforms lack specificity, and the scattered and numerous health information on the platforms has easily caused information overload; for another, most users lack professional medical knowledge and information literacy, so they cannot accurately express their information needs, have limited perspective of health information search, and are unable to accurately and completely find and effectively absorb the health information needed. Therefore, they cannot improve their level of health management by making full use of the platforms. Therefore, this paper will extract the real needs of the user group from the user question data of the existing online medical platforms to establish a user-oriented ontology model of AD and provide users with professional and comprehensive medical services, in the hope of realizing the new development of AD management and services with the joint participation of the state, society and individuals.

2 Related Research

Online medical platforms are online interactive platforms for people concerning about health to learn medical knowledge and share health information, knowledge, emotions and experiences with other users [5]. The platforms have reduced the cost of patients seeking health information and medical assistance and provided hospitals with opportunities to expand the market [6]. At present, scholars' research on online medical platforms mainly focuses on the following three aspects: (1) Design and algorithm improvement of online medical platforms. For example, an online medical appointment system was constructed based on the basic idea of web services [7]; a faceted navigation system was constructed based on the cardiovascular forum of dxy.cn from the perspective of UGC [8], and an automatic doctor matching algorithm based on online consultation records was studied [9], etc. (2) Research on the quality of online medical information services. For example, the key factors influencing the quality of online medical information services were identified through information gain and SVM based on the information ecology theory by using the questionnaire survey method [10]; (3) Research on group behavior in online medical communities. For example, the research on user interaction behaviors [11], the factors influencing doctor-patient interaction behaviors [12], the factors influencing doctor's word of mouth, the factors influencing doctor's contribution behaviors, patients' willingness to share information, the factors influencing doctor-patient trust, etc. in online medical communities.

Among them, currently the research on online medical platform users is a hot topic and has received extensive attention from scholars, including user participation, user needs, various behaviors and of different types of users and their influencing factors [13], etc. However, most of the previous studies used questionnaires, interviews and other methods that are easily influenced by subjective judgment to obtain users' views, and few directly used the real feedback data of users of the online medical platforms for research, so it is impossible to fundamentally mine the real health information needs of users in different disease fields to provide targeted online medical services.

On the other hand, some scholars have tried to gradually apply ontology technology to knowledge services for specific diseases. For example, Jonghun et al. and S.C. Christopoulou et al. respectively build ontology-based medical health information models to realize personalized medical services [14]. Xiong Huixiang et al. constructed a user-oriented chronic disease knowledge service model from a multi-dimensional perspective by reusing and optimizing the existing universal ontology model of diseases, and constructed ontology using coronary heart disease as an example [15]. However, on the whole, the existing ontology models do not reflect the real needs of users well, and there is no research on the ontology construction of AD, therefore they have poor practicability in the application for specific diseases. In addition, the studies on AD are basically epidemiological research, basic research and clinical trial research. There is very little research on the family burden and needs of AD patients, which is undoubtedly unfavorable to AD patients mainly depending on family care.

In the long-term service process, online medical platforms have accumulated mass user question data. These behavioral data are the real feedback of user needs, with high reliability and long data duration, which can reduce the influence of temporary subjective feelings or false data on the overall results and increase the reliability and validity of data analysis results. Therefore, this paper uses web crawlers to obtain the online medical platform users' question data on AD, mines users' needs and integrates them into the universal ontology of diseases, so as to build a practical AD ontology model, thus providing users with comprehensive and accurate knowledge services.

3 Topic Identification of AD-Related Users' Information Needs

In this section, typical online medical platforms are selected, and all the AD-related question text data on the platform are crawled; the topics of needs and the sub topics of AD-related users' needs are summarized and condensed through text feature extraction and content analysis to provide support for the construction of AD ontology.

3.1 Data Sources

With the support of policies such as Healthy China Strategy and "Internet + Medical Health", online medical platforms are growing vigorously, with various types and characteristics. They can be roughly divided into two categories: one is P2D (patient to doctor) community featuring doctor-patient interaction, such as Haodf (haodf.com), XYWY (xywy.com), WeDoctor (guahao.com), etc. the other is the P2P (patient to patient) community where patients communicate with each other, such as Sweet Home (bbs.tnbz. com) and Baidu Quit Smoking Bar. Since the purpose of this paper is to provide medical information services to meet the needs of non-professional AD patients and their families, P2D platforms are mainly used as the main data sources.

First of all, according to the 2019 China Online Medical Industry Research Report [16], the typical P2D platforms are selected for preliminary investigation and analysis. We found that, the existing online medical platforms have different types and quality of medical services. Some platforms have no Q&A or consultation feedback section, and some have less information in the classic Q&A section that cannot meet diversified needs. Moreover, the information on the platforms is scattered and messy, including a lot of low-quality information, which makes it difficult for users to easily obtain high-quality information services. Therefore, it is necessary to establish a universal ontology model for specific diseases to better meet the health information needs of users. This study intends to choose three platforms with a relatively perfect Q&A module, including Chunyu Doctor, XYWY and 120ask as data sources for further research.

3.2 Topic Identification Idea

This paper suggests that the user question data on the online medical platforms is a true reflection of users' understanding of diseases and can effectively represent users' health information needs. Therefore, need topic identification is based on question text data from three platforms. Firstly, Jieba word segmentation toolkit and TF-IDF text feature extraction algorithm were used to process text data to extract topic keywords of AD patients' questions, preliminarily understand several aspects of users' needs, and obtain major topics of needs. Secondly, content analysis method combined with professional knowledge and data text was used to construct analysis categories, and the sub topics under the topics of needs were obtained; the research samples were coded, and descriptive statistics were carried out on the coding results of AD-related users' needs, so as to understand and improve the frequency distribution of categories and sub-categories of users' needs, and further improve the AD-related user needs framework.

3.3 Identification Method and Procedure

User Questioning Data Collection. In this paper, Python crawler was used to collect the data of AD-related questions in the classic Q&A section of Chunyu Doctor, the Q&A section of the XYWY, and the Q&A section of the 120ask. In order to ensure the completeness of the questions, two keywords "Alzheimer's disease" and "senile dementia" were used in the search. A total of 3015 pieces of user question text data were initially obtained, with 659, 1437 and 919 pieces from the three platforms respectively.

Then, the text data were summarized and cleaned to eliminate the questions repeatedly asked by the same user, as well as the data irrelevant to the topic, and those with incomplete and unclear expression. For example, a user's question is only "my father suffers senile dementia", which is incomplete and does not clearly express the intention of the questioner, and needs to be deleted from the question text data set. Finally, 377 invalid questions were eliminated and 2,638 valid user questions were obtained for further analysis.

Topics of Needs Identification – Text Feature Extraction
(1) Word segmentation
Firstly, the question data after text deduplication was mechanically compressed to remove word repetition caused by crawling or user questions. For example, "Can Alzheimer's disease be cured? Can it be cured?" Such repeated corpus was caused by user input errors and is meaningless, and mechanical compression was required. After compression, it became "Can Alzheimer's disease be cured".

Then, the text data was segmented by using Jieba, a powerful Chinese word segmentation bank in Python. Jieba's word segmentation accuracy is as high as 97% and supports custom dictionaries. It is a word segmentation system with high efficiency and accuracy. As this paper involves specialized medical terms, in order to ensure better results, a dictionary of medical proper nouns for Alzheimer's disease was artificially constructed by referring to the vocabulary of relevant medical specialties, and added to help processing, such as drug names such as "nicergoline tablets", "cerebroprotein hydrolysate", "pyritinol", "aniracetam", "huperzine-A", "donepezil" and other proper nouns such as "deoxyribose glucose", "human immunodeficiency virus" and "Borrelia burgdorferi", so as to optimize the word segmentation effect.

Next, the result of word segmentation was processed to remove high-frequency meaningless stop words such as "of", "and" and "I", as well as words representing the disease such as "senile dementia" and "Alzheimer's disease" with a stop list.

Finally, semantic substitution was carried out. In order to improve the accuracy of analysis, words with similar semantics were replaced and merged, such as "section" and "department" were replaced with "department", "sign" and "precursor" were merged into "symptom", and "early stage" and "initial stage" were merged into "early stage".

(2) TF-IDF calculation
A document was developed with the preprocessed text data, and the TF-IDF value of each word in the document was calculated using TF-IDF algorithm; the results were arranged in descending order, thus the key topics of user needs were preliminarily obtained. The words with the top 50 TF-IDF values are shown in Table 1.

Table 1. TF-IDF calculation results (top 50)

Keywords	TF-IDF	Keywords	TF-IDF	Keywords	TF-IDF
Symptom	0.36	Forget	0.18	TCM	0.09
Where	0.35	Attention	0.16	Inheritance	0.09
Cure	0.32	Temper	0.16	Hypersomnia	0.08
Drug	0.32	Recovery	0.13	Beijing	0.08
Eat	0.31	Encephalanalosis	0.13	Life span	0.08
Sign	0.28	Diet	0.13	Treatment	0.08
Care	0.24	Amnesia	0.13	Hypertension	0.08
Hospital	0.23	Examination	0.13	Stay in bed	0.08
Prevention	0.23	Prank	0.11	Diabetes	0.08
Nursing	0.23	Elderly	0.10	Grandpa	0.08
Doctor	0.22	Food	0.10	Delay	0.08
Long time	0.20	Death	0.10	Defecation	0.08
Method	0.20	Know	0.10	Cerebral infarction	0.07
Have meal	0.20	Wander	0.10	Come home	0.07
Early stage	0.20	Evening	0.10	Mother	0.07
Department	0.18	Authority	0.10	Psychosis	0.07
Sleep	0.18	Family	0.09		

From the table above, it can be preliminarily known that the information needs of online medical platform users for AD are mainly concentrated in the following four aspects: 1) Medical treatment information. The results of text analysis show that the TF-IDF values of words related to patients' medical treatment, such as "cure", "where", "hospital", "drug", "department", "examination" and "Beijing", are relatively large. Users may have doubts about hospital recommendation and medical departments, and especially "where", "cure" and "hospital" are all ranked in the top 10, indicating that the quality consultation of hospitals is a problem that users are very concerned about. 2) Prevention. As can be seen from the table, users questions about "sign" and "prevention" also account for a large proportion, indicating that users are very concerned about how to prevent AD and how to identify signs of the disease to take measures. It can also be seen from symptomatic words such as "initial stage", "temper", "hypersomnia" and "amnesia". Since users are unable to keep in touch with doctors at all times to obtain medical help, they pay more attention to disease prevention knowledge and skills. 3) Prognosis. "Long time", "life span" and "delay" are all related to prognosis. Due to the long duration of AD, it is very important to understand the prognosis of patients. 4) Daily management. This part of the content accounts for the largest proportion in the word table, covering various nursing details such as diet and daily life. Since a large part of the questions about AD on the online medical platforms are from the families of the patients, the questions about nursing are urgent to be answered for many users.

Sub Topic Identification – Content Analysis Method

Firstly, the categories of analysis topics were established to determine the identification rules and coding content feature rules [17]. Based on the topics of needs extracted by text feature, the raw data of user questions related to the topic was browse to sum up the subdivision direction of user needs under this topic, and by referring to the research results of Lu Quan [18], Tang Xiaobo [19], Jin Biyi et al. [20] on disease ontology and knowledge service model, a table of Ad-related user information needs is constructed, which includes the four topics of medical treatment, prevention, prognosis and daily management and 11 sub topics, as shown in Table 2.

Table 2. Categories of ad-related users' information needs

Topics	Sub topic	Topics	Sub topic
Medical treatment	Hospital	Prognosis	Survival period
	Consultation department		Complication
	Related examinations	Daily management	Daily life management
Prevention	Primary prevention		Caregiver intervention
	Secondary prevention		Daily disease condition monitoring
	Tertiary prevention		

The content analysis unit is the actual calculation object of the coding process and they can be words, sentences, paragraphs or full texts [21]. In this paper, the raw data of 2638 user questions were used as analysis units for independent coding. For sub topics, the ones involved in the analysis unit are coded as "1" and the ones not involve are coded as "0". For the topics, if one or more sub topics under a topic are involved in the analysis unit, it is considered that the topic is involved in the analysis unit; If the analysis unit does not involve any sub topics under a certain topic, it is considered that the analysis unit does not involve this topic.

Coding was carried out according to the above rules; the coding results were counted, and the sub sub-topics were further summarized in the coding process. The analysis results are shown in Table 3.

Table 3. Frequency statistics

Topics			Sub topic			Sub sub-topic
User needs	Frequency	Ratio	User needs	Frequency	Ratio	
Medical treatment	878	33.30%	Hospital	681	77.60%	
			Consultation department	196	22.30%	
			Related examinations	75	8.50%	EEG, CT, MRI and RHG

(*continued*)

Table 3. (*continued*)

Topics			Sub topic			Sub sub-topic
User needs	Frequency	Ratio	User needs	Frequency	Ratio	
Prevention	218	8.70%	Primary prevention	13	6.00%	
			Secondary prevention	79	36.20%	
			Tertiary prevention	126	57.80%	
Prognosis	533	20.20%	Survival period	339	63.60%	
			Complication	185	34.70%	Pulmonary infection, urinary system infection, pressure ulcer
Daily management	1354	51.30%	Daily life management	976	72.10%	Medication nursing, safety nursing, psychological nursing, dietary nursing and daily life nursing
			Caregiver intervention	521	38.40%	Health intervention, psychological intervention
			Daily disease condition monitoring	566	41.80%	

(Note: Primary prevention refers to avoiding the disease; secondary prevention refers to the investigation of suspected cases, and tertiary prevention refers to delaying the development of the disease)

As can be seen from the table above, the sum of the proportions of the four major topics of medical treatment, prevention, prognosis and daily management mentioned is more than 100%, and the proportion of sub topics under each topic is also close to 100%, with relatively balanced distribution, indicating that the category table is a good representation of user needs. Moreover, the table is based on the existing analysis and research results, and has sufficient basis in both theory and practice, with a high level of content validity, so it can be used as a framework system for AD-related users' information needs for application.

In addition, according to the statistical results of topics, daily management information is the medical information most needed by users, followed by medical treatment, prognosis and prevention, which is consistent with the TF-IDF analysis results. Good daily management is the key to delaying AD, which is usually carried out by family caregivers. However, family caregivers usually lack professional knowledge and cannot obtain timely professional help from hospitals. Therefore, online medical platforms become the first choice to solve their confusions. Under the sub topics, the daily life management, hospital, survival period, etc. were mentioned more frequently.

3.4 User Needs Analysis Results

Through text feature extraction method and content analysis method, four user need topics that can be used to construct ontology and their sub topics are summed up in this section, specifically as follows:

1) Medical treatment. It includes hospital, department and related examinations, among which related examinations also include examination types such as EEG, CT scan, etc. "Which hospital is good at treating Alzheimer's disease?" and "which department does Alzheimer's disease patient should go to?" are the most frequently asked questions by platform users. However, from the results of previous platform analysis, such information is often included in other modules of the platform. This shows the low user needs centrality of the information organization of the current online medical platforms, and it also reflects the insufficient user information retrieval capability. Therefore, it is necessary to incorporate such needs into the ontology model of the disease and display them when users search the keywords.

2) Prevention. It includes primary, secondary and tertiary prevention. These three levels of prevention are aimed at users related to AD of different types and stages. Users at the primary prevention stage pay more attention to issues such as "whether AD is hereditary" and measures to avoid AD; users at the secondary prevention stage pay more attention to related symptoms of AD; users at the tertiary prevention stage are more interested in issues such as delaying the disease, administration, nursing, etc. By incorporating such needs into the ontology model, and establishing the relationship between three-level prevention and other subclasses to identify user problems and recommend relevant information, the user information needs can be more effectively met.

3) Prognosis. It includes survival period and complications, including pulmonary infection, urinary system infection and pressure ulcers. Due to the great differences in the conditions of different AD patients and the fact that patients and their families know little about the disease, the life span of patients and various complications are also the key concerns.

4) Daily management. It includes daily life management, daily disease condition monitoring and caregiver intervention, of which daily life management also includes medication nursing, safety nursing, psychological nursing, dietary nursing and daily life nursing. Daily management is the most important category of needs and related questions are more often raised by caregivers. Typical questions include "Can AD patients eat XX?", "What if AD patients are grumpy and do not sleep?", etc. Paying attention to such needs can effectively improve the quality of life of patients with AD and is conducive to improving the physical and mental health of caregivers.

4 Construction of Alzheimer's Disease Ontology

4.1 Ontology Design

At present, many universal top-level ontology models of diseases in medical research are universal and instructive for the construction of disease ontology. Therefore, in order to build an ontology model of AD oriented to online medical platforms, this paper will use the existing Maja Hadzic disease ontology model [22], which has been tested many times in practical research. It has good compatibility, and only the corresponding instance content needs to be appropriately added in the diagnosis and treatment of related diseases. Although the disease ontology model covers the general characteristics of various diseases, including types, symptoms, etiology and diagnosis and treatment, and can meet the general needs of patients for diseases, the four dimensions do not well reflect the real needs of patients with specific diseases for diagnosis, treatment and management. Therefore, in this paper, the four dimensions of "medical treatment", "prevention", "prognosis" and "daily management", which represent the needs of users with AD, and the semantic relationships involved were added to the general ontology model, as shown in the following figure, in order to realize the expansion of the ontology oriented to user needs (Fig. 1).

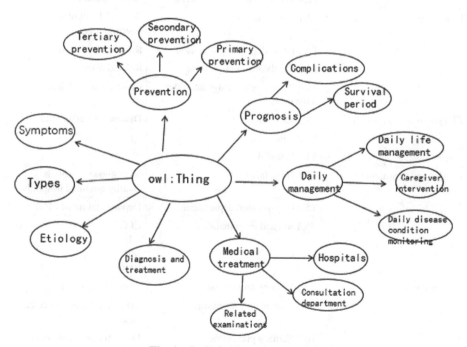

Fig. 1. Optimized ontology model

Then, using the optimized ontology model of AD, taking authoritative popular medical books and professional medical guidelines as the domain knowledge sources of the ontology, combining with the topic categories of user needs, and strictly following the relevant conceptual relationship description paradigm, the semantic relationships involved in the optimized ontology model were systematically sorted out, and the concept description is shown in the following table (Table 4).

Table 4. Semantic relationship and explanation of ontology model

Topic	Subclass	Concept interpretation
T1 Symptoms	T1.1 Pre-dementia symptoms	Observed characteristics during onset period
	T1.2 Mild symptoms	Stage symptoms and differentiation points
	T1.3 Moderate symptoms	
	T1.4 Severe symptoms	
T2 Diagnosis and treatment	T2.1 Drug therapy	Names and efficacy of western medicine
	T2.2 TCM therapy	TCM methods and efficacy
	T2.3 Support therapy	Associated symptoms and treatment methods
	T2.4 Rehabilitation physiotherapy	Methods and efficacy
T3 Etiology	T3.1 Inheritance	Gene and pathological interpretation
	T3.2 Brain degenerative disease	Related disease types
	T3.3 Cerebrovascular disease	Related disease types
	T3.4 Poisoning by drugs and other substances	Contraindicated drug names
T4 Types	T4.1 Early-onset	Disease characteristics
	T4.2 Late-onset	
	T4.3 Familial	
T5 Medical treatment	T5.1 Hospitals	Well-known hospitals Nearby qualified hospitals
	T5.2 Consultation department	Department name
	T5.3 Related examinations	EEG CT MRI RHG
T6 Prevention	T6.1 Primary prevention	Avoid the disease
	T6.2 Secondary prevention	Investigation of suspected cases
	T6.3 Tertiary prevention	Delay the development of the disease
T7 Prognosis	T7.1 Survival period	Patient's life span
	T7.2 Complications	Pulmonary infection Urinary system infection Pressure ulcer

(continued)

Table 4. (*continued*)

Topic	Subclass	Concept interpretation
T8 Daily management	T8.1 Daily life management	Medication nursing and safety nursing Psychological nursing and dietary nursing Daily life nursing
	T8.2 Caregiver intervention	Health intervention Psychological sensation
	T8.3 Daily disease condition monitoring	Means and method

4.2 Ontology Construction Process and Results

After defining each class and its subclasses in ontology, the ontology construction tool Protégé version 5.5 was used to construct the ontology of AD. The construction process is mainly divided into class construction, object attribute definition and data type construction. AD knowledge and its related relationships are displayed through the ontology construction.

(1) Construction of ontology class

Firstly, software function tags were used to create Owl project. The software will automatically provide the URL flag of the ontology and create a name related to AD, i.e. a new domain Owl ontology named after the flag is established. Select the tag class, create the basic class structure, set up eight major classes and define them respectively. The operation is shown in Fig. 2.

(2) Definition of ontology object attributes

Object attributes were defined for constructed classes, which were divided into symptoms, etiology, diagnosis and treatment, medical treatment, prevention and daily life, and are used to represent the relationship between classes, as shown in Fig. 3. The relationships and explanation are shown in the table below. Among them, "cure" and "need_cure", "lead_to" and "becuse_of", "get" and "from", "implement" and "be_implemented" are opposite object attributes and need to be defined in the description (Table 5).

(3) AD ontology classes and their hierarchy diagram

Through the above definitions of ontology classes, object attributes and data attributes, we can see AD ontology structure diagram. Ontology structure diagram is a description of the whole knowledge structure of AD. Among them, arrows represent different relationships. Solid arrows represent the relationships between classes and subclasses, dashed arrows represent the definitions of their object attributes, and dashed arrows of different colors represent different object attributes (Fig. 4).

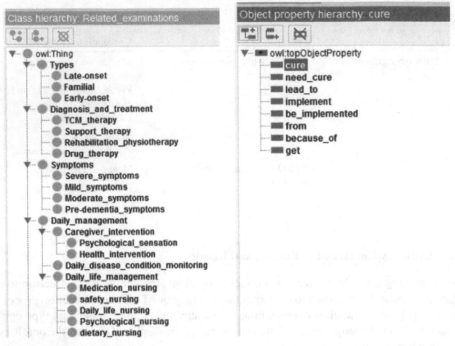

Fig. 2. Class definition   **Fig. 3.** Relationship definition

Table 5. Relationship annotation

Relationship	Annotation
cure	Diagnosis and treatment methods can relieve related symptoms
need_cure	Diagnosis and treatment methods required by related symptoms
lead_to	Related symptoms caused by a disease
because_of	Causes of related symptoms
get	Diagnosis and treatment available from medical department
from	Diagnosis and treatment should be obtained from the medical department
implement	Implement preventive measures in daily management
be_implemented	Preventive measures need to be implemented in daily management

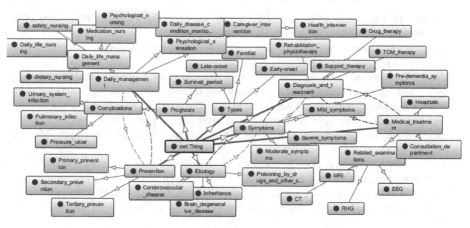

Fig. 4. Alzheimer's disease ontology structure diagram

5   Conclusion

Online medical platforms are an important means for AD patients and their families to obtain timely and useful medical information in the long process of fighting against the disease. Perfecting the platform construction and establishing a user-centered information organization and presentation mode are of great significance for improving the information utilization efficiency of AD-related users. In this paper, users' information needs are deeply mined from user question data on online medical platforms, and the framework of AD-related users' information needs is constructed and incorporated into the ontology model construction. An online medical platform oriented ontology model for AD-related users' information needs is proposed, which is helpful to establish a more comprehensive and complete AD knowledge base and provide more accurate information services for AD patients and their families.

At the same time, there are many deficiencies in this paper, for example, users' questions cannot reflect all the needs of patients and their families, and the author cannot have a deeper understanding of the medical data of AD due to the limited knowledge, which need to be further improved in future studies.

Acknowledgement. This research was supported by two grants respectively funded by the Natural Science Foundation of Guangdong (No.: 2018A030313706) and the National Natural Science Foundation of China (No.: 71974215).

References

1. Xinhua News Agency. Research Suggests 47 Million People Worldwide Affected by Dementia [EB/OL]. https://www.xinhuanet.com/world/2016-09/21/c_1119601736.htm. 2016-09-21/2020-03-24
2. Wang, J.: Challenges Faced by Dementia Family Caregivers and Expectations for Dementia Care Services. Central South University (2014)

3. Brodaty, H., Cumming, A.: Dementia services in Australia. Int. J. Geriatr. Psychiatry **25**(9), 887–995 (2010)
4. Brodaty, H., Donkin, M.: Family caregivers of people with dementia. Dialogues Clin. Neurosci. **11**(2), 217–228 (2009)
5. Zhang, W., Jiang, X.: A review of research on influencing factors of online health community users' participation behaviors [J/OL]. Library and Information Service, pp. 1–10, 29, April 2020. https://doi.org/10.13266/j.issn.0252-3116.2020.04.015
6. Wu, H., Lu, N.: How your colleagues' reputation impact your patients' odds of posting experiences: evidence from an online health community. Electron. Res. Appl. **16**, 7–17 (2016)
7. Li, L., Wang, C., Wang, K.: Design and research of online medical appointment system based on web service. Sci. Technol. Inf. (Acad. Ed.) (11), 160, 162 (2006)
8. Guo, C., Xiao, L., Jianjun, S.: Construction of faceted navigation system for online community - taking DXY Cardiovascular Forum as an example. Inf. Stud. Theory Appl. **40**(10), 112–116 (2017)
9. Liu, T.: Research on application of doctor automatic matching algorithm based on online consultation records. Inf. Stud. Theory Appl. **41**(06), 143–148+123 (2018)
10. Jiang, M., Xue, X., Yang, Y.: SVM-based research on key influencing factors of online medical information service quality. Inf. Sci. **38**(03), 70–77 (2020)
11. Wu, J., Shi, L.: Research on user interaction behaviors in online medical community based on social network analysis. Inf. Sci. (7), 120–125 (2017)
12. Ye, C.: Analysis of Influencing Factors of Doctor Interviews on Online Medical Platforms. Beijing Foreign Studies University, Beijing (2017)
13. Zhao, Y., Li, J., Zhou, L., Li, F.: Comparative analysis of needs and satisfaction of elderly and non-elderly users of online medical platforms - taking Chunyu doctor as an example. China J. Inf. Syst. (02), 67–80 (2018)
14. Kuziemsky, C.E., Lau, F.: A four stage approach for ontology-based health information system design. Artif. Intell. Med. **50**(3) (2010)
15. Xiong, H., Dai, Q., Mei, X.: Construction of chronic disease knowledge service model for online medical communities. Inf. Stud. Theory Appl. **43**(06), 123–130 (2020)
16. Alendarl: 2019 China Online Medical Industry Research Report [EB/OL]. https://wenku.baidu.com/view/cfc5a36805a1b0717fd5360cba1aa81144318f91.html. 2019-05-23/2020-03-24
17. Yang, J., Jia, S.: Identification of motivation of enterprise migration. Geogr. Sci. **31**(1), 15–21 (2011)
18. Lu, Q., Jiang, C., Chen, J.: Research on the organization of electronic medical record big data based on extended disease ontology. Doc. Inf. Knowl. **2019**(1), 109–118 (2019)
19. Tang, X., Zheng, D., Tan, M.: Research on the construction of knowledge service system model for chronic disease health education. Inf. Sci. **37**(1), 134–140 (2019)
20. Jin, B., Xu, X.: Research on topic characteristics in online healthy communities. Libr. Inf. Serv. **59**(12), 100–105 (2015)
21. Li, B.: Describing the characteristics of communication content and testing the hypothesis of communication research: a brief introduction to content analysis (2). Contemp. Commun. **1**, 47–51 (2000)
22. Hadzic, M., Chang, E.: Ontology-based support for human disease study. In: Hawaii International Conference on System Sciences. IEEE Computer Society (2005)

A Systematic Review of Information Quality of Artificial Intelligence Based Conversational Agents in Healthcare

Caihua Liu, Bingqian Zhang, and Guochao Peng[✉]

School of Information Management, Sun Yat-Sen University, Guangzhou 510275, Guangdong, China
penggch@mail.sysu.edu.cn

Abstract. Advances in artificial intelligence (AI) have led to an increase in the development of conversational agents used to deliver a variety of health-related services such as healthcare monitoring and personalized treatment. Essentially, the quality of these services relies heavily on the information quality of the agents. Recent literature shows a growing interest in investigating the quality of health-related information for AI-based conversational agents, while a systematic review of information quality on these agents has not been addressed. The current status of the art of the information quality of these agents in healthcare remains unclear. In this study, we conducted a systematic review of the 19 articles selected based on our inclusion and exclusion criteria to identify research purposes of using AI-based conversational agents in healthcare addressing information quality, research designs and user feedback on the information quality of the agents. The findings derived from this review suggest research possibilities for further exploration and provide implications for both theoretical and practical perspectives about achieving quality-assured information of the agents for health-related purposes.

Keywords: Information quality · Conversational agents · Healthcare · Systematic review

1 Introduction

To relieve the burden of clinical workforce and meet patient demands on health services, technologies have been increasingly used for health-related purposes [1]. Particularly, a recent increased interest in artificial intelligence (AI) has led to the popularity of conversational agents applied in healthcare that are "more or less autonomous and intelligent software entities" [2] understanding natural language input from users and providing corresponding services. The interactions between human and conversational agents allow users to access and communicate information for different needs such as healthcare monitoring and personalized treatment [3]. While the quality of health-related information of these agents is the baseline of quality-assured healthcare services. For example, inaccurate information provided by an AI-based conversational agent to address a health-related question that a patient concerns could result in harm including death [S5, S8].

© Springer Nature Switzerland AG 2021
N. Streitz and S. Konomi (Eds.): HCII 2021, LNCS 12782, pp. 331–347, 2021.
https://doi.org/10.1007/978-3-030-77015-0_24

The quality of the information thus should be considered as one issue of the priorities addressed in the development of AI-based conversational agents in healthcare.

The quality of information refers to fitness for use [4], and researchers have proposed dimensions to define and measure the quality of health-related information (e.g. completeness and accuracy) [5]. While information quality has been studied in healthcare for decades, the literature of the quality of health-related information in AI-based conversational agents still remains scattered. Prior literature reviews on these agents in healthcare only included information quality as an aspect in their study context [6, 7], however, limited attention has been directed towards the current states of the art in the field of information quality of these agents.

The aims of the present study are to identify research purposes of using AI-based conversational agents in healthcare, research designs and user feedback on the information quality of the agents by reviewing relevant literature on the agents involving information quality. This helps reveal research trends of this field and potential areas for further exploration. To achieve these aims, our study is guided by one specific research question (RQ):

RQ: How users perceived the information quality of AI-based conversation agents used in healthcare?

To address this RQ, following the guidelines of evidence-based paradigm [8], we conducted a systematic literature review (SLR) of the empirical studies that have investigated information quality of AI-based conversational agents in healthcare. The contributions of this study are twofold. Firstly, from the theoretical perspective, we identify research purposes, research designs and research findings addressing our RQ and establish links among these three themes that advances the knowledge in the area and reveal research possibilities. Secondly, from the practical perspective, the present study will increase the awareness of developers on the information quality matters when designing and developing the agents and call users, governments, and healthcare professionals to pay attention to achieving quality-assured health information of the agents.

The rest of this article is organized as follows: Sect. 2 gives a background about related studies; Sect. 3 presents research methods to conduct this study; Sect. 4 provides the results of this review; Sect. 5 discusses the findings, implications and limitations; and Sect. 6 concludes this study.

2   Related Studies

There is a body of literature that reviews the publications in relation to conversational agents in healthcare, as shown in Table 1. For instance, Laranjo et al. [9] examined the research facets of the included studies on conversational agents in healthcare (e.g. research designs and study contexts), technical characteristics (type of technology, dialogue management and initiative, and input and output modality), and evaluation measures of the agents (technical performance, user experience, and health research measures). Pereira and Díaz [10] reviewed healthy purposes of using conversational agents, behavior changes of patients who take advantages of the agents, and benefits introduced by the agents. Bendig et al. [11] also investigated the basic research facets of the included studies related to conversational agents such as location of study conducted, research

Table 1. Related studies on conversational agents in healthcare

Authors	Number of databases used for search	Timeframe of the included studies	Number of the included studies	Health context	Information quality focused?
Laranjo et al. [9]*	5	2003–2017	17	Any context	No
Pereira and Díaz [10]*	5	2014–2018	30	Any context	No
Bendig et al. [11]	7	2017–2018	6	Mental health	No
Vaidyam et al. [1]	6	2010–2017	10	Mental health	No
Montenegro et al. [12]*	10	2010–2018	40	Any context	No
Bibault et al. [13]	3	1980–2018	6	Any context	No
Schachner et al. [14]*	7	2010–2020	10	Chronic diseases	No
Gabarron et al. [15]	5	2015–2019	15	Public health	No
ter Stal et al. [2]	5	2001–2018	33	Any context	No
Milne-Ives et al. [16]	6	2008–2019	31	Any context	No
Tudor Car et al. [6]	10	2015–2018	47	Any context	Partially
Safi et al. [17]	8	2009–2019	45	Any context	No
Abd-Alrazaq et al. [7]	7	2003–2019	65	Any context	Partially
Our study*	6	Up to 2020	19	Any context	*Yes*

"*" indicates that the review study performed a systematic review

designs, statistical analysis population. Moreover, the researchers summarized opportunities, challenges, benefits and limitations of utilizing the agents in mental care. Similarly, Vaidyam et al. [1] looked at benefits and potential harms of conversational agents used in mental care. Montenegro et al. [12] analyzed interactions, dialog, and architectures attributes of conversational agents from the literature and reviewed the state of the art in this area as well as challenges, contexts for interaction, dialogue components, systems and techniques related to these agents in healthcare. Bibault et al. [13] reviewed the use of conversational agents in oncology including cancer screening, mental health, and lifestyle change and evaluated the ongoing trials on the agents in ontology. More recently, Schachner et al. [14] examined evaluation measures (e.g. usability measurement, technical performance, and health-related outcomes) of the identified AI-based conversational agents in the literature, technical characteristics of AI, types of chronic diseases involved in the agents, communication channels, dialogues initiatives, and interaction models of the agents. Gabarron et al. [15] reviewed the research of conversational agents in healthcare and divided these studies into interventional studies concerning health-related outcomes and development studies on usability evaluation and suggested improvements for future studies from the perspectives of agents' designs, research designs, and data analysis and reporting of results. While ter Stal et al. [2] focused on impacts of the functional features of conversational agents used in healthcare on the perception of the agent's (e.g. agent looks) and user's characteristics (e.g. speech and/or text output, facial and gaze expressions, and hand and body gestures). Milne-Ives et al. [16] summarized the characteristics of the included studies (e.g. types of AI-based conversational agents, health context, and study designs) and positive and/or mixed aspects of the agents in relation to their effectiveness, usability, and satisfactoriness. Tudor Car et al. [6] reviewed the characteristics of the included studies (e.g. countries of the studies conducted, study designs, and types of literature), the characteristics of the conversational agents studied, and evaluation outcomes of the agents. Safi et al. [17] investigated the components of conversational agents and grouped them into four modules: text understanding, dialogue management, data management, and text generation. Abd-Alrazaq et al. [7] reviewed different research facets (i.e. study metadata, population characteristics, and intervention characteristics) of technical evaluation for a conversational agent in healthcare and summarized metrics used to assess the agent as a whole and response generation, response understanding, and esthetics of the agent.

These literature reviews examined the studies on conversational agents from different perspectives to improve our understanding of this academic niche in the realm of healthcare, emphasizing technical characteristics of the agents and their related evaluation outcomes. Although Tudor Car et al. [6] included information accuracy of the agents as an aspect of evaluation outcomes investigated in the study context and Abd-Alrazaq et al. [7] identified the evaluation metrics of response generation and understanding for the agents that involve a few quality issues of the information provided by the agents (e.g. appropriateness and error rate of responses), an investigation on health-related information quality of AI-based conversational agents is not the focus of prior literature reviews. In this study, we not only review the research facets of the AI-based conversational agents' literature (i.e. publication year, research purposes of using the agents in healthcare, and research designs) but also look at user feedback on the information quality of these agents. In this light, we can have a better chance to improve the understanding of the topic of interest and explore potential areas for further investigation. Our SLR differs from prior published review studies in the following ways:

(1) Timeframe of review: The timeframe of our review is up to 2020 (inclusive) to capture all relevant developments; and

(2) Focus of review: This review looks at the studies where an AI-based conversational agent was applied in any health context. We conduct the content and thematic analysis on research purposes, research designs and how users perceived the information quality of the agents.

3 Research Methods

To conduct the SLR, we followed the guidelines of evidenced-based paradigm [8] that contain four main steps: (1) developing search strategy, (2) selecting relevant studies, (3) assessing the quality of relevant studies, and (4) extracting, analyzing, and synthesizing data from relevant studies.

3.1 Developing Search Strategy

We first developed our search strategy for searching all possible relevant articles for further study. This process includes three main activities: identifying major search terms, formulating search terms and selecting search sources [8].

Identifying Major Search Terms. Based on our aims and RQ, we generated the following major search terms: information, artificial intelligence, conversational agent, health.

Formulating Search Terms. Before developing our search terms, we conducted a preliminary survey on previous published review studies on conversational agents in healthcare. According to related studies (see Table 1) and Borges et al. [18], we came up with a set of alternative terms used to describe the major search terms, as presented in Table 2. These keywords selected were most frequently employed in the literature that assist us in identifying an exhaustive set of articles with respect to health-related information provided by AI-based conversational agents. Hence, the search strings used in this study were developed based on the selected keywords connected using the Boolean operators: (("information" OR "data" OR "content" OR "text" OR "message" OR "response") AND ("artificial intelligence" OR "machine learning" OR "deep learning" OR "representation learning" OR "neural network" OR "natural language processing" OR "natural language understanding") AND ("conversational agent" OR "conversational system" OR "dialog system" OR "dialogue system" OR "assistance technolog*" OR "relational agent" OR "digital agent" OR "digital assistant" OR "digital coach" OR "virtual advisor" OR "virtual assistant" OR "virtual coach" OR "virtual counsel" OR "virtual character" OR "chatterbot" OR "chatbot" OR "social bot" OR "social agent" OR "softbot" OR "software agent" OR "automated agent" OR "counsel agent" OR "motivational agent" OR "interface agent" OR "interface character") AND ("health" OR "healthcare" OR "health care" OR "*health" OR "*medic*" OR "illness" OR "disease")).

Selecting Search Sources. In this study we adopted six databases from previous published literature reviews (see Table 1) as the majority of them were the most frequently used databases to perform the search (at least employed in half of the review studies identified in this study as initial search sources and this implies that the databases can help researchers identify relevant publications as many as possible and are widely accepted in the area). The six databases utilized in this study are PubMed, EmBase, PsycINFO, IEEE Xplore Digital Library, ACM Digital Library, and Scopus[1].

Table 2. Alternative terms used to describe the major search terms in this review

Major term	Alternative terms
Information[a]	"data", "content", "text", "message", "response"
Artificial intelligence	"machine learning", "deep learning", "representation learning", "neural network", "natural language processing", "natural language understanding"
Conversational agent	"conversational system", "dialog system", "dialogue system", "assistance technolog*", "relational agent", "digital agent", "digital assistant", "digital coach", "virtual advisor", "virtual assistant", "virtual coach", "virtual counsel", "virtual character", "chatterbot", "chatbot", "social bot", "social agent", "softbot", "software agent", "automated agent", "counsel agent", "motivational agent", "interface agent", "interface character"
Health	"healthcare", "health care", "*health", "*medic*", "illness", "disease"

[a]In this SLR we applied "information" as the major term rather than using "information quality" because in our pilot search using "information quality" gave very limited results.

We applied the search strings to search publications in the fields of Title, Abstract and Keywords and also customized with the search strings in the databases based on their functional characteristics [19]. In this way, we had an initial list of articles for selection.

3.2 Selecting Relevant Studies

This step is to filter relevant articles from the initial identified publications. Referring to related studies (see Table 1), we developed the inclusion and exclusion criteria for study selection as shown in Table 3.

This primary search was conducted in December 2021. Using the search strings, we identified 504 articles in this study, of which 50 were discarded upon the title and abstract review using our exclusion criteria (from EC1 to EC3) (see Table 3). After full-text review, we included 37 articles achieving all inclusion criteria and further removed 18 from these articles based on the exclusion criteria (from EC4 to EC7). Finally, 19 articles appeared to be eligible for further analysis in our primary search. See Table 4. Each article was assigned with a unique identifier (the letter S followed by a number) that could be referenced in the analysis and reporting of the findings. All 19 studies included in this SLR are listed in Appendix 1.

---

[1] Although Scopus database was only used in three literature reviews identified in this study, it is an important source for search in the field of human computer interaction [2] and therefore we also included this database as our initial search sources.

Table 3. Inclusion and exclusion criteria used in this review

Criteria	Number of criteria	Description
Inclusion criteria	IC1	The studies included were published in English
	IC2	The studies included were published up to 2020
	IC3	The studies involved a conversational agent
	IC4	The studies addressed a health context
	IC5	The studies involved any kind of AI techniques for the agent
	IC6	The studies included users of the agent
Exclusion criteria	EC1	The studies are duplicates
	EC2	The studies are not accessible online
	EC3	The studies are not peer-reviewed research publications (e.g. thesis, book reviews, and editorial letters)
	EC4	The studies do not provide primary data themselves
	EC5	The studies utilized the "Wizard of Oz" method (responses given by a human operator rather than an automated agent) to interact with users
	EC6	The studies do not mention any health-related information matters about the agent
	EC7	The studies published have three pages or less in length

Table 4. Results of paper search and selection in this review

No	Database	NIP	NE1–3	NI	NNI	NE4–7	NR
DB1	PubMed	70	0	21	49	12	9
DB2	Embase	47	27	1	19	1	0
DB3	PsycINFO	21	11	4	6	1	3
DB4	IEEE Xplore Digital Library	9	0	4	5	0	4
DB5	ACM Digital Library	9	0	0	9	0	0
DB6	Scopus	348	12	7	329	4	3
Total		504	50	37	417	18	19

NIP: Number of initial identified papers
NE1–3: Number of papers matching one criterion from EC1 to EC3
NI: Number of papers matching all inclusion criteria
NNI: Number of papers that does not match one or more than one inclusion criteria
NE4–7: Number of papers matching one criterion from EC4 to EC7 from prior included papers
NR: Number of the papers remained in the primary search

3.3   Assessing the Quality of Relevant Studies

To assess the quality of the included studies we looked at the impact of these publications because the number of citations for a paper can be considered as an easy way of measuring the quality of a publication [20] that contributes to studying the impact of these publications on the relevant research community in this review. Figure 1 shows the citations of the included studies identified from Google Scholar (as on January 7th, 2021). In our results, 8 papers had over 10 citations and S11 had over 100 citations (see Fig. 1). We also observe that more than half of the included studies had less than 10 citations as the majority of them were published since 2020.

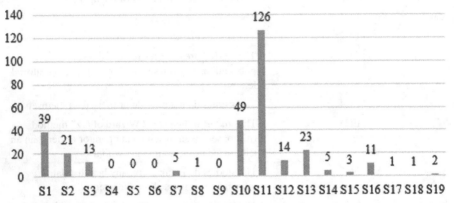

Fig. 1. Number of citations for the included studies identified in this review in Google Scholar.

3.4   Extracting, Analyzing, and Synthesizing Data from Relevant Studies

We extract the data from relevant studies including publication year, research purposes of using AI-based conversational agents in healthcare, and research design. Then we analysed and coded the responses from the text of each selected study relevant to our RQ. Thereafter, we grouped all extracted data based on these themes (i.e., research purposes, research designs, and responses to address the RQ), and conducted cross analysis to discuss our findings.

4   Results

This section gives the results of our SLR. First, we describe the characteristics of the included studies on the research purposes and research designs upon publication year, to give an overview of this field [6]. Then, we present the findings derived from the analysis of the reviewed studies based on our RQ.

4.1 Research Purposes

In this subsection, we present the research purposes of using AI-based conversational agents in healthcare that have been addressed in the reviewed studies based on publication year. The themes emerging from the data analysis were divided into six main groups: behaviors change, counselling, education, intervention, monitoring, and multiple purposes. These themes were named referring to the keywords explicitly used in the study context to describe the purposes of using the agents. See Fig. 2.

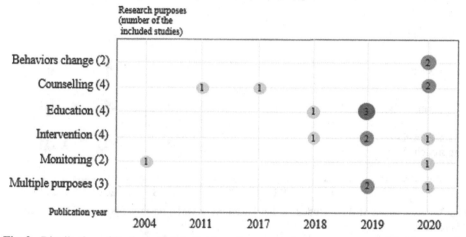

Fig. 2. Distribution of the included studies based on research purposes upon publication year in this review.

Figure 2 demonstrates that resent literature of the AI-based conversational agents used in healthcare has paid increasing attention to the quality of health information, addressing a variety of research purposes. For example, the agents can be applied to support patients in lifestyle behaviors change [S5, S17] (e.g., diet and exercise). A few patients utilized the agents for counselling alcohol and other drugs use [S6, S11], asking questions about plastic surgery [S8] and pre-test counseling of an HIV test [S16]. The users also took advantages of the agents to improve medication adherence through reminders and educational content of chronic disease [S2, S13] as well as knowledge and self-management regarding Juvenile Idiopathic Arthritis [S7], and to perform psychotherapy training [S12]. Some agents were used to support therapeutic interventions for mental health [S3, S9, S14] and palliative care [S15]. Other agents were mainly employed to follow up orthopedic patients [S4] and monitor homey hypertension [S19]. In the studies [S1, S10, S18], the users concerned diverse use of the agents in healthcare such as information seeking, personalized treatment, and self-management.

4.2 Research Designs

This subsection outlines the research designs adopted in the reviewed studies. These research designs that have been explicitly mentioned by the respective authors in the research are: case study [S7, S9], survey [S2, S8, S10], experiment [S3, S4, S5, S12, S14, S15, S16, S18, S19], and mixed-methods approach [S1, S6, S11, S13, S17]. Although few studies did not point out their research design, we referred to those studies which utilized similar research methods to assign. Figure 3 presents the distribution of the reviewed studies based on research designs upon publication year.

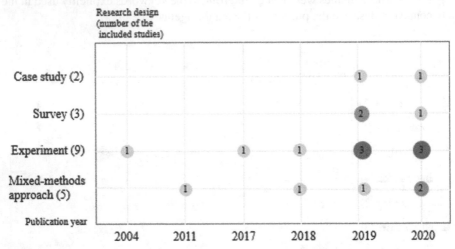

Fig. 3. Distribution of the included studies based on research designs upon publication year in this review.

As shown in Fig. 3, experiment was the most frequently adopted research design in our SLR. This could be due to that a few studies developed AI-based conversational agents for healthcare and recruited users to perform a usability evaluation. Mixed-methods approach followed as the second frequently used research design in this study and researchers benefited from multiple quantitative and qualitative approaches to facilitate their empirical findings. More recently, case study and survey emerged to (1) gain insights for the phenomena of applying a specific conversational agent in healthcare or (2) enhance the strength of causal inferences from research based on empirical data collected from a large number of participants.

4.3 Findings Addressing the RQ

The present subsection provides the findings derived from the included studies addressing our RQ. Table 5 depicts these findings that are classified into four categories including positive, negative, mixed, and not sure.

Table 5. Distribution of the included studies based on the categories of the feedback on the information quality of AI-based conversational agents in healthcare

Categories of the findings addressing the RQ	References	Percent
Positive (having only positive feedback on the information quality of the agents)	[S1, S2, S4, S11, S19]	26
Negative (having only negative feedback on the information quality of the agents)	[S5, S6, S16, S17]	21
Mixed (having both positive and negative feedback on the information quality of the agents)	[S3, S7, S8, S9, S10, S12, S13, S14, S15, S18]	53
Not sure (not sure about the information quality of the agents)	[S1]	5

Note that one study could have more than one category of the feedback in this review.

As shown in Table 5, 53% of the included studies reported mixed feedback from users on the information quality of the agents. Twenty-six of the included 19 studies had only positive feedback on the information quality, while twenty-one of the reviewed studies only indicated negative feedback in which the users also gave their suggestions on the aspects needed to improve. Only one study [S1] of this review revealed that the users were not sure about the quality of the information provided by a chatbot in their interviews. However, in the same study [S1], the results of the online survey disclosed a high level of chatbot acceptability from users about identifying accurate information.

5 Discussion

In this study, we followed the guidelines of evidenced-based paradigm [8] to conduct a systematic review on the publications of AI-based conversation agents applied in healthcare involving information quality. The analysis and synthesis of the resulting 19 studies selected based on our inclusion and exclusion criteria helps address our RQ:

RQ: How users perceived the information quality of AI-based conversation agents used in healthcare?
Findings: The feedback from the users on the information quality of the agents were categorized into four main groups: positive, negative, mixed and not sure (see Table 5).

The overall results of this study demonstrate that positive and negative comments on the information quality of the agents are neck and neck. This phenomenon has attracted an increasing research interest in recently three years. Furthermore, we found that the included studies tended to address more diverse research purposes since 2019 (see Fig. 2). More recently, multiple research designs appeared in investigating AI-based conversational agents in healthcare involving information quality (see Fig. 3).

To better disclose research possibilities, we conducted a cross analysis for research purposes, research designs and findings addressing the RQ, as shown in Table 6.

Table 6. A cross analysis of the included studied in this review

Research purposes	Results	Research design			
		Case study	Survey	Experiment	Mixed-methods approach
Behaviours change	P				
	N			[S5]	[S17]
	M				
	NS				
Counselling	P				[S11]
	N			[S16]	[S6]
	M		[S8]		
	NS				
Education	P		[S2]		
	N				
	M	[S7]		[S12]	[S13]
	NS				
Intervention	P				
	N				
	M	[S9]		[S3, S14, S15]	
	NS				
Monitoring	P	[S4, S19]			
	N				
	M				
	NS				
Multiple purposes	P				[S1]
	N				
	M		[S10]	[S18]	
	NS				[S1]

P: Positive (having only positive feedback on the information quality of the agents).
N: Negative (having only negative feedback on the information quality of the agents).
M: Mixed (having both positive and negative feedback on the information quality of the agents).
NS: Not Sure (not sure about the information quality of the agents).

Table 6 has many blank cells, implying these aspects have not been investigated in the literature that may be research areas for further exploration. For example, for the purpose of behaviors change, none of the included studies looked at (1) the information quality of AI-based conversational agents in healthcare from both positive and negative perspectives and (2) what are the concerns of users about the information quality when applying these agents. Meanwhile, research designs identified from this review could serve as candidates for selection based on a specific study context. Although the existing literature has paid attention to the information quality of the agents, the information quality matters were only included as an aspect of the study context for investigation. Defining and measuring the information quality of the agents based on specific dimensions of information quality has received limited attention. This may be due to that a unified system of information quality dimensions used for AI-based conversational agents in healthcare is missing in the literature. Positive and negative perspectives of the information quality of the agents have been investigated in the literature, while challenges and barriers to achieve high-quality information from the agents and information quality issues of the agents have not been fully addressed that could serve as a starting point to systematically govern and improve the information quality. Developing a framework of information quality governance for AI-based conversational agents in healthcare thus will be a research trend in this area. Additionally, in this review, the majority of the included studies utilized questionnaires or task completion rate to assess the information quality of the agents. None of them applied neuroscience methods [21] (e.g., eye tracking and electroencephalogram) to analyze how users determine the information quality of the agents. This assists in understanding the mechanisms of user behaviors on assessing the information quality, in order to better design and develop the agents that help users achieve quality-assured health information.

5.1 Implications for Academics

The theoretical contributions of this SLR includes a unique study of identifying user feedback on the information quality of AI-based conversational agents in healthcare and establishing links among research purposes, research designs and research findings addressing our RQ, which help improve the understanding of this area. The research purposes and research designs identified from the present study also assist in proposing and conducting similar studies in future to advance the research field. The research possibilities uncover in this study will become important themes in the research of AI-based conversational agents used for healthcare: (1) developing a system of information quality dimensions for defining and measuring information quality for the agents; (2) establishing a framework of information quality governance for these agents; and (3) applying neuroscience methods to analyze and understand user behaviors in relation to information quality assessment of the agents. Our future work will address these three research themes.

5.2 Implications for Practices

Our findings of research purposes in this study could receive the attention from developers to information quality of AI-based conversational agents developed for different purposes in healthcare. This review reveals that recent developments of the agents have both positive and negative feedback on the information quality. Developers should take into this feedback into account for improvement. Meanwhile, multiple aspects of the society (e.g., users, governments, and healthcare professionals) need to play their roles in achieving quality-assured health information of the agents and improving the awareness of the information quality matters of these agents is a starting point.

5.3 Limitations of This Study

While we have followed the SLR guidelines [8] to conduct the review, this study still has limitations. For example, our review was limited to the online databases with keywords advised by related studies (see Sect. 3) that could have resulted in potential articles missing in our study sample. We selected the articles based on our inclusion and exclusion criteria and extracted data from the articles based on our topics of interest. To ensure quality of coding text, we referred to the phrases and keywords explicitly used in the text and discussed any uncertain coding for resolution.

6   Conclusion

This article presents a systematic review of empirical studies of AI-based conversational agents involving information quality in healthcare. Our review answers a specific RQ based on the data extracted and analyzed from the selected 19 research articles published up to 2020 (inclusive) (Sect. 4.3). We conducted a cross analysis for the research purposes, research designs and findings addressing our RQ to establish links between these themes and reveal research possibilities (Sect. 5). Our findings also suggest implications for academics and practices.

Acknowledgement. This research was supported by two grants respectively funded by the Natural Science Foundation of Guangdong (No.: 2018A030313706) and the National Natural Science Foundation of China (No.: 71974215).

Appendix

Appendix 1. The included 19 studies in this SLR

Number of the study	Reference
S1	Nadarzynski, T., Miles, O., Cowie, A., Ridge, D.: Acceptability of artificial intelligence (AI)-led chatbot services in healthcare: A mixed-methods study. Digital health 5, p. 2055207619871808 (2019)
S2	Chaix, B., Bibault, J.E., Pienkowski, A., Delamon, G., Guillemassé, A., Nectoux, P., Brouard B.: When Chatbots meet patients: One-year prospective study of conversations between patients with breast cancer and a chatbot. JMIR Cancer 5(1), e12856 (2019)

(continued)

Appendix 1. (*continued*)

Number of the study	Reference
S3	Denecke, K., Hochreutener, S.L., Pöpel, A., May, R.: Self-anamnesis with a conversational user interface: Concept and usability study. Methods of information in medicine 57(05/06), 243–252 (2018)
S4	Bian, Y., Xiang, Y., Tong, B., Feng, B., Weng, X.: Artificial intelligence–assisted system in postoperative follow-up of orthopedic patients: Exploratory quantitative and qualitative study. Journal of Medical Internet Research 22(5), e16896 (2020)
S5	Chen, J., Lyell, D., Laranjo, L., Magrabi, F.: Effect of speech recognition on problem solving and recall in consumer digital health tasks: Controlled laboratory experiment. Journal of Medical Internet Research 22(6), e14827(2020)
S6	Barnett, A., Savic, M., Pienaar, K., Carter, A., Warren, N., Sandral, E., Manning, V., Lubman, D.I.: Enacting 'more-than-human'care: Clients' and counsellors' views on the multiple affordances of chatbots in alcohol and other drug counselling. International Journal of Drug Policy, 102910 (2020)
S7	Rose-Davis, B., Van Woensel, W., Stringer, E., Abidi, S., Abidi, S.S.: Using an artificial intelligence-based argument theory to generate automated patient education dialogues for families of children with juvenile idiopathic arthritis. In Ohno-Machado, L., Seroussi, B. (eds.) MedInfo 2019: Health and Welleing e-Networks for All, pp. 1337–1341. IOS Press, Incorporated (2019)
S8	Boczar D., Sisti A., Oliver J.D., Helmi H., Restrepo D.J., Huayllani M.T., Spaulding A.C., Carter R., Rinker B.D., Forte A.J.: Artificial intelligent virtual assistant for plastic surgery patient's frequently asked questions: A pilot study. Annals of Plastic Surgery 84(4), e16–21 (2020)
S9	Gaffney, H., Mansell, W., Tai, S.: Agents of change: Understanding the therapeutic processes associated with the helpfulness of therapy for mental health problems with relational agent MYLO. Digital Health 6, 2055207620911580 (2020)
S10	Palanica, A., Flaschner, P., Thommandram, A., Li, M., Fossat, Y.: Physicians' perceptions of chatbots in health care: Cross-sectional web-based survey. Journal of medical Internet research 21(4), e12887 (2019)
S11	Crutzen, R., Peters, G.J.Y., Portugal, S.D., Fisser, E.M., Grolleman, J.J.: An artificially intelligent chat agent that answers adolescents' questions related to sex, drugs, and alcohol: An exploratory study. Journal of Adolescent Health 48(5), 514–519 (2011)

(*continued*)

Appendix 1. (*continued*)

Number of the study	Reference
S12	Tanana, M.J., Soma, C.S., Srikumar, V., Atkins, D.C., Imel, Z.E.: Development and evaluation of ClientBot: Patient-like conversational agent to train basic counseling skills. Journal of medical Internet research 21(7), e12529 (2019)
S13	Hussain, S., Athula, G.: Extending a conventional chatbot knowledge base to external knowledge source and introducing user based sessions for diabetes education. In: Ogiela, L, Enokido, T., Ogiela, M.R., Javaid, N., Barolli, L., Takizawa, M. (eds.) International Conference on Advanced Information Networking and Applications Workshops, pp. 698–703. IEEE, Piscataway (2018)
S14	Ralston, K., Chen, Y., Isah, H., Zulkernine, F.: A voice interactive multilingual student support system using IBM Watson. In International Conference on Machine Learning and Applications, pp. 1924–1929. IEEE, Piscataway (2019)
S15	Chatzimina, M., Koumakis, L., Marias, K., Tsiknakis, M.: Employing conversational agents in palliative care: A feasibility study and preliminary assessment. In: International Conference on Bioinformatics and Bioengineering, pp. 489–496. IEEE, Piscataway (2019)
S16	van Heerden, A., Ntinga, X., Vilakazi, K.: The potential of conversational agents to provide a rapid HIV counseling and testing services. In International Conference on the Frontiers and Advances in Data Science, pp. 80–85. IEEE, Piscataway (2017)
S17	Balsa, J., Félix, I., Cláudio, A.P., Carmo, M.B., e Silva, I.C., Guerreiro, A., Guedes, M., Henriques, A., Guerreiro, M.P.: Usability of an intelligent virtual assistant for promoting behavior change and self-care in older people with Type 2 Diabetes. Journal of Medical Systems 44(7), 1–12 (2020)
S18	Prakash, A.V., Das, S.: Would you trust a bot for healthcare advice? An empirical investigation. In: Vogel, D., Shen, K. N., Ling, P. S. (eds.) Pacific Asia Conference on Information Systems, 62 (2020)
S19	Giorgino, T., Quaglini, S., Stefanelli, M.: Evaluation and usage patterns in the homey hypertension management dialog system. In AAAI Fall Symposium on Dialog Systems for Health Communication, FS-04-04 (2004)

References

1. Vaidyam, A.N., Wisniewski, H., Halamka, J.D., Kashavan, M.S., Torous, J.B.: Chatbots and conversational agents in mental health: a review of the psychiatric landscape. Can. J. Psychiatry **64**(7), 456–464 (2019)
2. ter Stal, S., Kramer, L.L., Tabak, M., op den Akker, H., Hermens, H.: Design features of embodied conversational agents in eHealth: a literature review. Int. J. Hum. Comput. Stud. **138**, 102409 (2020).

3. Palanica, A., Flaschner, P., Thommandram, A., Li, M., Fossat, Y.: Physicians' perceptions of chatbots in health care: cross-sectional web-based survey. J. Med. Internet Res. **21**(4), e12887 (2019)
4. Strong, D.M., Lee, Y.W., Wang, R.Y.: 10 potholes in the road to information quality. Computer **30**(8), 38–46 (1997)
5. Zhang, Y., Sun, Y., Xie, B.: Quality of health information for consumers on the web: a systematic review of indicators, criteria, tools, and evaluation results. J. Assoc. Inf. Sci. Technol. **66**(10), 2071–2084 (2015)
6. Car, L.T., et al.: Conversational agents in health care: scoping review and conceptual analysis. J. Med. Internet Res. **22**(8), e17158 (2020)
7. Abd-Alrazaq, A., Safi, Z., Alajlani, M., Warren, J., Househ, M., Denecke, K.: Technical metrics used to evaluate health care chatbots: scoping review. J. Med. Internet Res. **22**(6), e18301 (2020)
8. Kitchenham, B.A., Budgen, D., Brereton, P.: Evidence-Based Software Engineering and Systematic Reviews, 1st edn. CRC Press, Boca Raton, Florida (2016)
9. Laranjo, L., et al.: Conversational agents in healthcare: a systematic review. J. Am. Med. Inf. Assoc. **25**(9), 1248–1258 (2018)
10. Pereira, J., Díaz, Ó.: Using health chatbots for behavior change: a mapping study. J. Med. Syst. **43**(5), 135 (2019)
11. Bendig, E., Erb, B., Schulze-Thuesing, L., Baumeister, H.: The next generation: chatbots in clinical psychology and psychotherapy to foster mental health–a scoping review. Verhaltenstherapie, 1–13 (2019)
12. Montenegro, J.L.Z., da Costa, C.A., da Rosa Righi, R.: Survey of conversational agents in health. Exp. Syst. Appl. **129**, 56–67 (2019)
13. Bibault, J.-E., Chaix, B., Nectoux, P., Pienkowski, A., Guillemasé, A., Brouard, B.: Healthcare ex Machina: are conversational agents ready for prime time in oncology? Clin. Transl. Radiat. Oncol. **16**, 55–59 (2019)
14. Schachner, T., Keller, R., von Wangenheim, F.: Artificial intelligence-based conversational agents for chronic conditions: systematic literature review. J. Med. Internet Res. **22**(9), e20701 (2020)
15. Gabarron, E., Larbi, D., Denecke, K., Årsand, E.: What do we know about the use of chatbots for public health? Stud. Health Technol. Inf. **270**, 796–800 (2020)
16. Milne-Ives, M., et al.: The effectiveness of artificial intelligence conversational agents in health care: systematic review. J. Med. Internet Res. **22**(10), e20346 (2020)
17. Safi, Z., Abd-Alrazaq, A., Khalifa, M., Househ, M.: Technical aspects of developing chatbots for medical applications: scoping review. J. Med. Internet Res. **22**(12), e19127 (2020)
18. Borges, A.F., Laurindo, F.J., Spínola, M.M., Gonçalves, R.F., Mattos, C.A.: The strategic use of artificial intelligence in the digital era: systematic literature review and future research directions. Int. J. Inf. Manage. **57**, 102225 (2020)
19. Liu, C., Nitschke, P., Williams, S., Zowghi, D.: Data quality and the Internet of Things. Computing **102**(2), 573–599 (2019). https://doi.org/10.1007/s00607-019-00746-z
20. Bano, M., Zowghi, D.: A systematic review on the relationship between user involvement and system success. Inf. Softw. Technol. **58**, 148–169 (2015)
21. Khushaba, R.N., Wise, C., Kodagoda, S., Louviere, J., Kahn, B.E., Townsend, C.: Consumer neuroscience: assessing the brain response to marketing stimuli using electroencephalogram (EEG) and eye tracking. Exp. Syst. with Appl. **40**(9), 3803–3812 (2013)

Standard Dialogue Structure and Frequent Patterns in the Agent Dialogue System

Yoshimi Tominaga[1,2]([⊠]), Hideki Tanaka[1], Hiroshi Ishiguro[2], and Kohei Ogawa[3]

[1] Elvez, Inc., Tokyo, Japan
tominaga.yoshimi@irl.sys.es.osaka-u.ac.jp, {yoshimi.tominaga, hideki.tanaka}@elvez.co.jp
[2] Osaka University, Osaka, Japan
ishiguro@irl.sys.es.osaka-u.ac.jp
[3] Nagoya University, Nagoya, Aichi, Japan
k-ogawa@nuee.nagoya-u.ac.jp

Abstract. To design a dialogue well and easily implement it into an autonomous dialogue system, a dialogue with simple components in which interaction with the partners is smoothly achieved is required. In designing interactions to use in an autonomous dialogue system, we consider that there are typical dialogue structures that convey agency and facilitate the dialogue. In this paper, we focused on surveying such dialogue structures and defined this structure as the "Standard Dialogue Structure" for human-agent dialogue. It is constructed using the "Turn" that is one turn-taking between the dialogue participants, the "Topic" that is a series of Turns in which a single question is resolved, the "Topic-shift" that is short interaction to build consensus before moving to the next Topic, and the "Scene" that puts together each component. Using dialogue scenarios created based on the health checklist for elderly people, we confirmed that the Standard Dialogue Structure can be used in question-and-answer dialogues led by the agent. Furthermore, we investigated the frequent patterns of dialogue in the Topic by using the utterances in the Turns which were labeled by a four-quadrant impression. The results indicated that these frequent patterns could be an effective pattern for facilitating dialogue. Therefore, we investigate the possibility of expressing agency and promoting dialogue using these frequent patterns in the autonomous dialogue systems. In conclusion, we have shown that the Standard Dialogue Structure is possible to easily implement dialogues that effectively promote interaction, even for a novice in dialogue design.

Keywords: Natural interaction · Dialogue structure · Agent dialogue system · Topic-shift · Dialogue design

1 Introduction

Under the influence of the impact of COVID-19, the way we communicate has changed, and online communication through Information and Communication Technology has become essential worldwide. In the future, autonomous dialogue systems with virtual

© Springer Nature Switzerland AG 2021
N. Streitz and S. Konomi (Eds.): HCII 2021, LNCS 12782, pp. 348–360, 2021.
https://doi.org/10.1007/978-3-030-77015-0_25

agents will be used on a more usual basis. The change is not only limited to business and school but extends to daily communication between family members. Not only young people but also seniors will have more opportunities to communicate through smartphones. The elderly population aged 65 and over is 18.1% of the world's population and will continue to increase. In particular, the elderly population ratio in Japan is 28.7%, the highest in the world [1]. However, for the disabled and elderly, current autonomous dialogue systems are complex and difficult to use. According to Gray et al. [2], compared to human adults, robots do not give the "agency" that is the felt impression of it is acting according to its own judgments. With current autonomous dialogue systems, it is difficult to convey intentions and consents indirectly due to limited nonverbal outputs.

Therefore, an autonomous dialogue system should cooperate with users. For example, the following methods have been empirically established. In task-oriented dialogue, to elicit from the dialogue partner that is necessary to accomplish the task, it is possible to guide the other person's answer by communicating the goal and narrowing down the future options. Also, repeating the dialogue partner's statements can give the impression of empathy or agreement with the answer and also readiness to move on to the next Topic. On the other hand, a simple repetition of a matter of fact can give the impression of boredom.

In designing dialogues for an autonomous dialogue system, therefore, the system should not only listen to the necessary information required to accomplish the task but also consider how to proceed with the dialogue and how to interact with each dialogue partner cooperatively to proceed smoothly. However, it is very difficult for a novice to design a dialogue. To design a dialogue well and implement it into an autonomous dialogue system easily, it is necessary to design a dialogue with simple components.

We have been developing a mobile application for elderly people using a selection-based dialogue system that displays choices on a screen and asks participants to choose a response. Our feasibility study shows that even elderly people could effectively use the dialogue system on a smartphone app without any problems. But, on the other hand, longer dialogues tended to be avoided by users and were used less frequently [3]. In developing our application, we asked various people to create dialogue scenarios related to their work or questionnaires they are using in their work. However, most of them had a hard time creating dialogue scenarios. As autonomous dialogue systems become more common, it will be necessary for people who are not familiar with dialogue systems to be able to design dialogues easily. In continuing to develop of our dialogue system, we have come to consider that there are typical dialogue structures that can be used to design dialogues for autonomous dialogue systems. Clarifying these elements, such as the structure and typical patterns of dialogues, would facilitate easier dialogue design. In this study, therefore, we have focused on these structures of human-agent dialogue and have surveyed typical patterns in question-and-answer dialogues.

2 Standard Dialogue Structure

Our goal is to facilitate the design and implementation of dialogues for autonomous dialogue systems. Therefore, we investigated the structure of dialogues with the aim of implementing dialogues in dialogue system. In a study on the definition of dialogue structure, Bangalore et al. [4] proposed a model in which a task-oriented dialogue is divided into subtasks. They compared the chunk-based model and the hierarchical model for tagging dialogue acts in the subtask structure. Wolfbauer et al. [5] designed a dialogue structure for reflection guidance. They defined levels for pre-defined questions to control the dialogue content and order. Galitsky et al. [6] built a dialogue tree structure by analyzing a customer support dialogue dataset. They evaluated the features of personalization, recommendation, and clarification within dialogue scenarios. Watanabe et al. [7, 8] described a dialogue strategy and dialogue scenarios that evoke consumers' emotions. Through a field experiment featuring product sales using a touch panel, they assumed a mental distance from the customer and changed the phrases of the sales dialogue. However, these examples concern specified tasks, and it is difficult to say that the results of these studies can be applied to general dialogues including non-task-oriented dialogues.

Based on our experience of creating dialogue scenarios both through continuing to operate our application and carrying out feasibility studies, we concluded that different topics feature a similar way of proceeding within the dialogue. Although the ways of promoting dialogue are different for each person, they can be organized into a simple structure. We defined such a structure as the "Standard Dialogue Structure" for human-agent dialogue. The following is a description of the Standard Dialogue Structure.

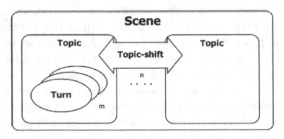

Fig. 1. Standard dialogue structure

Table 1. Components of standard dialogue structure

Component	Description
Scene	The Scene is the situation in which the dialogue takes place. The participants have one major purpose, either to convey or receive some message
Topic	The Topic is the one theme or purpose that should be heard or be communicated. Each Topic is independent of the other Topics
Topic-shift	Topic-shift is a short interaction that occurs when there is a change of Topic. Topic-shift builds consensus for each participant and changes the dialogue's mood
Turn	The Turn is a minimal interaction and turn-taking consists of the speaker's utterance and the response of other participants

Figure 1 shows the structure of the Standard Dialogue Structure. The details of each component are shown in Table 1. The minimum component of the dialogue is the Turn, which can be considered of as one episode of turn-taking between the speaker's question and the dialogue partner's response. In general, it needs a series of Turns to resolve a single question. In addition to question-answering dialogue, the dialogues in which an overview and guiding actions are given are also considered as one of series of Turns. We call this series of Turns the "Topic". The Topic has a simple purpose, and each are independent of the other Topics. When moving on to the next Topic, a short interaction is needed in which participants question each other and reach a consensus. We call this the "Topic-shift". The connection between a series of Topics and Topic-shifts is called the "Scene". The Scene is a situation in which a dialogue takes place.

Looking at the Standard Dialogue Structure in terms of the overall dialogue progression, the Scene has a major goal throughout the dialogue, and the dialogue is about some Topics which aims to achieve the goal. Each Topic is independent of the others and swapping their orders around does not affect the progress of the dialogue in the entire Scene. Also, when Topic-shift occurs and the dialogue moves on to the next Topic, a consensus is formed among the dialogue participants.

In designing an autonomous dialogue system, following the Standard Dialogue Structure makes it easy to design a dialogue that gives the intended impression. For example, although the Topic-shift is a short interaction, even a difference in the expression of the Topic-shift can change the impression of the speaker. Therefore, Topic-shift can be used to express personality without this being influenced by the content of the task.

Although the Standard Dialogue Structure is very limited, we believe that it can be applied to many question-answer dialogue systems. To show that the Standard Dialogue Structure is useful for analyzing and designing dialogues, we will show that dialogue scenarios created for autonomous dialogue systems can be represented by the Standard Dialogue Structure. We will also show that some typical dialogue patterns can be used to analyze dialogue scenarios and facilitate dialogue according to the Standard Dialogue Structure.

3   Dialogue Structure Analysis of Dialogue Scenarios

In our application for the elderly, we use an autonomous dialogue system to perform simple checks on the daily living conditions and health status of the elderly. In this paper, we analyzed the basic dialogue structure using a dialogue scenario that was created based on the "Basic Checklist" [9] used to check the physical condition of elderly people. The Basic Checklist is a health-related checklist for the elderly created by Japan's Ministry of Health, Labor, and Welfare. It consists of 25 yes/no questions about daily life and physical and mental health, such as whether the elderly people go out or seek advice from family and friends. Local governments in Japan regularly conduct surveys using this checklist as part of their welfare measures for elderly people. However, we have heard some people say that the monotonous face-to-face surveys with many questions make the respondents angry. By using a dialogue system, it would be possible to ask questions equivalent to this checklist progressively on a daily basis.

We created dialogue scenarios by asking participants about all 25 items in the Basic Checklist using "Chabot" [10] which is a flowchart-style scenario editor. The creation of dialogue scenarios was conducted through crowd-sourcing. In creating dialogue scenarios, the following instructions were given to create a dialogue that asks all the questions in the Basic Checklist. The scenario should be written separately for each question item. The human-side utterance should have no more than four choices. Also, for reference, we showed the example of dialogues that are not related to the Basic Checklist. We collected dialogue scenarios for 17 people, and the data produced were analyzed by correcting obvious typos and errors in connecting flowcharts and excluding some of the 25 questions that were incomplete or omitted.

The data were analyzed by applying the Standard Dialogue Structure to confirm whether the created dialogue scenarios can be applied to the Standard Dialogue Structure. We also discussed the points to note when incorporating the questionnaire into the dialogue scenario. In addition, we confirmed whether there are typical patterns in the analyzed data by applying it to the standard dialogue structure. Specifically, we categorize the intentions of each Turn, labelled "teach", "empathy", "survey" and "listen", and show the frequently occurring dialogue patterns.

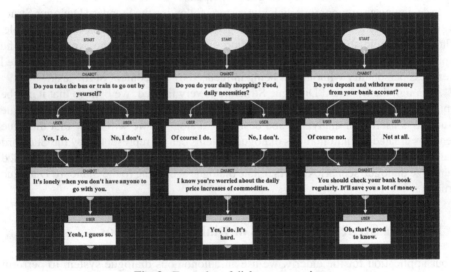

Fig. 2. Examples of dialogue scenarios

3.1 Analysis of Dialogue Components

We applied the created dialogue scenarios to the Standard Dialogue Structure and confirmed their characteristics. Figure 2 shows an example of the dialogue scenarios that were created. In the flowchart, the "Chabot" box is the agent's speech, and the "User" box is the dialogue system user's choices. These scenarios were created by the same person. The smallest interaction in the dialogue is the turn-taking between speakers. When applied to the flowchart of the dialogue scenario created in this study, the agent's utterance and the user's choice in response can be considered as one Turn. In the dialogue scenario shown in Fig. 2, we can see that each question in the Basic Checklist consists of an interaction of two Turns. Comparing the contents of each scenario in Fig. 2, we can see that contents are independent of each other. From this, we can consider each one of the question items as a Topic.

The following are the results of the analysis of each component of the Standard Dialogue Structure as applied to the dialogue scenarios.

Topic and Turn

We checked the content of the dialogue scenarios created and investigated whether the dialogue scenario for each question item changed its content concerning the results of answering another question item or the state of the dialogue. Specifically, scenarios that branched out depending on the content of the aforementioned questions, or scenarios that referred to the content of the aforementioned questions, were considered relevant.

As a result, all scenario creators did not create dialogue scenarios with contents that depended on other question items. Therefore, it can be said that it is possible to create a dialogue with each question item of the Basic Checklist as one Topic.

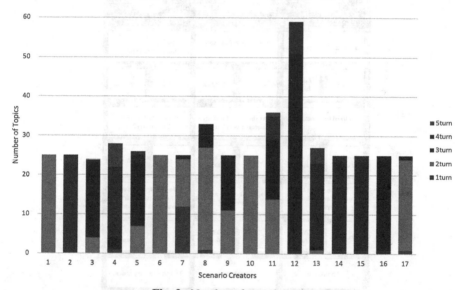

Fig. 3. Number of turns in topic

Also, we considered that there are typical patterns for each scenario creator and dialogue scenarios created by the same creator consist of almost the same number of Turns per Topic. We followed the flowcharts of dialogue scenarios in order and divided the choices of the agent and the user into Turns. If the agent's speech branched after a choice, the flowchart is traced and tabulated separately for each branch.

As a result of dividing the dialogue scenario into Turns while taking branching into account, 483 Topic data were obtained. For each creator, the number of Turns per Topic is shown in Fig. 3. For creator 3, 4, and 8, there was an incomplete preparation of one questionnaire item, and those data were removed.

When the number of Turns in Topic was analyzed, 457 out of 483 Topics consisted of two to four Turns of interaction. When looking at the number of Turns in one Topic for each creator, 7 creators had the same number of Turns in all Topics of his or her created dialogue scenario. In addition, 15 creators had the same number of Turns in more than half of the Topics. We found that the interaction between the agent and the user in each Topic could be expressed in a few Turns. We also found that many scenario creators have a typical dialogue pattern and create dialogue scenarios with a similar pattern for each question item.

Scene and Topic-Shift

Next, we analyzed the connections between Topics. Scenes consists of multiple Topics in the Standard Dialogue Structure. If a dialogue scenario regarding each of the above questions is considered as a Topic, Topic-shift, which performs the role of connecting Topics, is necessary for smooth dialogue.

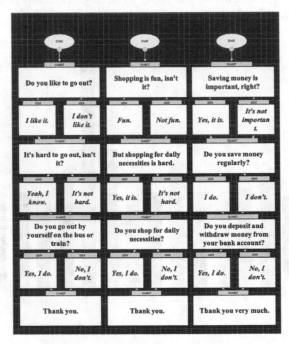

Fig. 4. Example of topics for everyday life

We investigated whether the dialogue scenarios created in this study contain interactions that can be considered Topic-shifts. The questions in the Basic Checklist, which was used as the subject of scenario creation in this study, can be divided into six evaluation groups: "daily life", "exercise", "nutrition and oral health", "withdrawal", "cognition", and "mental". Considering the implementation of a survey for the Basic Checklist, it is common to ask all 25 questions or at least the questions related to one assessment group together. This is because if the survey is conducted at different times, the Basic Checklist cannot be judged correctly.

We considered a dialogue about one of the evaluation groups in the Basic Checklist to be one Scene in the Standard Dialogue Structure and checked the contents of the dialogue scenario created. Figure 4 shows a series of dialogue scenarios related to daily life. As can be seen from the results of the Topic verification, there is no relevance between Topics for each question item, so simply sequencing the dialogue scenarios for the Topic would result in unnatural transition to the next Topic. To facilitate the dialogue, a short preamble is necessary at the beginning of the dialogue and at the transition of Topic, and a closing statement is necessary at the end.

Discussion

From the results of the analysis, it is clear that the dialogue scenarios created based on the Basic Checklist can be expressed in the basic dialogue structure. In particular, by dividing and organizing the dialogue into Turns and Topics, the question items of the Basic Checklist can be easily incorporated into the dialogue. In addition, simply tailoring the questions into a dialogue format will result in a dialogue that is not connected when viewed throughout Scene. Therefore, it can be said that the existence of Topic-shift as well as Topic content is necessary to realize a smooth dialogue.

The Standard Dialogue Structure facilitates the design of human-agent dialogue. This is because Topic-shift does not depend on the Topic content. When designing a survey or a question-and-answer dialogue, the designer should first focus on Topic and then design a dialogue in which each question is successfully asked. In addition, Topic-shift interaction can be added to connect the Topics. Topic-shifts vary depending on the progress of the dialogue, whether the conversation is going well, and whether the other person is in a good mood, but there are not many variations of Topic-shift for each person. In other words, we can say that we can prepare a typical pattern regardless of the Topic. Since Topic-shift alone gives a different impression to the other party, it can also express the individuality of the agent independently of the Topic content.

In summary, we have found that it is possible to easily design a smooth dialogue by applying the Standard Dialogue Structure. In particular, it was suggested that the typical pattern can be used in human-agent dialogues where the system can take the initiative in advancing the dialogue.

3.2 Frequent Patterns of a Dialogue

The analysis so far has shown that it is relatively easy to design human-agent dialogues by using the Standard Dialogue Structure. On the other hand, to create a positive impression while fulfilling the task of dialogue, such as answering questions, it is important to know how to proceed with the dialogue within the Topic. Although there seem to be many variations in the way people carry out dialogue within the Topic, each person seems to have some typical patterns.

We wanted to identify typical patterns in the way dialogue proceeds within Topics and the composition of the Turns. As mentioned earlier, in human-agent dialogues, the agent can take the lead in advancing the dialogue. Therefore, by looking at the intentions of each Turn from the agent's perspective, we can clarify the composition of the Topic. Specifically, the characteristics of the Turn are evaluated on two axes and analyzed in a four-quadrant classification. Then, each Turn is labeled, and the combinations of labels that appear frequently are analyzed. We then analyzed the combinations of labels that appear most frequently in each Turn. This allows us to identify the combinations of

Turns that are most frequently used, and thus to identify the preferred way of conducting dialogue on the Topic.

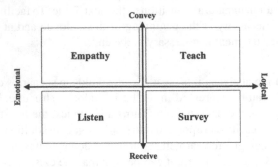

Fig. 5. For-quadrant labels for turn

Four-Quadrants Labeling

We analyzed and labeled the content of each Turn's utterance from the agent's point of view. Specifically, we analyzed the content of each Turn's utterance along two axes: "convey-receive", and "logical-emotional". The reasons for the analysis of these two axes are as follows. First, since dialogue is an exchange of information between speakers, it is possible to clearly distinguish the purpose of the dialogue, whether it is to convey information or to receive it. Also, in question-answer dialogue, clarifying whether each speaker is a communicator or a receiver can facilitate the task. While the first axis focuses on the speaker's role, the second, the "logical-emotional" axis, focuses on the speaker's impression.

We evaluated each Turn in Topic data evaluated in Sect. 3.1 on two axes. Furthermore, based on the ratings on the two axes, we labeled the content of each Turn with impressions in four quadrants: "teach" (logical-convey), "empathy" (emotional-convey), "survey" (logical-receive), and "listen" (emotional-receive) as shown in Fig. 5.

Frequent Pattern Mining

The aforementioned efforts have allowed the Turn to be represented by a combination of four labels. We conducted a frequent pattern analysis of the frequency of occurrence of these labels for each Topic to identify typical dialogue patterns. To perform the frequent pattern analysis, we transformed the dialogue data of one Topic into a sequence of labeled Turns. For these label sequences, we conducted a frequent pattern mining using Prefix Span algorithm [11], and counted the number of occurrences of the label sequences and their occurrence rates.

Result

As a result, the number of label sequence data to be analyzed was 483. Table 2 shows the results of the frequent pattern analysis for the label sequences with an appearance rate of 10% or higher. In this analysis, combinations of labels with two or more are considered as patterns. From the results in Table 2, the most frequently appearing pattern was the combination "survey-teach". This was followed by the patterns of "survey-empathy,"

Table 2. Appearance rates in result of frequent pattern mining

Label pattern	Appearance rate	Counts
N/A	100.0%	483
survey	96.7%	468
teach	60.5%	292
empathy	52.6%	254
survey-teach	**40.4%**	**195**
survey-empathy	**36.2%**	**175**
survey-survey	**29.0%**	**140**
teach-survey	28.0%	135
empathy-survey	21.7%	105
survey-survey-empathy	**15.5%**	**75**
listen	15.5%	75
teach-empathy	14.1%	68
teach-teach	13.5%	65
empathy-empathy	12.6%	61
empathy-teach	10.8%	52

"survey-survey," and "teach-survey. The most frequently appearance pattern with three or more labels was "survey-survey-empathy".

Discussion

From the above results, in the dialogues based on the Basic Checklist, there were many patterns such as "survey-teach" and "survey-empathy," in which a question was posed and then the other person's answer was used to show feedback through teaching or empathy. It is the "survey-survey-empathy" pattern that appeared most frequently in three or more Turns. An example of a dialogue scenario for this pattern is shown in Fig. 6. In this pattern, the question is asked twice, and the answers are narrowed down. At the end of Topic, the speaker gives empathetic feedback indicating that the autonomous dialogue system has listened to the dialogue partner's answer. This can be said to be a combination of "survey-survey" and "survey-empathy" patterns.

From the above analysis, we were able to identify examples of typical patterns that facilitate dialogue in designing dialogue within Topic.

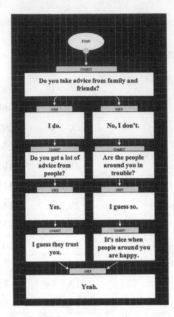

Fig. 6. Example of a dialogue pattern (survey-survey-empathy)

4 Discussion

We proposed to analyze and design dialogues using the Standard Dialogue Structure to facilitate dialogue design for an autonomous dialogue system. The above results showed that a dialogue scenario created based on the Basic Checklist can be represented by the Standard Dialogue Structure. Also, the results showed that there are typical patterns in the series of Turns in Topic. We consider that these frequent patterns could be effective to facilitate a dialogue. These frequent patterns could be used to facilitate dialogue in an autonomous dialogue system that has weak non-verbal output.

In designing dialogue for an autonomous dialogue system, the Standard Dialogue Structures has the following advantages. The first is that it is easy to incorporate current resources into the dialogue. Normally, when providing a service or collecting information through an autonomous dialogue system, there is a list of possible contents and questionnaire items. The Basic Checklist used in this study is one such example. Since the Standard Dialogue Structure can treat each question involved as a Topic, it is possible to incorporate them into the dialogue without worrying too much about the overall dialogue structure. Secondly, Topic-shift can be used to smoothly connect Topics. Since Topic-shift design does not require much awareness of the content of the Topic, there is no need to consider complex conditional branching, nor does it vary greatly depending on the task being handled. Third, typical patterns can be used for organization within Topics. By using phrases that give an impression according to the pattern in each Turn of the dialogue, an impression-like interaction can be realized instead of a simple question and answer.

In conjunction these advantages can reduce complex dialogue structures to simple problems and facilitate the preparation of templates for dialogue patterns. Therefore, even for a novice in dialogue design, the Dialogue Structure can easily facilitate the implementation of a smooth dialogue by combining repetition of typical patterns of Topics and Topic-shifts. In addition, this makes the automation and systematization of dialogue scenario generation simpler.

On the other hand, the dialogue scenario analyzed was created based on the Basic Checklist which takes the form of a questionnaire. Further study is needed to determine whether the Standard Dialogue Structure and the patterns presented in this study can be applied to more complex task-oriented dialogues. In addition, it is necessary to investigate whether an autonomous dialogue system that follows the patterns in this study could give a positive impression to users as intended by the patterns in an actual system.

5   Conclusion

In this study, we proposed the Standard Dialogue Structure that is a structure of human-agent dialogue which aims to facilitate the analysis and design of dialogues, which are expected to be increasingly used in the future. In the Standard Dialogue Structure, the Turn is defined as one turn-taking of between an agent and a user that is the minimum component, and the Topic is defined as a set of Turns on a single question item. To facilitate dialogue, Topic-shift is necessary to connect these Topics, and we defined a series of Topics and Topic-shifts as the Scene.

We analyzed dialogue scenarios created based on the Basic Checklists for the health check adopted in welfare policies in Japan and showed that they can be expressed in the Standard Dialogue Structure. As a result of our analysis, we found that the questions in the Basic Checklist correspond to Topics, and that each Topic consists of approximately 2–4 Turns. A typical pattern of organization within the Topic was identified. Specifically, the characteristics of the Turn were represented by four-quadrant labels consisting of the two axes of "convey-receive" and "logical-emotional", and frequent pattern analysis was conducted. The results showed that typical patterns such as question refinement patterns and empathy patterns were used.

The above results show that the Standard Dialogue Structure reduces dialogues into simple components and facilitates their design. We have shown that the Standard Dialogue Structure can be used to easily implement dialogues that effectively promote interaction, even for people who are novices in dialogue design.

These findings are of social benefit. We are providing an application for elderly people to inform their families about their daily health, as face-to-face communication is becoming increasingly difficult. Though this application, we are trying to smoothly find out about their daily health conditions and problems using a dialogue.

References

1. Statistics Bureau of Japan, Elderly people in Japan from the viewpoint of statistics, Named after Respect for the Aged Day. https://www.stat.go.jp/data/topics/topi1260.html. Accessed 24 Oct 2020

2. Gray, H.M., Gray, K., Wegner, D.M.: Dimensions of mind perception. Science **315**, 619 (2007)
3. Tominaga, Y., Tanaka, H., Narumoto, J., Ishiguro, H., Ogawa, K.: Development of applications for community building in a declining population society. J. Digit. Pract. **11**(2), 389–413 (2020)
4. Bangalore, S., Fabbrizio, G.D., Stent, A.: Learning the structure of task-driven human-human dialogs. In: Proceedings of the 21st International Conference on Computational Linguistics and 44th Annual Meeting of the Association for Computational Linguistics, Sydney, Australia (2006)
5. Wolfbauer, I., Pammer-Schindler, V., Rose, C.P.: Rebo junior: analysis of dialogue structure quality for a reflection guidance chatbot. In: EC-TEL Impact Paper Proceedings 2020: 15th European Conference on Technology Enhanced Learning (2020)
6. Galitsky, B., Ilvovsky, D.: Building dialogue structure from discourse tree of a question. In: Proceedings of the 2018 EMNLP Workshop SCAI: The 2nd International Workshop on Search-Oriented Conversational AI, Brussels, Belgium (2018)
7. Watanabe, M., Ogawa, K., Ishiguro, H.: Can androids be salespeople in the real world? In: Conference on Human Factors in Computing Systems (2015)
8. Watanabe, M., Ogawa, K., Ishiguro, H.: Minami-chan: application and verification of androids to society through selling. IPSJ J. **57**(4), 1251–1261 (2016)
9. Ministry of Health, Labor and Welfare, Related regulations for comprehensive project - Comprehensive Project Guidelines. https://www.mhlw.go.jp/stf/seisakunitsuite/bunya/000 0184585.html. Accessed 15 Jan 2021
10. Elvez, Inc., Chabot. https://chabot.elvez.jp/. Accessed 6 Jan 2021
11. Pei, J., et al.: PrefixSpan: mining sequential patterns by prefix-projected growth. In: Proceedings the 17th International Conference on Data Engineering (2001)

Intelligent Product Design with Natural Interaction

Rui Wang[1], Feng Wang[1(✉)], and Jun Hu[2]

[1] School of Design, Jiangnan University, Wuxi, China
wangfeng@jiangnan.edu.cn
[2] Department of Industrial Design, Eindhoven University of Technology, Eindhoven,
The Netherlands

Abstract. This paper analyzes intelligent products' design from the perspective of enhancing the user experience to understand natural interaction in intelligent products' development. According to the people-oriented natural interaction characteristics, this paper analyzes intelligent products' development and discusses the future development trends. From the perspective of information processing psychology, this paper analyzes why "intelligent speakers" are so popular and clarifies the situational factors in intelligent product design based on situational awareness theory, which leads to the natural interaction direction of intelligent product design. Finally, a case of an intelligent speaker's design process is presented. The case shows that the core of intelligent product design is to reduce user information transformation workload on the one hand. On the other hand, it predicts the user's action or the result that the user wants to produce. The intelligent product should respond to users' unexpressed needs in advance and provide users with a more humanized and personalized user experience.

Keywords: Natural interaction · Intelligent products · User experience · Situational awareness

1 Introduction

Since the new century, we have experienced the explosive growth of scientific and technological achievements. The computer and Internet technologies mature gradually for the increasing demand for high-quality life in health, safety, convenience, and comfort. Most people worldwide have passed the era of not having enough food and warm clothes. Consumers are no longer satisfied with the essential functions of products; they prefer a more convenient, efficient, and high-quality, time-saving life [1]. Pushed by the Internet of things technology, intelligent products became popular. The wide application of intelligent products had become the new trend. It brings new challenges and new opportunities. According to expert analysis [2], China's intelligent product industry chain is not yet mature, and it is still in the growth stage. There is also a lack of unified industry standards. At present, most smart home products are simply equipped with WIFI connectivity or embedded chip for hardware improvements. Many do not realize real intelligent learning. Moreover, due to the numerous platforms and different ways of connecting smart products to different services, users need to download

© Springer Nature Switzerland AG 2021
N. Streitz and S. Konomi (Eds.): HCII 2021, LNCS 12782, pp. 361–373, 2021.
https://doi.org/10.1007/978-3-030-77015-0_26

multiple apps to control different smart products. Many of these products do not systematically realize functions such as interconnection between smart products, making the user experience worse. Finally and most importantly, intelligent product designers and manufacturers misunderstand the essence of intelligent product design. They focus their product development on technology upgrading and fail to accurately grasp users' real needs.

Except for natural creations, all human-created artifacts are made for "use" [3]. Product design is essentially a creative act of artificial creation, which is to "create a more reasonable way to live (use)" [4]. According to Norman, a successful product can be described by a three-legged stool. Technology, marketing, and user experience support the right product [5]. Therefore, the focus of intelligent product design is not only on technology upgrading but also on user experience for a more comfortable, convenient, and natural life. In terms of research on intelligent product design, Cui et al. pointed out that product design in the intelligent era should meet the needs of users, design the operation mode that is easy for users to understand and master, and achieve barrier-free man-machine communication [6]; Song Fenglin introduced that the purpose of intelligence is to simplify operation steps and realize efficient application through complex structures, in which intelligent products have thinking ability is the core of its intelligence[7]; In the product design research based on user experience system, Mu Feng et al. also mentioned that design should communicate with people [8]. To enhance the user experience and change the user's very stiff feeling brought by the current intelligent products, intelligent products design should pay attention to the design of interaction mode between people and products to make it more natural. In the research on the interaction mode of intelligent products, Li Shiguo introduced that the design of interaction system should follow the principle of acceptability, that technology should adapt to people's lifestyle, and emphasized that it is more appropriate for people to use what technology to do what they want under what conditions [9]. Therefore, exploring natural interaction in intelligent products can further clarify intelligent products' core design direction.

2   Concept of Natural Interaction

Natural interaction is considered to be a kind of experience. People can naturally communicate through gestures, language expressions, behaviors, and actions, and they can also understand the world through watching and operating [10]. Now users are allowed to communicate with technology and machines to interact with the real world in daily life, named human-computer natural interaction. It is also called a natural user interface. This concept first originated from the research field of human-computer interaction. The user operates the computer through the most natural mode, such as action, gesture, language, etc., to get rid of the mouse and keyboard [11].

In product design, natural interaction means that people communicate and operate products through voice, action, behavior and other communication means in pre-language society. But in the actual interaction process, people may use "unnatural" actions or behaviors derived from life skills to interact with products. It mainly refers to learning and using abstract symbols such as text and graphics, including the acquired learning of remote control graphics rules and the learning and interactive interface with a smartphone. This kind of interactive way still belongs to the natural interaction behavior. Thus, natural interaction also derives another meaning: people interact naturally with products through their skills and habits that grasp daily life [12] (see Fig. 1).

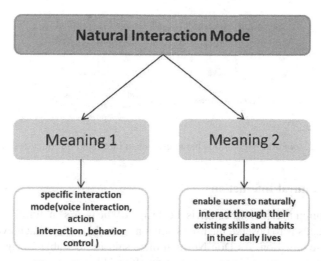

Fig. 1. Two layers of meaning of natural interaction.

Don Norman [13], in his book "Design for Future Products, "mentioned that the direction of future design is to "naturally" solve the problem of communication between users and products through natural interaction. Natural interaction mode studies the interaction mode between users and products, including the "natural" operation mode of users and the appropriate feedback mode.

3   Natural Interaction and Intelligent Product Design

Human-computer natural interaction can be divided into explicit human-computer natural interaction and implicit human-computer natural interaction: the former refers to the device system passively responds to the user's active command operation mode corresponds to the user's natural behavior in daily life. The latter means that the device system actively identifies and understands the user behavior and then acts the understood information on the human-computer interaction process [14]. This is the process that the machine adapts to the human. In this case, users needn't pay too much attention to the interaction process and needn't overthink using the device system either.

In the specific use scenarios of intelligent products, users and products have explicit natural interaction and implicit natural interaction (see Fig. 2). Explicit natural interaction means that intelligent products passively respond to the user's active demand, such as the user says "light on" command by voice, and then the light is on accordingly. Implicit natural interaction means that intelligent products predict users' unexpressed demands and respond to users' demands in advance. For example, when users get up from their bed at night, the smart light nearby will automatically turn.

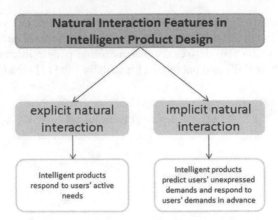

Fig. 2. Natural interaction characteristics in intelligent product design.

3.1 Explicit Natural Interaction

The core of explicit natural interaction is the design of the user's "natural" way of using a product. The focus is to observe the user's subconscious behavior to achieve its purpose in a specific use situation. As Don Norman once said in "Useable Design, "knee-jerk activity is quick and automatic and requires no effort" [15].

Information Processing Psychology
Information processing psychology is generated in the late 1950s. It emphasizes that cognition is the process of transforming, simplifying, storing, extracting, and using sensory information. Its activities include pattern recognition, attention, memory, strategy, knowledge representation, concept formation, problem-solving, judgment, reasoning, speech, and cognitive development [16].

Analysis of the Reasons for the Popularity of "Intelligent Speakers"
The gradual maturity and development of technology have brought voice interaction, gesture interaction, and other interactive ways. Smart home appliances can automatically perceive their own state and perceive the surrounding environment, automatically control and receive all kinds of instructions from users. In just a few years, a wide variety of intelligent household appliances are emerging on the market. Among them, the smart speaker market is scorching. The most significant difference between smart speakers and traditional speakers is the function of human-computer interaction. Voice interaction is the core of smart speakers. Researchers and relevant institutions have conducted in-depth research on voice interaction, making smart speakers understand human language to the maximum extent.

The reason why voice interaction is so popular with users is that voice interaction returns to human nature. Hence, it is primarily "natural" for users to operate from the perspective of the history of human information dissemination (see Fig. 3), the primitive human society communicated through language (sound) and body movements. Later, with material civilization development, merely relying on voice or body communication can no longer meet human communication needs, so words were created. As an abstract symbol, written language can only be grasped after learning. The reception of character information requires readers to transform the multiple symbol information they have learned in their minds to understand the content that writing language wants to convey.

However, people's lives are full of information in the information age. Simultaneously, people's pace of life and work has also accelerated. Therefore, it is a heavy burden for people to rely on words for communication. Therefore, to reduce the amount of information conversion, human beings have entered the era of picture reading. Image information is very intuitive for humans. People can understand without learning multiple written language symbols. Still, they need to be familiar and stored in the brain to understand specific symbols under social and cultural background and the meaning of symbols expressed by some specific images.

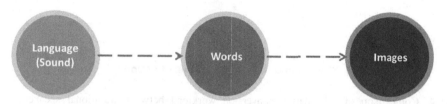

Fig. 3. The development history of information communication.

From the perspective of information processing psychology, users only need to send voice instructions through the most authentic way to complete voice interaction operation. While traditional speakers require users to extract the symbol information (text/image), they have learned to match the desired operation information (text/image) before pressing the operation key (see Fig. 4).

Therefore, compared with the traditional speaker operation way, the voice does not need brain conversion, significantly reducing the workload of information conversion for users. Therefore, voice interaction is a very "natural" operation mode for users.

3.2 Implicit Natural Interaction

The core of implicit natural interaction is to predict the behavior that users will or want to do. The focus is to perceive the situational information in the product's specific use process and then actively predict the demand according to the user's living habits, hobbies, use habits, etc.

Situational Awareness Theory
In 1994, Schilit et al. [17] put forward the concept of situational awareness for the first time. The core purpose of situational awareness is to actively perceive the changes of situational information around users and provide appropriate information and services at the right time according to the needs of current tasks. Situational awareness research mainly includes two points: one is to study people's perception, understanding, and feedback of the surrounding situation from the perspective of users, and the other is to

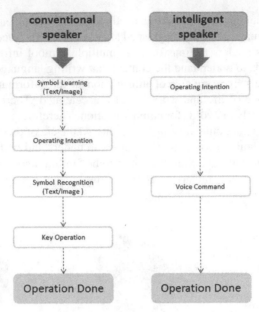

Fig. 4. Comparison of information conversion workload between traditional speakers and intelligent speakers.

study how to build a situational awareness system to perceive users and serve users by studying users' situational awareness principles.

Situational Factors Intelligent Product Design

In the design of intelligent products, the second point of situational awareness research is mainly applied. Intelligent products build their intelligent system by studying the user's perception of the surrounding situation when using the product and predicting users' potential unexpressed needs by perceiving the situational information.

The primary situational information that intelligent products need to perceive is summarized as environmental situation, user situation, and cultural situation (see Fig. 5). Among them, the perception of cultural context is advanced. The deeper the intelligent product system understands the cultural context, the more it can reflect intelligent products' development depth. Only by giving users the most appropriate feedback at the right time and on the right occasion can it provide users with a more excellent user experience.

The environmental situation is the natural environment information in the use situation, mainly including light environment, sound environment, temperature and humidity environment, and other information. Intelligent products perceive relevant information through various sensors, such as temperature and humidity sensors, photosensitive sensors, etc. These sensors are like human facial features, making intelligent products that have the sensory functions of seeing, listening, smelling, touching, and systematically recording the change of the surrounding environment information. Take the intelligent air purifier as an example to illustrate the influence of these factors on the design of intelligent products: when the air sensor in the air purifier detects the odor or smoke and

Environment Situation   **User Situation**   **Cultural Situation**

Fig. 5. Environment situation, user situation, the cultural situation in intelligent product design.

other polluting gases in the air, it will automatically turn on the purification mode, and the continuous detection of the sensor is more sensitive than people's sense of smell, so it can intelligently provide users with considerate user experience without people's active operation.

User situation is related to user characteristics, including users' habits of using the product, lifestyle, personal preferences, and other information. A corresponding user model can be built for each user based on user situational information collection. Through data analysis, intelligent products intelligently understand and learn from each user to provide a more considerate and personalized user experience. For example, a smart home housekeeper may need to manually set most of the actions in the early stage of use. It will learn your lifestyle and understand the scenes, times, and rules you set during this period. And then, after a particular time, it can intelligently manage your appliances. When you go out to work in the morning, the smart Housekeeper will help turn off all the appliances. Besides, when it's time to go home from work in summer, the smart Housekeeper has already turned on the air conditioner for you in advance, so you can enjoy the cool indoor space as soon as you go home.

Cultural situation is associated with the user's cultural background, including the comprehensive information of group culture, customs, values, etc. By understanding the cultural situation, intelligent products need to comprehensively judge the user's behavior or wants to do in this situation. People's behavior of making appropriate feedback through a comprehensive judgment of situational perception is regarded as "situational aware-ness." For example, when someone around you is answering the phone, you will pay attention to communicate with others in a low voice. The word "situational awareness" is used to describe people. Chinese people pay attention to the cultivation of situational awareness and think highly of etiquette. Japanese people pay attention to cultivating children's situational awareness when their children are very young and emphasize not to cause trouble to others. Civic education in Europe and the United States also reflects the emphasis on the cultivation of rules and occasion sense. Intelligent products need to perceive users in context and adapt to people's lives, so intelligent products should also have "situational awareness," which could contribute to a better user experience. For example, when the smart speaker is playing out at a high volume, suddenly someone nearby answers the phone. In this case, the smart speaker is expected to intelligently reduce the volume, not to affect others' telephone communication.

4   Intelligent Product Design Process Based on Natural Interaction

The core design direction of explicit natural interactions aims to design users' "natural" user mode. Hence, the essential point is that we need to observe users' "natural" behavior in their daily life to find more suitable interactive ways in line with the user's natural behavior and reduce the information conversion workload of the user to a greater extent. The core design of implicit natural interaction is to predict what the user is going to do or want to do, so we need to perceive the user and the surrounding situation, analyze the situation information, and then comprehensively judge and predict the user needs to determine the active interaction function of the product.

Based on the analysis of the characteristics of explicit natural interaction and implicit natural interaction in intelligent product design, the intelligent product's design steps based on natural interaction are proposed (see Fig. 6).

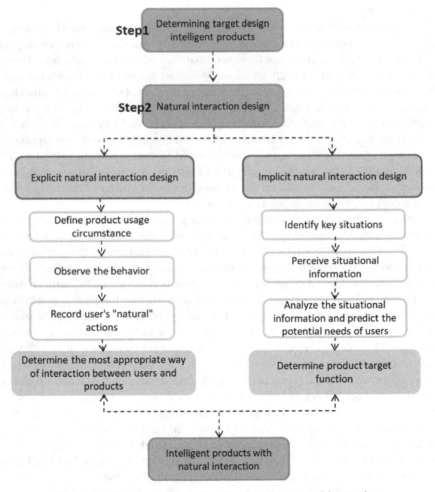

Fig. 6. Intelligent product design steps based on natural interaction.

4.1 Determining Target Design Intelligent Products

This step is a general starting step in product design. At the beginning of the design, specific design categories should be selected. Therefore, this step will not be explained in detail. This paper focuses on the design method of natural interaction function in intelligent products.

4.2 Natural Interaction Design

Explicit Natural Interaction Design - Behavior Observation

To determine the most appropriate and natural interaction mode, we need to start by observing users' "natural" behavior, including users' subconscious behavior, unconditional response behavior, and conditional response behavior.

Subconscious behavior is the tendency of people's unconscious behavior, which can be revealed naturally without any effort, and even can't be controlled and concealed subjectively. For example, some people's ears will turn red as soon as they communicate with others.

Unconditioned reaction behavior is reflex behavior, a kind of "natural" reaction behavior of human physiology without learning, such as knee jump reflex behavior.

Conditioned response behavior is a kind of matching reaction behavior left by accumulated learning or experience in our life. For example, if we set a song as a mobile phone ringtone for a long time, then we would think it's our mobile phone ringing when we hear this song in another place.

Therefore, it is necessary to observe the user's behavior habits in the specific product use circumstance in intelligent product design. And record the user's natural behavior to screen out the most natural interaction model that best matches the function of the intelligent product, which has the less information conversion workload of users naturally.

Implicit Natural Interaction Design - Situational Analysis

To determine the product's target functions, we first need to identify the critical use situation and then collect the situational factors related to the product's critical use situation. The primary situational information that intelligent products need to perceive is summarized as environmental context, user context, and cultural context. Among them, the perception of cultural context is high-level perception. The deeper the intelligent product system understands the cultural context, the more it can reflect intelligent product development depth.

Next, through comprehensive analysis and judgment, we can predict the behavior that the user will or wants to produce so as to give the user appropriate feedback in the appropriate situation and achieve the goal of according to the user's behavior to predict the user's next behavior and respond to the user's unexpressed demand in advance.

5 Case Study: Design an Intelligent Speaker

5.1 Determining Target Design Intelligent Products

As the voice control terminal of all kinds of intelligent products, intelligent speakers have a high degree of correlation with the user's life. Therefore, this paper takes the optimization design of intelligent speakers as an example to verify the feasibility of the intelligent product design method based on natural interaction.

5.2 Natural Interaction Design

Explicit Natural Interaction Design

At present, voice interaction is a common and main operation mode of the intelligent speaker, which is also in line with the user's natural behavior. But the operation mode of voice interaction is not suitable for smart speakers' scenarios. For example, when the smart speaker is playing music, and someone in the user's home suddenly answers the phone, the user wants to pause the music, and in this case, the voice command is not the most appropriate way.

Therefore, in the above user situations, we found that the user needs to stop music. Then, through observing the user's subconscious behavior, we recorded that when people try to control the volume, there are two kinds of natural behaviors: one is that the subconscious reaction is to cover the vocal position; the other is to make the "Shh" gesture (see Fig. 7).

Fig. 7. Two kinds of natural behaviors when people try to control the volume: 1. cover the vocal position [18]; 2. make the "Shh" gesture [19].

Next, combined with the specific user scenarios and evaluating the difficulty of existing technology implementation, we finally decided that covering the vocal position with a hand is more appropriate and natural.

So in the end of the explicit natural interaction design part, it is concluded that to meet the need of users who want to pause music, except for the voice interaction, the auxiliary interaction way that needs to be added is that the user could cover the voice point of the intelligent speaker with his hand to make the music stop.

Implicit Natural Interaction Design

In this optimization example, the analysis and functional design are mainly focused on high-level perception, that is, cultural context.

Through interviews with smart speaker users, we screened out the critical situation: at night, users immerse themselves in music but unintentionally affect their neighbors' sleep. After a comprehensive analysis of the environmental situation factors - night time, user situation factors - preference for listening to music loud at night, cultural situation factors - group culture, we determined that the active interaction function of the intelligent speaker is to set the maximum volume limit from 22:00 to 6:00, so as to avoid the possible negative impact of user behavior and provide a more humanized user experience.

After the above design steps, we get two optimization functions of an intelligent speaker based on natural interaction: one is that the user covers the speaker with his hand and the music is suspended; the other is a maximum volume limit of dB between 22:00 and 6:00.

5.3 Prototype Production

The prototype consists of hardware and software. The hardware includes the appearance modeling (see Fig. 8) and internal functional components. Bamboo board environmental-friendly materials are used for appearance modeling, and CNC machine tools are used to make model parts and assemble them. The internal functional components consist of an ultrasonic rangefinder, Bluetooth audio amplifier board, loudspeaker, etc. The software part uses Arduino IDE to program. Users can connect mobile phones and smart speakers through Bluetooth to play music. When the user covers the bell, the feedback distance of the ultrasonic rangefinder is less than 10, and the music is suspended.

Fig. 8. The product prototype.

5.4 Instructions for Natural Interactive Speakers

This intelligent speaker has the following functions: first, it can pause music more naturally. When someone in the user's home suddenly answers the phone or wants to pause the music, they can use the natural "natural" behavior - covering the voice with their hands (see Fig. 9). Second, the decibel limit function at night. When the user is immersed in music at night, the smart speaker will automatically turn on its "situational awareness" function, automatically help you adjust the maximum volume that can be played. To avoid the user's unintentional influence on neighbors' nights of sleep, promote harmony between neighbors (see Fig. 10).

Fig. 9. Stop the music by covering the vocal place with their hands.

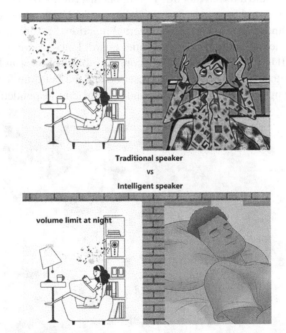

Fig. 10. The smart speaker's "situational awareness" [20].

6   Conclusions

The design of intelligent products based on natural interaction enhances the user experience, captures the user's real needs, and implements the actual user-centered design. Based on the theories, the core of intelligent product design reduces the user's information workload and predicts user behavior and the user needs. It is about situational awareness: to respond to the user's needs, not expressed. The presented design case demonstrated a process that tries to enhance the smart speakers' user experience, improve the design efficiency, and provide the user with a more personal and personalized experience.

References

1. Tan, Y.-Y., Geng, D.: Household Smart Product Design under the lifestyle. Packag. Eng. **37**, 22108–22113 (2016)
2. Wen, X.: Development status and suggestions of china's intelligent hardware industry. High Technol. Industr. **02**, 80–85 (2016)
3. Zhan, K.: Creation and Production, Xinhua (abstract), pp. 85–88 (2005)
4. Liu, G.-Z.: Taking the road of China's contemporary industrial design. In: Proceedings of China International Industrial Design, pp. 86–110 (2004)
5. Norman, D.A.: Emotional Design, Translated by Fu Qiu-fang. Electronic Industry Press, Beijing (2005)
6. Cui, T.-J., Xu, B., Shen, Z.: Product design in the intelligent era. Packag. Eng. **31**(16), 31–34 (2010)
7. Song, F.: Product design in the era of wisdom. Intel. Manuf. (2016)
8. Mou, F., Chu, J.-J.: Study of product design based on user experience system. Packag. Eng., 142–144 (2008)
9. Li, S.-G.: Interaction system design – a new perspective of product design. Decoration, 12–13 (2007)
10. Valli, A.: The design of natural interaction. Multimedia Tools Appl. **38**(3), 295–305 (2008)
11. Tan, H.: A Study on Natural Interaction in Digital Entertainment Products. Jiang Nan University (2011)
12. Yuan, X.: Intelligent Home User Interface Design Based on Natural Interaction. Zhe Jiang University (2016)
13. Norman, D.A.: Future Product Design. Electronic Industry Press, Beijing (2009)
14. Wache, J.: Implicit human-computer interaction: two complementary approaches. In: Proceedings of the 2015 ACM International Conference on Multimodal Interaction, Seattle, Washington, United State, pp. 599–603 (2015)
15. Norman, D.A.: The Design of Everyday Things. China Citic Press (2007)
16. Ning-Jian, L.: Applied Cognitive Psychology. Shanghai Education Press, Shanghai (2009)
17. Zuo, Z., Jiang, X.: Design of mobile shopping application based on context-aware. Packag. Eng. **38**(24), 156–159 (2017)
18. Picture from: https://gimg2.baidu.com/image_search/src=http%3A%2F%2Fwww.planpr.cn%2Fuploads%2Fallimg%2F160825%2F2160r5104600926.jpg&refer=http%3A%2F%2Fwww.planpr.cn&app=2002&size=f9999,10000&q=a80&n=0&g=0n&fmt=jpeg?sec=1614826399&t=6cffcaab7394f2ca05629c2c36ffbe92
19. Picture from: https://ss0.baidu.com/6ON1bjeh1BF3odCf/it/u=2096610984,519361857&fm=27&gp=0.jpg
20. Picture from: https://cms.111yao.com/ueditor/php/upload/image/20160512/1463034306394967.jpg

HUD Information Design for IoV Intelligent Navigation System

Qingshu Zeng[1(✉)] and Tianyu Wu[2]

[1] School of Design Art and Media, Nanjing University of Science and Technology,
200, Xiaolingwei Street, Nanjing 210094, Jiangsu, People's Republic of China
[2] School of Design, Royal College of Art, Kensington Gore, South Kensington,
London SW7 2EU, UK

Abstract. The car navigation function is mainly realized through the smartphone and the central control interface, both of which are not in the driver's best field of vision, bringing potential safety hazards. Head-Up Display (HUD) projects information to the upper part of the ambitious vision, such as the car's front windshield, which has a better driving experience and safety. This article adopts the case analysis method to analyze the classic design cases of navigation head-up display and proposes the information organization strategy and visual design strategy of HUD. It combines design examples to verify the feasibility of the information organization strategy and design strategy and provides a theoretical basis for the car interaction design.

Keywords: HUD · Information organization · Visual design · Navigation system

1 Introduction

The Internet of Vehicles (IoV) uses sensors, networks and control technologies to make drivers, vehicles, environment, roads, roadside facilities and pedestrians an organic whole, providing car navigation systems with richer types and quantities of information, and improving the accuracy of the information, It also provides a channel for users to publish navigation-related information [1]. At present, the car navigation of the IoV includes the following features: Heterogeneous information content, which comes from the Internet, infrastructure, and mobile devices, has a wide variety of content. In addition to static traffic information such as road names, it also includes dynamic road condition information and even event information [2]. The form of information includes text, graphics, sound, animation and even video information. The multi-state interaction mode, diversified service terminal equipment provides a multi-state interaction mode for the service. In addition to physical buttons, knobs, touch screens, voice and somatosensory, interactions can also be achieved with wearable smart devices such as Google Glass and Apple Watch. The development of augmented reality and head-up displays also provide convenience and safety for services a specific guarantee.

Services are interactive, including "human-computer interaction" and reflects the characteristics of "human-human interaction". The user's role in the service process is no longer just the receiver of information, but also the producer and creator of information.

N. Streitz and S. Konomi (Eds.): HCII 2021, LNCS 12782, pp. 374–384, 2021.
https://doi.org/10.1007/978-3-030-77015-0_27

Therefore, the navigation system is a critical information carrier for the driver to interact with the car's human-machine system. At present, the navigation function is mainly realized through the smartphone and the central control interface, but both are not in the driver's best field of view, bringing potential safety hazards. HUD projects information on the car's front windshield, reducing the risk of the driver's sight deviation caused by bowing his head while reducing driving load and improving driving safety experience [3]. This article adopts the case analysis method, based on the classic design case of navigation head-up display, and analyzes and studies from the aspects of information organization criteria, information content, information structure and visual design, and combines design practice on this basis to initially verify the feasibility of the research, Laid a particular theoretical foundation for the subsequent research on the design of the automotive interactive visual display.

2 Related Work

About 80% of the driver's information is obtained through the visual channel. Therefore, the design of the vehicle interactive visual information display interface is highly problematic [4]. The perspective of information interaction includes a natural display interface for front road conditions, a display interface for assisted driving, an interface for information interaction and entertainment inside and outside the car, and an integrated interface between mobile devices and cars [5]. In the traditional car interior, the primary and auxiliary instrument panels and the central control area are the realization carriers of the information display interface, the so-called head-down display (HDD). However, with the massive involvement of the Internet of Vehicles and information, the display position and display carrier of the car's information will also change accordingly [6].

In the future, smart cars' display will no longer be limited to areas such as traditional dashboards, centre consoles, and rearview mirrors. Any physical equipment and environment may be embedded in the display device and become a medium for information display [7]. The original driving-centric information architecture will be broken down according to entertainment, interaction, and personalized settings, and displayed in different areas of the car.

In terms of display mode, smart cars' display will no longer be limited to a single physical device, but the integration of multiple locations and multiple display forms. From the perspective of human-computer interaction, the most significant advantage of head-up display is that the driver can obtain all kinds of information without leaving the road ahead, effectively improving driving safety, and is considered the safest display method the future one. Smart cars are transitioning to unmanned driving, and driving behaviour will still be vital in automotive human-computer interaction design in the next few years [8]. Therefore, the head-up display has the advantages of improving driving safety and reducing the driver's cognitive load to have a more extensive application scene and space. Even if fully automatic driving is realized in the future, users still have many demands for obtaining information through the front windshield, and the head-up display also has a vast design space [9].

It can be seen from the design research on production cars and concept cars that a significant trend is that the HUD interface will become an essential part of the car's interactive interface. Recent trends indicate that HUD displays mainly essential driving information (such as vehicle speed, navigation information, etc.) directly related to assisted driving. On this basis, a small amount of unimportant information (such as music in the entertainment system, etc.) can be displayed, but it is in an unimportant area. The future trend is likely to be that HUD, virtual reality, and the 3D display will be combined with the dashboard and even the centre console to form an integrated display interface [10]. The display content will integrate car control, navigation, entertainment, communication and network applications, and future car systems Will form a rugged network terminal. Therefore, this article is based on the classic case of car navigation HUD, analyzes it from the perspective of information organization and visual design, and validates it with design practice.

3   Information Structure of the HUD Interface of the Car Navigation System

The application of HUD in the in-car display system can be traced back to the 1980s, displaying vehicle speed and fuel level with monochrome numbers and symbols. Driven by imaging materials and technology, HUD's display function is also becoming more and more perfect. Taking the navigation system as an example, BMW of Germany and Pioneer of Japan are pioneers in successfully applying navigation system to HUD display. Both are in the navigation product information. The organization, visual design and other aspects all reflect their design characteristics.

3.1   Information Organization Guidelines

The so-called information organization refers to the organization and definition of screen layout, workflow, and interactive behaviour from the interaction framework level. It aims to define product functions, data elements, and the definition of product function modules and operational levels. The navigation system provides users with an information-rich experience based on spatial cognition. Therefore, the driver's recognition and understanding of navigation complex information is the core of HUD information organization guidelines [11]. From the perspective of recognition, attention should be paid to the consistency of the interface layout. The driver can maintain a consistent sense of direction and association in different situations to understand the corresponding association with less cognitive cycles.

For example, the Pioneer HUD display interface is divided into a stable information display area and an iterative information display area. The display content and location of the stable information area are relatively stable, such as place name, direction, time, etc.; while the iterative information area displays different information as the driving situation changes [12]. The content is the real-time push of external driving environment information. For example, when approaching an intersection 50 m, the pre-selected lane reminder icon will be pushed in the iteration area, and it will disappear after passing. The block layout of stable information and iterative information allows users to more quickly and accurately identify changes in the external situation and make driving decisions [13]. From a comprehensible point of view, visual elements familiar to drivers should be used to organize information to form cognitive migration. For example, the speed limit reminder sign on the BMW HUD navigation interface is the same as the speed limit sign design on real road conditions; the number representing the distance and the arrow indicating the direction are laid out in the same horizontal dimension, which is very similar to the actual road sign design.

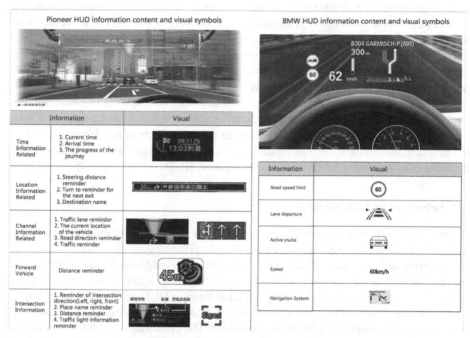

Fig. 1. Pioneer (upper left) from https://jpn.pioneer/ja/. BMW (upper right) from https://www.bmw.com/en/. HUD information content and visual symbols analyzed by the authors

3.2 Information Content

From the perspective of information content, including functions and data elements. Traditional car navigation product information data elements include maps, numbers, text, graphics, and voice. The data elements presented by the HUD navigation system are mainly numbers, icons, text, and characters, which are represented by visual symbols in the interface [14]. Functional elements are the conversion of functional requirements and the manipulation of data elements. The core function of the navigation system is destination guidance, which can be summarized into location information related (place name, distance reminder), channel information related (direction, lane selection), and assisted driving information related (vehicle speed, progress information reminder, etc.) on the HUD interface. Take the information content of Pioneer and BMW HUD as examples to analyze functions and data elements.

The Pioneer HUD's functional elements shown on the left side of Fig. 1 cover five categories, and each category is further subdivided into functions, namely: time information, location information, channel information, vehicle locking, and intersection information. Taking time information as an example, the functional elements can be subdivided into three items: current time, arrival time, and progress preview. The data elements used in the interface are numbers, characters, and icons. Each functional element corresponds to a combination of data elements. For example, the combination of numbers and clock icons conveys the functional meaning of the current time; the combination of numbers and text conveys the functional meaning of arrival time; the flags and circular track icons convey destination and time progress's functional meaning. The BMW HUD's functional elements include place name, distance, direction, navigation lane, speed, speed limit, and assisted driving. Each function corresponds to the corresponding data element. For example, the speed reminder corresponds to a number, and the direction reminder corresponds to an icon, as shown in Fig. 1 on the right. It can be seen that Pioneer and BMW HUD have certain commonalities in the definition of data and practical information, such as distance, direction, and place name reminders. These elements constitute the core functions of navigation HUD.

3.3 Information Architecture

The purpose of information architecture is to organize several information to quickly and accurately find the information they need. From the point of view of cognitive economy, summarizing and processing diverse visual information through modularization can save drivers' limited cognitive resources, and at the same time, it can make the processing of visual information more timely [15]. Take the Pioneer HUD interface as an example. The information level of the system is wide and shallow. The necessary information is distributed in the interface in the form of modules. The information modules are divided into time information, location information, channel information, etc., and these modules are subdivided into different Functional elements, for example, the location information module contains distance, direction, and destination reminders.

In contrast, the channel information module contains functional elements such as traffic lights, real-time road conditions, and distance reminders of the preceding vehicle, as shown on the left side of Fig. 2. The BMW's HUD display interface organizes information in an "immersive" page. The information module can be divided into two modules: the navigation system and driving assistance. The navigation system module comprises functional elements such as destination name, distance reminder, route reminder, and progress preview. In contrast, the auxiliary driving module comprises practical information such as lane-keeping, active cruise, and speed limit reminder, as shown on the right side of Fig. 2. From the analysis of these two cases, it can be seen that the information module is the integration of information content, and the division of information levels is the basis for the layout of the information module in the interface.

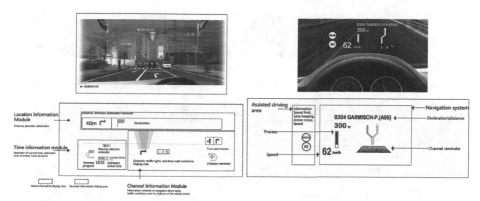

Fig. 2. Pioneer (upper left) from https://jpn.pioneer/ja/. BMW (upper right) from https://www.bmw.com/en/. HUD information architecture analyzed by the authors

4 Visual Design Analysis of the HUD of the Car Navigation System

Overall, the HUD interface should follow the general rules of visual design, such as interface clarity, readability, style consistency, avoiding visual noise, and having a sense of aesthetic pleasure [14]. In the design details, attention should be paid to HUD's media properties near the HUD imaging materials and lighting environment. For example, the early projection technology was based on a transparent high-refractive-index coating on the front windshield, and the thickness of the film was precisely the peak wavelength of the green selective reflection, which is why the early information display was mostly green. Shana Smith et al. conducted research based on automobile HUD images and driver's perceptual engineering and proposed that colour, font, location and other elements are the key to HUD visual graphic design [15]. Through analyzing the visual interface of BMW and Pioneer HUD, it can be seen that fonts, linearity, auxiliary visual symbols, colours, and auxiliary colour blocks are the design elements that constitute the visual interface of the interface. Among them, colour, text, and icons are the key elements of the HUD visual interface design, as shown in Fig. 3. Also, the HUD interface, the main instrument panel, the auxiliary instrument panel, and the central control interface together constitute the vehicle interactive visual information display interface, so the visual style also needs to be consistent. Taking the interface icons as an example, they are divided into three categories: arrows indicating directions, graphics indicating states (such as time, travel progress), and symbols indicating assisted driving functions (such as lane departure) [16]. These icons are displayed on the HUD interface and the central control and main instrument interface. Therefore, the difference between the HUD display medium and other display media should be considered in the design [3]. The central control display interface is an LCD screen with higher resolution and more prosperous and more delicate colour levels of the icons. HUD is a projection-based windshield display interface with low colour reproduction. This requires designers to determine the hue, brightness, and brightness of the same icon. Saturation needs to be treated differently [17].

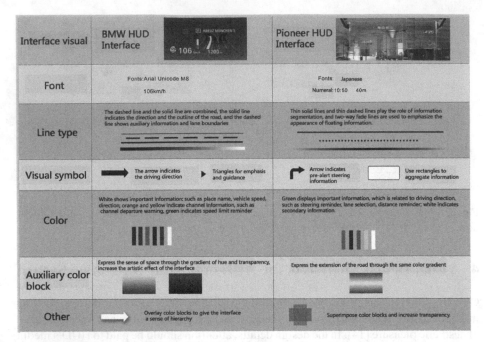

Fig. 3. Pioneer and BMW HUD visual design analysis (Color figure online)

5 Design Practice of Head-Up Display (HUD) of the Car Navigation System

The design strategies are summarized from information organization design and visual design and verified by design practice through the above case analysis.

Follow HUD's information organization guidelines, design with recognition and understanding as to the core. According to the information organization and visual design strategy, the design process can be divided into two steps: 1. Information organization; 2. Visual design.

5.1 Information Organization

First, define the information content, that is, determine the functional elements like direction, distance, place name, navigation lane, pre-selected lane, and speed limit reminder. According to the division of HUD information levels, the above functional elements are summarized into primary channel information related and auxiliary information related to the hierarchical relationship. The purpose is to provide a basis for the spatial layout of information modules.

Second, follow the design guidelines of consistency, reduce cognitive cycles, and structure information according to the information content level, as shown in Fig. 4.

The interface is divided into two modules: the main channel information module and the auxiliary information module. The functional elements contained in the main channel information module are of great significance to the user's driving decision-making. Therefore, the layout is in the centre of the interface and coincides with the vision's main driving field. The structure is stable and consists of direction, distance, place name, and channel reminders. The auxiliary information module presents iterative information, which is only displayed in the context that needs to be displayed, so the layout is on the upper right of the interface to avoid interference with the A-pillar. For example, the current speed and speed limit reminder icon will only appear in a speeding situation.

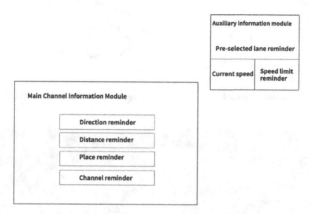

Fig. 4. Information architecture

5.2 Visual Design, that is, Visual Symbol and Interface Design

According to the above-defined functional elements, visual symbols are designed, and the data elements used are a combination of numbers, characters and icons. Follow the comprehensibility principle, and indicate functions such as lane reminders and speed limit reminders based on road signs familiar to drivers, as shown in Fig. 5. In this case, the HUD display position is in the driver's primary field of view. To reduce interference, follow the visual design strategy and repeatedly scrutinize the size and colour of arrow symbols, numbers, and characters. For example, when dealing with visual symbols' proportional relationship, The division of information levels is the basis, and the direction reminder function is the primary information, as shown in Fig. 6. Therefore, the arrow symbol takes a larger proportion in the main channel information module than the distance and place name reminder icons. When dealing with the relationship between the channel reminder and the road surface change, the method adopted expresses the road extension distance and space relationship through three colour band symbols with gradual transparency, as shown in Fig. 7.

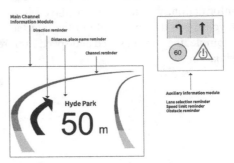

Fig. 5. Visual symbol

Fig. 6. V interface low-fidelity prototype

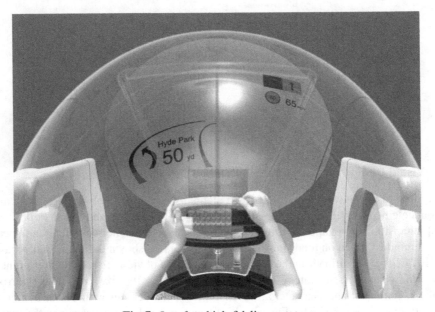

Fig. 7. Interface high-fidelity prototype

6 Conclusion

The use of HUD as the navigation system's display interface has mature applications in the aviation field. However, the HUD as a car navigation interface is still in the stage of continuous exploration and improvement, which is also the practical significance of this paper. This paper analyzes Pioneer and BMW's HUD navigation system, proposes the HUD interface information organization strategy and visual design strategy, and has been initially verified through design practice. This research provides an essential theoretical, and practical basis for designing an automotive interactive visual information display interface.

Acknowledgments. This research was supported by Humanities and Social Sciences Research Funds of the Ministry of Education of the People's Republic of China (19C10288009/19YJC760004), Fundamental Research Funds for the Central Universities (1171090797/30917013111). The authors would like to thank editors and reviewers for their comments.

References

1. Zeng, Q., Shi, M.: Story board tools and methods for user-knowledge-based automotive human-machine interface design. In: Rau, P.-L. (ed.) CCD 2018. LNCS, vol. 10911, pp. 108–119. Springer, Cham (2018). https://doi.org/10.1007/978-3-319-92141-9_8
2. Lee, S., Harada, A.: A design approach by objective and subjective evaluation of kansei information. In: China-Japan, Korea Design Symposium, pp. 961–968 (1998)
3. Bella, M., Hanington, B.: Universal Methods of Design. Central Compilation Translation Press, Beijing (2013)
4. Zhao, J.-H., Tan, H., Tan, Z.-Y.: Car Styling: Theory, Research and Application. Beijing Institute of Technology Press, Beijing (2011)
5. Zeng, Q., Duan, Q., Shi, M., He, X., Hassan, M.M.: Design framework and intelligent in-vehicle information system for sensor-cloud platform and applications. IEEE Access **8**, 201675–201685 (2020)
6. Yoshimoto, K., Suetomi, T.C.: The history of research and development of driving simulator in Japan. In: Proceedings of Driving Simulation Conference Asia/Pacific, Tsukuba, Japan, pp. 113–120 (2016)
7. Pruitt, J., Adlin, T.: The Persona Lifecycle: Keeping People in Mind Throughout Product Design, pp. 45–48. Elsevier, San Francisco (2006)
8. Sommer, R., Sommer, B.: A Practical Guide to Behavioral Research: Tools and Techniques, pp. 143–145. Oxford University Press, New York (2002)
9. Serenko, A.: The use of interface agents for email notification in critical incidents. Int. J. Hum.-Comput. Stud. **64**(11), 1084–1098 (2006)
10. Spencer, D.: Card sorting: Designing Usable Categories, pp. 115–118. Rosenfeld Media, New York (2009)
11. Zeng, Q., Duan, Q.: A study on integrated design process of software and hardware interfaces for automotive human-machine interaction. In: Rau, P.-L. (ed.) HCII 2019. LNCS, vol. 11576, pp. 105–123. Springer, Cham (2019). https://doi.org/10.1007/978-3-030-22577-3_8
12. Hankey, J.M., Dingus, T.A., Hanowski, R.J., Andrews, C.: In-vehicle information systems behavioral model and design support, pp. 145–150. Virginia Tech Transportation Institute, Blacksburg (2001)
13. Mills, E.: The Art of Visual Notetaking: An Interactive Guide to Visual Communication and Sketchnoting. Walter Foster Publishing, Mission Viejo (2019)
14. Zeng, Q., Hu, M.: Mood board tool - an innovation method in vehicle HMI design. In: Streitz, N., Konomi, S. (eds.) HCII 2020. LNCS, vol. 12203, pp. 138–149. Springer, Cham (2020). https://doi.org/10.1007/978-3-030-50344-4_11
15. McDonagh, D., Storer, I.: Mood boards as a design catalyst and resource: researching an under-researched area. Des. J. **7**(3), 16–31 (2004)

16. Eckert, C., Stacey, M.: Sources of inspiration: a language of design. Des. Stud. **21**(5), 523–538 (2000)
17. Zeng, Q., Jiang, B., Duan, Q.: Integrated evaluation of hardware and software interfaces for automotive human–machine interaction. IET Cyber-Phys. Syst. Theory Appl, (2019). https://doi.org/10.1049/iet-cps.2019.0002

Author Index

Printed in the United States
by Baker & Taylor Publisher Services